MILLER'S
CollectableS
PRICE ◆ GUIDE
1993-94

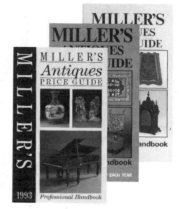

MILLER'S

CollectableS

PRICE ◆ GUIDE

1993-94

(Volume V)

Compiled and Edited by
Judith and Martin Miller

General Editor: Robert Murfin

BCA

LONDON   NEW YORK   SYDNEY   TORONTO

MILLER'S COLLECTABLES PRICE GUIDE 1993/94

Compiled, edited and designed by
Millers Publications
The Cellars, High Street,
Tenterden, Kent. TN30 6BN
Telephone (05806) 6411

This edition published 1993
by BCA by arrangement with
Millers Publications

Compiled and edited by
Judith & Martin Miller

General Editor: Robert Murfin
Editorial Co-ordinator: Sue Boyd
Editorial Assistants: Marion Rickman, Jo Wood, Jill Charles
Artwork: Stephen Parry, Jody Taylor, Darren Manser
Photographic Co-ordinator and Advertising Executive: Elizabeth Smith
Display Advertisements: Elizabeth Warwick, Sally Marshall
Index compiled: DD Editorial Services, Beccles
Additional photography: Ian Booth, Robin Saker

Copyright © 1993 Millers Publications

CN 9775

Bromide output: The Final Word, Tonbridge, Kent
Illustrations: G. H. Graphics, St. Leonards-on-Sea
Colour origination: Scantrans, Singapore
Printed and bound in England by William Clowes Ltd.,
Beccles and London

CONTENTS

Acknowledgements

The publishers would like to acknowledge the great assistance given by our consultants.

ART DECO:	**Beverley,** 30 Church Street, London NW8
BOOKS:	**Peter Harrington,** Harrington Bros. The Chelsea Antique Market, 253 King's Road, London SW3
CONTINENTAL CRACKLE WARE:	**David & Sylvia Powell,** Decorative Arts 1860-1960, 28 The Mall, Camden Passage, N1
GOSS & CRESTED WARE:	**Nicholas Pine,** Goss & Crested China Ltd., 62 Murray Road, Horndean, Hants
SCOTTISH POTTERY:	**George Haggarty,** Bow Well Antiques, 103 West Bow, Edinburgh
EPHEMERA:	**Trevor Vennett-Smith, FRICS, FSVA, CAAV,** 11 Nottingham Road, Gotham, Nottingham
COMICS:	**Phil Clark,** Nostalgia & Comics, 14-16 Smallbrook Queensway, City Centre, Birmingham
SIXTIES & SEVENTIES:	**Liam Woolnough,** 130 Queens Road, Nuneaton, Warwickshire
STANHOPES:	**Douglas Jull,** Cissbury, Worthing, Sussex
ROCKING HORSES:	**Stevenson Brothers,** The Workshop, Ashford Road, Bethersden, Ashford, Kent

A teddy-dog, a prototype from Chad Valley, stuffed with straw, with glass eyes and mohair coat, c1930, 12in (31cm) long.
£100-150 *STK*

This toy was not popular so, therefore, rare.

INDEX TO ADVERTISERS

A Lyons' Milk Chocolate 1d Bar
box, c1920, 11in (28cm) wide.
£20-25 *ACh*

A Rowntree's insert, c1928, 8in
(20cm) high. **£10-15** *ACh*

A Cadbury's Milk Tray box,
in purple and gold, c1950
4in (10cm) high.
£2-3 *ACh*

A Fry's Chocolate Crunchies
advertisement, c1930,
9.5in (24cm) wide.
£18-25 *ACh*

An advertising die-cut show
card, 10in (25cm) high.
£20-25 *ACh*

Key to Illustrations

Each illustration and descriptive caption is accompanied by a letter code. By reference to the following list of Auctioneers (denoted by *) and Dealers (•), the source of any item may be immediately determined. In no way does this constitute or imply a contract or binding offer on the part of any of our contributors to supply or sell the goods illustrated, or similar articles, at the prices stated. Advertisers in this year's directory are denoted by †.

AA • Ambeline Antiques, By George Antique Centre, St. Albans, Herts Tel: 0727 53032 & 081 445 8025

AAM • Anything American (Chris Pearce), 33-35 Duddenhill Lane, London NW10. Tel: 081 451 0320

AAR * Amersham Auction Rooms, 125 Station Road, Amersham, Bucks. Tel: 0494 729292

ABS • Abstract, 58-60 Kensington Church Street, London W8. Tel: 071 376 2652

ACC •† Albert's, 113 London Road, Twickenham, Middx. Tel: 081 891 3067

ACh • Alan Chappell Tel: 0938 84543

ACL • Academy Costumes Ltd., 25 Murphy Street, London SE1. Tel: 071 620 0771

ADC • Art Deco Ceramics, Sheep Street Antique Centre and Ely Street Antique Market, Stratford-upon-Avon, Warwicks. Tel: 0789 297496/297244

AGM • The Button Museum, Kyrle Street, Ross-on-Wye, Hereford & Worcs. Tel: 0989 66089

AH * Andrew Hartley, Victoria Hall, Little Lane, Ilkley, W. Yorks. Tel: 0943 816363

AI • Antiques & Interiors, 22 Ashford Road, Tenterden, Kent. Tel: 05806 5462

AL •† Ann Lingard, Ropewalk Antiques, Ropewalk, Rye, East Sussex. Tel: 0797 223486

ALL * Allen & Harris, Bristol Auction Rooms, St. John's Place, Apsley Road, Clifton, Bristol, Avon. Tel: 0272 737201

AMH • Amhurst Antiques, 23 London Road, Riverhead, Kent. Tel: 0732 455047

AOS •† Antiques on the Square, Church Stretton, Shropshire. Tel: 0694 724111

APO • Apollo Antiques Ltd., The Saltisford, Birmingham Road, Warwick. Tel: 0926 494746

ASA • AS Antiques & Decorative Arts, 26 Broad Street, Pendleton, Salford 6, Manchester. Tel: 061 737 5938

ASB •† Andrew Spencer Bottomley, The Coach House, 173A Huddersfield Road, Thongsbridge, Holmfirth, Huddersfield, Yorks. Tel: 0484 685234

ASc • Ascott Antiques, Narborough, Leics. Tel: 0533 863190

ASH • Ashburton Marbles, Grate Hall, North Street, Ashburton, Devon. Tel: 0364 53189

B * Boardman, Station Road Corner, Haverhill, Suffolk. Tel: 0440 703784

BBA * Bloomsbury Book Auctions, 3/4 Hardwick Street, Off Rosebery Avenue, London EC1. Tel: 071 833 2636/6361945

BBR *† BBR Auctions, c/o Elsecar Project, Wath Road, Elsecar, Barnsley, S. Yorks. Tel: 0226 745156.

Bea * Bearnes, Rainbow, Avenue Road, Torquay, Devon. Tel: 0803 296277

BEE •† Beehive House, Janice Paull, 125 Warwick Road, Kenilworth, Warwickshire CV8 1HY Tel: 0926 55253

BGA • By George Antique Centre, 23 George Street, St. Albans, Herts. Tel: 0727 53032

BHE •† British Heritage Telephones, 11 Rhodes Drive, Unsworth, Bury, Lancs. Tel: 061-767 9259

Bon *† Bonhams, Montpelier Galleries, Montpelier Street, Knightsbridge, London SW7. Tel: 071 584 9161

BOW •† Simon Bowler, Smith Street Antique Centre, Warwick. Tel: 0926 400554 & 021 783 8930

BWA • Bow-Well Antiques, 103 West Bow, Edinburgh. Tel: 031 225 3335.

BWe * Biddle & Webb of Birmingham, Ladywood Middleway, Birmingham. Tel: 021 455 8042

C * Christie, Manson & Woods Ltd., 8 King Street, St James's, London SW1. Tel: 071 839 9060

CAA • Central Antique Arms & Militaria, Smith Street Antique Centre, 7 Smith Street, Warwick, CV34 4JA Tel: 0926 400554

CAB •† Candlestick & Bakelite, PO Box 308, Orpington, Kent. Tel: 081 467 3743.

CAG * Canterbury Auction Galleries, 40 Station Road West, Canterbury, Kent. Tel: 0227 763337.

CB • Christine Bridge Antiques, 78 Castlenau, London SW1 Tel: 081 741 5501

CCC •† The Crested China Co., The Station House, Driffield, E. Yorks. Tel: 0377 47042

CD • The China Doll, 31 Walcot Street, Bath, Avon. Tel: 0225 465849

C(G) * Christie's (International) S.A., 8 Place de la Tocannerie, 1204 Geneva. Tel: 010 4122 311 1766

CHa • Carol Hammond, Unit 8, Kensington Church Street Antiques Centre, 58/60 Kensington Church Street, London W8. Tel: 071 938 4405

CHA • Chapel House Antiques, 32 Pentood Industrial Estate, Pendre, Cardigan, Dyfed. Tel: 0239 614868 & 613268

CJS • Collectable Jukeboxes (Terry Price), PO Box 1964, Selly Oak, Birmingham B29 4B2. Tel: 021 475 6540.

CLA • Classic Costumes, Northcote Road Antique Market, 155a Northcote Road, Battersea, London SW11. Tel: 081 764 8858

COB •† Cobwebs, 78 Northam Road, Southampton. Tel: 0703 227458

COL •† Collectables, P.O. Box 130, Chatham, Kent. Tel: 0634 828767

CNY * Christie, Manson & Woods International Inc., 502 Park Avenue, New York, NY 10022, USA. Tel: (212) 546 1000 (including Christie's East)

CP •† Cat Pottery, 1 Grammar School Road, North Walsham, Norfolk Tel: 0692 402962

CPT • Chris Partington, 41 Berwick Road, Shrewsbury, Shropshire SY1 2LS Tel: 0743 369373

CS •† Christopher Sykes Antiques, The Old Parsonage, Woburn, Bucks. Tel: 0525 290259/290467

C(S) * Christie's Scotland Ltd., 164-166 Bath Street, Glasgow. Tel: 041 332 8134

CSA • Church Street Antiques, 15 Church Street, Godalming, Surrey. Tel: 0483 860894

CSC • The Chicago Sound Company, Northmoor House, Colesbrook, Gillingham, Dorset. Tel: 0747 824338

CSK *† Christie's (South Kensington) Ltd., 85 Old Brompton Road, London SW7. Tel: 071 581 7611

DA * Dee & Atkinson, The Exchange Saleroom, Driffield, Yorks YO25 7LJ. Tel: 0377 43151

DaD • David Dockree, 224 Moss Lane, Bramhall, Stockport Cheshire. Tel: 061 485 1258

DHO • Derek Howard, The Original Chelsea Antiques Market, 245/253 King's Road, London SW3. Tel: 071-352 4113

DID • Didier Antiques, 58-60 Kensington Church Street, London W8. Tel: 071 938 2537 & 0836 232634

DN * Dreweatt Neate, Donnington Priory, Donnington, Newbury, Berks. Tel: 0635 31234

DRU • Drummonds of Bramley, Birtley Farm, Horsham Road, Bramley, Guildford, Surrey. Tel: 0483 898766.

EB • E. Brook, Smith Street Antique Centre, Warwick. Tel: 0926 497864

EP * Evans & Partridge, Agriculture House, High Street, Stockbridge, Hants. Tel: 0264 810702

FAB • FAB, 130 Queen's Road, Nuneaton, Warwicks. Tel: 0203 382399

FMN •† Forget Me Not Antiques (Heather Sharp), By George Antique Centre, 23 George Street, St. Albans, Herts. Tel: 0727 53032 & 0923 261172

G&CC •† Goss and Crested China Ltd. (Nicholas J. Pine), 62 Murray Road, Horndean, Hants. Tel: 0705 597440

GAK • G. A. Key, 8 Market Place, Aylsham, Norwich, Norfolk. Tel: 0263 733195

GAZ • Gazelles, 31 Northam Road, Southampton. Tel: 0703 235291/780798

GH * Giles Haywood, The Auction House, St. John's Road, Stourbridge, W. Midlands. Tel: 0384 370891

GHA • Garden House Antiques, 116-118 High Street, Tenterden, Kent. Tel: 05806 3664

GRF • Grange Farm Ltd., Grange Farm, Tongham, Surrey. Tel: 0258 2993/2804

HB •† Harrington Bros., The Chelsea Antique Market, 253 King's Road, London SW3 5EL. Tel: 071 352 5689 & 1720.

HCH * Hobbs & Chambers, Market Place, Cirencester, Glos. Tel: 0285 4736

HEG • Stuart Heggie, 58 Northgate, Canterbury, Kent CT1 1BB Tel: 0227 470422

HEW •† Muir Hewett, Halifax Antiques Centre, Queen's Road Mills, Queen's Road/Gibbet Street, Halifax, W. Yorks. Tel: 0422 366657

HEY • Heyford Antiques, 7 Church Street, Nether Heyford, Northampton. Tel: 0327 40749

HOW • Howards Antiques, 10 Alexandra Road, Aberystwyth, Dyfed. Tel: 0970 624973

HSS * Henry Spencer & Sons, 20 The Square, Retford, Notts. Tel: 0777 708633.

ING • Inglewood Antiques, Ely St. Antique Centre, Stratford-upon-Avon, Warwicks. Tel: 0789 297496

IS •† Ian Sharp Antiques, 23 Front Street, Tynemouth. Tel: 091-296 0656

IW	•†	Islwyn Watkins, 1 High Street, 29 Market Street, Knighton, Powys. Tel: 0547 520145 & 528940
JAC	•	John & Anne Clegg, 12 Old Street, Ludlow, Shropshire Tel: 0584 873176
JBB	•†	Jessie's Button Box, Great Western Antique Centre, Bartlett Street, Bath, Avon. Tel: 0225 310388
JH	*	Jacobs & Hunt, Lavant Street, Petersfield, Hants. Tel: 0730 62744
JHo	•	Jonathan Horne (Antiques) Ltd., 66B & C Kensington Church Street, London W8. Tel: 071 221 5658.
JMC	•	J & M Collectables, The Cranbrook Antique Centre, High Street, Cranbrook, Kent. Tel: 0580 891657
JMG	•†	Jamie Maxtone Graham, Lyne Haugh, Lyne Station, Peebles, Scotland. Tel: 07214 304.
K	•†	Keith Gretton, Unit 14 Northcote Road Antique Market, Battersea, London SW11. Tel: 071 228 0741 & 071 228 6850
KAC	•	Kensington Antique Centre, 58-60 Kensington Church Street, London W8. Tel: 071 376 0425
L	*	Lawrence Fine Art, South Street, Crewkerne, Somerset. Tel: 0460 73041
LB	•	The Lace Basket, la East Cross, Tenterden, Kent. Tel: 05806 3923/3664
LBL	•	Laurance Black Ltd. Antiques of Scotland, 45 Cumberland Street, Edinburgh. Tel: 031 557 4545
LF	*	Lambert & Foster, 102 High Street, Tenterden, Kent. TN30 6HU. Tel: 05806 3233.
LIO	•†	Lion's Den, 31 Henley Street, Stratford-upon-Avon, Warwicks. Tel: 0789 415802.
LR	•	Leonard Russell, 21 King's Avenue, Mount Pleasant, Newhaven, E. Sussex. Tel: 0273 515153
LRG	•	Lots Road Galleries, 71 Lots Road, London SW10 0RN. Tel: 071 351 7771
MA	•	Manor Antiques, 2a High Street, Westerham, Kent. Tel: 0959 64810
MAS	•	Maskerade (Lynn Waller), Unit 15, The Antique Centre, 58 Kensington Church Street, London W8. Tel: 071 937 8974
MCA	*	Mervyn Carey Auctions, Twysden Cottage, Benenden, Cranbrook, Kent. Tel: 0580 240283
MJB	*	Michael J. Bowman, 6 Haccombe House, Netherton, Newton Abbot, Devon. Tel: 0626 872890
ML	•	Magic Lantern (Josie Marsden), By George Antique Centre, 23 George Street, St. Albans, Herts. Tel: 0727 53032
MR	*	Martyn Rowe, The Truro Auction Centre, Calenick Street, Truro, Cornwall TR1 2SG. Tel: 0872 260020.
MRT	•	Mark Rees Tools, Barrow Mead Cottage, Rush Hill, Bath BA2 2QR Tel: 0225 837031
N	*	Neales, 192-194 Mansfield Road, Nottingham NG1 3HX Tel: 0602 624141
NA	•	Nostalgia Amusements, 22 Greenwood Close, Thames Ditton, Surrey. Tel: 081 398 2141
NB	•	Nicolaus Boston, Kensington Church Street Antique Centre, London W8. Tel: 071 376 0425 & 0722 326906
NCA	•†	New Century Art Pottery, 69 Kensington Church Street, London W8. Tel: 071 376 2810
ND	*†	Nock Deighton, Livestock & Auction Centre, Tasley, Bridgnorth, Shropshire WV16 40R. Tel: 0746 762666
NF	•	Nick Fletcher, PO Box 411, Longton, Stoke-on-Trent ST3 4SS.
NOS	•	Nostalgia Comics, 14-16 Smallbrook Queensway, City Centre, Birmingham. Tel: 021 643 0143
NOW	•	Now & Then, 7 & 9 West Crosscauseway, Edinburgh EH8 9JW. Tel: 031 668 2927/0860 278774
NP	•†	Neville Pundole, PO Box 6, Attleborough, Norfolk. Tel: 0953 454106
OD	•	Offa's Dyke Antique Centre, 4 High Street, Knighton, Powys, Wales. Tel: 0547 528635
ONS	*	Onslow's Metrostore, Townmead Road, London SW6. Tel: 071 793 0240
ORG	•	Oriental Rug Gallery, 42 Verulam Road, St. Albans, Herts AL3 4DQ Tel: 0727 41046
PAG	•	Prinny's Antiques Gallery (F. Whitney Antiques), 3 Meeting House Lane, Brighton. Tel: 0273 204554
PAR	•	Park House Antiques, Park Street, Stow-on-the-Wold, Nr Cheltenham, Glos.
PC		Private Collection
PCh	*	Peter Cheney, Western Road Auction Rooms, Western Road, Littlehampton, Sussex. Tel: 0903 722264 & 713418
P(L)	*	Phillips, Hepper House, 17a East Parade, Leeds LS1 2BU Tel: 0532 448011
PLO	•	Mrs I. Morton-Smith, The Plough, Maysleith, Milland, Nr. Liphook, Hants Tel: 0428 76323
POW	•†	Sylvia Powell Decorative Arts, 28 The Mall, Camden Passage, London N1. Tel: 071 354 2977/081 458 4543.
PR	•	Pamela Richards, Sheep Street Antique Centre, Stratford-upon-Avon, Warwicks.
P(S)	*	Phillips, 49 London Road, Sevenoaks, Kent. Tel: 0732 740310
PSA	•	Pantiles Spa Antiques, 6 Union House, Eridge Road, Tunbridge Wells, Kent. Tel: 0892 541377
RAG	*	Rye Auction Galleries, Rock Channel, Rye, Sussex. Tel: 0797 222124.
RBB	*	Russell, Baldwin & Bright, Fine Art Salerooms, Ryelands Road, Leominster, Hereford. Tel: 0568 611166

RdeR• Rogers de Rin, 76 Hospital Road, Paradise Walk, London SW3. Tel: 071 352 9007

RE • Ron's Emporium, 98 Church Lane, Sholden, Deal, Kent. Tel: 0304 374784

REL • Relic Antiques at Brillscote Farm, Lea, Malmesbury, Wilts. Tel: 0666 822332

RFA • Rochester Fine Arts, 86 High Street, Rochester, Kent. Tel: 0634 814129

RIC • Rich Designs, 11 Union Street, Stratford-upon-Avon, Warwicks. Tel: 0789 772111.

RID * Riddetts of Bournemouth, 26 Richmond Hill, Bournemouth, Dorset Tel: 0202 555686

ROS • Roses, 60 King's Street, Sandwich, Kent. Tel: 0304 615303

ROW • Rowena Blackford at Penny Lampard's Antique Centre, 31-33 High Street, Headcorn, Kent. Tel: 0622 890682 & 861360

RP • Robert Pugh, Pennard House Antiques, 3/4 Piccadilly, London Road, Bath. Tel: 0225 314713/313791

RR • Jonathan Hill, 2-4 Brook Street, Bampton, Devon. Tel: 0398 331532

RWB • Roy W. Bunn Antiques, 34-36 Church Street, Barnoldswick, Colne, Lancs. Tel: 0282 813703

S * Sotheby's, 34-35 New Bond Street, London W1. Tel: 071 493 8080

S(AM)* Sotheby's, 102 Rokin, 1012 KZ, Amsterdam, Holland. Tel: 31 (20) 627 56 56

S(Mon)* Sotheby's Monaco, BP 45-98001, Monaco. Tel: 93 30 88 80

S(NY)* Sotheby's New York, 1334 York Avenue, New York, NY 10021. Tel: 212 606 7000

S(S) * Sotheby's Sussex, Summers Place, Billingshurst, W. Sussex. Tel: 0403 783933

SAM • Samarkand Galleries, 2 Brewery Yard, Sheep Street, Stow-on-the-Wold, Glos. Tel: 0451 832322

SCO • Scot Hay House Antiques, 7 Nantwich Road, Woore, Shropshire. Tel: 063081 7118

SCR •† The Scripophily Shop, Britannia House, Grosvenor Square, London W1. Tel: 071 495 0580

SCW • The Sussex Commemorative Ware Centre, 88 Western Road, Hove, Sussex BN3 1JB. Tel: 0273 773911.

Sim * Simmons & Sons, 32 Bell Street, Henley-on-Thames, Oxon. Tel: 0491 591111

Som • Somervale Antiques, 6 Radstock Road, Midsomer Norton, Bath, Avon. Tel: 0761 412686

SRA *† Sheffield Railwayana Auctions, 43 Little Norton Lane, Sheffield, Yorks. Tel: 0742 745085 & 0860 921519

STE •† Stevenson Brothers, The Workshop, Ashford Road, Bethersden, Ashford, Kent. Tel: 0233 820580

STK •† Stockbridge Antiques, 8 Deanhaugh Street, Edinburgh EH4 1LY. Tel: 031 332 1366

SUF • Suffolk Sales, Half Moon House, High Street, Clare, Suffolk. Tel: 0787 277993

SWO * Sworders, G. E. Sworder & Sons, 15 Northgate End, Bishops Stortford, Herts. Tel: 0279 51388

TED •† Teddy Bears of Witney, 99 High Street, Witney, Oxon. Tel: 0993 702616

TEM • Teddy's Emporium, 50 Northgate, Canterbury, Kent CT1 1BE Tel: 0227 769987

TH • Tony Horsley. Tel: 0273 732163

TOR • Tortoiseshell (Pixie Taylor), Trebedw Guest House, Henllan, Llandysul, Dyfed, Wales. Tel: 0559 370943.

TRU • The Trumpet, West End, Minchinhampton, Glos. Tel: 0453 883027

TS • Tim's Spot, Ely St. Antique Centre, Stratford-upon-Avon, Warwicks. Tel: 0789 297496

TVA • Teme Valley Antiques, 1 The Bull Ring, Ludlow, Shropshire. Tel: 0584 874686.

VB • Variety Box, 16 Chapel Place, Tunbridge Wells, Kent. Tel: 0892 31868 & 21589

VBu •† Valerie Burman, Market Fayre, 69 High Street, Broadstairs, Kent. Tel: 0843 862563

VH • Valerie Howard, 131e Kensington Church Street, London W8. Tel: 071 792 9702

VS *† T. Vennett-Smith, 11 Nottingham Road, Gotham, Nottingham. Tel: 0602 830541

WA •† Windmill Antiques, 4 Montpelier Mews, Harrogate, Yorks. Tel: 0423 530502 & 0845 401330

WAC •† Walsall Antiques Centre, 7a Digbeth Arcade, Walsall, W. Midlands. Tel: 0922 725163/5

WAL *† Wallis & Wallis, West Street Auction Galleries, Lewes, E. Sussex. Tel: 0273 480208

WEL • Wells Reclamation & Co., The Old Cider Farm, Coxley, Nr Wells, Somerset Tel: 0749 77087/77484

Wil • Willcocks Antiques, G3 Chenil Galleries, 181-183 King's Road, London SW3. Tel: 071 351 6816.

WIL * Peter Wilson, Victoria Gallery, Market Street, Nantwich, Cheshire. Tel: 0270 623878

WW * Woolley & Wallis, The Castle Auction Mart, Castle Street, Salisbury, Wilts Tel: 0722 321711

YV • Yvonne Willcocks, K3 Chenil Galleries, 183 King's Road, Chelsea, London SW3. Tel: 071 352 7384

ZEI • Zeitgeist, 58 Kensington Church Street, London W8. Tel: 071 938 4817

Aeronautica

A presentation silver salver and other memorabilia relating to Lt. G.L. Brinton, RN, (Flying Officer RAF), a member of the Schneider Trophy Team, 1931.
£2,900-3,000 *S(S)*

A Gloster Meteor control column handgrip, with firing buttons, in as new condition with packing, in original box, 8in (20cm) wide.
£125-150 *CSK*

A portrait of a WRAF pilot, 26in (66cm) long.
£125-175 *RE*

An RAF sector clock, with 5 minute red, blue and yellow sectors, mahogany case stamped on the back S.Davall & Sons, Goswell Road, dated 1939, lacking glass and winding key, case with traces of paint.
£850-900 *S(S)*

A bomb aimer's computer, 1940s.
£15-18 *COB*

An RAF World War II period sector clock, the case stamped MCA21B713, with RAF crest, 17.25in (43.8cm) diam., unrestored.
£1,800-2,000 *CSK*

Air Chief Marshal Lord Dowding's handwritten draft 'farewell' message to Fighter Command, November 1940.
£9,000-10,000 *S(S)*

A Supermarine Spitfire blind flying panel, with connecting pipes, 14in (30.5cm) wide.
£460-480 *CSK*

A rare RNAS station bell, with original clapper and white painted rope handle, 16in (40.5cm) high.
£1,600-1,700 *S(S)*

An Air Ministry pattern astro-compass manufactured by Sperti Inc. Cincinnati, Ohio; an RAF sextant MkV; and an aircraft octant in case, 8.25in (21cm) wide.
£25-30 *CSK*
and a bubble sextant Mk VIII by H. Hughes & Son Limited, 10.5in (27cm) wide, in case and a U.S. pattern Army Air Force pattern bubble sextant, in case 12.75in (32.5cm) wide.
£60-70 *CSK*

A Brooklands Aero Club car badge, nickel plated with enamelling in 5 colours, the reverse numbered 130, some damage, early 1930s.
£575-600 *S(S)*

A Luftwaffe pilot's wristwatch, 1940s. **£450-500** *S(S)*

Cross Reference
Wristwatches

An 'Aviation' board game, The Aerial Tactics Game of Attack and Defence, with original printed cards on metal stands and board, in original box.
£80-100 *CSK*

Part of the propellor of a Mark I Spitfire, 1940s, 6.5in (16cm) square.
£15-20 *OD*

A silver and enamelled RFC cigarette case, the gilt interior engraved Capt. A. D. Pass. RFC 23 Queens Gate Terrace, S.W., some enamel missing, hallmarked London 1916, 5in (13.5cm) high.
£100-120 *S(S)*

An RAF Operations Room Sector clock, with painted dial divided into coloured triangles of red, yellow and blue for 2.5 minute periods, in mahogany case, stamped 16573 Made by W. Elliott Ltd. England 1941, 14in (35.5cm) diam, with key.
£1,500-1,600 *CSK*

A complete Kelvin Hughes Craig computer, for course and speed calculation, with original instruction book in mint condition, in original transit case, 28in (71cm) long.
£275-300 *CSK*

Part of a crashed spitfire.
£25-28 *COB*

A teddy bear, Edward St. John Biggin, complete with flying outfit decorated with numerous badges and a Flying Log Book, showing many types flown, with photographs and display case containing further badges.
£450-500 *S(S)*

A bronze medallion commemorating the Montgolfier brothers' ascent, with moulded signature N. Galteaux, 1.5in (4cm) diam. **£150-200** *CSK*

Cross Reference
Teddy Bears

A silk Union Jack, inscribed in ink 'Flown on Apollo 15 26th July- 7th Aug 1971' and signed by the astronaut Al Worden, with silk crew badge for Scott, Worden and Irwin, framed and glazed, with hand written card by Al Worden certifying authenticity.
£1,800-1,900 *CSK*

A gilt bronze medallion, embossed 'Lindbergh Medal of the Congress of the United States of America', signed 'Lavra Gardia Fraser Sculptor', 'Act May 4 1928', 2.75in (7cm).
£120-140 *CSK*

A collection of World War II period wooden scale model construction kits.
£120-150 *CSK*

Dress

A USAAF issue silk lined leather flying jacket, the back decorated with an F86 Sabre surrounded by stars. **£200-220** *CSK*

A RAF flying helmet, complete with visor, microphones, etc, 1970s. **£60-65** *COB*

A USAAF flying suit and helmet, the lightweight suit in orange cotton with Colonel insignia, type K-2B, label dated 13 November 1963, and transfers, including 155th Fighter Group. **£650-700** *S(S)*

A WRAF pilot's helmet and spats, c1930. **£90-110** RE

A USAAF officer's service tunic and trousers, WWII period. **£250-275** *S(S)*

A rare group of early RAF uniform and flying clothing, 1918. **£950-1,100** *S(S)*

An Air Transport Auxiliary (Ferry Pilots) blue service tunic, skirt and side cap, with ATA wings and First Officer rank. **£475-525** *ONS*

Ephemera

A Qantas flying boat luggage label, 1940. **£3-4** *COB*

A box of approximately 200 1940s aircraft recognition cards. **£40-45** *COB*

H.S. Williamson, Imperial Airways, London, Scylla, lithograph in colours, 1934, backed on linen, 20 by 25in (51 by 64cm).
£625-650 *CSK*

A World War II period Royal Air Force pilot's flying log book for G.A.F. Edmiston, qualified as pilot 22nd July 1940.
£320-350 *CSK*

A selection of illustrated German aviation books, with original dust jackets.
£10-20 each *CSK*

Models

A Tippco clockwork lithographed tinplate high wing bomber, cat. ref. 29, with operating propeller, undercarriage and bomb dropping action, c1936, pilot, bombs and bombing mechanism missing.
£375-400 *CSK*

A flying scale model of Junkers D1 single seat fighter, wooden airframe covered with simulated corrugated aluminium, with working control surfaces, finished in green and purple camouflage, wingspan 76in (193cm).
£1,250-1,350 *CSK*

A 1:72 scale aluminium model of a Fokker DR1, 'The Red Baron Werner Voss' by D. Vann, wingspan 7.5in (19.5cm).
£225-250 *CSK*

A flying scale model of a Fokker DVII, the single seat fighter with fabric covered wooden airframe and working control surfaces, finished in camouflage red, blue and white, wingspan 57in (145cm).   **£350-375** *CSK*

A flying scale model of a Hawker Fury, with fabric covered wooden airframe and working control surfaces, finished in the colours of No. 43 Sqn. RAF the famous 'Fighting Cocks', wingspan 60in (152.5cm).
£460-480 *CSK*

A flying scale model of a Sparmann P-1, with fabric covered wooden airframe and working control surfaces, finished in Swedish Air Force silver livery, wingspan 82in (208cm). **£575-600** CSK

A detailed flying scale model of a Bristol Bulldog, with fabric covered wooden airframe, and working control surfaces, finished in the colours of No. 3 Sqn. RAF, wingspan 64in (162.5cm). **£450-475** *CSK*

A model aircraft centrepiece, by Doug Vann, modern, 8in (20.5cm) high. **£900-1,000** *S(S)*

A flying scale model of a Curtis Owl, finished in USAAF camouflage, wingspan 82in (208cm). **£400-425** *CSK*

A 1:144 scale aluminium model of the Hawker Hurricane, mounted by D. Vann, wingspan, 6.75in (17.2cm). **£120-130** *CSK*

A flying scale model of a de Havilland Mosquito FB.VI, with wooden airframe, working rudder, elevators, ailerons and flaps, finished in RCAF camouflage of 418 (City of Edmonton), wingspan 72in (183cm). **£1,500-1,600** *CSK*

A flying scale model of a Bucker Bu131 Jungmann, with fabric covered wooden airframe and working control surfaces, finished in Luftwaffe markings and camouflage, wingspan 72in (183cm). **£650-680** *CSK*

A flying scale model of a Hawker Hurricane, with working control surfaces, finished in blue, wingspan 66in (177.5cm). **£475-500** *CSK*

l. A static display model of a Sopwith Pup, with cockpit with flying and engine controls, 9.5in (24cm) long.   **£300-325**

r. A detailed scale static display model of the Sopwith 5F.1. Dolphin, Serial No. E5429, with fabric covered wings fuselage and empennage, cockpit with flying and engine controls, windscreen and 2 machine guns with telescopic sight, 9 cylinder rotary engine, propeller, undercarriage and other details, finished in RFC camouflage 9.5in (24cm) long. **£420-450** *CSK*

A flying scale model of the Gloster Gladiator, with wooden airframe and working control surfaces, finished in the colours of No. 43 Sqn. RAF, wingspan 56in (142cm). **£460-480** *CSK*

A flying scale model of a Fokker DVI, with fabric covered wooden airframe, working control surfaces, finished in green, purple and white with markings, wingspan 73in (185.5cm). **£1,250-1,400** *CSK*

Photographs

Postcards

A set of 9 World War II Luftwaffe photo mechanical colour reproductions, slight tear, 10 by 11.5in (25 by 29cm). **£200-225** *CSK*

A collection of 35 signed commemorative philatelic covers related to the NASA Space Programme, including Mercury, Apollo, Gemini and Space Shuttle flights. **£850-875** *CSK*

Signatures include: Major General Walter Dornberger, ex commandant, Peenemunde, Wernher von Braun, Willy Messerschmitt, John Glenn, Cdr. Scott Carpenter, Col. James McDivitt, Capt. James Lovell, Neil Armstrong, 'Buzz' Aldrin, Alexander Ivanchenkov, Vladimir Kovalenok and many others.

Cross Reference
Postcards

A collection of 13 photographs, some in colour, including Avro Lancaster ED 592, and a selection of aviation 'Profile' booklets.   **£50-60** *CSK*

A collection of 10 coloured and photographic postcards. **£170-190** *CSK*

A collection of 20 early aviation postcards. **£110-125** *CSK*

A collection of 11 official photographic reproduction postcards depicting LZ 127, 'Graf Zeppelin'. **£210-230** *CSK*

Cross Reference
Zeppelins

Prints

James Goulding, Heinkel He 162 A 2, 19.5 by 15in (49.5 by 38cm). **£210-230** *CSK*

Original artwork for 'Profile' and other publications.

Posters

DORNIER-WERKE

DMZ Deutsche Motor-Zeitshrift, various issues 1933-39, unbound, some complete years, containing advertisements for German aircraft manufacturers, and a quantity of technical books. **£75-85** *CSK*

An Imperial Airways lithograph in colours, backed on linen, c1936, 38 by 25in (98 by 63cm). **£725-750** *CSK*

Frank Wootton, born 1911, Lockheed Super Constellation of Linea Aeropostal Venezuela, signed and inscribed, oil sketch on board, unframed, 21.25 by 25.25in (54 by 64cm). **£775-800** *CSK*

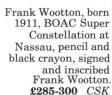

Frank Wootton, born 1911, BOAC Super Constellation at Nassau, pencil and black crayon, signed and inscribed Frank Wootton. **£285-300** *CSK*

An Imperial Airways flying boat map, 1930s. **£20-25** *COB*

A collection of 6 aircraft pictures, including a Dewoitine 730, 9.5 by 12.5in (24 by 32cm). **£120-140** *CSK*

A Short built Felixtowe F5s, in 'dazzle' camouflage on convoy patrol, watercolour, 17 by 22in (43 by 56cm). **£60-80** *CSK*

Munro, 'Wapiti', signed, inscribed and dated, pencil and watercolour, 12.5 by 19.25in (32 by 49cm). **£60-70** *CSK*

C. Rupert Moore, a Dragon Rapide of North Sea Air Transport Ltd., airborne, signed and dated 1947, pencil and bodycolour heightened with white, 23.5 by 17.25in (60 by 44cm). **£80-100** *CSK*

A rare Vickers Supermarine Spitfire Sales Brochure, dated June 1939, spiral bound, sepia and blue, photos and text. **£620-640** *CSK*
Provenance: ex R.J. Mitchell and thence by descent.

A collection of 14 original artworks for 'Profile' publications. **£350-370** *CSK*

Ross Nicoll, The Vickers Valiant prototype, signed, gouache and watercolour, 16.25 by 22.75in (41 by 58cm). **£125-145** *CSK*

W.J. Gaskin, Handley Page Heyford bombers in mock combat with flight of Hawker Furies, signed, pencil and watercolour, 10.75 by 15.5in (27.5 by 40cm). **£100-120** *CSK*

Roffe, Fokker triplanes, and SE5s about to close for action, gouache, signed, 12.25 by 18.25in (31 by 46.5cm).
£80-100 *CSK*

A limited edition print, Return of the Few, after Robert Taylor, 7/50, signed in pencil by 52 Battle of Britain pilots, including Brian Kingcome, Bob Stanford-Tuck, Frank Carey, Pete Brothers and Al Deere, 24 by 16in (61 by 41cm), mounted, framed and glazed.
£850-1,000 *S(S)*

A collection of original artworks including de Havilland Rapide, for 'Profile' publications.
£350-370 *CSK*

A collection of 16 original artworks for 'Profile' publications.
£220-240 *CSK*

Propellers

A laminated mahogany 2-blade propeller, with canvas covered tips and brass leading edges, the boss stamped 'DRG No.Z64 80 HP. CIRRUS MkII. D 6'4". P4'8" A G 51482 DEC/33', one blade with transfer The Airscrew Co. Weybridge Surrey, 76in (193cm) diam.
£160-180 *CSK*

A 4-bladed laminated mahogany aircraft propeller, the boss stamped G64N51, D2366P3340, T28096 LH, 200HP, Hispano Suiza, SE5, 94in (239cm) diam.
£650-700 *CSK*

A rare 4-blade laminated wood propeller, the 4 tips with brass sheaths stamped around the shaft hull '2869 Darracq Motor Engineering Co. Ltd., London, 100hp Monosoupape Gnome FE8, W.D. 17586 T 7928' bearing the original Darracq circular transfer to the reverse of the blade.
£800-900 *MR*

This propeller is one of a batch of 245 plus 50 more completed by Vickers of the Durracq-built FE8 Biplane Fighter with pusher propeller of late 1916. It was used by No. 40 or No. 41 Squadron Royal Flying Corps.
With full provenance from its retainment after World War I to its present owner.

A two-bladed laminated mahogany propeller, boss stamped D2500 P1800 886, 98in (249cm) span.
£475-525 *S(S)*

A laminated mahogany two-blade propeller, applied with transfers for F Tibbenham, Ipswich, 104in (264cm) diam.
£450-460 *CSK*

A laminated mahogany 4-blade propeller, built in 2 sections and with brass leading edges, the bosses stamped GF 0572 No.2 (the other 2A) DRG.No.5097.4.25 D 2660P2180 De H 50, 107in (271.8cm).
£950-1,000 *CSK*

Zeppelins

The Graf Zeppelin
OVER NEW YORK
(THE SHERRY-NETHERLAND HOTEL)

A menu card, The Graf Zeppelin over New York, from the first Europe Pan-American flight, issued by the Louis Sherry Hotel N.Y.
£250-275 *CSK*

» Die Zeppeline tanken vor jeder Weltfahrt frisches Oel «

Schonen auch Sie Ihren Motor durch regelmäßigen Oelwechsel
laut Fabrikempfehlung unabhängig von Sommer und Winter
nur mit

VEEDOL
MOTORENOEL
HAMBURG-AMERIKANISCHE MINERALÖL-GESELLSCHAFT M B H
HAMBURG 30

A collection of photographs from the personal album of Heinrich Kubis, some taken on board LZ 127 'Graf Zeppelin', and a chromium plated shaped entrée dish carried aboard LZ 129 'Hindenburg' during the 1936 'Olympiafahrt', 11.5in (28.9cm) wide.
£3,400-3,500 *CSK*

A Veedol lithograph poster in colours, backed on linen, 50 by 29.5in (127 by 75cm).
£575-600 *CSK*

A clockwork lithographed tinplate Graf Zeppelin D LZ 127, equipped for electric light, bulb holder missing.
£350-375 *CSK*

A leatherette and silk lined correspondence folder, embossed in gilt 'Graf Zeppelin', with a pictorial representation of LZ 127, 17.5in (44.5cm) wide open, and a collection of original Deutsche Zeppelin-Reedcrei notepaper, envelopes and a broadsheet, carried aboard, c1929.
£550-575 *CSK*

A collection of 6 commemorative postcards, 3 colour including one dated 17-9-29 'Au Bord des Luftschiffes Graf Zeppelin,', and a photograph of LZ127 Graf Zeppelin alighting on the Bodensee.
£110-125 *CSK*

A gilt-bronze and enamel commemorative plaque, inscribed ZIELFAHRT ZUR ZEPPELIN-LANDUNG, 1931, 3.25in (8.2cm) wide.
£220-240 *CSK*

A wood and plated metal Art Deco period window static display model of Graf Zeppelin, 16.75 by 30in (42.5 by 76.2cm).
£950-1,000 *CSK*

FURTHER READING

History of British Aviation, Brett R. Dallas, 2 vols 1908-14 and 1913-14
British Flying Boats and Amphibians, G. R. Duval, 1909-52 London 1953
The Fighters: The Men and Machines of the First Air War, Thomas R. Funderburk, London 1966
The History of Aeronautics in Britain, J. E. Hodgson, 1924
Janes All The World's Aircraft - Published annually
Airmails 1870-1970, James A. Mackay, London 1971.
Combat Aircraft of the World, F. C. Swanborough, London 1962

A scarce commemorative painted metal money box, recording a zeppelin landing on 5th August, 1908, made by Märklin, 5in (13cm).
£525-575 *S(S)*

A LZ130 'Graf Zeppelin' folding broadsheet, with detailed cut-away and publicity information for this, the last Zeppelin built, dated 5/39.
£175-200 *CSK*

Automobilia

A BP Motor Spirit double sided union flag, 16 by 24in (41 by 62cm). **£150-170** *ONS*

A Bedford Drivers Club badge, 3.25in (11cm) diam. **£2-5** *PC*

A Price's Motorine Motor Oil, double sided sign, 18in (46cm) diam. **£80-100** *ONS*

A Jaguar car badge, 4in (10cm) long. **£4-6** *RE*

A Runeasy cycle oil can, 1920s. **£9-11** *COB*

A Henry Le Monnier Automobile Unic Poster, lithograph in colours, 1928, backed on linen, 45 by 61in (115 by 155cm). **£1,000-1,200** *CSK*

A Louis Vuitton fine tan leather small accessory trunk, with leather corners, leather strap and carrying handles, brass studded, on casters, inside lid and base lined with brown felt, labelled LV No 789794, lock No 073685, 24 by 19 by 15.5in (62 by 48 by 39cm). **£1,500-1,700** *ONS*

Three tinplate clockwork toy racing cars, English, 1930-1940s. **£110-120** *S*

Cross Reference
Toys/Tinplate

A collection of 6 posters advertising Concours d'Elegance, Pebble Beach, California, from the 1960s. **£950-1,200** *CNY*

Two wood scratch built models of Bluebird, c1936, the largest 20in (51cm) long. **£175-200** *S*

Cross Reference
Toys

Mascots

A Mohican Indian Head chromium plated bronze mascot, mounded on wood base, by Darel, c1930, 4.75in (12cm) high.
£200-220 *CSK*

A monkey mascot, with an elongated mouth, brass mounted on brass base, c1920, 4in (10.5cm) high.
£150-160 *CSK*

It is believed this is one of 5 manufactured by Napier Cars for an Indian prince who commissioned a gold one as a wedding gift.

A Wolseley radiator cap, 4.75in (12cm) long.
£10-15 *RE*

A Lalique smoked grey glass 'Sanglier' mascot, etched and moulded R. Lalique, 2 small chips, 1930s, 2.75in (7cm) high.
£450-490 *S*

A Farman Icarus mascot, chromium plated bronze, stamped and marked Colin George, 20 782, Made in France, 10, base stamped Finnigans London, 1922, 6in (15cm) high.
£600-650 *S*

A Lalique car mascot, moulded in the form of a dragonfly with wings closed, moulded mark Lalique and engraved R. Lalique, France, c1920s, 6.25in (15.5cm) long.
£700-730 *WIL*

Art Deco

Art Deco, the style that epitomises the twenties and thirties, derived its name from the Paris Exhibition of 1925. The 'Exposition des Arts Decoratifs et Industriels Modernes', sponsored by the French Government, was a showcase of all that was modern. Designed to generate trade in post war Europe, it was a huge success. The Exhibition coupled with the launch of the liner SS Normandie in 1935 established Art Deco as one of the most innovative and exciting styles of the 20thC. Almost everything imaginable on the Normandie, from the glasses and tableware to the bathroom tiles, demonstrated the Art Deco style, establishing the designers as leaders in their respective fields.

Art Deco took a long time to become recognised by collectors. It was not until the sixties that attentions moved from the Art Nouveau period to Art Deco with the jewellery of Jean Fouquet and the glass of René Lalique leading the field.

Most modern collectors seem attracted to the practical wares; ceramics, glass and household accessories, particularly as furniture and those wonderful figures and sculptures became prohibitively expensive.

We have included a good selection of household goods in this year's edition and would remind you to cross reference to the glass and ceramic sections.

A chrome covered tea and coffee pot, c1930.
£25-35 each *CAB*

A Christofle 'Gallia' sugar shaker, in original box, c1920, 4.5in (12cm) high.
£300-350 *ABS*

An Art Deco chrome photograph frame, 6in (15cm) high.
£12-15 *ROW*

Cross Reference
Picture Frames

A French Art Deco gilt bronze and glass lamp, c1930.
£200-400
ASA

An Art Deco coffee and liqueur set, tray 17in (43.5cm) wide.
£400-600 *ASA*

Cross Reference
Radios

A radio by Walter Dorwin Teague, with mirrored glass and painted wood case, c1936, 17.5in (44.5cm) wide.
£850-900 *S*

An Art Deco figure lamp, with alabaster orb and shade. **£500-650** *ASA*

A lacquer cigarette case, c1920. **£300-350** *ABS*

A Ziggurat Art Deco oak photograph frame, 6in (15cm) high. **£12-15** *ROW*

Cross Reference
Smoking

A cold painted bronze, ivory, and marble 'Bat Dancer' clock, by Ferdinand Preiss, marked F. Preiss, c1925, 15in (39cm) high. **£4,250-4,750** *S*

An Art Deco chrome and black barometer, c1935 10in (25cm) wide. **£80-100** *CAB*

A set of 5 Art Deco ceiling and wall lights. **£600-1,000** *ASA*

Cross Reference
Continental Art Deco Ceramics

An Art Deco cold painted metal figure lamp, c1930. **£450-650** *ASA*

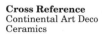

An Art Deco mirror, hand painted under the glass and signed P. A. Pilley, in a dark green lacquered frame, 25.5in (65cm) high. **£65-75** *ROW*

An Art Deco tea tray, with a coloured silver paper crinoline lady under black glass, in an oak frame, 16in (40.5cm) long. **£20-25** *ROW*

Clocks

A Modernist nickel plated metal and glass clock, attributed to Léon Hatot, c1930, 13in (33cm) high.
£675-700 *S*

A silver coloured metal clock with lightly hammered gilt metal finish, VII numeral missing, marked Imhof, 6in (16cm) high.
£700-750 *S*

A silver mounted clock with 30 hour movement, Birmingham 1923, 6in (15cm) high.
£100-125 *TRU*

Figures

A spelter figure of a girl fencer, 9.5in (24cm) high.
£300-350 *HEW*

'Scarf Dancer', a silvered bronze and onyx figure, by Demetre H. Chiparus, marked D H Chiparus, c1925, 26in (67cm) high.
£4,250-4,750 *S*

'Oriental Dancer', a cold painted bronze and onyx figure, by Demetre H. Chiparus, marked Chiparus, c1920, 16in (40cm) high.
£3,750-4,000 *S*

A cold painted bronze and ivory Devil and Girl, marked Roland Paris, on a marble stand, minor damage, c1920, 16in (40cm) high.
£1,600-1,700 *S*

An Art Deco carved wooden sculpture of frogs, 8in (20cm) high.
£80-150 *ASA*

Art Nouveau

The Art Nouveau style which had developed by about 1880 traced its origins to the earlier Arts and Crafts Movement. The same flowing floral designs were incorporated with the use of modern materials and craftsmanship. The styles were a great success at the Paris Exhibition of 1900 and artists and designers sold their wares at the gallery 'Maison de l'Art Nouveau' owned by the entrepreneur Siegfried Bing. Artists such as Tiffany, Gailliard and Emile Gallé soon became very popular. The term Art Nouveau is traditionally reputed to have derived from the title of Bing's gallery. The French referred to the movement as 'Le Style Anglais' and the Italians as 'Stile Liberty', much to the surprise of the founder of the store Arthur Liberty who constantly called it Art Nouveau!

Art Nouveau was a natural progression for collectors as the art and designs of the Victorian period became harder to find and consequently more expensive. By the 1960s Art Nouveau was firmly established as a collecting area in its own right.

We have concentrated our selection on more affordable practical household items, but would strongly recommend you to cross refer to the ceramic and glass sections, and particularly the work of Alphonse Mucha and Aubrey Beardsley in the Ephemera Section.

A pair of Keswick copper repoussé vases, by W.H. Mawson, 10in (25cm). **£150-175** *ZEI*

A Zsolnay ewer, in stoneware and gilt, c1900, 21.5in (55cm) high. **£600-800** *ABS*

A Keswick copper muffin dish, 9in (23cm). **£100-150** *ZEI*

A Newlyn copper punch bowl, with repoussé fruit and foliage, 11in (28cm). **£200-300** *ZEI*

A pair of WMF classical vases, in silvered pewter with cut crystal liners, 13in (33cm). **£600-800** *ZEI*

A neo-Gothic tea set in silvered Britannia metal for Spurrier and Cornforth, 1880s. **£600-800** *ZEI*

An iridescent glass three-handled dish, attributed to Marie Kirschner, for Loetz, c1905, 10in (25cm) diam. **£600-625** *S*

A pair of Liberty Tudric pewter vases, designed by Knox. **£500-600** *ZEI*

An Art Nouveau silver standing bowl, on shaped square base with 4 curved supports to the shaped square bowl top, London 1907, by Mappin & Webb, 18.5ozs.
£280-320 *GAK*

A lightly hammered silver inkwell, with cabochons, maker's mark London, inscribed Omar Ramsden et Alwyn Carr me fecerunt, c1912, 3.5in (9cm).
£875-925 *S*

A Keswick copper charger with repoussé design, 19in (48cm).
£200-300 *ZEI*

A Victorian terracotta planter, Arts & Crafts Movement, 26in (66cm) high.
£300-350 *GRF*

An Austrian pewter mounted vase, by Loetz, 9in (23cm).
£200-300 *ZEI*

A WMF Art Nouveau centrepiece, in silvered pewter with cut crystal liners, 20in (51cm) high.
£800-1,000 *ZEI*

A WMF oval flower dish, in silver plated pewter with green cut crystal liner, 15in (38cm).
£500-600 *ZEI*

A Della Robbia vase, by Anne David, 10in (25cm).
£250-300 *ZEI*

A Silberzinn wine cooler in the Art Nouveau Whiplash style.
£400-600 *ZEI*

A WMF Gothic revival silver on brass jewel casket.
£100-150 *ZEI*

A pair of carved wood mirrors, with easel supports, c1905, 16.5in (42cm).
£1,100-1,300 *S*

An Art Nouveau oil lamp stand, painted green with yellow flowers, 35in (89cm) high.
£250-300 *PC*

Candlesticks

A pair of WMF Arts & Crafts style candlesticks, 10in (25cm).
£300-350 *ZEI*

A pair of Goberg German Arts & Crafts candlesticks.
£100-150 *ZEI*

Picture Frames

A WMF silver plated toilet mirror, 12in (32in).
£700-800 *ZEI*

An English Art Nouveau style silver photograph frame, with large flowerheads on undulating leafy stems, blue velvet easel back, 11in (27.9cm) high.
£135-150 *CNY*

A pair of George V Art Nouveau style photograph frames, Chester 1913, 10in (25cm) high.
£650-675 *HSS*

Bells

A celluloid table or desk bell, moulded as an owl's head, with beak operating wind-up bell mechanism, c1930, 4in (10cm) diam.
£80-100 *PC*

For a further selection of bells please refer to Miller's Collectables Guide, Volume IV, pages 46-47

Books

Twentieth Century book collecting is currently a very popular area attracting some very good prices. Currently sought after are early P. G. Wodehouse and Stephen King. Cookery books are always in demand.

As with all collectables, condition is paramount, the classic catalogue description is 'As new with similar dust jacket', however books showing signs of use should not be discarded, but condition must be reflected in the price.

What constitutes a valuable book? Is it the age, author, title, condition, first edition, the illustrator, the illustrations, the fact that it is signed by the author, the leather binding or the rarity? In truth it is generally a combination of all or some of these things.

Desirability together with availability have created a great interest in 20thC books. They are accessible, bargains can still be found and one can start with little capital. Popular authors are, by definition, printed in large quantities, although this may not be the case with their early works. If a film or T.V. series has been made of the work this will help it achieve a wider audience. If the author is American then the U.S. printing is generally preferred although it may not necessarily be the true first. Ernest Hemingway's 'Across the River and into the Trees' was first published in the U.K. and Winston Churchill's 'History of the Second World War' was first issued in America, for example.

In the end the best way to learn about books is to handle them, seek out reliable dealers and ask questions.

The Dryads and Other Tales, by Frank White, illustrated by A. M. Corah, published by Frederick Warne & Co., Copyright 1936. **£18-20** *TRU*

The Boy's Own Book of Indoor Games, c1920s. **£2.50-3.50** *TRU*

The Sleeping Beauty, retold by A.T. Quiller-Couch, illustrated by Edmund Dulac, 11 by 9in (28 by 23cm). **£160-180** *HB*

Round the World in Eighty Days, Jules Verne, published by Hutchinson & Co., poor condition, c1890s. **£2-3** *TRU*

The Admirable Crichton, by J.M. Barrie, published by Hodder & Stoughton, illustrated by Hugh Thomson, 10.75 by 8.25in (27 by 21cm). **£50-60** *HB*

Cross Reference
Colour Review

Four Kate Greenaway Almanacks, 1886/87/90/91, 4 by 3in (10 by 8cm) each.
£125-150 each *HB*

Boy's Own Annuals, 1915-16 and 1919-20.
£2-3 each *TRU*

Little Lord Fauntleroy, by Frances Hodgson Burnett, published by Frederick Warne & Co., 1890.
£2.50-3.50 *TRU*

Eagle Annual, No.7.
£3-4.50 *TRU*

Ruthless Rhymes, published by Edward Arnold, London, c1920.
£10-12.50 *TRU*

Nursery Songs, published by T.C. & E. C. Jac, London, songs arranged by Joseph Moorat and pictures by Paul Woodroffe.
£10-12.50 *TRU*

The Golden Age, by
Kenneth Grahame,
illustrated by Ernest
H. Shepard, 1st edition
and signed by Shepard,
7.5 by 5in (19 by 13cm).
£125-150 *HB*

Swinburne, selected
poems published by
The Bodley Head, 1st
edition 1928,
illustrated by Harry
Clarke, 9.75 by 6.5in
(24 by 16cm).
£65-75 *HB*

King Arthur and His Knights, by Harry G. Theaker,
published by Ward Lock & Co., c1930, some
tears to plates, 10 by 7.5in (25 by 19cm).
£30-40 *Wil*

Poems of Childhood, by Eugene
Field, published by Charles
Scribners & Sons, New York, 1st
edition, 1904, illustrated by
Maxfield Parrish, 9.5 by 7.25in
(24 by 18cm).
£55-60 *HB*

A Song of the English, by
Rudyard Kipling, published by
Hodder & Stoughton, illustrated
by W. Heath Robinson, 1st
edition, 11.25 by 9in (29 by 23cm).
£140-150 *HB*

Through The Looking Glass,
by Lewis Carroll, published
by MacMillan & Co., 1893,
7.5 by 5in (19 by 13cm).
£40-45 *Wil*

The Tapestry Room, by Mrs
Molesworth, published by
MacMillan & Co, illustrated
by Walter Crane, reprint
1904, 7.5 by 5in (19 by 13cm).
£15-20 *Wil*

Le Village Aérien - Voyages
Extraordinaires, Collection
Hetzel, by Jules Verne, 1st
edition, 11 by 7.5in
(28 by 19cm).
£225-250 *HB*

Alice Through the Looking Glass, and what Alice found there, The Pennyroyal Edition, published by University of California Press 1983, illustrated by Barry Moser, 13.5 by 8.75in (34 by 22cm).
£40-45 *Wil*

Peter Pan in Kensington Gardens, by J.M. Barrie, illustrated by Arthur Rackham, 1st edition, 1906, 10 by 7.75in (25 by 20cm).
£150-180 *HB*

Flower Legends for Children, told by Hilda Murray, published by Longmans Green & Co., pictured by J.S. Eland, 8.75 by 11.25in (22 by 29cm).
£65-70 *Wil*

The Water Babies, by Charles Kingsley, published by Hodder & Stoughton for Boots Pure Drug Co., illustrated by Jessie Willcox Smith.
£65-75 *Wil*

A Midsummer Night's Dream, published by Constable & Co. Ltd., London, 1st edition, 1914, illustrated by W. Heath Robinson, 11.5 by 9in (29 by 23cm).
£125-150 *HB*

The Complete Alice & The Hunting Of The Snark, by Lewis Carroll, published by Jonathan Cape, 1st edition 1975, illustrated by Ralph Steadman, 11.5 by 8.25in (29 by 21cm).
£40-45 *Wil*

The Tale of Two Bad Mice, by Beatrix Potter, published by F. Warne & Co., 1st edition 1904, 5.75 by 4.25in (15 by 11cm).
£125-145 *HB*

Alice's Adventures in Wonderland, by Lewis Carroll, published by William Heinemann, illustrated by Arthur Rackham, 1st edition 1907, with a poem by Austin Dobson, 8.25 by 6.25in (21 by 16cm).
£100-120 *HB*

The Princess And Curdie, published by Blackie, illustrated by Helen Stratton, 12 colour illustrations and 29 text illustrations in black and white, 8 by 6in (20 by 15cm).
£80-85 *Wil*

The Tale of Mr Tod, by Beatrix Potter, published F. Warne & Co., 1st edition 1912, 5.5 by 4.5in (14 by 12cm).
£125-150 *HB*

Bunter The Ventriloquist, by Frank Richards, 1st edition, 1961, 7.5 by 5in (19 by 13cm).
£20-25 *HB*

A complete set of 23 titles in presentation Peter Rabbit's Book Shelf, published by F. Warne & Co. Ltd., c1970.
£45-55 *ROW*

Winnie-The-Pooh And Eeyore's Tail, by A.A. Milne, published by Methuen & Co. Ltd., 9.5 by 7.5in (24 by 19cm).
£60-70 *HB*

The Tale of Tom Kitten, by Beatrix Potter, published by F. Warne & Co., 1st edition 1907, 5.5 by 4.5in (14 by 12cm).
£125-150 *HB*

The Tale of Peter Rabbit, by Beatrix Potter, published by F. Warne & Co., early edition. **£70-75** *HB*

The Art of Walt Disney, by Robert D. Field, 1st edition, 1944, 11 by 8.5in (29 by 21cm). **£65-75** *HB*

The Tale of Mrs Tiggy-Winkle, by Beatrix Potter, published by F. Warne & Co., 1st edition 1905, 5.5 by 4.5in (14 by 12cm). **£125-150** *HB*

Billy Bunter's Bargain, by Frank Richards, 1st edition, 1958, 7.5 by 5in (19 by 13cm). **£25-30** *HB*

The Tale of The Flopsy Bunnies, by Beatrix Potter, published by F. Warne & Co., 1st edition 1909, 5.5 by 4.5in (14 by 12cm). **£125-150** *HB*

Maigret's Memoirs, by Simenon, published by Hamish Hamilton, 1st edition, 1963, 7.5 by 5.25in (19 by 13cm). **£30-35** *HB*

Set of 12 newspaper books of Financial Times 1967-74, 23.5 by 16in (60 by 41cm). **£200-300** *APO*

Maigret's Little Joke, by Simenon, published by Hamish Hamilton, 1957, 7.5 by 5in (19 by 13cm). **£30-35** *HB*

Maigret and the Burglar's Wife, by Simenon, published by Hamish Hamilton, 1st edition, 1955, 7.5 by 5.25in (19 by 13cm). **£30-35** *HB*

Language of Flowers, published by George Routledge & Sons, London, 1st edition, c1888, illustrated by Kate Greenaway, with 125 flower illustrations, 6 by 5in (15 by 13cm). **£100-120** *HB*

The Wonder Book of Tell Me Why, 1930s. **£3.50-4.50** *TRU*

Gnomeland, Teatime Tales for Tiny Tots, by Uncle Elgo. **£1-2** *TRU*

Hawthorne's Wonder Book, published by Hodder & Stoughton, 1st edition, illustrated by Arthur Rackham, 10 by 8in (25 by 20cm). **£120-180** *HB*

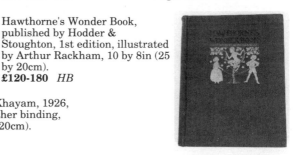

Rubáiyát of Omar Khayam, 1926, with decorative leather binding, 10.25 by 8in (26 by 20cm). **£100-120** *HB*

The Legend of Sleepy Hollow, published by George G. Harrap & Co. Ltd., London, 1928, illustrated by Arthur Rackham, 8 colour illustrations, black and white line drawings, pictorial end papers, 10 by 8in (25 by 20cm). **£140-150** *HB*

The Tempest, published by Heinemann, 1st edition, illustrated by Arthur Rackham, 10 by 7.5in (25 by 19cm). **£170-180** *HB*

Undine, by De La Motte Fouqué, adapted from the German by W.L. Courtney, published by William Heinemann, London 1909, illustrated by Arthur Rackham, 15 colour plates, 10.5 by 7.5in (26 by 19cm). **£80-90** *HB*

The Wood Rangers, by Captain Mayne Reid, G. Roulledge & Sons, reasonable condition. **£3-4** *TRU*

London, by A.R. Hope Moncrieff, published by A & C Black, 1916, 9 by 6.5in (23 by 16cm). **£50-60** *HB*

The Arthur Rackham Fairy Book, re-print George Harrap & Co., reprint 1939, 9 by 6.25in (23 by 16cm).
£50-55 *Wil*

Bunter Out Of Bounds, by Frank Richards, 1st edition, 1959, 7.5 by 5in (19 by 13cm).
£25-30 *HB*

The Tale of Pigling Bland, by Beatrix Potter, published by Frederick Warne & Co., 1st edition 1913, 5.5 by 4.5in (14 by 12cm).
£120-140 *HB*

Rogues in Porcelain, compiled and decorated by John Austen, 1924, 10 by 6.5in (25 by 16cm). **£80-85** *Wil*

Ask Mamma or The Richest Commoner in England, published by Bradley Agnew & Co., March 31, 1858, illustrated by John Leech, 9 by 6in (23 by 15cm).
£45-50 *Wil*

Boot Scrapers

A cast iron boot scraper,
11.5in (29cm) high.
£30-40 *DRU*

A cast iron wall mounted boot
scraper from the Chinese
Embassy, No. 41 Portland Place,
c1880, 16in (41cm) high.
£30-40 *DRU*

A wrought iron boot scraper, from
The Nurses' Home, Charing Cross
Hospital, c1900, 15in (38cm) wide.
£45-50 *DRU*

Cross Reference

Metalware
Kitchenalia
Tools

A cast iron boot scraper,
20in (51cm) high.
£40-50 *DRU*

A wall mounted boot scraper, 12in
(31cm) wide.
£20-30 *DRU*

A cast iron boot scraper, 10in
(25cm) high.
£30-40 *DRU*

A boot scraper,
late 19thC,
12.5in (32cm)
high.
£30-40 *DRU*

A Victorian wall mounted
cast iron boot scraper,
16.5in (42cm) high.
£40-60 *DRU*

A foot scraper from the extension
to Chelsea Police Station, 10in (25
cm) high.
£40-50 *DRU*

A boot scraper, late 18thC,
7.5in (19cm).
£30-40 *DRU*

Bottles

A Persian green bottle, c1700, 11.5in (29cm) high.
£55-75 *LIO*

A Staffordshire pottery potato flask, c1785, 7.5in (19cm) long.
£55-75 *LIO*

An English wine bottle, c1765, 12in (31cm) high.
£75-95 *LIO*

An English onion bottle, c1705, 6in (15cm) high.
£140-160 *LIO*

An Indian green bottle, c1700, 11in (28cm) high.
£50-70 *LIO*

A Dalby's deep aqua glass cone shaped pontilled bottle, embossed 'Dalby's, Gell's, Carminative', 3.75in (9cm).
£60-65 *BBR*

An early clear glass feeder, 8.75in (22cm) long.
£35-40 *BBR*

A Hamilton aqua glass embossed bottle, 'A S Watson & Co Ltd, Hong Kong, China & Manila', cracked, 9.25in (24cm) long.
£15-20 *BBR*

A blue cylinder glass with blob lip, front embossed 'Jas Mackie & Sons, Est 1835, Newcastle', some wear, 6.75in (17cm) high.
£40-45 *BBR*

A round bottomed aqua glass cylinder, embossed in ribbon around shoulder. 'Carrara Water Maughams Patent Registered 31 May 1845'
£40-45 *BBR*

A plated Hamilton stand, for 3 bottles, stamped 'Mappin Brothers, 2062/A', slight tarnishing, 13in (33cm) high.
£60-65 *BBR*

A Barrett & Elers aqua glass bottle, embossed 'Barrett & Co Vauxhall, London', and around base edge 'Lumb & Co/Makers, Castleford', 9.25in (24cm) high.
£15-17 *BBR*

A Hamilton aqua glass bottle, embossed 'N Paul & Burrow, Real, Soda Water, 5 Bow Street, Covent Garden 1802', 8.5in (21cm) long.
£40-45 *BBR*

Cross Reference
Glass

Medicine Bottles

A round cobalt poison bottle, with 'Liq Arsenic' in white lettering to front panel and 'Poison' near base, chipped, 7.25in (18cm).
£60-65 *BBR*

An aqua glass medicine bottle, embossed 'Man Or Animals', and triangular 'T.M. RD296 969', embossed around base, 4.75in (12cm).
£16-18 *BBR*

A Tipper & Son cobalt blue glass bottle, embossed 'Tipper & Son M.R.C.V.S./By Examination Birmingham, Not To Be Taken', 6.75in (17cm) high.
£75-80 *BBR*

A ribbed circular cobalt poison bottle, with 'Liq. Ammon. Fort' in white lettering on front panel, and 'Poison' in orange lettering near base, with stopper, chipped, 9in (23cm) high.
£85-95 *BBR*

A Quines patent light blue aqua bottle, unusual circular wedge shape, rising upwards at an angle, embossed 'Poison' both sides and '2oz' beneath neck, 4.75in (12cm) long.
£225-250 *BBR*

One of the U.K.'s rarest glass poison bottles.

A cobalt 'Admiralty' poison bottle, ribbed on 3 sides, '16ozN' on front, complete with stopper, 6.5in (16cm) high.
£60-65 *BBR*

Stoneware

A bottle inscribed
'R.A.C.S., Olde
Fashioned,
Stone Ginger Beer',
green top, with small
chips, 7in (18cm) high.
£60-65 *BBR*

A stone bottle inscribed
'The Cyclists Favourite
Ginger Beer
Dorchester', with
transfer of cyclists,
6.75in (17cm) high.
£40-45 *BBR*

A stone bottle, inscribed
'J Robertson & Co
Edinburgh Brewed
Ginger Beer', 8.25in
(21cm) high.
£40-45 *BBR*

A Jenner &
Butterworth stone
bottle, with Crown
cork closure,
picture of Blackpool
Tower, 8.5in
(21cm) high.
£90-100 *BBR*

Cross Reference
Packaging & Advertising

A bottle inscribed 'Underwoods,
Brewed Ginger Beer, Carlisle', a
picture of the factory and
'Awarded Certificate of Merit
1896', 8in (20cm) high.
£75-80 *BBR*

A stone bottle, 10in
(25cm) high.
£6-8 *SCO*

A stone bottle inscribed
'Probyn's Ginger Beer/Gold
Medal Brewers Exhibition
1896' with picture of a
Grecian lady, 6.75in (17cm)
high.   **£30-35** *BBR*

Boxes

Cross Reference
Tea Caddies

A Continental silver gilt and enamelled box, the lid painted with a maiden, the sides with resting maidens and cherubs, base sepia painted with landscape, enamelled interior with centre panel of birds and flowers, 19thC, 2.5in (6cm) diam.
£1,100-1,200 *GAK*

A brass mounted stationery box, with single long drawer, fall front and fitted interior, early 20thC, 12.5in (32in high).
£200-220 *GAK*

A selection of ivory, bone and coquilla nut egg boxes.
£9-13 each *VB*

A Victorian figured walnut brass bound lap desk, with fitted interior, 11in (28cm) wide.
£165-185 *GAK*

An Anglo Indian Vizigapatnam ivory sewing box, with incised design of flowers and fitted interior, early 19thC.
£450-500 *LRG*

An Ottaviani crested crane box, in palisander wood, enamel, and silver coloured metal, engraved 'Ottaviani' and stamped '8 MC', 1960s, 9.5in (24cm) wide.
£700-775 *S*

A walnut and brass bound stationery box with dome top, late 19thC, 9.5in (24cm) wide.
£130-150 *PCh*

A pair of boxes in olive wood and walnut, 19thC.
£200-225 *Sim*

An enamelled steel deed box, 15.75in (40cm). **£60-70** *LBL*

Buckles

A Liberty Cymric buckle, Birmingham 1903, 3in (8cm).
£250-280 *JBB*

A silver buckle by Archibald Knox for Liberty & Co., stamped Cymric, maker's mark and number '5', Birmingham, c1902, 3.5in (9cm) wide.
£550-600 *S*

An Art Deco celluloid buckle, 1.25in (3cm) square.
£2-3 *COL*

A paste clasp with centre pink stone, c1900, 3.5in (9cm).
£30-40 *JBB*

A silver plated clasp, 3.5in (9cm).
£30-40 *JBB*

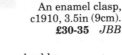

An Art Nouveau parcel gilt and silver coloured metal buckle, stamped '24', c1900, 3.5in (9cm).
£425-475 *S*

A Victorian cloak clasp, 4.5in (12cm).
£20-25 *JBB*

An enamel clasp, c1910, 3.5in (9cm).
£30-35 *JBB*

A brass buckle, with diamanté and black stones, 3in (8cm) wide.
£4-6 *COL*

Button Hooks

A silver button hook, set with Scottish agate, c1880, 7in (18cm) long.　　**£40-60** *BWA*

For a further selection of Button Hooks, please refer to previous editions of Miller's Collectables Price Guides.

An early Victorian cut steel clasp.
£50-55 *JBB*

Buttons

A selection of gentlemens trouser
buttons, from bespoke tailors.
5-10p each *AGM*

*Local research can identify the
location and dates of the shops.*

A mogul painting on ivory button,
c1840.
£70-75 *JBB*

Peanuts character buttons.
5-10p each *AGM*

A ceramic button.
£2-3 *JBB*

Cross Reference
Art Deco

An Artid button, 1940s.
£1-2 *JBB*

Art Deco inlaid wood
buttons. **£25-30** *JBB*

FURTHER READING
*The Complete Button
Book,* Lilian Smith Albert and
Cathryn Kent, London 1952
*The Collector's Encyclopedia
of Buttons,* Sally C. Luscomb,
New York 1967
Buttons: A Guide for Collectors,
Gwen Squire, London 1972
Buttons, Diana Epstein and
Millicent Safro, Newleaf
Publications, Maine, USA,
1991

A set of six carved mother-of-pearl
sphinx buttons.
£30-40 each *JBB*

A set of 6 silver buttons, boxed.
£60-70 *TRU*

Fossilized walrus tooth buttons,
Scrimshaw from Alaska buttons.
£25-30 each *JBB*

Two boxes of Imari seven Gods of
Wisdom buttons.
£40-45 each and
One box of Imari five Gods of
Wisdom buttons.
£30-40 *JBB*

Cross Reference
Paperweights

An enamel on silver buckle and
button set, Birmingham 1910.
£120-140 *JBB*

A paperweight button.
£10-12 each *JBB*

A lady's head button.
£8-10 *JBB*

Victorian porcelain buttons.
£50-60 each *JBB*

An ivory netsuke button.
£30-35 *JBB*

An embroidered swan button.
£6-8 *JBB*

Fox head
horn buttons.
£1-3 each
JBB

Beatrix Potter character buttons.
5-10p each *AGM*

A boxed set of 8
Victorian
enamelled
buttons.
£200-225
JBB

Cameras

This year we have concentrated on the more unusual cameras that collectors may come across. We have focused in particular on a fascinating selection of 'Spy' cameras.

We recommend you refer to previous editions of Collectables, especially Volume IV, 1992-93, pages 62-70, for the more usual plate and modern single lens reflex cameras.

The camera market is steady and the more unusual items, as featured here, are keenly sought by collectors and dealers alike. Please note the cross reference to the Scientific Instrument section.

A Rollei-Werke, West Germany, 16mm Rollei 16S camera, with chrome and snakeskin trim body covering, a Rollei Honeywell badge, and a Carl Zeiss Tessar f2.8 25mm lens, in maker's ever ready case, in maker's fitted presentation case.
£190-200 *CSK*

A Contessa-Nettel 6 x 9cm tropical Deck-Rullo camera, with polished teak body, nickel fittings, tan leather bellows and a Carl Zeiss Jena Tessar f4.5 12cm lens.
£1,400-1,600 *CSK*

An Expo Camera Co., 30 x 28mm focal-plane police camera with black metal body, nickel fittings, rotating viewfinder, focal-plane shutter, film holder, and instruction booklet, in maker's box.
£1,100-1,200 *CSK*

The focal-plane Expo police camera was advertised for a very brief period. This is the only known example. The original sold for $7.50 rather than the $5 for the ordinary model which may explain its apparent rarity. The camera features a rotating waist level and a slightly different body construction.

A Thornton-Pickard Mfg. Co. Ltd., London, 6 x 9cm tropical Duplex Ruby reflex camera, with polished teak body, brass binding, tan leather viewing hood and bellows and a T.T.H. Cooke Anastigmat 6.25 in f158mm lens.
£1,300-1,400 *CSK*

A Phönix 9 x 12cm tropical camera, with polished teak body, brass fittings, tan coloured bellows and a Schneider Xenar f/4.5 13.5cm lens, in a dial set Compur shutter. **£375-400** *CSK*

A Bernard Wolf, Switzerland, 4.5 x 6cm collapsible camera, with hinged clam section, chromed struts, inset sports finder engraved + 80703, unpleated soft leather bellows, lens section with sliding apertures, meniscus lens, single speed shutter and ground glass focusing screen.
£1,600-1,700 *CSK*

The number marked on the camera related to a Swiss patent dated 25 November 1918 granted to Bernard Wolf of Basle, Switzerland.

A Molteni, Paris, 9 x 12cm detective camera, with polished mahogany body, brass fittings, hinged front and back sections, internally contained dark slides and a brass bound lens, signed.
£375-400 *CSK*

An A. Ross, London, 3.5 x 3.5in mahogany body boxform camera, with removable focusing screen and a brass bound A. Ross lens, with rack and pinion focusing.
£2,750-2,850 *CSK*

An F. Koristka, Milan, 1.5 x 1.5in mahogany body boxform camera, with brass fittings, internally contained single metal plate holders and a brass bound Zeiss Anastigmat f2.5 62mm lens.
£1,000-1,100 *CSK*

A Dr Adolf Hesekiel & Co., Berlin, 9 x 12cm reflex camera, with polished wood body, brass fittings, black cloth viewing hood, a Dopple-Anastigmat 120mm lens.
£3,000-3,250 *CSK*

A Houghton-Butcher Mfg. Co. Ltd., London 6 x 9cm tropical Ensign Cameo camera, with brass and brown metal fittings, tan leather bellows and a Dallmeyer, London Dalmac f3.5 4.75in lens, in a rimset Compur shutter.
£240-260 *CSK*

A George Hare, London, quarter plate brass and mahogany tailboard camera, with red leather square cut bellows, a brass bound Perken, Son and Rayment 5 x 4 Rapid Euryscope Optimus lens and maker's plate.
£475-525 *CSK*

A Rowland Ward & Co., London, 1.25 x 1.25in Naturalist's camera, with wood body, brass fittings, rotary shutter, direct vision finder, side mounted rack and plate advancing mechanism, base mounted 12 plate plateholder, instruction sheet and maker's box with printed instruction label.
£5,250-5,500 *CSK*

The Naturalist's camera is virtually identical to Marion and Cos Academy camera and the instruction sheet carries the name Academy.

A J. Lancaster & Son, Birmingham, quarter plate The Rover camera, with polished mahogany body and brass bound lens, in a Lancaster See-Saw shutter.
£450-500 *CSK*

A 4 x 5in wood body American pattern boxform camera, with inlay decoration, focusing screen and a brass bound lens.
£175-200 *CSK*

A G.G.S., Italy, 35mm Luckyflex camera, with a Solar Anastigmat f3.2 50mm viewing lens and a Solar Anastigmat f3.2 50mm lens.
£1,275-1,350 *CSK*

A Nettel, Sontheim, 9 x 12cm tropical Sonnet camera, with polished teak and tan leather body, brass fittings, tan leather bellows and a Carl Zeiss Jena Tessar f4.5 15cm lens, in a Compound shutter.
£200-250 *CSK*

A Steinheil, München, 9 x 12cm wood body detective camera, with brass fittings, internally contained single metal slides, maker's plate and a brass bound lens. **£480-500** *CSK*

A Soho Ltd., London, 127-rollfilm collapsible camera, No. 2202 with bronzed metal body, red leather bellows and a Kershaw Annar f8 lens. **£110-120** *CSK*

A Bell Camera Co., Grinnell, 11.5 x 3.5in rollfilm Bell's Straight Working Panoram camera no. 72, with red leather bellows and a Wollensak lens. **£675-700** *CSK*

A 1.5 x 1.5in mahogany boxform camera, with waist level viewfinder, lens and dark slide, camera body stamped, Gesetzl Geschletzt. **£425-475** *CSK*

A Voigtländer, Germany, 4.5 x 6cm Bergheil deluxe camera, with tan leather body covering and bellows, gilt fittings and a Voigtländer Heliar 75mm f4.5 lens in a dial set Compur shutter.
£950-1,000 *CSK*

A Showa Optical Works Ltd., Japan, 14 x 14mm Gemflex twin lens reflex camera, with metal and black leather covered body, side panel with aperture adjustment and winding knob, opposite side panel with viewing hood release button, back plate engraved Made in Occupied Japan, a Gem viewing lens, Gem f3.5 25mm taking lens in a Swallow shutter.
£525-575 *CSK*

A 14 x 14mm triangular shaped Sun camera, with black body covering and chrome top and baseplates, waistlevel finder, I and B shutter and a Sanko 35mm lens.
£550-575 *CSK*

An H.J. Redding & Gyles, London, 120-rollfilm 6 x 6cm mahogany body Luzo camera, with round viewfinder, film punch, lens, shutter, maker's plate and in maker's leather case.
£875-925 *CSK*

A Graflex camera and case, 11in (28cm) wide.
£150-160 *BWA*

A W. Kunik, West Germany, 14 x 14mm Petietux camera, with built in light meter, flash syncronisation and a helical focusing Kratz Optic f2.8 25mm lens.
£350-380 *CSK*

A replica Doppel-Sport pigeon camera, with black metal body and alloy fittings, rotating shutter and fixing straps.
£680-700 *CSK*

A Sanwa Syokai Ltd., Tokyo, 14 x 14mm Myracle model II camera, with black body covering and chrome top and baseplates and a Hope Anastigmat f4.5 lens, in maker's leather ever ready case, in maker's box stamped Made in Occupied Japan.
£275-300 *CSK*

A S.C.A.T., Italy, 16mm camera, with black body covering, a f3.5 lens with helical focusing and a yellow filter, in a green case and instruction leaflet, in maker's box.
£180-220 *CSK*

A Schatz & Son, Germany, 16mm Sola camera, with polished metal and black leather covered body, swinging waist level viewfinder, top plate mounted sportsfinder, baseplate mounted clockwork film advance and a Schneider Kinoplan f3 2.5cm lens.
£2,600-2,800 *CSK*

The Sola was patented on 29 October 1934 and started sales in c1938. It could take up to 6 photographs at around 1.5 frames per second, using 16mm film in special cassettes. The camera featured one of the first spring wound motors which could advance the whole film at one winding. The camera was used by the German Schutz-Staffel who used it to take rapid sequence photographs.

A Petal Optical Co., Japan., 22mm diameter octagonal Evarax A camera, with polished chrome body, front plate with red and blue decorative floral engraving, legend Evarax A Patents, 25 and B shutter, release engraved Made in Occupied Japan, a box of panchromatic Petal film.
£1,850-1,950 *CSK*

A Minica O.L., Japan, 17 x 17mm Mini camera, with black body covering and chrome finished trim, top plate with swinging frame finder, lens panel and back plate engraved Minica O.L. Made in Occupied Japan.
£975-1,000 *CSK*

An Expo Camera Co., New York, 1.25 x 1in Expo Police camera, with black metal body, nickel fittings, waist level finder, shutter, interior transfer Expo Police Camera Pat. throughout the world, US Pat. Jan 31st 1911, and film holder, direction book for Expo Police camera and slip case, in maker's box.
£575-600 *CSK*

An E. B. Koopman 1.5in square hand camera, The Presto with metal body, top plate mounted film or plate advance, front mounted wheel stops and internal four plate holder.
£350-375 *CSK*

This was invented by Herman Casler.

The American Camera Co., London, 1.75in diam. metal body camera, The Demon, with spring shutter, metal plate cover and back plate.
£1,250-1,350 *CSK*

A Lancart, Paris, 12 x 15mm XYZ camera, with nickel plated body, side panel with film advance, top plate with collapsible sportsfinder, back panel and front panel decoratively engraved, Kynor f3.5 lens and one film spool.
£1,800-2,000 *CSK*

The XYZ camera dates from c1935.

An S.P.S. Co., Japan, 12 x 14mm Peace Baby Flex twin lens reflex camera, with black leather and metal body, a 20mm taking lens in a Time and Instantaneous shutter and two film spools.
£1,500-1,600 *CSK*

A Fotofex-Kameras, Berlin, 16mm Mini Fex camera, with black leather covered body, chrome trim, a direct vision optical viewfinder and a Ludwig Victar f3.5 25mm lens in a Vario shutter. **£730-780** *CSK*

The Mini Fex is considered the first serious sophisticated subminiature of the 20thC.

An O.I.P., Brussels, 35mm Cinescopie camera, with polished metal, leather covered and black enamel body, top-plate with film winding knob, removable lens section with removable parallax correcting viewfinder stamped 5, a f3.5 50mm. lens, in a self setting Ibsor shutter.
£875-925 *CSK*

This was an early 35mm camera for 24 x 24mm negatives.

A 14 x 14mm Baby Flex twin lens reflex camera with black leather and metal body, a Sanko f3.5 20mm taking lens in a Peace III R.K. Instantaneous and Time shutter and one film spool.
£1,200-1,300 *CSK*

A Carmen, France, 25mm square Pygmee camera, with black metal and nickel fitted body, viewfinder, *P* and *I* shutter, lens and interior with label, in maker's box.
£125-150 *CSK*

The Pygmee was also sold under the name Carmen.

A James A. Sinclair & Co. Ltd.,London quarter plate tropical Una camera, with polished mahogany body, brass binding, leather bellows and a Contessa-Nettel Sonnar anastigmat f4.5 13.5cm lens.
£1,600-1,800 *CSK*

A Riken Optical Co., Japan, 16mm Ricoh 16 camera, with black covered and chrome body and a Riken Ricoh f2.8 2.5cm lens, a 16mm Golden Ricoh 16 camera, with black covered and gold plated body, a gold plated barrel Riken Ricoh f3.5 2.5cm. lens and gold plated tripod adapter and instruction booklet.
£275-300 *CSK*

A Concava S.A.,16mm Tessina camera, Switzerland, with red metal and chrome body, waist level finder, a Tessina 25mm f/2.8 lens, removable Tessina 17 jewel watch mounted on accessory shoe and a leather wrist strap with camera mounting plate.
£3,000-£3,250 *CSK*

The Tessina watch is a very rare accessory, and probably only 100 were made for the American market.

An A. Dubroni, Paris, 5 x 5cm boxform camera, with a brass bound Dubroni lens, spirit burner and 6 glass chemical bottles, in maker's fitted wood box.
£2,500-2,700 *CSK*

A Waldes & Co., Dresden 4 x 4cm Foto-Fips cardboard body camera, comprising bellows and shutter and metal support structs, mounted in a box, with chemical bottle and plates.
£340-360 *CSK*

The camera is labelled in Czechoslovakian and dates to c1925. This example is in very good condition.

l. A Concava S.A., Switzerland, 35mm Tessina Automat 35 camera, with chrome body, waist level finder and a Tessinon 25mm f2.8 lens, and a removable accessory shoe-mounted Metraphot 2 photo-electric light meter.
£750-775 *CSK*

This camera was reputedly made for the Tessina designer Dr. Steineck. It has a different finished metal and fittings.

r. A Concava S.A., 35mm Tessina 35 camera, with polished chrome body, waist level finder, a 25mm f2.8 lens, nickel-prototype automatic clockwork winder, and a black leather Tessina wriststrap.
£1,300-1,400 *CSK*

An E. & H.T. Anthony, New York, quarter plate wood body Schmidt patent detective, camera No. 36, with brass fittings, rotary shutter and lens.
£2,500-2,750 *CSK*

The Canadian mounted police ordered Tessina cameras with motor winders and it is possible that this is a prototype for these.

A Compendica Vaduz, Liechtenstein, 16mm Compendica 88/16a camera, No. 504, with green crackle metal body, rear mounted combined shutter/aperture control, light meter, and a helically focusing Compendica f/2.9 25mm lens, camera blueprint, press print and press handout. **£2,250-2,500** *CSK*

The American Safety Razor Corp., USA, 22 x 24mm ASR Fotodisc camera, with black crackle and polished metal body, direct vision finder, a Rapodis 32mm lens and backplate, with user instructions, and a Fotodisc film magazine.
£740-780 *CSK*

A C. P. Goerz, Vienna, 16mm Minicord camera, with a black leather covered metal body, and a C. P. Goerz Helgor f2 2.5cm lens. **£185-200** *CSK*

Spy Cameras

A C. P. Stirn, Germany, 1.75in diam. Concealed Vest camera, with polished metal body, top mounted back opening catch, front panel with 6 position exposure counter lens, back plate engraved Pat'd July 27. 1886, and internally contained 5in diam. exposed plate, in maker's fitted mahogany box opening door, nickel handle and base mounted tripod bush.
£2,750-3,000 *CSK*

An A. Lehmann, Berlin, replica Ben Akiba walking stick camera, with polished chrome plated body with decorative engraving, film winding key, shutter, lens and 5 internally contained film spools.
£1,750-2,000 *CSK*

Binocular Cameras

A 1.5in square replica Krugener Photo-Carnet camera, with wooden body, sector shutter, lens, leather panel stamped Photo-Carnet de Dr Krugener inventeur A. Schaeffner, and single metal slides.
£1,000-1,100 *CSK*

A Toko Photo Co., 10 x 14mm Teleca combined binocular camera, with a pair of leather covered barrel binocular lenses, a Telesigmar f4.5 3.5in and a film cassette, in maker's leather case.
£980-1,250 *CSK*

A Binoca Co., Japan, 16mm Binoca combined opera glass camera, with white plastic casing and brassed metal fittings, an integral pair of individually focusing 2.5 by 25 binocular lenses, a Bicon f4.5 40mm taking lens and film cassette.
£575-600 *CSK*

A Möller Wedel, West Germany, 16mm CamBinox combined camera/binocular, with a pair of binocular lenses with individual rear sight adjustment, a central camera section with a top section, back section with combined exposure counter and shutter setting knob and an interchangeable J. D. Möller Jdemar f3.5 90mm taking lens and instruction booklet.
£1,100-1,200 *CSK*

A Toko Photo Co., Japan, 10 x 14mm Cyclops combined binocular camera, with a pair of leather covered binocular lenses and a Telesigmar f4.5 3.5in taking lens, in maker's fitted leather case.
£1,100-1,200 *CSK*

A Nichiryo International Co., Japan, 35mm Nicnon binocular camera, with a pair of 7 x 50 binocular lenses with dioptre adjustment, an integral Nicnon 165mm f3.5 taking lens and an attached camera section with clockwork wind.
£480-500 *CSK*

Cigarette Packet Cameras

Four 110-film disguised cigarette packet cameras, each with plastic casing and integral cameras, comprising Peer 100, Marlboro, Mild Seven and 555.
£300-400 each *CSK*

A 16mm disguised cigarette box camera with black paint body with gilt JPS logo, integral shutter and 23mm f3.5 lens.
£750-780 *CSK*

A W. Kunik, West Germany, brown Vanity lighter outfit, comprising a 16mm Petie camera, with black crackle and chrome metal body and a 25mm f11 lens, in a tan coloured leather covered body with integral petrol lighter. **£750-775** *CSK*

Cigarette Lighter Cameras

Advertisements for this camera began to appear in 1987. It had similar specifications to a camera made by Nikkoh and was designated the 2000 CL camera by one US distributor.

A 8 x 13mm gold plated cigarette lighter camera, with film advance, single speed shutter, lighter, Minox film chamber and baseplate engraved 18K-20my SIPE-Germany.
£3,750-3,950 *CSK*

l. A Suzuki Optical Works, Japan, 6 x 6mm Echo 8 camera lighter, inside camera section with waist level finder, 2 film cassettes and lighter section, and original instruction sheet.
£1,800-2,000 *CSK*

r. A Suzuki Optical Co. 6 x 6mm Camera-Lite camera lighter with chrome body, 2 film cassettes and metal lighter section, in maker's grey plastic slip case, and original instruction sheet.
£2,000-2,250 *CSK*

A Speccam combined camera/table top cigarette lighter with gold plated and black snakeskin covered body.
£350-400 *CSK*

Gun Cameras

A Doryu Camera Co. Ltd., Japan, 16mm Doryu 2-16 flash camera, with black plastic and polished metal body and a Dorymar wide angle 15mm f2.2 lens, mounted on an integral pistol stock and facility for magnesium flash pellets.
£13,000-15,000 *CSK*

The Doryu pistol camera was introduced in 1955.

An E. Krauss, Paris, 28 x 21mm Le Photo-Revolver camera, with black metal and nickel body section, top plate with folding sportsfinder and front panel with helical focusing lens and shutter controls, mounted on a leather covered and nickel magazine back.
£2,500-2,700 *CSK*

An ERAC Selling Company Ltd., London, 16mm Erac pistol camera, with a metal body camera mounted in a black plastic casing shaped as a pistol.
£375-400 *CSK*

Matchbox Cameras

A metal body Matchbox camera with collapsible sportsfinder, 2 sliding apertures, and a Carl Zeiss Jena Tessar f2.7 2.5cm lens, baseplate painted to resemble a matchbox.
£6,250-6,500 *CSK*

The camera was made in Germany c1938, and was extremely well made. Its underside had a Nazi eagle painted on a blue-grey background to resemble a matchbox.

An Eastman Kodak Co., Rochester, NY, 0.5 by 0.5in Matchbox camera model 2, with black Bakelite body, outer metal sleeve, winding knob with markings at 180° and simple Time and Instantaneous shutter, in maker's purse.
£2,500-2,800 *CSK*

The Kodak Matchbox camera was made between 1944 and 1945 and around 1,000 were made for the American Office of Secret Services in 2 batches of 500. The second model was made for reels of film.

A 16mm matchbox camera with nickel body, top plate with adjustable aperture control, side plate with shutter control.
£4,500-4,800 *CSK*

Two examples are known of which one had a fixed aperture (as in this case) and the other had an adjustable aperture. The action of pushing the camera forward inside the matchbox opened the front flap and released the shutter which was then reset on the reverse action.

Minox

A VEF, Riga, Latvia, 13 x 8mm Minox camera, with stainless steel body, top plate with focusing dial from 8"-∞, shutter release button, sliding yellow filter, baseplate engraved VEF Riga Minox. Made in Latvia. Pat. app. and a Minostigmat f3.5 15mm lens.
£580-600 *CSK*

A VEF, Riga, Minox enlarger, with brown Bakelite body, VEF light bulb, lens, electric cable and 2.25 x 3.25in paper holder, in maker's box; postcard paper holder in box, and a VEF Minox film processing tank, in maker's box.
£900-1,000 *CSK*

A VEF, Riga, 13 x8mm camera, with stainless steel body, top plate with focusing dial, exposure counter, shutter release button and shutter speed, casing locked, a Minostigmat 15mm f3.5 lens, baseplate engraved VEF Minox Riga., Made in Latvia and front plate engraved WA 506 with Nazi eagle insignia.
£2,750-3,000 *CSK*

This camera dates from the German occupation of the Baltic states before the advancing Red Army occupied Latvia.

A 8 x 11mm L'Appareil Espion Français camera, with ribbed brassed metal body, top plate, combined lens cover and shutter release, and direct vision viewfinder, lacking lens.
£800-850 *CSK*

The French espionage camera was made because of the shortage of Minox cameras and its design was based on Minox features. It took 45 frames 8 x 11mm on 9mm film. The camera was only made from 1939-41 and it is believed that fewer than 1,000 were made. They are usually found lacking their taking lens.

The Stylophot with right angle finder was made in very small numbers.

Pen Cameras

A Secam 16mm secret Stylophot colour camera, with black plastic body, right angle and direct vision finders, film advance with no coloured filter, aperture setting marked Noir Color, and 2 film cassettes, in maker's box marked Secreto.
£225-250 *CSK*

l. A Minox 8 x 11mm LX selection camera, with gold plated body, top plate with LED indicator lights, shutter release button and green, red and yellow LED's and a Minox f3.5 15mm lens, in maker's presentation box. **£680-700**

r. A 8 by 13mm dummy Minox B camera, with dummy lens and viewfinder and baseplate engraved Minox, Wetzlar F1589, Made in Germany.
£130-150 *CSK*

A Secam, France, 16mm Private Eye camera, with black plastic casing, film advance with inset orange filter, 2 position aperture Noir Color, blue lens shade and 2 film cassettes.
£275-300 *CSK*

A Harukawa, Japan, 16mm Septon pen camera, with plastic body, chrome and alloy fittings, direct vision finder, a Septon f2.8 20mm lens, integral propelling pencil, with instruction leaflet and maker's box.
£1,100-1,200 *CSK*

Radio Cameras

A Bell International Corp. 16mm Bell Kamra combined camera/radio, model KTC-62 No. 16728, in red plastic casing with metal trim, Prominar f3.5 23mm lens, in fitted presentation box; 3 Kowa Optical Co. 16mm Ramera combined camera/radio model KTC-62, in blue, black and white plastic casings, each with a Prominar f3.5 23mm lens, 2 in fitted presentation box. **£700-775** *CSK*

A Minolta Camera Co., Japan, 16mm Sonocon 16 combined camera/radio, with a black finish body, Rokkor f2.8 22mm lens, integral 7 transistor radio and charger.
£1,100-1,200 *CSK*

Ring Cameras

A Buttrio, Udine, Italy, 25mm diam. GF 81 ring camera No. 14, with polished gold plated body, helical focusing, depth of field indicator, rotary shutter, and removable waist level viewfinder, in turned wood case, 10 packets of unexposed disc films and 2 sets of instructions in Italian and English, in maker's box.
£3,750-4,000 *CSK*

The GF.81 camera appeared in 1981 and was made by Gian Paolo Ferro of Udine. Twenty of each of 2 models were made in polished or brushed gold.

A 3.5 x 5mm chrome metal body ring camera, with a Trioplan f2.8 10mm lens, iris diaphragm, single speed shutter, removable brass film insert section.
£5,750-6,000 *CSK*

Vanity Case Cameras

A W. Kunik, Petie vanity outfit, comprising a 16mm Petie camera with black crackle and chrome metal body and a 25mm f11 lens, in a vanity case covered in green, orange and black coloured leather with gilt tooling, powder compact, lipstick holder and film holder.
£1,300-1,500 *CSK*

A W. Kunik, West Germany, gilt Petie vanity outfit, comprising a 16mm Petie camera with grey-green and gilt metal body and a Röschlein Achromat 25mm f11 lens, in a mottled blue enamel finish and gilt metal trimmed vanity case with powder compact, lipstick holder and film holder.
£800-850 *CSK*

Watch Cameras

A Houghtons pattern Ticka camera, with lens cap, swinging viewfinder and interior label.
£1,100-1,200 *CSK*

An Expo Camera Co., USA, watch camera, with polished metal body, top plate, lens cap attached to body by chain, with instruction leaflet, in maker's box.
£1,100-1,300 *CSK*

A Houghtons Ltd., Ticka camera, with polished metal body with top plate, lens cap attached to body by chain, in maker's box, a Ticka film in maker's box, and an empty Ticka film box.
£800-900 *CSK*

A Steineck Camera-Werk, West Germany, 25mm diam. Steineck ABC wristwatch camera, with alloy body, waist level mirror finder, a Steinheil VL f2.5 12.5mm lens, close-up lens, and a red leather strap, in maker's presentation case, body 42 by 32mm.
£3,250-3,500 *CSK*

An Expo Camera Co., USA, watch camera, with polished metal body with top plate, swinging viewfinder and spare film spool, in maker's fitted box with printed label.
£800-900 *CSK*

FURTHER READING

An Age of Cameras, Edward Holmes, 1974. *Subminiature Photography,* White, 1990.

Candle Extinguishers

A Royal Worcester candle extinguisher, 'Hush', shape no. 2844, with rare colour variation of cream dress edged with blue, blue ribbon and blonde hair, date code 1956, 3.5in (8cm) high.
£200-250 *TVA*

For a further selection of candle extinguishers refer to Miller's Collectables Price Guide Volume IV pages 71 to 73

Card Cases

A mother-of-pearl card case, 4 by 3in (10 by 8cm).
£90-100 *COL*

For a further selection of Card Cases, please refer to Miller's Collectables Price Guide, Volume IV page 290.

Candlesticks

A copper and brass weighted candle holder, after a design by W.A.S. Benson.
£100-150 *ZEI*

A pair of early George III style silver candlesticks, with detachable nozzles, Sheffield 1903, 9in (23cm).
£375-400 *GAK*

Cross Reference
Art Nouveau

A pair of Lauder candlesticks, with bird, 12in (31cm) high.
£325-350 *NCA*

A pair of Liberty Archibald Knox pewter and enamelled candlesticks.
£800-1,000 *ABS*

The Old Man and the Sea, by Ernest Hemingway, published by Jonathan Cape, lst Edition, 1953. **£30-35** *HB*

Billy Bunter The Hiker, by Frank Richards, 1st edition, 1958. **£25-30** *HB*

Thunderball, by Ian Fleming, published by Jonathan Cape, 1st edition, 1961. **£70-75** *HB*

The Lord of the Rings, 1st edition, by J.R.R. Tolkien, signed. **£700-750** *HB*

From Damascus to Palmyra, by John Kelman, illustrated by Margaret Thomas, 1908. **£65-75** *HB*

The Spy Who Loved Me, by Ian Fleming, published by Jonathan Cape, 1st edition, 1962. **£70-75** *HB*

Maigret has Scruples, by Simenon, published by Hamish Hamilton, 1st edition, 1959. **£30-35** *HB*

The Eyes of the Dragon, by Stephen King, signed, 1st edition, 1987. **£80-85** *HB*

Sunset at Blandings, by P.G. Wodehouse, 1st edition, 1977. **£25-30** *HB*

A set of 8 horse racing waistcoat buttons, 1890s-1920s. **£25-50 the set** *AGM*

A Glasgow University Athletic Club button. **50p-£2** *AGM*

A gentleman's sporting button, late 19thC. **50p-£2** *AGM*

A P S A Fencing Club button. **50p-£2** *AGM*

A York Rugby Football Union button. **50p-£2** *AGM*

A set of gaiety girls buttons, worn on waistcoats, c1890s. **£25-50** *AGM*

A selection of silver Golf Club buttons, given as prizes, dated between 1920 and 1938. **£5-10 each** *AGM*

Four Golf Club blazer buttons. **£1-5 each** *AGM*

A gentleman's sporting button, late 19thC. **50p-£2** *AGM*

A set of footballers buttons. **£25-50** *AGM*

A gentleman's sporting button, late 19thC. **50p-£2** *AGM*

l. A selection of various yacht club buttons. **50p-£2 each** *AGM*

r. An early Victorian man and horse button. **£2-5** *AGM*

A Belleek caberet, 2nd period. **£280-300 the set.** Kettle. **£350-375** *PC*

A collection of Belleek Echinus, 1st period, bowls **£60-75 each.** Kettle and teapots **£300-395** *PC*

A Belleek mirror and boudoir candlestick, 1st period. **£750-800 each** *PC*

A collection of Belleek, 2nd period. **£150-200 each** *PC*

Two pairs of Belleek spill vases, 1st period. **£600-650 each pair** *PC*

A Belleek Echinus bread plate, 1st period. **£320-350** *PC*

A collection of Belleek crested pieces, 2nd period. **£60-150 each** *PC*

Two menu holders, with applied flowers, 2nd period. **£125-150 each** *PC*

Three Belleek amphora jars, 1st period. **£300-350 each** *PC*

A Masonic mantle plaque, by Obadiah Sherratt, c1825. **£1,500-1,800** *LR*

Thirty seven pieces of Spode dinner ware, early 19thC, each piece damaged or repaired. **£550-600** *PCh*

A barge ware teapot and lid, 'A present to Mrs. Pinkey from Florrie, 1914'. **£125-150** *PCh*

A printed lustre jug, c1830, 5in (12.5cm). **£200-250** *IW*

A Masonic creamware jug, Tyneside School, c1825, 6in (15cm). **£180-220** *IS*

A Sunderland pottery jug, with transfer commemorating 'Crimea', c1845. **£200-250** *HOW*

A Victorian hat pin holder, 5in (12.5cm). **£28-35** *AA*

A William Greatbatch teapot, Staffordshire, c1775, 5.5in (14cm). **£1,500-1,650** *JHo*

A Victorian toothbrush dish, with lid, 8in (20.5cm) long. **£40-50** *AI*

A pair of Ridgway's chamber pots, with moulded handles. **£100-150** *CB*

A Mason's Ironstone vase. **£220-245** *VH*

A Sunderland lustre jug, c1830. **£280-320** *RP*

A Mason's Ironstone punch bowl, impressed mark, c1820, 13in (33cm) diam. **£1,500-1,950** *BEE*

Ironstone china was introduced by Josiah Spode in Staffordshire in about 1805.

C. J. Mason patented his 'Ironstone China' in 1813 and it was made exclusively by his factory until 1827.

A Mason's Ironstone tureen and cover, printed and impressed mark, c1820. **£1,000-1,250** *BEE*

Two Mason's Ironstone jugs, c1815:
Footbath jug. **£1,000-1,200**
Toy jug. **£250-320** *BEE*

A Mason's Ironstone footbath, impressed mark, c1815, 15in (38cm) wide. **£1,750-2,000** *BEE*

l. A Mason's Ironstone letter rack, c1820. **£650-750**
r. A Mason's Ironstone spill vase, c1815. **£300-350** *BEE*

A Charlotte Rhead
vase.
£80-140 *AOS*

A Royal Doulton
vase, numbered 32,
1903, 10in (25cm)
high. **£80-95** *POW*

A pair of Brannam
vases, 1894, 9in (23cm)
high. **£280-300** *NCA*

A Doulton Lambeth
vase, signed, impressed
mark H.B. 911.
£575-600 *PCh*

A Moorcroft
pomegranate vase,
1914, 4in (10cm) high.
£250-350 *LIO*

A Charlotte
Rhead vase with
Lotus Leaves
pattern, c1932,
8.5in (21cm) high.
£100-150 *AOS*

A Devonware
Hawk vase, 12in
(31cm).
£40-65 *AOS*

A Gouda pottery vase, 7in
(18cm) high.
£50-60 *NCA*

A Minton 'Tube Line' jug,
14in (36cm) high.
£200-300 *ASA*

A Royal Doulton vase, Margaret
Thompson, c1920, 6in (15cm)
high. **£200-235** *POW*

Two Royal Doulton vases, Christine
Abbot, 1923, 4.5in (11cm) high
£55-65, 9in (23cm) **£90-105** *POW*

A Crown Devon posy bowl, 10in (25cm) diam. **£50-85** *AOS*

A Clarice Cliff vase, 6in (15cm) high. **£800-900** *RIC*

A Clarice Cliff lotus jug, 1929, 12in (31cm). **£1,500-2,000** *GAZ*

A Clarice Cliff vase, 1929, 8in (20cm). **£1,200-1,400** *GAZ*

A pair of Carlton Ware vases. **£300-400** *AOS*

A Forrester's Phoenix ware jug, Fuchsia pattern. **£70-80** *HEW*

A Burleigh jug, 8.5in (21cm) high. **£75-125** *AOS*

A Decoro vase, 1930s, 8in (20cm) high. **£50-75** *AOS*

A Clarice Cliff vase, for Newport Pottery, 1930s, 11.75in (30cm) high. **£575-600** *S*

r. A Clarice Cliff vase, shape No. 342. **£750-800** *ADC*

A Clarice Cliff Bizarre bowl, for Wilkinson Ltd., 1920s, 7.5in (19cm) diam. **£1,350-1,500** *S*

A Bough lady's powder bowl, marked, 1915. **£150-200** *BWA*

l. A Forrester's Phoenix ware bowl, c1930, 11in (28cm) diam. **£150-175** *HEW*

A Clarice Cliff ashtray, Gibraltar pattern. **£220-250** *RIC*

A Royal Doulton embossed jug, one of a limited edition of 600, 8in (20cm) high. **£200-260** *PCh*

A Longwy dish, c1900, marked, 7in (18cm) high. **£220-250** *CHa*

A pottery stove, complete with oil lamp, c1880. **£300-350** *LBL*

A Kingsware jug, Doulton base mark, 9in (23cm) high. **£175-200** *BBR*

Price's Cottage Ware, teapot, milk jug and sugar basin. **£10-30 each** *COL*

An earthenware grotesque dog, probably North Devon, c1900, 8in (20cm). **£50-60** *OD*

A Crown Ducal Charlotte Rhead decorated dish. **£55-65** *PCh*

A Moorcroft Liberty mug, c1919. **£450-500** *WAC*

A Brannam jug, c1883, 5.5in (14cm) high. **£100-120** *NCA*

A Burleigh parrot jug, c1935, 7in (18cm) high. **£50-60** *PAG*

Two Moorcroft commemorative mugs. **£300-350 each** *NA*

A Moorcroft commemorative flambé beaker. **£455-500** *WAC*

A blue crackleglaze bowl and pot, Boch Frères La Louvière, c1920, bowl **£200-225**, pot **£145-165**   *POW*

A pair of Keramis 'La Maîtrise' vases, c1920. **£575-600**   *POW*

A Bourne Denby owl jug **£30-45** and matching vase. **£40-55**   *AOS*

A Longwy crackleglaze dove, c1920. **£295-325**   *POW*

A Longwy 'Prima Vera' , c1920. **£545-585**   *POW*

A Keramis vase, c1920. **£275-300**   *POW*

A Chameleon ware vase, George Clews. **£80-100**   *NCA*

A Bough jug, in crocus design, marked, 6in (15cm) high. **£200-250** *BWA*

A Dunmore pottery jardinière, 8in (20cm) high. **£250-300** *BWA*

A Bough bowl, marked J.E.A. 1923, 8.5in (21cm) diam. **£200-250** *BWA*

A selection of Dunmore pottery pigs, including a money box. **£250-300 each** *BWA*

r. A Dunmore pottery toad, 6in (15cm). **£300-400** *BWA*

A Bough vase and cover, 15in (38cm) high. **£300-350** *BWA*

A Dunmore bust of General Gordon, 12in (31cm) high. **£500-700** *BWA*

A Bough Toby jug, marked E.A., 1922. **£400-500** *BWA*

A Bough vase, damaged, marked E.A. **£100-125** *BWA*

A Dunmore pottery toad, 6in (15cm) high. **£300-400** *BWA*

A Bough pottery biscuit barrel. **£200-250** *BWA*

A Dunmore pottery bear dish, 10in (25cm) long. **£700-1,000** *BWA*

r. A Bough teapot, marked C.C.A., 4.5in (12cm) high. **£200-250** *BWA*

A Dunmore pottery jardinière, with dragon design. **£500-600** *BWA*

A Dunmore pottery owl jar, with removable head. **£1,000-1,200** *BWA*

A Dunmore pottery fish wall plaque, 9in (23cm) long. **£200-250** *BWA*

A pair of Dunmore pottery chargers, 15.5in (39cm) diam. **£1,000-1,500** *BWA*

A Dunmore pottery teapot, milk jug and sugar basin, teapot 4.5in (11cm) high. **£250-300 the set** *BWA*

A Dunmore pottery copy of a medieval cooking pot, 8in (20cm) high. **£200-250** *BWA*

l. A Dunmore pottery jardinière, 9in (23cm) high. **£200-250** *BWA*

A Dunmore tobacco jar, 11.5in (29cm) high. **£1,000-1,200** *BWA*

Two Dunmore pottery Burns character figures, 7.5 and 8in (19 and 20cm) high. **£300-400** *BWA*

A Dunmore pottery toad, 10in (25cm) high. **£800-1,200** *BWA*

A painted bowl, by Morven MaCleod, 7.5in (19m) diam. **£200-220** *BWA*

A Strathyre jug, painted by Jessie Wilson. **£100-120** *BWA*

A Bough three-handled loving cup, 7.5in (19cm) high. **£400-500** *BWA*

A Dunmore dragon jug, 13in (33cm). **£250-300** *BWA*

A Dunmore wall pocket. **£200-300** *BWA*

A Wemyss vase, with painted peacock. **£200-350** *RdeR*

A Strathyre jug, painted by Jessica Wilson, 6in (15cm) high. **£100-150** *BWA*

A Dunmore pottery crab wall pocket, 6in (15cm) long. **£300-350** *BWA*

A Macmerry cup and saucer. **£100-120** *BWA*

A Macmerry painted teapot, 8in (20cm) wide. **£400-450** *BWA*

A Wemyss chamber pot, with peaches, 8.25in (21cm) diam. **£250-350** *BWA*

A Prestonpans tea caddy, 5.5in (14cm) high. **£500-600** *BWA*

A zoo plate, 7.75in (19cm) diam. **£200-250** *BWA*

A bowl, by Peggy Foy, c1945.
£20-30 *IW*

A hand painted bowl, signed Florrie
Cliff, c1930. **£100-120** *ACh*

A wall mask, 7.5in
(19cm). **£100-120** *HEW*

Two Sylvac dogs, large
£85-130, small **£15-25** *AOS*

A Sadler teapot, c1950, 7.5in
(19cm). **£20-25** *OD*

A Cartlon Ware hand painted
plate. **£220-240** *GAZ*

A Wade trio, 'Hedgerow'.
£10-12 *COL*

r. Aunt Jemima, a hollow
doorstop, 1920s.
£70-100 *PC*

r. A Chinese
enamelled lamp, 9in
(23cm) high.
£100-125 *ML*

A Goebels hand painted
figure, 1930, 12in (31.5cm).
£320-350 *GAZ*

l. A Crown Devon lamp
base, 4.75in (12cm) high.
£250-275 *HEW*

A Myott fruit basket, 14in (36cm) wide.
£50-85 *AOS*

A pottery plate, probably Yorkshire, c1800.
£280-300 *RP*

A set of 4 Sèvres hand painted plates with gilt edges, 9.5in (24cm) diam.
£120-130 *PCh*

A Continental cabinet plate, with masks in gilding, c1840. **£180-220** *LIO*

A Quimper dish, marked H3 Quimper, c1900, 14.5in (37cm) wide. **£250-275** *VH*

A Victorian cabinet plate, unmarked, 9.5in (24cm) diam.
£100-140 *LIO*

A Crescent cabinet plate, decorated by Birbeck, c1910. **£110-140** *LIO*

A Doulton Series Ware fruit bowl.
£25-40 *AOS*

A pair of gilt decorated plates, with Okehampton Castle and Monks Rock Tenby, late 19thC. **£35-40** *PCh*

A Poole pottery commemorative plate, 11in (28cm) diam.
£50-60 *PCh*

A Wedgwood dessert dish, coloured in enamels, c1810, 10in (25cm) wide.
£180-200 *VH*

A Davenport cabinet plate, c1850, 9.5in (24cm) diam.
£120-150 *LIO*

A Fourmaintrau Frères pottery charger, marked, late 19thC.
£200-220 *VH*

A musical mug, 'I love Cyprus', plays 'Sing a Song of Sixpence', c1992. **£8-10** *PC*

A musical commemorative mug, plays 'Congratulations', 1986, 3.5in (9cm) high. **£50-100** *PC*

A George VI commemorative jug which plays 'For He's a Jolly Good Fellow', 1937. **£150-200** *PC*

A selection of Goss crested pottery, and Willow Art parian bust of Burns. **£65-75** *PCh*

A Crown Devon Fieldings musical Coronation jug, plays 'God Save The King', 1937. **£200-300** *PC*

A Worcester candle snuffer, 'The Witch', c1890. **£180-220** *TH*

A collection of Worcester candle snuffers, a monk, French cook, Japanese owl, old lady and Granny Snow. **£180-260 each** *TH*

A George V and Queen Mary Coronation plate, 1911, 8in (20cm) diam. **£30-40** *LIO*

A George V and Queen Mary Coronation mug, 1911, 4in (10cm) high. **£15-20** *LIO*

A Crown Devon one pint musical Coronation mug, plays 'Here's Health Unto His Majesty', May 12, 1937, 6.25in (16cm) high. **£200-250** *PC*

The Eaton Boating Song musical jug. **£400-500** *PC*

Twinkle Twinkle Little Star musical figure. **£150-200** *PC*

A Crown Devon musical Toby jug, There's a Tavern in the Town, 9in (23cm). **£150-200** *PC*

A musical Toby jug, The Night That We Danced. **£150-200** *PC*

Sally In Our Alley musical 1pt jug. **£400-500** *PC*

A John Peel whisky musical flagon. **£180-250** *PC*

A Crown Devon Fieldings Widdicombe Fair musical 1 pint jug. **£170-220** *PC*

l. A musical tankard, Roll Out The Barrel. **£50-100** *PC*

On Ilka Moor Baht'at 1 pint tankard. **£150-200** *PC*

A John Peel 1 pint musical tankard. **£100-150** *PC*

A Crown Devon musical 1 pint tankard, Daisy Daisy, 6in (15cm). **£130-180** *PC*

A Cherry Brandy musical bottle, The Hunting Song. **£50-100** *PC*

CERAMICS

This year we have arranged our Ceramics section slightly differently, to complement our Art Nouveau section. We have still maintained our basic principles to aid identification; that is we have grouped the featured items by factory, when the factory is clearly marked, and we have illustrated the main factory marks where necessary. We have also included the salient points of manufacturers' history, dates, locations and major artists and designers. In addition, this year we have featured particular geographical areas of production, notably the Low Countries and Scotland. These ceramics are becoming very collectable at the moment and offer new and varied fields for collectors who perhaps cannot manage the financial resources required for the more fashionable Art Deco pieces. It is worth reiterating that every year the ceramic section is wholly different and reflects market trends in popularity as well as prices. It is essential that previous editions are consulted to see, for example, Susie Cooper or Clarice Cliff, as featured last year, and refer to the cross references.

We have then, as usual, covered areas that are collected as particular items, for example teapots, which obviously come from a variety of makers.

Ceramics are as popular as ever with collectors of all ages, regardless of budgets, and if we have not yet featured what you collect please let us know.

Finally, remember that perfect pieces command the best prices and will prove to be the best investment, and as we always say, research your subject and buy the best you can afford.

Ault

● Founded by William Ault at Swadlincote, Nr Burton-on-Trent, Staffordshire.

● Produced earthenwares between 1887 and 1923.

● Became Ault Potteries in 1937, still producing earthenwares.

● Printed or impressed marks from 1887 onwards.

● Christopher Dresser (1834-1904) designed products for Ault and marked his work with his name (1891-96). He later worked for both Minton and Wedgwood.

Beswick

● Founded by John Beswick at Gold Street, Longton, Staffordshire, and produced earthenwares from c1936.

● Early wares not marked; later wares' printed marks as shown.

A yellow flower holder, designed by Christopher Dresser, 4in (10cm) diam.
£80-100 *NCA*

A yellow flower basket, by Christopher Dresser, 8in (20cm) high.
£280-300 *NCA*

BESWICK ENGLAND

Beswick Ware.
MADE IN ENGLAND

A hand painted wall mask, 1930s, 8in (20cm).
£150-200 *GAZ*

A terrier, 3.5in (9cm) long.
£15-20 *WAC*

A panda 2.75in (7cm) long.
£8-12 *WAC*

A retriever, 8in (20cm) long.
£25-30 *WAC*

A pigeon, 8in (20cm) long.
£30-35 *WAC*

A matt blue/green vase, 8in
(20cm) high. **£15-25** *AOS*

A joker mask, 5in (13cm) high.
£85-95 *WAC*

Bourne Denby

A Glyn Colledge vase, 7.5in (19cm) high. **£50-60** *NCA*

A Glyn Colledge vase, 8.5in (21cm) high. **£55-65** *NCA*

A Glyn Colledge vase, 14in (36cm) high. **£80-100** *NCA*

A Glyn Colledge jug, 7.5in (19cm) high. **£40-50** *NCA*

A Glyn Colledge bowl, 12.5in (32cm) diam. **£70-80** *NCA*

A Glyn Colledge ewer, 13in (33cm) high. **£80-100** *NCA*

Brannam

● C.H. Brannam Ltd produced earthenwares at the Litchdon Pottery, Barnstaple, Devon, from about 1879.

● Marks consisted of incised letters C.H. BRANNAM, sometimes dated and BARUM (the Roman name for Barnstaple).

For a further selection of Brannam earthenware refer to previous volumes of Miller's Collectables Price Guides, available from Millers Publications.

A vase, c1886, 7in (18cm) high. **£280-300** *NCA*

An oval green flower holder, 4in (10cm) high. **£250-280** *NCA*

A jug with mythical bird decoration, 1881, 8in (20cm) high. **£250-275** *NCA*

A blue puffin jug, 6.25in (16cm) high. **£60-70** *NCA*

A bowl, c1883, 3.25in (9cm) high. **£80-100** *NCA*

A frog vase, 1894, 3in (8cm) high. **£100-120** *NCA*

An 'Oriental' bowl, 7in (18cm) diam. **£60-70** *NCA*

Bretby

● Bretby Art Pottery was a partnership formed during the early 1880s by Willam Tooth (Linthorpe Art Pottery) and William Ault.

● Factory was at Woodville, near Burton-on-Trent, Derbyshire.

● Products marked as shown. The word 'ENGLAND' was added from c1891.

● William Ault left the partnership in 1886. The company became 'Tooth and Co' from the 1920s.

A vase, 4.5in (11cm) high. **£20-30** *NCA*

A two-handled loving cup, 4.5in (11cm). **£60-70** *NCA*

A ceramic cat with green glass eyes, 7.5in (19cm) high. **£60-100** *ZEI*

A pair of 'Oriental' bowls, 8in (20cm) diam. **£60-75** *NCA*

An 'Oriental' vase, 8in (20cm) high. **£90-100** *NCA*

Buckley

A rustic garden trio, comprising a seat and 2 urns, possibly different potteries, seat 17in (43cm) high, urns 26.5in (67cm) high.
£800-900 the set *IW*

A bird whistle, c1880, 9in (23cm) high.
£240-260 *IW*

Burgess & Leigh

A flower jug, 'The Kingfisher', 1930s, 7in (18cm) high.
£45-55 *GAZ*

A flower jug, 'Parrot' design, 1930s, 7in (18cm) high.
£45-55 *GAZ*

> **Cross Reference**
> Jugs

A flower jug, 'The Highwayman', c1930, 8in (20cm) high. **£200-250** *GAZ*

Burmantofts

● Burmantofts Art Pottery was produced by Messrs Wilcox & Co. (Ltd) of Leeds, Yorkshire, between 1882-1904.

● The Art Pottery was discontinued in 1904, some later terracotta ware was marked Leeds Fire-Clay Co. Ltd.

Two V. Kremer vases, 5in (13cm) high.
£120-130 each *NCA*

A two-handled vase,
10in (25cm)
high.
£140-160 *NCA*

A dragon chamberstick,
4.5in (11cm) high.
£180-200 *NCA*

An Isnik onion shaped vase, with
white and blue flower decoration
on deep blue ground, impressed
and printed mark, 19thC, 9.75in
(25cm) high. **£530-550** *AH*

> **Cross Reference**
> Art Nouveau

Carlton Ware

● Produced since 1890 at the Carlton
Works at Stoke-on-Trent.

● Art Pottery produced during the
1920s; household domestic wares very
heavily Art Deco influenced.

● Particularly famous for Guinness
advertising figures and animals.

● Later marks sometimes feature
previous name Wiltshaw & Robinson
Ltd.

A mug, c1925, 3.75in (9cm) high. **£20-25** *OD*

An Australian one-person set, 12in (31cm) long.
£230-260 *GAZ*

An Australian grape pattern
milk jug, 6.5in (16cm) high.
£120-140 *GAZ*

> **Cross Reference**
>
> Commemorative

A mushroom
cruet, 5.5in
(14cm) diam.
£20-25
WAC

A black cat teapot, c1960, 7.5in (19cm) high. **£30-40** *LIO*

A green vase with poppy and daisy design, 8in (20cm) high. **£250-300** *GAZ*

An Australian raspberry design jug, 5.5in (14cm) high. **£120-150** *GAZ*

George Clews & Co.

A pair of Chameleon Ware vases, 5.5in (14cm) high. **£80-100** *NCA*

A Chameleon Ware vase, in shades of yellow ochre, 10in (25cm) high. **£90-110** *NCA*

A Chameleon Ware Aladdin's Lamp, 8.5in (21cm) high. **£90-110** *NCA*

A Chameleon Ware vase, 9.5in (24cm) high. **£90-110** *NCA*

A two-handled Chameleon Ware vase, 6.5in (16cm) high. **£60-75** *NCA*

Charlotte Rhead

A tube line design plaque, by Crown Ducal Co., 1930, 14.5in (37cm).
£160-200 *GAZ*

A pottery wall plaque by Crown Ducal, 16.5in (42cm).
£430-450 *GAK*

A bowl in pattern no. 5802, c1939.
£100-150 *AOS*

An octagonal bowl.
£75-125 *AOS*

Clarice Cliff

> **Cross Reference**
> Night Lights

● Originally Clarice Cliff worked for Arthur J. Wilkinson (Ltd).

● Produced designs for Newport Pottery marked as below from 1938.

A Goblin Ware child's night light, 3.5in (9cm) high.
£150-250 *RIC*

An Orange and Plums design preserve pot.
£50-75 *AOS*

A Trees and House pattern plate.
£100-150 *AOS*

Clarice Cliff
NEWPORT POTTERY
ENGLAND

A sandwich plate, 11.5in (29cm) long. **£250-275** *RIC*

Note the difference in price on these sandwich plates, the pattern used is vital to the value of a piece - not the shape.

A Floral Latona vase, hairline crack, 6in (15cm) high.
£120-165 *RIC*

A Chloris pattern vase, shape 358, 8in (20cm) high. **£175-275** *AOS*

A Bizarre pattern sandwich plate, 11.5in (29cm) long.
£35-45 *RIC*

Part of a table centrepiece, in Bamboo pattern, 5in (13cm) wide.
£60-75 *RIC*

A Biarritz shaped bowl, 6in (15cm) wide.
£18-22 *RIC*

A biscuit barrel in Marguerite pattern, 7in (18cm) high.
£175-200 *RIC*

An ashtray, 5in (13cm) square.
£75-80 *RIC*

A Capri Orange squat candlestick, 3in (8cm) high.
£90-110 *RIC*

A conical milk jug in blue Autumn pattern, from a tea-for-6 set, 4in (10cm) high.   **£175-200** *RIC*

A Marigold pattern sandwich plate, 11.5in (29cm) long.   **£400-450** *RIC*

An early Geometric pattern sandwich plate, 11.5in (29cm) long.
£175-200 *RIC*

Part of a salad draining set, orange colourway, in Trees and House design, 8in (20cm).
£400-500 *GAZ*

A Bizarre shaped vase, in Secrets pattern, first produced 1939, 8in (20cm).
£500-600 *GAZ*

A Sunray pattern biscuit barrel, c1930, 6.5in (16cm).
£500-600 *GAZ*

A Bizarre glazed earthenware vase in Fir Tree pattern, marked Hand painted Bizarre by Clarice Cliff, Wilkinson Ltd, England, 1930s, 12.5in (32cm).
£575-600 *S*

A Celtic Harvest pattern preserve pot, with chrome lid, 4.5in (11cm) high.
£30-40 *RIC*

Decoro

● Decoro Pottery Co. (a part of R.H. & S.L. Plant Ltd) produced earthenwares at the Tuscan Works, Longton, Staffordshire, between 1933-49.

Decoro Pottery
MADE IN
ENGLAND

USCAN
DECORO
POTTERY
MADE IN
ENGLAND

An octagonal fruit bowl, 8in (20cm) diam.
£75-125 *AOS*

A gourd shaped vase, Reg. No. 429479, 8in (20cm) high.
£75-125 *AOS*

MAKE THE MOST OF MILLERS
Condition is absolutely vital when assessing the value of any item. Damaged pieces appreciate much less than perfect examples. However, a rare, desirable piece may command a high price even when damaged.

Devon Ware

A Honiton vase, 3in (8cm) high.
£8-10 *COL*

A Longpark cockerel teapot and
cover, reverse with 'From Dawlish
Dawntee be fraid 'aut now', 6in
(15cm) diam.
£30-35 *PAR*

A Longpark cockerel coffee pot
and cover, reverse with 'It's an ill
wind that blows nobody good', 7in
(18cm).
£30-35 *PAR*

A Longpark cockerel
jam dish, impressed
mark, 6in (15cm).
£18-20 *PAR*

A Longpark water jug,
7in (18cm) high.
£30-45 *AOS*

A Crown Devon cake plate, with
stylised flowers pattern, 8in
(20cm) diam.
£38-45 *ADC*

A Crown Devon coffee set, in
geometric design, with lustre
interior, c1930, coffee pot 7in
(18cm) high.
£350-400 *GAZ*

A Crown Devon hand painted
plate, 10.25in (26cm).
£85-95 *ADC*

A teapot, 6in
(15cm) high.
£20-30 *AOS*

A Honiton
'Kenton' pattern
jug, 7.75in
(19cm) high.
£20-25 *COL*

Doulton

'Gladiator' D 6550, designed by M. Henk, and produced between 1961-67, 7.5in (19cm) high.
£230-250 *WIL*

A character jug, in the form of Field Marshal Smuts, withdrawn 1948.
£560-580 *Bea*

A baluster form stoneware jar, painted by Margaret E. Thompson, in blue and black enamels with the light brown body showing through, impressed and painted marks, 14.5in (37cm) high.
£330-350 *Bea*

A model of a bulldog, in a Union Jack cloak, printed mark, Rd.no. 645658, 6.25in (16cm) high.
£110-130 *P(S)*

For a further selection of Doulton refer to Miller's Collectables Price Guide Volume I page 69, Volume III page 71 and Volume IV pages 82 and 83

'Gondolier' D 6589, designed by D. Biggs, produced from 1964-69, 8in (20cm) high.
£180-200 *WIL*

Jackfield Ware

A jug, 6.5in (16cm) high. **£25-30** *AA*

A jug, with pewter lid, 5.5in (14cm) high.
£25-30 *AA*

Two cups and saucers, cups 2.75in and 3in (8cm) diam. **£28-30 each** *AA*

Two teapot stands, 6 and 7.5in (15 and 19cm) diam.
£6-8 each *AA*

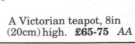

A cheese dish, 8in (20cm) diam.
£85-95 *AA*

A Victorian teapot, 8in (20cm) high. **£65-75** *AA*

A teapot, 5.5in (14cm) high.
£65-75 *AA*

Cross Reference
Tea Pots

A teapot, 5.5in (14cm) high. **£50-60** *AA*

A teapot.
£75-85
AA

A jug, with pewter lid, 6in
(15cm) high.
£30-35 *AA*

George Jones & Sons

● These items were manufactured by one company George Jones & Son Ltd. who traded as the Trent Potteries and Crescent Potteries in South Wolfe Street, Stoke-on-Trent between 1861-1951

● Upon the death of George Jones, the founder, the business was carried on by several of his sons, one of whom, Horace Overton Jones, was an artist specialising in floral and topographical subjects.

● Some examples bear a monogram H.O.J. within the design.

A chocolate pot set, tray 12in(31cm) diam, pot 6in (15cm) high.
£180-200
WAC

A trio, marked George Jones Sons, Pyrethrum, plate 7in (18cm) diam. dated 1884,
£25-35 *WAC*

An afternoon tea cup and plate, 8.25in (21cm) wide. **£40-50 each** *WAC*

A violet design cream jug, sugar bowl and trio, plate 7in (18cm) cream and sugar **£30-36** Trio **£40-45** *WAC*

A Crescent china plate c1880, 8.75in (22cm) diam. **£20-25** *WAC*

A sucrier, 6in (15cm) high. **£35-40** *WAC*

A plate, unmarked, 9.75in (24cm) diam. **£12-15** *WAC*

An oval dish, marked Stoke Crescent, signed H.O.J., 8.75in (22cm) wide. **£45-50** *WAC*

A Crescent trio, marked George Jones & Sons, plate 7.25in (18cm) diam. **£18-25** *WAC*

A trio signed H.O.J. **£45-55 each** *WAC*

A plate, 8.25in (21cm) diam. **£25-30** *WAC*

A birds and bloom plate, marked George Jones & Sons, c1884, 9.75in (24cm) diam. **£12-18** *WAC*

A Crescent butter dish, George Jones & Sons, 6in (15cm) wide. **£15-20** *WAC*

A Stoke Crescent vase, George Jones & Sons, 5.75in (15cm) high. **£55-65** *WAC*

Lauder

A chamberstick, 8in (20cm) high. **£75-85** *NCA*

A vase, 6in (15cm) high. **£80-90** *NCA*

Linthorpe

● Linthorpe pottery was produced at Middlesbrough, Yorks, between 1879-1889.

● Simple block lettered impressed mark - LINTHORPE (sometimes with the outline of a vase).

● Christopher Dresser designed works had an incised, impressed or painted signature.

● Managed by Henry Tooth before 1883 and monogrammed as below.

Ħ   HT

Cross Reference
Art Nouveau

A Christopher Dresser yellow floral jug, 6.5in (16cm) high. **£500-550** *NCA*

A Christopher Dresser plate, 8.5in (21cm) diam. **£90-110** *NCA*

A butterscotch glaze bowl, designed by Christopher Dresser with studding to sides, 9.5in (24cm) diam. **£200-300** *ZEI*

Moorcroft

● W. Moorcroft (Ltd) produced earthenwares at the Washington Works, Burslem, Staffordshire, from 1913.

● Simple impressed block lettered mark MOORCROFT BURSLEM.

● William Moorcroft's signature, was registered as a trademark in 1919. He died in 1945.

● Walter Moorcroft continued pottery in the traditional Moorcroft style with an initialled mark.

● Modern wares also have a printed mark MOORCROFT MADE IN ENGLAND.

A MacIntyre goblet, with red cornflowers, c1910, 9in (23cm).
£1,500-1,600 *NP*

A MacIntyre Flamminian vase, c1906, 8in (20cm).
£275-300 *NP*

A Moorcroft/MacIntyre ring holder, decorated with the poppy design, c1903, 4in (10cm) diam.
£300-350 *LIO*

A flambé glazed vase, in Clematis design, 12.5in (32cm). **£900-1,000** *NP*

A buttercup vase, c1992, 16in (40.5cm) high.
£375-400 *NP*

A jardinière, Fairy Rings, design by Philip Richardson, introduced 1987, impressed Made in England and factory mark, John Moorcroft monogram, 9in (23cm) high.
£250-325 *VBu*

A pansy design bowl, c1918, 6in (15cm) high.
£1,100-1,200 *NP*

A MacIntyre Florian bowl with inverted rim, with blue cornflowers, minor damage, c1900, 8in (20cm) diam.
£300-350 *NP*

An arum lily pot, c1960, 6in (15cm) high. **£200-250** *NP*

A MacIntyre Aurelian vase, in cobalt blue and gold, c1898, 6in (15cm).
£250-300 *NP*

A William Moorcroft salt glaze bowl, impressed marks and facsimile signature, 1930s, 10in (25.5cm).
£350-450 *VBu*

A carp plate, from a limited edition of 250, 1989.
£175-200 *NP*

A Walter Moorcroft bowl, impressed Made in England, facsimile signature and royal warrant, 10in (25.5cm) diam.
£200-300 *VBu*

A pottery pedestal
jardinière, painted with
mushrooms and toadstools
on a mottled green ground,
impressed No. 995,
signed W. Moorcroft, with
printed mark made for
Liberty & Co., 8in
(20cm) high.
£900-950 *Bea*

A pomegranate vase,
c1924, 12in (30.5cm)
high. **£300-325** *NP*

A pomegranate
parasol top,
made for the
ladies at Ascot,
c1917.
£80-100 *LIO*

A MacIntyre
commemorative
mug, inscribed
from Mr & Mrs
Lasenby,
Liberty, 4in
(10cm).
£350-400 *NP*

A dandelion
vase, from
a limited
edition of 200,
1992.
£190-225 *NP*

Pilkington Lancastrian

● Pilkington's Tile & Pottery Co. Ltd, of Clifton Junction, Nr. Manchester, Lancs, produced earthenwares and lustre and glazed finishes.

● Art Pottery produced from about 1897-1938 and some later c1948-57.

● Early wares, if marked, had an incised 'P'.

● Several trade marks registered from 1904.

● Royal Lancastrian mark often accompanied by initial of designer.

A Pilkington Lancastrian pottery bowl, designed by Walter Crane, 6in (15cm).
£200-300 *ZEI*

> **Cross Reference**
> Art Nouveau

later mark c1948-1957

A Pilkington Lancastrian vase, designed by Gladys Rodgers, in grey matt glaze with multi-coloured chevrons, 17in (43cm) high.
£300-400 *ZEI*

Royal Winton

A moulded jug, 7in (18cm) high.
£25-45 *AOS*

A comport, c1935, 9.5in (24cm) diam.
£80-90 *COL*

> **DID YOU KNOW?**
> Miller's Collectables Price Guide is designed to build up, year by year, into the most comprehensive reference system available.

A sugar shaker in Paradise pattern.
£20-30 *AOS*

A jam pot in Springtime pattern.
£20-30 *AOS*

Royal Worcester

A plate painted with Roseck Abbey, probably by Robert Perling, impressed mark, c1870, 8.75in (22cm) diam.
£150-160 *TVA*

A stork vase, shape no. 238, the ivory tusk section pierced and covered with flowering prunus, with a brown and gilt stork, bronze and green glaze rock formed base with tortoises, c1872, 11in (28cm) high.
£1,200-1,300 *GAK*

A Locke & Co. triple vase pattern no. 363, c1900, 7in (18cm) high.
£100-145 *TVA*

A honey pot and cover, pattern W5171, c1895, 4.5in (13cm).
£150-185 *TVA*

A Bamboo Rose jar and cover, shape 1326, 1898 date code, 4.5in (11cm) diam.
£100-150 *TVA*

A vase, shape 1727, slight restoration, date code for 1897, 3.75in (9cm) high.
£100-150 *TVA*

A tusk ice jug, shape 106, date 1886, 9in (23cm) high.
£400-500 *TVA*

A pair of bowls, with elephant supports, c1890, 5in (13cm) square.
£190-235 *TVA*

A Locke & Co vase, decorated with a mirror image pattern, c1900, 3.25in (8cm) high.
£50-80 *TVA*

A shell dish, shape no 1413, date 1906, 4.5in (11cm) wide.
£100-140 *TVA*

A Locke & Co. vase, with finely painted pattern, shape no. 423, cracked, c1900, 5in (13cm) high.
£70-80 *TVA*

A globe vase, with violet pattern, shape 916, slight restoration, date code 1903, 4.5in (11cm) high.
£80-135 *TVA*

A pair of leaf dishes, c1892, 5in (13cm) wide.
£100-120 *AMH*

A porcelain model of Napoleon Bonaparte on a white charger, from the series of famous military commanders by Bernard Winskill, No. 18 of a limited edition of 750, complete with certificate and wood stand.
£2,000-2,250 *Bea*

A dish, small chips, date code for 1900, 4.5in (11cm) diam.
£50-55 *AMH*

A model of H.R.H. The Duke of Edinburgh on his polo pony, modelled by Doris Lindner, No. 18 of a limited edition of 750, complete with certificate and wood stand.
£275-290 *Bea*

A crinoline figure with cap, modelled as a tea cosy top, shape 2620, introduced 1916, 3in (8cm) high.
£400-450 *TVA*

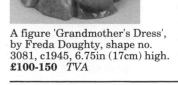

A figure 'Grandmother's Dress', by Freda Doughty, shape no. 3081, c1945, 6.75in (17cm) high.
£100-150 *TVA*

A miniature patch box and cover, with hand painted birds, 1924, 1.5in (4cm) diam.
£100-150 *TVA*

A figure 'Marking Stones', 7.5in (19cm) high.
£400-500 *TH*

A figure of 'Ye Rat Catcher', 7.5in (19cm) high.
£400-500 *TH*

A figure of 'Ye Brush Man', 7.25in (18cm) high.
£400-500 *TH*

A figure 'Ye Prison Basket', 7.5in (19cm) high.
£400-500 *TH*

A figure of 'Ye Watchman' from the Cries of London series, 7.25in (18cm) high.
£400-500 *TH*

A pair of bird models, from the American game bird series, male and female Mallard, by Ronald Van Ruyckevelt, each No. 140 of a limited edition of 500, complete with certificates and wood stands.
£1,500-1,750 *Bea*

MAKE THE MOST OF MILLERS
Condition is absolutely vital when assessing the value of any item. Damaged pieces appreciate much less than perfect examples. However, a rare, desirable piece may command a high price even when damaged.

Ruskin

● Ruskin Pottery (W. Howson Taylor) of Smethwick, Birmingham, produced earthenwares between 1898 and 1935.

● Early wares were simply impressed TAYLOR.

● Painted or incised marks as below.

A crystaline glazed vase, 8in (20cm) high.
£100-150 *ZEI*

Cross Reference
Art Nouveau

A crystaline glazed vase, signed by W. Howson Taylor, 15in (38cm) high.
£600-800 *ZEI*

Rye

A bowl, with flecked body covered with applied green hops and leaves, the rim banded with sprigs, marked on base S.R.W. Rye, 9in (23cm).
£300-350 *RAG*

For a further selection of Rye Pottery, please refer to Miller's Collectables Price Guide, Volume III, page 62.

Salopian

● The Salopian Art Pottery of Benthall, Nr Broseley, Shropshire, produced earthenwares between c1882 and 1912.

● Simple impressed mark on earthenwares SALOPIAN.

A blue vase, 5.5in (14cm) high. **£30-35** *NCA*

A vase, 4in (10cm) high. **£30-35** *NCA*

Sylvac

A rabbit, 5.5in (14cm) high.
£15-20 *WAC*

A dog, 5.5in (14cm) high. **£15-22** *AOS*

A vase, 6in (15cm) high. **£22-25** *COL*

A child's mug, 3in (8cm) high.
£10-12 *COL*

Cross Reference
Childrens & Nursery
Ceramics

A selection of Sylvac. **£18-25 each** *WAC*

A cat, 7in (18cm) high.
£15-20 *WAC*

A spill holder/vase, 6.75in (17cm) high.
£10-15 *WAC*

A blue dog, 5.25in (13cm) high.
£10-15 *WAC*

A poodle.
£15-25 *AOS*

A pixie, 4in (10cm) long.
£12-14 *WAC*

A sunflower plate.
£10-15 *AOS*

A dog, 8in (20cm) long.
£15-20 *WAC*

A money box, 6in (15cm) high.
£10-12 *COL*

A posy planter, 13in (33cm) long.   **£15-20** *COL*

A green and cream toast rack, 8in (20cm) long.
£15-20 *COL*

Upchurch

● The Upchurch Pottery (William and James Baker) produced earthenwares at Rainham in Kent between 1913 and 1961.

● Simple impressed marks UPCHURCH or UPCHURCH SEEBY.

● Seeby were their agents at Reading and Seeby sometimes appears as a painted mark.

> **Cross Reference**
> Art Nouveau

A matt glazed vase, 7in (18cm). **£50-70** *ZEI*

A matt glazed vase, 10in (25cm).
£70-100 *ZEI*

A twin handled vase with matt glaze, 6in (15cm).
£70-100 *ZEI*

Wade Heath

● Formerly Wade & Colclough, Union Pottery, Burslem, Staffordshire, subsequently Wade Heath and Co., produced earthenwares between 1887 and 1927.

● Wade Heath and Co. (Ltd), High Street Works, also Royal Victoria Pottery from 1938 marked their products in a variety of ways, all printed or impressed and including the word Wade.

> **FURTHER READING**
> *The World of Wade Collectible Pottery & Porcelain,* Ian Warner and Mike Posgay, 1991

A vase, c1935, 6.5in (16cm) high.
£25-35 *AOS*

A two-handled vase, c1935, 5in (13cm) high. **£20-30** *AOS*

A vase, c1935, 6in (15cm) high.
£25-35 *AOS*

Wedgwood

A plate, with transfer printed harbour scene, c1867, 9in (23cm) diam.
£120-150 *TVA*

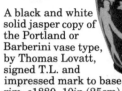

A black basalt encaustic decorated two-handled oviform vase, painted in red, damaged and repaired, c1800, 10in (25cm) high.
£450-500 *C*

A black and white solid jasper copy of the Portland or Barberini vase type, by Thomas Lovatt, signed T.L. and impressed mark to base rim, c1880, 10in (25cm) **£1,100-1,200** *C*

A blue jasper dipped stoneware copy of the Portland or Barberini vase type, impressed mark and date code for 1887, 10in (25cm) high.
£575-600 *C*

A creamware oviform teapot and cover, painted in the manner of David Rhodes in yellow, iron red, pale green, dark brown and black, slight chips to rim of cover, c1768, 5.5in (14cm) high.
£1,900-2,000 *C*

Winstanley

A tabby cat licking its back, with closed eyes, marked J.Winstanley, England, 3, c1970, 8in (20cm) long.
£20-25 *CP*

A seated cat, marked J. Winstanley, 3, England, 8in (20cm) high.
£20-25 *CP*

A grey persian cat with white paws, marked J. Winstanley, England, 4, 8in (20cm) high.
£22-26 *CP*

A grey tabby cat, marked 5 J. Winstanley, England, 11.9.91, 12.5in (32cm) long. **£27-30** *CP*

A tabby cat with white crossed paws, marked J. Winstanley, England, 7, 9.9.91, 14.5in (37cm) long. **£35-40** *CP*

A tabby cat with white paws, marked J. Winstanley, 4, England, 9.5in (24cm) long. **£22-26** *CP*

Continental Art Deco Crackleware

A Boch Frères Keramis kingfisher, marked Ch. Catteau, c1920, 6.25in (16cm) high. **£80-95** *POW*

'Pierrot & Pierrette' by L. Fontinelle, in crackleglaze, c1925, 11.5in (29cm) long. **£450-475** *POW*

'Danse Moderne', pale pink banjo player and 2 dancers, Boch Frères Keramis, marked Ch. Catteau, c1920, 14.5in (37cm) long. **£475-525** *POW*

White crackleglaze cats, Odyv, c1915, 13in (33cm) long. **£140-165** *POW*

A dove, Adnet, c1930, 8in (20cm) high. **£150-185** *POW*

White crackleglaze Flamenco dancers, Auguste Maizin et Cie, c1920, 15in (38cm) high. **£170-195** *POW*

A pair of cockatoo book ends in white crackleglaze, Faiencerie Auguste Mouzin et Cie, c1925, 8in (20cm) high. **£150-175** *POW*

A white elephant, Zuid-Holland, 9in (23cm) high. **£180-200** *POW*

A pale pink crackleglaze double fish, c1920, 15in (38cm) high.
£150-195 *POW*

A pair of crackleglaze doves with gold tails, L. Guiraud Vallauris, 4in (10cm) long.
£150-195 *POW*

A pink crackleglaze fish, Saint Clement, c1920, 7in (18cm) high.
£50-75 *POW*

Three dancers, Etha Lempke, Zuid-Holland, c1930, 8in (20cm) high.
£220-260 *POW*

A crackleglaze figure, Marcel Guillard, Editions Etling, c1925, 9in (23cm) high.
£200-225 *POW*

A green crackleglaze fish, Le Jan, c1925, 16in (41cm) long.
£150-185 *POW*

A seal, Zuid-Holland c1930, 9in (23cm) high.
£120-145 *POW*

A dove ashtray, Boch Frères Keramis, Ch. Catteau, c1918, 5.25in (13cm) diam.
£100-135 *POW*

A white crackleglaze sailing boat, Le Jan, c1920, 19in (48cm) high.
£220-265 *POW*

A pair of Pierrot white crackleglaze book ends, Odyv, c1925, 7in (18cm) high.
£225-265 *POW*

A turquoise squirrel, Auguste Mouzin et Cie, c1925, 11in (28cm) high. **£100-125** *POW*

Cross Reference
Art Deco

A white crackleglaze cubist knight on horseback, Odyv, c1925, 9in (23cm) high. **£140-165** *POW*

A turquoise crackleglaze dog, Le Jan, c1910, 13in (33cm) long. **£80-100** *POW*

Cubist crackleglaze birds, Angelo Hecq, c1930, limited edition 1/150, 13in (33cm) high. **£350-400** *POW*

A pair of crackleglaze fox book ends, Joset, c1930, 6.5in (16cm) high. **£75-95** *POW*

A pale green dove, Boch Frères Keramis, Ch. Catteau, c1920, 9in (23cm) high. **£150-185** *POW*

Dutch Art Deco/Art Nouveau Ceramics

A Zuid-Holland earthenware cache pot, in shades of blue, green, yellow and mauve, painted marks Gouda Juliana Ivora, c1915, 9in (22cm) diam. **£385-400** *S(AM)*

A pair of book ends D'Larrieu, c1910, 8.25in (21cm) high. **£400-425** *POW*

A crackleglaze peacock, Guillemin, c1920, 14in (36cm) long. **£120-145** *POW*

A pair of Zuid-Holland vases, amphora shape with loop handles, in shades of green, mauve and cream, chipped to base, painted marks, c1910, 14.5in (37cm) high. **£550-600** *S(AM)*

Two earthenware Gouda Ivora vases, with painted marks, c1915, 10.5in (26cm) high. **£200-225** *S(AM)*

SCOTTISH CERAMICS
Dunmore

- Situated on Dunmore Ness in Stirlingshire.

- Dunmore wares enjoyed royal patronage in the 1870s and were exhibited regularly in Edinburgh and Glasgow.

- Noted for grotesque animals, pedestals and commemorative busts; classic 19thC Scottish Art Pottery.

A pottery twig handled dish, 11in (28cm) wide.
£150-200
BWA

A pale green moon flask, 8.5in (21cm) high.
£150-200 *BWA*

A green, brown and ochre pottery planter, 8.5in (21cm) high.
£250-300 *BWA*

A bambo stick spill vase, 7.5in (19cm) high.
£100-130 *BWA*

A green and brown mottled pottery teapot, 7.5in (19cm) high.
£200-220 *BWA*

A green and ochre tazza, 8.5in (21cm) high.
£300-350 *BWA*

A two-handled brown treacle glazed frog mug, with 2 frogs, brown and cream, 6.5in (16cm) high.
£300-350 *BWA*

Four posy jars, 5in (13cm) high.
£100-130 *BWA*

A green chamberstick, 7.25in (18cm) wide.
£150-200 *BWA*

A red and ochre fern leaf design vase, 10in (25cm) high. **£200-250** *BWA*

A green snake handled vase, 9.5in (24cm) high. **£200-250** *BWA*

A blue owl, 6in (15cm) high **£380-400** *BWA*

A black and green two-handled bowl, 11in (28cm) wide. **£175-200** *BWA*

A pair of blue Grecian vases, 13.5in (34cm) high. **£700-800** *BWA*

A pair of glazed blue candlesticks, c1860, 13.5in (34cm) high. **£700-800** *BWA*

Cross Reference Candlesticks

Holyrood

- Henry Taylor Wyse, 1870-1951, an accomplished artist, produced his first catalogue Simple Furniture in 1900.

- His pottery designs were produced during the first quarter of 20thC.

- Some blanks were purchased from David Methven & Sons of Kirkaldy and sold locally and exported to the Empire.

- Although Wyse's Holyrood Pottery became quite successful, his main interest was his full-time art teacher's job; he often encouraged both teachers and students to use his factory.

A blue, green and pink pottery vase, 8in (20cm) high. **£150-175** *BWA*

A red and green glazed vase, 8in (20cm) high. **£150-175** *BWA*

A blue and red vase, 6in (15cm)high. **£100-120** *BWA*

Prestonpans

● Industrial potteries date back to the mid-18thC. The original pottery was founded by William Cadell in 1750.

● The early wares were unmarked.

● Belfield & Co. established in mid-1830s by Charles Belfield at Seacliff.

A Gordon's green plate, with impressed mark, c1820, 8.5in (21cm) diam. **£30-50** *BWA*

Prestonpans Pottery mark

A Belfields teapot, early 20thC, 8.5in (21cm) high. **£75-85** *BWA*

A Gordon's Queen Caroline plate, in Pratt colours, 9in (23cm) diam. **£350-450** *BWA*

Strathyre

● Strathyre is a small town in Perthshire which, as well as producing its own pottery, also bought in 'blanks' for decoration by their 'Lady Artists' notably Mary Ramsey and Jessie Wilson.

● Most Strathyre pieces are clearly marked and generally signed or initialled by the artist.

● Industrial potteries date back to the mid-18thC. The original pottery was founded by William Cadell in 1750.

● The early wares were unmarked.

● Belfield & Co. established in mid-1830s by Charles Belfield at Seacliff.

A plate decorated by J.D. Wilson, 6.75in (17cm) diam. **£100-150** *BWA*

A dish, decorated by Mary A Ramsay, 11in (28cm) diam. **£150-200** *BWA*

Kilcoddy

A zoo jug, painted by Miles
Johnson, 4.5in (11cm) high.
£150-175 *BWA*

A Morrison &
Crawford blue and
green named money
box, 6.5in (16cm)
high.
£100-120 *BWA*

A whisky flask, blue, red, green
and yellow, dated 1832, 9in
(23cm) high. **£200-300** *BWA*

A zoo jug, painted by Miles
Johnson, 4.5in (11cm) high.
£150-175 *BWA*

A hand painted bowl, c1850,
11.75in (30cm) diam.
£100-150 *BWA*

Portobello

A Rathbone's blue and
white bowl, variation
of the Fallow Deer
pattern, c1830,
7in (18cm) diam.
£100-150 *BWA*

A W & J A Bailey, Alloa,
green and brown glazed
plate, 9in (23cm) diam.
£30-40 *BWA*

A lustre jug, c1840,
3.5in (9cm)
high.
£50-75 *BWA*

Wemyss

A jam pot, with plums
design, 5.5in (14cm) high.
£150-200 *BWA*

A vase, in wild roses
pattern, 6.5in (16cm)
high.
£200-250 *BWA*

A teapot, with sweet
peas design,
5in (13cm) high.
£250-300 *BWA*

A cockerel cream jug, 2.5in (6cm) high and a Bonjour bowl, 2in (5cm) high.
£200-250 the pair *BWA*

A chamber pot, with plums pattern, 8.5in (21cm) diam.
£200-250 *BWA*

A cat with black spots, green glass eyes and pink paws, with painted black mark, 12.25in (31cm) high.
£1,300-1,500 *AH*

A pair of 'Jazzy' vases, 7.5in (19cm) high.
£200-250 *BWA*

A goose vase, 8in (20cm) high.
£600-900 *BWA*

A teapot, with rose design, 5in (13cm) high.
£250-300 *BWA*

A tankard, with peacock, 5.75in (14cm) high.
£400-600 *BWA*

Welsh

A pitcher, probably Newport, with contemporary paint, c1880, 14.5in (37cm) high.
£60-70 *IW*

A set of four salt glaze lions, based on a pressed glass original, probably North Wales, c1860, 6.5in (17cm) high.
£380-420 the set *IW*

A Sweeney Mountain tobacco jar, 7.5in (19cm), early 19thC.
£40-45 *IW*

For a further selection of Welsh Pottery please refer to Miller's Collectables Price Guide Volume IV, p103.

Bowls & Dishes

A Phoenix Ware bowl, by Thomas Forester & Sons Ltd, peacock blue, exterior decorated with cream roses and gilt on black, c1920, 11.5in (29.5cm) diam.
£30-40 *ROW*

A bowl by John Pearson, 5in (13cm) wide.
£180-200 *NCA*

A shell shaped dessert dish, by Charles Bourne, pattern no. 60, c1820, 8.5in (21.5cm) wide.
£600-700 *TVA*

Barge Ware

A Measham Ware teapot, with cream body, and green, blue and red applied design, c1880, 12in (30cm) high.
£350-450 *HEY*

A Measham Ware teapot, decorated in typical treacle glaze, applied with blue, white and print motifs, the cartouche reads 'A Present From A Friend', c1890, 12.5in (32cm) high.
£200-300 *HEY*

A jug, c1896, 8in (20cm) high.
£75-95 *AA*

A teapot, c1900, 8in (20cm) high.
£115-165 *AA*

A jug, c1885, 7.5in (19cm) high.
£75-95 *AA*

A Measham Ware teapot, decorated in typical brown treacle glaze, with blue, pink and white applied decoration, c1890, 13.5in (34cm) high.
£300-400 *HEY*

Children's & Nursery Ware

A child's plate, with purple print, spurious Wedgwood type mark, c1840, 7in (17.5cm) diam.
£50-60 *IW*

A Doulton Bunnykins special edition two-handled mug, 1984, 3in (8cm) high. **£10-12** *COL*

A child's tea set, comprising: teapot, milk jug, sugar bowl, 2 cups, 2 saucers and 2 plates, each piece illustrated with a different nursery rhyme, teapot 4in (10cm) high. **£65-75** *ROW*

Two Victorian nursery plates, with black transfer printed picture, hand coloured in green and red, c1850, 6.5in (41cm) diam.
£50-60 each *HEY*

A Doulton Bunnykins mug, 3in (7.5cm) high.
£5-8 *COL*

A Victorian nursery plate, in naturalistic underglaze colours and lustre under, with Joseph dressed in turquoise cloak, c1850, 7in (17.5cm) diam.
£35-45 *HEY*

A child's plate, possibly Davenport, 'Visit to the Zebra', c1840, 6.5in (16cm) diam.
£100-130 *IW*

A Doulton Bunnykins mug, 3.5in (8.5cm) high.
£5-6 *COL*

A Grimwades Peter Rabbit small tea set, comprising: 2 teapots, 2 jugs, bowl, 4 cups, saucers and plates, all decorated with scenes of Beatrix Potter's Peter Rabbit, on white ground with gilt edging, slight damage, cups 2in (5.5cm) high, in original box. **£500-550** *S(S)*

Coffee Pots

A Tams Ware hand painted green and white coffee set, c1930. **£40-50** *ROW*

A Wellington China coffee pot, sugar basin and cream jug, coffee pot 6in (15cm) high. **£10-15** *COL*

A pottery coffee pot, c1800, 11in (28cm) high. **£300-350** *JAC*

Commemorative

A commemorative cup and saucer, transfer painted enamel with gold decoration, saucer, c1880, saucer 6in (15cm) diam. **£55-65** *OD*

An earthenware jug with satirical print of Napoleon, overglaze print and enamel with lustre,some damage, c1814, 5.5in (14cm) high. **£130-150** *IW*

A Sunderland commemorative frog mug, with black transfer print, 4.5in (11.5cm) high. **£350-385** *JHo*

A Royal Doulton 'Peace' mug, 1919. **£30-35** *TRU*

A Denby Dale Pie plate, c1928, 9.5in (24cm) diam. **£60-70** *RP*

A commemorative frog mug, by Dixon Austin & Co., Sunderland, black transfer print with 'God Speed The Plough', 5in (13cm) high. **£345-365** *JHo*

Churchill

A Winston Churchill head, modelled by Frank A. Potts, 1941, 6.5in (16.5cm) high.
£60-70 *WAC*

A Royal Doulton Winston Churchill Toby jug, 5.5in (14cm) high.
£20-25 *WAC*

Produced until 1991

A Wedgwood bust of Churchill, modelled by Arnold Machin R.A., 1940, 7.5in (19cm) high.
£250-275 *WAC*

A Roosevelt and Churchill cup, with 'Let's Drink To Peace', and 'Let's Drink To Victory', 5.5in (14cm) high.
£140-150 *WAC*

Political

A Wedgwood cream glazed pottery jug, commemorating Thomas Carlisle, dated for 30th April, 1881, 9in (23cm) high.
£120-140 *GAK*

A Burleigh Ware cup, Champion of Democracy, with Roosevelt and Churchill, 6in (15cm) high.
£140-150 *WAC*

A Robert Peel jug, 5in (13cm).
£100-125 *WAC*

A blue printed commemorative jug of Sir R. Peel, M.P., c1840, slight damage, 4in (10cm) high. **£60-80** *LIO*

A mug from a limited edition of 250 items commemorating 3 election victories, Hayle, Cornwall, 3.5in (9cm). **£25-30** *WAC*

A Paragon mug, No 34 of a limited edition of 50 mugs, commemorating Neville Chamberlain, 'I am myself a man of Peace to the depths of my soul', 5in (13cm) high. **£600-650** *WAC*

A Reform jug, with re-used Napoleonic war print with added words 'Union Reform', c1832, 5.5in (14cm) high. **£180-220** *IW*

Royalty

A Paragon bone china jug, made for the 150th anniversary of Admiral Nelson's death, c1955, 4.5in (11.5cm) high. **£75-85** *WAC*

A Silver Jubilee 1910-1935 commemorative mug, 4in (10cm) high. **£18-22** *COL*

A Goodwin Bridgwood & Harris George IV commemorative silver-form jug, printed in black, damaged, black printed mark of lion over G.B.H. c1830, 5.5in (13.5cm) high. **£350-550** *S(S)*

Modern Royalty

A plate commemorating the wedding of Prince Andrew and Sarah Ferguson, by Sutherland China for Peter Jones Collection, Wakefield, 8.5in (21.5cm) diam.
£20-25 *WAC*

A Staffordshire pottery beaker, commemorating the wedding of Princess Anne and Captain Mark Phillips, 3.5in (8.5cm) high.
£8-12 *WAC*

A Sutherland plate, the Prince and Princess of Wales and bridesmaids, for Peter Jones Collection, Wakefield, 8.5in (21.5cm) diam.
£25-30 *WAC*

A Royal Wedding money box, 1981, 3.5in (9cm).
£8-12 *WAC*

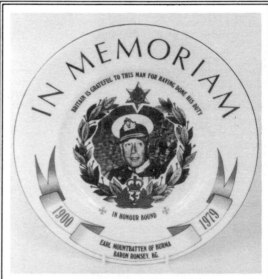

A plate designed and produced by Panorama Studies, Ashburton Devon, depicting Earl Mountbatten, 10.5in (26.5cm) diam. **£45-50** *WAC*

A Duchy of Cornwall mug, Panorama Studies of Ashburton, Devon, John Bell design, 3.5in (9cm) high.
£15-20 *WAC*

A Wedgwood mug, commemorating the wedding of Princess Anne and Captain Mark Phillips, 4in (10cm) high.
£45-50 *WAC*

A child's part tea set. **£25-35** *WAC*

A mug commemorating H. M. Queen Elizabeth II's Silver Jubilee, black transfer ware. **£6-8** *COL*

A mug commemorating the Coronation, 2 June 1953, 2.5in (6.5cm) high. **£6-8** *COL*

A Coalport mug commemorating the birth of Prince William, 21 June 1982, 3.5in (9cm) high. **£30-35** *WAC*

A two-handled mug, 'Long Live Prince Henry Charles Albert David', 13 September 1984, 3.5in (9cm) high. **£20-25** *WAC*

Moorcroft Commemorative

A flambé square box, by Moorcroft, commemorating the Coronation of Edward VIII, damaged, 3. 5in (9cm). **£485-500** *WAC*

A Moorcroft tankard, commemorating King George VI, 4.5in (11.5cm) high. **£525-550** *WAC*

A Moorcroft salt glaze pot, commemorating King Edward VIII, 5in (13cm) diam. **£135-155** *WAC*

A mug commemorating the Coronation of King Edward VII and Queen Alexandra, given by Mr and Mrs Lasenby of Liberty's to all their staff, c1902, 3.5in (8.5cm) high. **£250-350** *WAC*

A Moorcroft jar commemorating King Edward VIII, 6in (15cm) high. **£285-300** *WAC*

A mug commemorating Edward VIII, 4.5in (11.5cm). **£575-600** *WAC*

Cruets

Faience

A monkey cruet, made in Japan, 4in (10cm) high. **£7-8** ` *WAC*

For a further selection of Cruets please refer to Miller's Collectables Price Guide Volume IV, pages 74-75.

A French tureen and cover, modelled as a duck on a leaf-moulded circular base, glaze cracked, 15in (38cm) high. **£575-600** *CSK*

A plate, c1900, 5in (12.5cm) diam. **£7-8** *OD*

A dish, marked S.B., c1900, 9in (22.5cm) wide. **£15-20** *OD*

A plate, c1900, 8in (20cm) diam. **£20-25** *OD*   Two plates, c1900, 5in (12.5cm) diam. **£7-8 each** *OD*

Ironstone

A Mason's Ironstone jug and basin set, 19thC. **£265-285** *JH*

A pair of Ashwoods Real Ironstone china tureens, white with blue, red and gilt underglaze c1880. **£250-300** *LRG*

Goss China

- Goss factory started producing Parian Ware in 1858.

- Historical models in porcelain were first produced in 1881 to be sold as souvenirs for trippers and holiday-makers.

- Only one agent was appointed in each town and by 1914 sixteen hundred agents had been appointed.

- 2,500 shapes were available with over 8,000 different coats-of-arms.

A selection of view ware. **£35-85 each** *CCC*

A group of 'Royal' interest ware. **£30-150 each** *CCC*

A Pompeian ewer. **£8-10** *G&CC*

John Knox's house. **£450-500** *CCC*

A Carew cross. **£100-125** *G&CC*

A bread platter, inscribed 'Give Us This Day Our Daily Bread', with the Brussels crest. **£100-125** *G&CC*

A Dr Kenealy spill vase. **£150-200** *G&CC*

'Meditation' figurine. **£300-350** *G&CC*

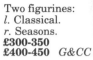

Two figurines:
l. Classical.
r. Seasons.
£300-350
£400-450   *G&CC*

A Llewellyn Jewitt bust.
£2,250-2,500   *G&CC*

An Apollo bust.
£800-850   *G&CC*

FURTHER READING

The Concise Encyclopedia and Price Guide to Goss China and *The Price Guide to Arms and Decorations on Goss China,* Nicholas Pine (Milestone Publications), 62 Murray Road, Horndean, Hants.
William Henry Goss, The Story of the Staffordshire Family of Potters Who Invented Heraldic Porcelain, Lynda and Nicholas Pine.

Crested China

● Crested China was produced by many factories between about 1880 and 1940.

● Most famous main manufacturers were Arcadian, Carlton, Grafton, Shelley and Willow Art.

● More diverse model subjects than Goss, especially buildings, hats, animals, shoes etc.

● Many military subjects produced during the First World War to stimulate dwindling sales.

● Most companies were out of business by the start of the Second World War.

A selection of larger models. **£10-40 each**   *CCC*

A selection of busts.
£45-95   *CCC*

A selection of World War I figures and busts.
£50-80 each   *CCC*

A selection of birds,   **£20-50 each**   *CCC*

A selection of crested chairs.
£6-20 each *G&CC*

A selection of seaside souvenirs.
£3.50-25 each *G&CC*

An Arcadian jug,
£100-120 and a
figure,
£150-175 CCC

A selection of dogs.
£15-35 each *CCC*

Crested chess pieces. **£7-30 each** *G&CC*

A selection of
figures, various
factories.
£35-120 each
CCC

FURTHER READING
Crested China, Sandy Andrews.
*The Price Guide to Crested
China*, Nicholas Pine
(Milestone Publications), 62
Murray Road, Horndean, Hants.

Jugs

A nature jug after Bernard
Pallissy, 19thC.
£100-150 *AOS*

An Arthur Wood moulded jug
depicting Jack and The
Beanstalk, c1935, 8.5in (21.5cm)
high. **£50-80** *AOS*

A Spode New Oval shape cream
jug, pattern No. 889, c1805, 5.5in
(14cm) wide.
£100-150 *TVA*

A German Hunter jug, 19thC,
4.5in (11.5cm) high.
£8-10 *OD*

A jug depicting spinners, c1930,
5in (13cm) high.
£12-15 *OD*

An Empire Ware jug, c1938.
£15-20 *AOS*

| Cross Reference |
| Drinking |
| Pub Jugs |

A set of 3 Arthur Wood jugs, 5.5
to 6.5in (14 to 16.5cm) high.
£65-85 *COL*

An Arthur Wood jug, c1935, 7in
(17.5cm) high.
£20-30 *AOS*

Musical Jugs

● First launched in 1930 with the introduction of 'John Peel' series of half pint mug, pint mug and jug, shortly followed by a cigarette box, salad bowl and a whisky flagon.

● Further musical subjects included Widdicombe Fair, On Ilkla Moor Baht'at, Killarney and Auld Lang Syne.

● Rarer titles followed, including the Eton Boating Song and Gracie Fields.

● The production of musical novelties dwindled after World War II and had ceased by 1951.

A tankard playing The Floral Dance, 6in (15cm) high. **£150-200** *PC*

A Carlton Ware musical tankard, depicting Grandfather's Clock, 5in (13cm) high. **£150-200** *PC*

A Crown Devon Fielding painted one pint jug, playing 'Auld Lang Syne', 8.5in (21cm) high. **£125-200** *PC*

A half pint jug, depicting Windsor Castle, made at Burslem Pottery, playing 'Here's Health Unto His Majesty', 6in (15cm) high. **£200-250** *PC*

A Long John Silver musical Toby jug, unmarked, 10.5in (26.5cm) high. **£150-200** *PC*

> **Cross Reference**
> Toby Jugs

A half pint and a pint Sylvan Pottery tankard, playing John Peel, 6 and 7.5in (16.5 and 19cm) high.
£75-125 *PC*

A King George VI and Queen Elizabeth musical jug, playing 'God Save The King', 9in (23cm) high.
£250-350 *PC*

A half pint tankard, 'The Irish Jaunting Car', playing Killarney, 5in (13cm) high.
£150-200 *PC*

A half pint tankard, probably Winton, with Thorens movement playing Killarney, 6in (15cm) high.   **£100-200** *PC*

A musical tankard, 'Widdicombe Fair', 5in (13cm) high. **£150-200** *PC*

A one pint jug, 'The Irish Jaunting Car', playing Killarney, 8in (20cm) high.
£200-250 *PC*

A Royal Doulton 'Old Charlie' jug, playing 'Here's Health Unto His Majesty', 5.5in (14cm) high.
£400-500 *PC*

Cross Reference
Doulton

A half pint Royal Winton Grimwades George VI Coronation tankard, playing the National Anthem, 6in (15cm) high.
£250-300 *PC*

Cross Reference
Colour Section

A half pint musical tankard depicting John Peel, 4.5in (11.5cm) high.
£100-150 *PC*

A half-pint tankard playing 'On Ilkla Moor Baht 'At', 4.5in (11.5cm) high.   **£150-200** *PC*

Lustre Ware

A set of 3 graduated copper lustre jugs, slight damage.
£45-55 *LF*

A pink lustre tobacco jar, c1920, 4.5in (11.5cm) high.
£8-10 *OD*

A Gray's Gloria lustre jug, orange and black on white with gilding to rim and handle, c1925, 4.5in (11.5cm) high.
£45-50 *ROW*

Gloria lustre was developed by Susie Cooper in collaberation with Gordon Forsyth between 1925 and 1930.

Majolica

An Egyptian revival jug, 8.5in (21.5cm) high.
£80-100 *NCA*

A modern Bavarian green lustre moustache cup and saucer, c1910, cup 6.5in (16.5cm) diam.
£20-25 *OD*

For further selection of Lustre Ware refer to Miller's Collectables, Price Guide, Volume IV, page 116.

A Minton parrot, c1900, 11in (28cm) high.
£300-350 *NB*

Two Minton wall tiles, c1870, 8in (20cm).
£25-30 each *NB*

A Holdcroft sugar bowl, c1870, 4in (10cm) high.
£200-250 *NB*

A majolica fish flower holder, c1890, 14in (35.5cm) long.
£130-150 *NB*

A French majolica vase, c1890, 10in (25.5cm).
£110-130 *NB*

A Minton jug, c1860, 7in (18cm).
£130-150 *NB*

A French majolica flower holder, c1880, 6.5in (16cm) long.
£110-130 *NB*

A kettle with fish design, c1875, 8in (20.5cm).
£200-250 *NB*

A majolica strawberry dish, c1870, 12in (30.5cm).
£150-180 *NB*

A French majolica plate, c1890, 7in (18cm).
£20-25 *NB*

A pitcher, c1870, 9in (23cm).
£50-75 *NB*

A Wedgwood shell plate, c1870, 7.5in (19cm).
£40-50 *NB*

A French majolica figure, c1900, 6in (15cm) high.
£30-40 *NB*

Mugs

A Pearlware blue painted quart mug, inscribed H. Rouse, c1800, 6in (15cm) high.
£100-120 *OD*

A French majolica jug, c1890, 5in (13cm) high.
£20-25 *NB*

A majolica pitcher, c1880, 8in (20cm) high.
£50-60 *NB*

An earthenware mug with black and blue banded decoration, possibly Swansea, c1840, 5in (13cm) high.
£70-75 *OD*

Plates

A green china wall plate, with yellow daffodils, c1920, 9in (23cm) diam.
£25-30 *ROW*

A green Keith Murray dish and 5 plates.
£100-150 *ASA*

A British Anchor China cake plate, with chrome handle, c1932, 9in (23cm) diam.
£8-10 *COL*

A Hollinshead & Kirkham plate, 'Autumn' pattern, 9in (22cm) wide.
£35-45 *ADC*

A Bassano plate painted in the manner of Bartolomeo Terchi, c1740, 9in (22.5cm) diam.
£1,550-1,650 *C*

A blue and white delftware plate, painted in inky blue, inscribed Thos. Stevens, 1784, 9in (23cm) diam.
£350-450 *S(S)*

A Ridgway plate, pattern no. 941, c1815, 9in (23cm) diam.
£200-225 *TVA*

An underglaze blue painted plaque, c1795, 6in (15cm) diam.
£100-130 *IW*

A set of 6 Meir Ware dessert plates.
£25-35 *AOS*

Ribbon Plates

Two ribbon plates, typically to decorate a narrow boat, the left coloured black and red, the right blue and silver, c1900, 7.5in (19cm) diam. **£25-35 each** *HEY*

For a further selection of Ribbon Plates, refer to Miller's Collectables, Price Guide, Volume IV, pages 122 and 123.

Pot Lids

Stamp's Myrrhine Tooth
Paste, 3.75in (9cm) wide.
£35-40 *BBR*

Russian Bear's Grease,
3.75in (9cm) diam.
£170-190 *BBR*

Pratt Ware coloured pot lid of
Shakespeare's house, c1865,
4.25in (11cm) diam.
£55-75 *LIO*

Bear's Grease,
2.25in (6cm) diam.
£80-90 *BBR*

The Alexandra
Cherry Tooth Paste.
£185-200 *BBR*

Shakespeare, mauve transfer
print, 3.25in (8cm) diam.
£70-80 *BBR*

Bear's Grease, c1865, 3in (8cm) diam.
£45-65 *LIO*

Mrs Ellen Hales, 3in
(7.5cm) diam.
£45-50 *BBR*

Teapots

For a further selection of
Pot Lids, refer to
Miller's Collectables
Price Guide, Volume IV
pages 119 to 121.

A train teapot, by Ellgreaves, c1930.
£300-325 *KAC*

An Empire Ware airman
teapot, possibly to
commemorate the Battle
of Britain, c1940.
£250-300 *KAC*

A cat teapot, creamer
and sugar, by
Crown Ducal, c1930.
£100-125 *KAC*

A black cat teapot, with
a red bow, c1950.
£30-40 *KAC*

A Simple Simon teapot, with Georgie Porgie sugar, and Old Mother Hubbard creamer, by Devonmoor Pottery, c1930.
£130-150 *KAC*

A Price's Cottage Ware teapot, 5in (13cm) high.
£20-25 *COL*

A Price Brothers jester teapot, c1940.
£100-125 *KAC*

A Shelley bathing tent teapot, and a bucket for sugar and sea shell for creamer, designed by Hilda Cowham, 1928. **£950-1,100** *KAC*

A cottage teapot.
£20-25 *ROW*

A German teddy bear teapot, c1940.
£60-75 *KAC*

A teapot in the form of Cinderella's pumpkin coach, with Mac and Jaq the mice helpers as creamer and sugar bowl, by Weetman, for Walt Disney Productions, 1960. **£125-150** *KAC*

A Soho Pottery teapot in the form of corn on the cob, with stand, made to imitate earlier majolica pieces, c1930.
£130-150 *KAC*

A 'Scottie' golfer teapot, by Wade, and golf bag creamer and golf ball sugar, c1950. **£150-175** *KAC*

Tea Sets

A trio by Barker Brothers, hand painted design by John Guildford, c1930, plate 7in (18cm) diam.
£50-60 *GAZ*

A Foley bone china tea cup and saucer, white with gilded handle and rim, and pink interior to cup, c1896. **£15-18** *ROW*

A cup and saucer, by H. & R. Daniel, c1820, saucer 6in (15cm) diam.
£130-150 *TVA*

A bowl, 6in (15cm) diam.
£100-125 *TVA*

A Chamberlain trio, comprising coffee cup, tea cup, and saucer, pattern no. 886, c1820, saucer 5in (13cm) diam. **£150-225** *TVA*

A tea bowl and saucer, by Penningtons, Liverpool, printed with floral sprays, tea bowl with hairline crack, c1750, saucer 5.5in (14cm) diam. **£100-120** *TVA*

A Foley bone china tea cup and saucer, white with pink rose buds and gilding to rim, c1896.
£15-18 *ROW*

A tea set, design 2194, decorated with blue pansies, with WMF mounts, on a tray.
£100-130 *ASA*

A Wade trio, 'Mode', c1950.
£8-10 *COL*

A tea cup and saucer, hand painted in Paris, with silver lemon slice holder, Birmingham, c1905. **£35-45** *AMH*

A Derby tea cup and saucer, painted with Shropshire landscapes, by Robert Brewer, slight rubbing, c1810.
£650-700 *TVA*

A Pratt Ware cup and saucer with turquoise body, c1860.
£100-150 *HEY*

A trio, by Dunn Bennett & Co., 6in (15cm) diam.
£18-20   *OD*

A Charles Bourne, London, trio, pattern no. 208, c1820, saucer 5.5in (14cm) diam.
£300-400   *TVA*

Toby Jugs

The Snuff Taker, by Brampton, salt glazed, c1840, 9in (23cm) high.
£240-280   *IW*

Three modern limited edition Toby jugs: William Moorcroft, c1992, 8.5in (21.5cm) high, **£220- 240**, Clarice Cliff, 9in (22cm) high and Charlotte Rhead, 9.5in (23cm) high.
£350-450 each   *ADC*

A character jug of John Peel, by Wilkinsons, signed by J. H. Thorpe, 14in (36cm) high.
£300-450   *AOS*

A Pratt type pearlware toby jug, sponged in blue, c1800, 10in (25cm) high.
£900-1,200   *S(S)*

A Yorkshire toby jug, decorated in Pratt colours, with impressed crown under base, c1810, 10in (25cm) high.
£800-900   *RWB*

A Ralph Wood style toby jug, some restoration, 9.5in (24cm) high.
£280-300   *Bea*

A Ralph Wood style Toby jug, with blue coat and ochre breeches, holding a jug of ale in one hand and beaker in the other, 9.5in (24cm) high.   **£280-300**   *Bea*

Toothbrush Trays

An Edwardian toothbrush dish and lid, 8in (20cm) long. **£18-20** *AI*

An Edwardian toothbrush dish and lid, 8.5in (21.5cm) long. **£20-25** *AI*

Vases

A pottery flower holder, by J. R. Malley & Co., 5in (13cm) wide. **£25-30** *NCA*

A green William Baron vase, 6in (15cm) high. **£80-100** *NCA*

A Mason's Ironstone Vase and Table pattern toothstick box and cover, c1815, 8in (20cm) long. **£270-300** *VH*

> **Cross Reference**
> Oriental

Two Noritake Japanese porcelain vases, with tube line design, c1930, largest 4in (10cm) high. **£60-80 each** *GAZ*

A pair of Kutani porcelain vases, one with damaged rim, red three character seal mark, 14.5in (37cm) high. **£800-1,000** *P(S)*

A pottery two-handled amphora vase, decorated with owls, 5.5in (14cm) high. **£40-50** *NCA*

> **Cross Reference**
> Devon Ware

A Poole Pottery 'freeform' vase, c1950, 8.5in (21.5cm) high. **£140-180** *KAC*

A Copeland and Garrett spill vase, c1840, 4in (10cm) high. **£120-130** *TVA*

A Lauder Barum red pottery bottle vase, inscribed and painted, minor glaze damage, 17.5in (44cm) high. **£270-290** *Bea*

A Minton Hollins Astra Ware
pink and grey mottled vase, 8.5in
(21.5cm) high.
£80-100 *NCA*

A Chameleon Ware two-handled
vase, designed by George Clews,
1930.
£85-135 *AOS*

Cross Reference
Art Nouveau

A Rookwood Pottery matt glazed
vase, 9in (23cm) high.
£200-300 *ZEI*

A Royal Cauldon
vase, by Edith
Gaiter, c1935,
8.5in (21.5cm) high.
£35-50 *AOS*

Victorian Staffordshire Pottery

A Staffordshire
ochre, green
and cream
figure, c1800,
3.5in (9cm)
long.
£1,600-1,700
JHo

A Staffordshire cow and calf spill
holders, 19thC, 13in (33cm) high.
£350-375 *AA*

Two Staffordshire pottery figures of highlanders,
19thC: *l.* With horse and dead game, 10.5in (26cm).
£200-250 *r.* With spaniel, wearing blue frock coat
and tartan sash, 11in (28cm). **£70-100** *AH*

A Staffordshire sheep, 19thC, 3in
(8cm) long. **£60-70** *AA*

A pair of Staffordshire poodles and families, on
blue bases, 5in (12.5cm). **£160-180** *GAK*

137

A Staffordshire figure of a Highlander, 19thC, 12in (31cm) high.
£100-120 *AA*

A Staffordshire earthenware jug, transfer printed in black and hand coloured, inscribed John Matthews, Bricklayer's Arms, 1863, 9in (23cm). **£300-330** *S(S)*

A Staffordshire inkpot, 19thC.
£75-85 *AA*

A Staffordshire inkwell, 'The Cobbler', 19thC, 4.5in (11cm) high. **£170-180** *AA*

A grey transfer printed drainer, 19thC, 12in (31cm) wide.
£90-100 *TRU*

Two Staffordshire poodles, 19thC, 7 and 8in (18 and 20cm) high.
£120-130 *AA*

A pair of Staffordshire spaniels, with glass eyes, 19thC, 13in (33cm) high. **£180-190** *AA*

A pair of pearlware groups, the Sailors 'Departure' and 'Return', in enamel colours, both on red titled bases, c1810, 9in (23cm) high. **£500-600** *HEY*

A Staffordshire porcellaneous inkwell, modelled as a harpist and decorated in gilt, with shamrocks, c1840, 4.75in (12cm). **£160-180** *RWB*

A Walton pearlware group of 'Tenderness', on a titled green base moulded with blue scrolls, chipped, impressed mark, c1820, 7.5in (19cm) high. **£700-800** *S(S)*

A Staffordshire pearlware figure entitled Show Woman, c1830. **£400-500** *S(S)*

A Staffordshire sheep spill holder, 19thC, 8in (20cm) high. **£140-150** *AA*

A Staffordshire pottery figure of a woman standing by a birdcage, with a bird seated on her arm, c1855, 11.5in (29cm). **£145-160** *RWB*

A pair of Staffordshire vases, one damaged, 19thC. **£100-120** *SUF*

A late Victorian ceramic corner wash hand basin, white, decorated with blue floral transfers, hair line crack, back stamp for J. Dimmock & Co., Hanley. **£80-90** *WIL*

A Staffordshire spill vase, 19thC, 9in (23cm) high. **£125-135** *AA*

A Staffordshire figure of Giuseppe Garibaldi, c1864, 13.25in (34cm). **£250-280** *RWB*

A Staffordshire figure of Pope Pius IV, titled 'His Holiness the Pope', c1875, 18.25in (46cm). **£320-360** *RWB*

A Staffordshire porcellaneous figure of a girl with a flower basket, c1840, 6in (15cm). **£160-180** *RWB*

A Staffordshire pastille burner, modelled as a house, c1840, 4.5in (11cm). **£170-190** *RWB*

A Walton pearlware figure of a youth, on a green mound base, some damage, impressed mark, c1820, 6in (15cm) high. **£350-450** *S(S)*

A Staffordshire spill vase, 19thC, 7in (18cm) high. **£90-100** *AA*

A Staffordshire Highland Couple, clock piece, 19thC, 15in (38cm) high. **£90-100** *AA*

A jug, bowl, potty and matching dressing table set, decorated with pheasants and foliage, on a cream ground. **£150-160** *TRU*

A selection of brown and white Staffordshire spaniels, 19thC, 3.5 to 9in (9 to 23cm). **£85-130 each** *AA*

A pair of Staffordshire figures of poodles with pups, c1850, 7in (18cm) high. **£380-420** *RWB*

A pair of Staffordshire Prussian generals, sparsely coloured in gilt, red and yellow, c1870, 12in (30cm) high. **£100-150 each** *HEY*

A pair of Willow pattern tureens, late 19thC, 11in (28cm) wide. **£90-100** *TRU*

A Staffordshire spaniel and puppy, on cobalt blue base, 19thC, 6in (15cm) high. **£190-200** *AA*

Contemporary Ceramics

A Winchcombe pottery two- handled bowl, possibly by Michael Cardew, c1938, 8in (20cm) diam. **£200-240** *IW*

A Winchcombe cider jug, by Raymond Finch, 1938, 9.5in (24cm) high. **£85-95** *IW*

A mead bottle by John Leach, Michelney pottery, 1968, 7.5in (19cm) high. **£40-50** *IW*

A green salt kit, Weatheriggs pottery, Cumbria, c1930, 10.5in (26cm) high. **£30-40** *IW*

A buff coloured stoneware jug, Carter Stabler & Adams, Poole, c1920, 6in (15cm) high. **£60-70** *OD*

A Winchcombe Studio Pottery jug, with impressed pottery mark of Sydney Justin, c1930, 5.25in (13cm) high. **£40-50** *OD*

A Winchcombe pottery jug, by Raymond Finch,firing defects, 1954, 11.5in (29cm) high. **£75-85** *IW*

Wall Plaques

A Czechoslovakian hand painted wall masque, 1930s. **£200-250** *GAZ*

Cross Reference
Children's & Nursery Ware

A Czechoslovakian hand painted wall masque, c1930. **£200-250** *GAZ*

A celadon bowl by J.F. Walford, Redhill, Surrey, c1950, 3.25in (8cm) high. **£50-60** *IW*

Chimneypots

These Victorian chimney pots are mainly from the Lancashire area - predominantly Manchester - and are collected for use as flower pots.

A Victorian chimneypot, 16in (41cm) high.
£15-20 *AA*

A Victorian glazed chimneypot, 36in (91.5cm) high
£30-35 *AA*

A Victorian glazed chimneypot, 21in (53cm) high. **£30-35** *AA*

A Victorian unglazed chimneypot, 27in (68.5cm) high.
£25-30 *AA*

A Victorian glazed chimneypot, 23in (59cm) high. **£30-35** *AA*

A Victorian glazed chimneypot, 16in (41cm) high.
£20-25 *AA*

A Victorian unglazed chimneypot, 33.5in (85cm) high.
£55-65 *AA*

A Victorian chimneypot, 33.5in (85cm) high.
£55-65 *AA*

A Victorian chimneypot,
20in (50.5cm) high.
£15-20 *AA*

A Victorian glazed chimneypot,
25in (64cm) high.
£25-30 *AA*

A Victorian
unglazed
chimneypot,
15.5in
(39.5cm) high.
£10-15 *AA*

A Victorian glazed chimneypot,
23in (59cm) high.
£30-35 *AA*

A Victorian
unglazed
chimneypot,16.5in
(42cm) high.
£15-20 *AA*

A Victorian glazed
chimneypot,38in
(96.5cm) high.
£30-35 *AA*

A Victorian glazed
chimney pot,
26in (66.5cm)
high. **£25-30** *AA*

A Victorian glazed chimneypot,
27in (69cm) high. **£30-35** *AA*

A Victorian
chimneypot, 32in
(81cm) high.
£35-40 *AA*

A Victorian glazed
chimneypot,22.5in
(56cm) high.
£30-35 *AA*

Diana, No.18, D. C.
Thompson, 1963.
£3-4 *NOS*

Popular Comics, No. 45,
Dell Comics, 1939.
£30-32 *NOS*

Rover, Nos 1148 and 1152, D. C.
Thompson, 1946.
£4-5 each *NOS*

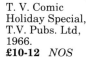

Plastic Man, No.
64, last issue,
1956.
£35-37 *NOS*

T. V. Comic
Holiday Special,
T.V. Pubs. Ltd,
1966.
£10-12 *NOS*

Misty, No.1, Fleetway,
1978. **£2-3** *NOS*

Solo, No.8, City
Magazines/Century 21,
1967,
£4-5 *NOS*

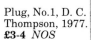

Plug, No.1, D. C.
Thompson, 1977.
£3-4 *NOS*

All American, No. 68,
D. C. Comics, 1945.
£80-85 *NOS*

Magic,
No.1, D. C.
Thompson,
features
nephews of
Dandy and
Beano
characters.
£2.50-3
NOS

Goofy, No.1, I.P.C.,
with Disney strips,
1973.
£2-3 *NOS*

Tom and
Jerry, No.1,
Spotlight
Publications
Ltd, 1973.
£2-3 *NOS*

32 Captain Marvel Junior comics, 1946-52.
£1,200-1,400 *S(NY)*

Captain Marvel Thrill Book, 1941, near mint condition.
£1,900-2,200 *S(NY)*

Marvel Comics, No.2 prototype cover, Bill Everett, c1938.
£9,000-9,500 *S(NY)*

Pep Comics, No.1, M.J.L. Magazines, January 1941.
£750-800 *S(NY)*

Captain Britain, No.1, with cut out mask.
£2-3 *NOS*

Marvel Mystery Comics, No.5, March 1940, Timely Publications.
£2,500-3,000 *S(NY)*

Captain America, No.1, March 1941, Timely Publications.
£2,800-3,000 *S(NY)*

Whiz Comics, No.3, April 1940, Fawcett Publications.
£2,500-3,000 *S(NY)*

Popeye Feature Book, 1937, David McKay Publications.
£1,750-2,000 *S(NY)*

12 Weird Fantasy comic books,
by artists Frank Frazetta and
Al Williamson, E. C.
Publications, 1950s.
£520-560 *S(NY)*

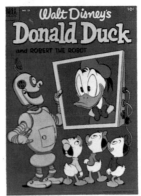

24 Donald Duck comic
books, covers by artist Carl
Barks, by Dell Publications,
1950s.
£500-520 *S(NY)*

A group of 94 Classic
Comics, by Gilbertson
Publications, 1940-1960.
£11,000-13,000 *S(NY)*

Two Daredevil comics by
Lev Gleason Publications,
1941.
£7,000-7,500 *S(NY)*

Five Blue Beetle comics,
Nos. 1-5, artist Will
Eisner, by Fox
Publications, c1939.
£3,200-3,500 *S(NY)*

Ten Shadow comics, by
Street and Smith
Publications, 1943-44.
£2,500-2,800 *S(NY)*

Twenty seven Walt Disney
comics and stories, covers by
Walt Kelly, Dell Publications.
£600-700 *S(NY)*

Four Flash Gordon comics,
artist Alex Raymond, 1953.
£700-800 *S(NY)*

15 Bulletman comics,
artist Mac Rayboy,
Fawcett Pubs, 1941-46.
£6,300-6,600 *S(NY)*

A bébé, by E. Denamur, wearing original underclothes and dress, c1885.
£2,000-3,000 *STK*

A German bisque headed doll, with papier mâché toddler body.
£150-195 *PAR*

A Bru walking and kiss throwing bébé, original clothing, marked Bru Jne R9, 23in (59cm) high. **£3,500-4,500** *STK*

A pale bisque baby doll, by Swaine & Co., German, marked M 232, c1910, 22in (56cm). **£1,700-2,000** *STK*

An Ernst Heubach character baby, marked, c1915.
£450-550 *STK*

A Kammer & Reinhardt Kaiser Baby, with flock hair, wearing original crochet dress, 10in (25cm).
£400-600 *STK*

A Max Handwerck Bébé Elite, with jointed wood and papier mâché body, 24in (62cm).
£450-500 *PAR*

A Bru bébé, with original kid body, bisque arms, turned wooden legs, and mohair wig, marked Bru Jne 8, c1880.
£7,500-9,500 *STK*

A doll's dress, hand made using antique materials.
£45-50 *PAR*

A Mulatto bisque headed character doll, impressed Simon & Halbig.
£2,600-3,000 *CSK*

Two dolls using heads from the same mould, c1890: *l.* Roullet & Decamps. **£1,600-1,700** *r.* Simon & Halbig **£750-950** *STK*

A doll's dress, hand made using antique materials.
£50-55 *PAR*

A Jules Steiner bisque headed bébé, impressed J. Steiner Bte SGDG FLRE A15. **£4,500-5,000** *PAR*

A pale bisque character boy doll, with toddler body, dressed in original suit, mohair wig, by Porzellanfabrik Mengers-gereuth, 15in (38.5cm).
£500-600 *STK*

A Jules Steiner bisque doll.
£1,800-2,500 *STK*

A doll's dress and bonnet, hand made from antique materials and lace.
£50-55 *PAR*

Mr Punch

'Boris', a red Steiff bear, c1920, 21in (53.5cm) high. **£3,000-5,000** *STK*

'Knickerbocker', an American bear, c1930, 18in (46cm). **£150-250** *STK*

Judy and the Baby

A set of Punch and Judy show characters, c1920, 9 to 19in (22.5 to 48.5cm) high. **£350-450 the set** *NOW*

The Devil and the Skeleton

The Crocodile

The Clown

A Decamps clockwork toy, 19thC. **£300-500** *NOW*

A Steiff bear, c1908. **£1,800-2,500** *NOW*

A Steiff teddy bear, with button in his ear, c1904. **£1,500-1,800** *TED*

A heart shaped mohair cushion with bear and musical box, German, c1930. **£200-300** *TED*

A mohair bear, by Twyfords, 1950s. **£70-100** *TED*

An English bear, stuffed with wood wool, 1920s. **£400-450** *TED*

A Schuco mohair lipstick and powder compact bear, 1930s. **£250-300** *TED*

r. A complete Steiff King Skittle set, with 8 other animals, c1895. **£3,000-5,000** *TED*

A traditional English bear, 1940s. **£60-80** *TED*

A Petit et Dumontier pressed bisque bébé, impressed P 5 D, c1880. **£13,500-14,500** *S*

A Bru Jeune et Cie bisque swivel head bébé, unmarked, c1875. **£16,000-17,500** *S*

An A. Thuillier pressed bisque bébé, impressed A 14 T, c1875, 26in (66cm). **£35,000-38,000** *S*

l. A Kämmer & Reinhardt c1910 **£2,000-2,500**
c. A Gebrüder Heubach, c1912 **£2,250-2,750**
r. A François Gaultier, c1880. **£650-750** *S*

l. A bisque character doll. **£5,000-5,500** *S*

An Emile Jumeau pressed bisque doll, c1880. **£9,000-10,000** *S*

A Jumeau pressed bisque portrait doll, impressed 1, together with trunk containing 6 outfits. **£7,500-8,000** *S*

A Jules Steiner bisque bourgoin doll, with impressed mark, c1885. **£2,750-3,250** *S*

A Mothereau pressed bisque bébé doll, impressed B 6 M, c1885. **£10,500-11,500** *S*

Chocolate

This is another example of how a variety of goods and products with a single theme can be amassed to produce a magnificent and fascinating collection - in this case, chocolate.

A Cadbury's label from a wooden box, c1920, 11in (28cm) high.
£25-35 *ACh*

A Rowntree's insert for a free casket, c1920, 7in 17.5cm) wide.
Insert £5-6, Casket £8-12 *ACh*

A selection of chocolate wrappers, c1940.
£2-3 each *ACh*

Chocolate wrappers, c1930.
£2-3 each *ACh*

Two Bourneville Cocoa tins, with contents, poor condition, 5in (12.5cm) high.
l. unopened, c1930, **£4-5**
r. c1940, **£2-3** *ACh*

A Fry's original postcard, c1910. **£25-30** *ACh*

A Rowntree's insert, c1928, 8in (20cm) high. **£3-4** *ACh*

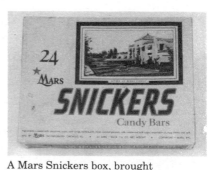

A Mars Snickers box, brought over by an American GI, c1941, 9in (22.5cm) wide. **£3-4** *ACh*

A Cadbury's chromolithograph label, c1900, 9.5in (24cm) wide.
£40-50 *ACh*

A Cadbury's Dairy Milk Chocolate box, with chromolithograph label, c1910, 12in (30.5cm) wide.
£40-50 *ACh*

Cross Reference
Packaging & Advertising

Two chocolate wrappers, c1950.
50p-£1 each *ACh*

A Fry's advertisement
show card, c1930, 15in
(38.5cm) high.
£40-60 *ACh*

Chocolate wrappers with
figures, **£5-6 each** *ACh*

Coca-Cola

A cardboard Coca-Cola bottle
carrier, 1960s.
£5-6 *COB*

A Coca-Cola wooden
guitar case, 1970s.
£30-35 *COB*

Cross Reference
Drinking

A Cadbury's Chocolate Coffee
Crèmes box, c1900.
£40-50 *ACh*

A glass Coca-Cola
advertisement, 1940s.
£20-25 *COB*

Cross Reference
Packaging &
Advertising

A Fry's Chocolate Cream box
label, c1930, 8.5in (21cm) wide.
£15-18 *ACh*

A Coca-Cola metal flask in
a case, 1960s. **£9-10** *COB*

DOLLS

We have followed, as before, the generally accepted rules for the categorization of dolls; that is, by the medium from which the head is made. The French and German bisque headed dolls are further divided by manufacturer where clearly marked, but it is worth remembering that manufacturers often made heads for other doll makers and that the body may be made from some other material.

The market remains good, as always, for top quality examples. It is very important to check carefully for damage and restoration. Very early dolls before c1750 are commanding good prices despite the comparative crudeness of construction, detail and lack of original clothing.

A parian swivelhead shoulder doll, with closed mouth, fixed blue eyes, moulded hair and cloth body with bisque lower arms, legs missing, c1880, 9in (23cm) high .
£485-525 *S(S)*

A group of original googlie eye dolls, all bisque with jointed shoulders, c1912, 2.5 to 5in (6 to 13cm) high.
£350-400 *STK*

A papoose rubber doll, in buckskin outfit, made by Ojibwa, c1940, sold at Niagara Falls, 5in (13cm).
£25-35 *STK*

An Indonesian carved hardwood doll, with articulated arms, one-piece head and body, 19thC.
£150-200 *STK*

A German papier mâché shoulder doll, with closed mouth, painted features, brush-stroke hair and straight kid body, in original costume, 10in (26cm) high. **£275-300** *S(S)*

A Norah Wellings doll, wearing Victorian knickerbockers, c1925, 14in (36cm) high. **£60-70** *LB*

A Russian composition doll, in original costume, c1930, 10in (25cm) high. **£25-35** *STK*

A R & B Drink'N Babe doll, completely original with trunk of accessories and original tag, marked Dream Baby, made for the American market, c1920. **£350-450** *STK*

A Scandinavian costume doll, c1930, 8in (20cm) high. **£15-20** *STK*

A Pierotti-type poured wax shoulder doll, with closed mouth, fixed blue eyes, inserted blonde hair and cloth body, poured wax lower limbs and original costume, c1880, 16.5in (42cm) high. **£450-475** *S(S)*

Peruvian dolls, made from ancient ancestral cloth, approx. 1000 years old, but dolls made this century by Cuancay Indians, 5.5 and 9in (14 and 23cm) high. **£25-35 each group** *STK*

A Japanese doll, with 6 wigs, in original wooden box, c1935. **£75-100** *STK*

A French mechanical swimming bisque doll 'Ondine', with clockwork mechanism wound at navel, in original box, repaired and wear to box, with instruction sheets, 7in (18cm) high. **£1,200-1,300** *S*

A celluloid costume doll, c1915, 6in (15cm) high, **£15-20** *STK*

A Dean's rag doll, c1925, 25in (64cm) high. **£20-25** *OD*

A Farnell felt doll of Jean Harlow, with a blonde wig, and painted facial features, label on foot, Farnell's, Alpha Toys, Made in England, added Lenci label on clothes, 26in (66cm) high. **£400-450** *S(NY)*

A costume doll pen wiper, c1925, 3in (8cm) high. **£15-20** *STK*

'Margie' composition doll, Cameo Doll Company, with painted and moulded hair and painted facial features, and original paper label in its original box, 9 in (23cm) high.
£60-70 *S(NY)*

A celluloid character lady doll, with inset brown eyes, blonde mohair wig and adult body, with turtle mark, 14.5in (37cm) high.
£675-700 *CSK*

A German child doll, with bisque head and limbs, c1890, 5.5in (14cm) high.
£100-150 *STK*

An Irish Rosebud doll, in original box, c1950, 6in (15cm).
£45-60 *STK*

A Chad Valley Mabel Lucie Attwell cloth doll, with pressed felt face, glass eyes and 5-piece velvet covered body, in original costume, c1936, 14in (36cm) high, in original cardboard box. **£240-250** *S(S)*

A half doll clothes brush, 4.5in (11cm)
£15-20 *LB*

A black dolls house man, c1880, 5in (13cm) high.
£60-80 *STK*

A Scottish costume doll, with original mohair wig, c1930, 8in (20cm) high.
£20-30 *STK*

Bisque Headed Dolls

The finest French and German dolls are bisque headed. Bisque is porcelain at the unglazed stage of manufacture and very easily damaged, therefore prospective purchases must be closely examined for damage and repair. Porcelain or china headed dolls are easily identified as they are glazed and appear shiny.

A DEP bisque doll, with weighted blue glass eyes, pierced ears and jointed wood and composition body, in original silk dress and bonnet, silk damaged, impressed DEP8, c1910. **£425-450** *S(S)*

A bisque headed character baby doll, with blue sleeping eyes, wig, baby's body and embroidered dress, impressed J.D.K. 257 36, 14.5in (37cm) high. **£250-275** *CSK*

A C.M. Bergmann bisque socket head character baby doll, 16in (41cm) high. **£150-200** *HSS*

A bisque head doll, with blue sleeping eyes, wood and composition ball jointed body, AM 390 A3M DRGM 246/1, 20in (51cm) high. **£270-300** *PAR*

An Einco character boy doll, wearing original velvet and lace outfit, c1915, 10in (25cm). **£480-580** *STK*

A Willi Weyh Mulatto bisque doll, with closed mouth, weighted brown eyes, domed head and cloth body, impressed W Weyh 2, c1926, 10.5in (27cm) high.
£300-350 *S(S)*

A French bisque head doll, with cork pate, brown wig, blue paperweight eyes, pierced ears and a closed mouth, on a 5-piece composition body, incised EDEN BEBE/Paris/M, 23in (59cm) high.
£500-550 *S(NY)*

A CET & Co. German character báby doll, with dimpled face and bright blue eyes, original mohair wig, underwear marked CET & Co. 66-7, c1910, 14in (36cm) high.
£250-350 *STK*

A bisque headed googlie-eyed doll, with water melon mouth, moulded curls and bent limbed composition body, broken thumb and foot, rub to cheek, impressed 172-1, 12in (31cm) high.
£850-900 *CSK*

FURTHER READING

Delightful Dolls, Thelma Bateman, Washington 1966.
The American Doll Artist, Helen Bullard, Boston 1965.
Dolls: Makers and Marks, Elizabeth A. Coleman, Washington 1963
The Collector's Encyclopedia of Dolls, Dorothy S., Elizabeth A. and Evelyn J. Coleman, New York 1968.
Dolls, Lady Antonia Fraser, London 1963.
Wonderful Dolls of Wax, Jo Elizabeth Gerken, Lincoln (Nebraska) 1964.
Directories of British, French and German Dolls, Luella Hart, Oaklands (Calif) 1964-65.
Dolls and Dollmakers, Mary Hillier, London 1968.
Dressing Dolls, A. Johnson, London 1969.
Dolls & Dolls Houses, Constance King, London 1977.
Dolls, J. Noble, London 1968.
Dolls of the World, G. White, London 1962.
European and American Dolls, G. White, London 1966.
Miller's Antiques Checklist, Dolls and Teddy Bears, Mitchell Beazley International Ltd., 1992

A French doll, with bisque head, real hair wig and jointed composition limbs, marked Fabrication Française A H & C Limoges, A6.
£250-275 *LF*

A Belgium bisque shoulderhead, with a blonde mohair wig, light blue painted eyes, eye shadow and a closed mouth, incised D.F./B./F.1., 6in (15cm) high.
£200-250 *S(NY)*

The head was made by the De Fuisseau around 1910 in Bandour, Belgium.

A German bisque headed black baby doll, with composition bent limb body, sleeping eyes, marked 241-3, 17in (43cm) high. **£225-250** *PAR*

A French bisque head doll, blue glass eyes, pierced ears and open mouth inset with upper teeth, on a jointed composition body, incised Limoges/France, 26in (66cm) high. **£300-350** *S(NY)*

An A.T. bisque headed doll, with socket head, blue paperweight eyes, pierced ears, closed mouth, blonde wig, on a wood and composition body, damaged and repaired, incised A6T, 19in (48cm) high. **£5,000-5,500** *CNY*

A French swivel head bisque fashion doll, with closed mouth, fixed blue glass paperweight eyes, blonde wig and gussetted kid body, in original costume, cracks to face, impressed 4, c1880, 17in (44cm) high. **£850-900** *S(S)*

A Walthier & Son googlie eye doll, with bisque head, mohair wig and wearing original outfit, c1910, 8in (20cm) high. **£350-650** *STK*

A Limbach character boy, 'Walter', marked with the shamrock incised 8687, wearing original sailor suit, with flapper legs, c1920.
£350-450 *STK*

Dolls with flapper legs have joints half-way up the thigh so that it is covered when girl dolls wear flapper dresses.

A French bisque headed bébé, probably Petit & Dumontier, incised P 5 D, with a brown wig, pierced ears, brown paperweight eyes and an outlined closed mouth, on a wood and composition 8 ball-jointed body with metal hands, left small finger missing, hands repainted, 26in (66cm) high. **£10,500-11,500** *S(NY)*

A French bisque swivel head fashion doll, with brown wig, blue threaded glass eyes, pierced ears and closed mouth, on a kid body with individually stitched fingers, incised 3, 17in (43cm) high.
£1,300-1,500 *S(NY)*

A 'Kaiser Baby' character doll, marked K * R 100, credited as being the first character baby doll made by Kammer & Reinhardt, c1910, 15in (38cm) high.
£450-650 *STK*

A Schoenau & Hoffmeister child doll, original wig, 1906, 24in (61cm) high.
£400-700 *STK*

A French bisque headed child doll, with dark lashed sleeping eyes, fair mohair wig and jointed body, with original paper covered wardrobe, with complete trousseau, including iron, skipping rope, hot water bottle, buttons on card, mirror, brush and comb, wardrobe 15.5in (40cm) high.
£800-900 *CSK*

A Bruno Schmidt bisque head doll, with ball jointed wood and composition body, brown glass eyes, c1910, 31in (79cm) high.
£1,400-1,500 *PAR*

Armand Marseille

Two child dolls produced from the same mould, marked 1894, AM 8/O dep 2/O., 16in (40.5cm):
l. with elaborate painting for the French market. with single stroke brows.
£350-500
r. with single stroke brows and slightly less elaborate painting for the German market,
£300-400 *STK*

An Armand Marseille doll.
£180-200 *MR*

A dream baby No. 351.with original wickerwork layette, original outfit and spare clothes, c1920.
£350-450 *STK*

Bru

A French bisque headed bébé, with a blonde wig, cork pate, brown sleeping eyes, pierced ears and an outlined open mouth inset with upper teeth, on a wood and composition jointed body with straight legs, the doll throws kisses and has a voice box, one hand replaced, marked Bru, incised Bru Jne R/9, 21in (53cm) high.
£1,300-2,000 *S(NY)*

A bisque head doll, with blue-grey sleeping eyes, straight arms and legs and composition body, AM390 A6M, 10in (25cm) high.
£180-200 *PAR*

A Bébé Brevete, with carved wood body, paperweight eyes, wearing original costume, c1875, 14in (36cm) high.
£3,000-4,000 *STK*

A Bru swivel head fashion doll, with closed mouth, fixed blue eyes, sparse wig over cork pate, gussetted pink kid body, one arm detached, impressed A DEPOSE on left shoulder and B. Jne on right, c1866, 12in (31cm) high. **£1,000-1,100** *S(S)*

A bisque headed bébé, with cork pate, Bru metal neck joint, brown paperweight eyes, pierced ears and an outlined closed mouth, on a gussetted kid body with bisque lower arms, mark to face and one small finger broken, marked Bébé Brevete Bru, incised 5/0, 10.5in (26cm) high, **£3,500-4,500** *S(NY)*

Heubach

A character baby doll, in blue knitted suit, c1915, 10in (25cm) high. **£400-550** *STK*

A laughing baby boy doll, with bisque head, intaglio eyes, original rompers, No. 7604, c1920. **£300-400** *STK*

An Ernst Heubach doll, with replacement clothes made from old material of the period. **£225-250** *PAR*

A bisque character 'Crying' doll, with open/closed crying mouth, intaglio eyes, domed head and curved limb composition body, impressed 8, c1912, 14.5in (37cm) high. **£1,200-1,300** *S(S)*

An all bisque 'Piano Baby' with painted features, moulded hair and oversized boots, c1914, 10in (25.5cm) high. **£450-480** *S(S)*

Jumeau

A bisque bébé doll, with brown hair, and azure eyes, silk dress, head marked Tête Jumeau, body marked Jumeau Médaille d'Or, c1885, 24.5in (62cm) high. **£1,500-2,500** *STK*

A bisque headed bébé doll, with cork pate, blonde wig, blue paperweight eyes, pierced ears, on 8-ball wood and composition body, 17in (43cm) high. **£5,000-6,000** *S(NY)*

A small bisque doll, with open mouth, fixed brown eyes, and jointed wood and composition body, slight damage, impressed 1 at neck socket, c1890. **£425-475** *S(S)*

A bisque headed bébé, with cork pate, spiral spring neck joint, blue threaded glass eyes, pierced ears, on a wood and composition ball-jointed body, arms replaced, head incised 1, stamped in blue Jumeau/Medaille D'Or/Paris, 11in (28cm) high. **£1,500-2,000** *S(NY)*

A bisque headed bébé, with cork pate, brown wig, blue paperweight eyes, pierced ears, closed mouth, on a jointed composition body with straight wrists, original dress and gloves, fingers scuffed, body stamped in blue Jumeau/ Medaille d'Or/Paris, head stamped in red Depose/Tête Jumeau/BTe. S.G.D.G./8, 18in (46cm) high. **£2,500-3,500** *S(NY)*

A Mulatto bisque doll, with open mouth, fixed brown eyes, pierced ears, black wig, cork pate, jointed wood and composition body, slight wig pull chips, impressed 4, c1907, 13in (34cm) high.
£750-800 *S(S)*

A bisque headed bébé, with cork pate, brown wig, brown threaded paperweight eyes, pierced ears, purple plush over eyes and closed mouth, on a jointed composition body with paper label Bébé Jumeau/Diplome d'Honneur, incised 4, 23in (59cm) high.
£7,500-8,500 *S(NY)*

A bisque headed bébé, with paperweight eyes, pierced ears, outlined mouth, on a wood and composition jointed body, stamped in blue Jumeau/Medaille d'Or /Paris, head stamped in red Depose/Tête Jumeau/BTe. S.G.D.G./9, with a voice box, 19.5in (50cm) high.
£2,000-3,000 *S(NY)*

A bisque headed bébé doll, with brown pate, original blonde wig, paperweight eyes, pierced ears, open mouth inset with upper teeth, on a jointed composition body, stamped in blue Bébé Jumeau/BTe. S.G.D.G./Depose, original size 12 Bee marked shoes, 26in (66cm) high. **£1,500-2,000** *S(NY)*

A bisque headed bébé doll, with pierced ears, brown wig and jointed wood and composition body, dressed in spotted muslin and brown Jumeau shoes, crack to head, hands replaced, impressed 8, 20in (51cm) high.
£950-1,000 *CSK*

A bisque headed bébé, with cork pate, blonde wig, brown paperweight eyes, pierced ears, outlined closed mouth, on a jointed composition body with straight wrists, stamped in blue Jumeau/Diplome d'Honneur, head incised Depose/Tête Jumeau/12, 26in (66cm) high.
£2,000-3,000 *S(NY)*

A pressed bisque swivel headed fashion doll, with closed mouth, fixed blue paperweight eyes, pierced ears, blonde mohair wig over cork pate and gussetted kid body with separately stitched fingers, original dress and straw bonnet, head impressed 9, stamped on body Jumeau Medaille d'Or Paris, 23in (59cm) high. **£3,250-3,500** *S*

Kestner

A bisque headed doll, with closed mouth, original fleece wig and peg jointed body, wearing original outfit, marked 9, 9in (23cm) high. **£650-750** *STK*

A doll with closed mouth, painted face and eyes and wearing original outfit, marked 3917, probably by Kestner, c1880. **£350-450** *STK*

Rabery & Delphieu

A bisque headed doll, with blonde wig, blue sleeping eyes, open mouth, on a wood and composition ball-jointed body, incised made in/K14/Germany/146, stamped in red Excelsior/D.R.P.No. 70685/Germany/4, 23in (59cm) high. **£300-350** *S(NY)*

S.F.B.J.

A bisque bébé, with blue paperweight eyes, and closed mouth, wearing original outfit, c1880, 24in (62cm) high. **£2,500-3,500** *STK*

A bisque headed bébé, with cork pate, original blonde wig, blue paperweight eyes, pierced ears, closed mouth, on a jointed composition jointed body with straight wrists, incised R.2.D., 21.5in (54cm) high. **£2,200-3,000** *S(NY)*

A bisque headed character boy doll, with moulded hair, brown glass eyes, open/closed mouth with 2 moulded upper teeth, on a repainted jointed composition body, incised S.F.B.J./235/Paris/8, 19in (48cm) high. **£450-550** *S(NY)*

Simon & Halbig

A bisque headed doll, with blue glass eyes, pierced ears, open mouth, on a wood composition jointed body, wearing original dress, head incised Simon & Halbig/K*R/13, with Le Petit Parisien 1889 paper label on body, 17.5in (44cm) high.
£350-400 *S(NY)*

A bisque headed character doll, with blonde wig, blue sleeping eyes, an open/closed mouth, on a 5-piece composition baby body, incised 1428/4, 11in (28cm) high. **£500-550** *S(NY)*

A doll, with blue sleeping eyes and brown wig, 10.5in (27cm) high.
£200-250 *PAR*

Steiner

A bisque headed bébé, with blonde wig, blue paperweight eyes, pierced ears, closed mouth, on a jointed composition body, wearing a white cotton c1890 chemise trimmed with lace, and leather shoes, head incised Sie C 6, body with J.St stamp, 21in (54cm) high.
£3,000-4,000 *S(NY)*

A bisque headed bébé doll, with blonde wig, cork pate, blue paperweight eyes, closed mouth, pierced ears, on a wood and composition jointed body, hairline crack to face, head incised A-13/Paris, stamped Le Parisien, 20.5in (52cm) high.
£900-1,000 *S(NY)*

A bisque headed doll, with mohair wig and original silk underwear and cotton dress, marked HS3, 16in (41cm) high.
£450-550 *STK*

A bisque headed bébé, fixed blue eyes, pierced ears, and jointed papier mâché body with bisque hands, with new wig, impressed A-13 Paris, stamped on the hip Le Petit Parisien A. St Ste S.G.D.G. by Steiner.
£1,000-1,150 *CSK*

Felt Dolls

Two Lenci felt dolls, from the 300 series, girl and boy doll with brown hair and painted facial features, 16 and 17in (41 and 43cm) high.   **£850-950** *S(NY)*

A Lenci felt doll of a boy in a smoking jacket, from the 300 series, with a painted facial features, Lenci marked pipe in pocket and a tobacco pouch, c1925, 17in (43cm) high. **£2,000-2,500** *S(NY)*

A pair of Maggie and Jiggs cloth dolls, Maggie holding a rolling pin, Jiggs smoking the usual cigar, c1925, 18 and 18.5in (46 and 47cm) high. **£2,000-3,000** *CNY*

Pedlar Dolls

A pair of Lenci Scottish felt dolls, the boy and girl with blonde hair and painted facial features, 17in (43cm) high each. **£2,000-3,000** *S(NY)*

These are from the 300 series with the hollow torsos. His hair is knotted as a hooked rug, her hair is in strips.

An early wooden pedlar doll in glass case. **£275-300** *PAR*

Wooden Dolls

A pedlar doll in glass dome. **£275-300** *PAR*

An antique pedlar doll in glass dome. **£400-450** *PAR*

A Georgian oak doll, 12.5in (32cm) high. **£400-450** *JAC*

A Grödnertal wooden doll, with painted features, black painted skull, c1830, 8.5in (21cm) high. **£450-500** *S(S)*

Dolls Houses

An Edwardian dolls house.
£330-360 *DaD*

A wooden dolls house, with papered brick facade, 2 bay windows, central front door, side opening to reveal the base with pull-out drawer forming a stylised garden, slight damage, English, c1860, 26in (66cm) high.
£1,700-2,500 *S(S)*

A further selection of dolls houses is featured in previous editions of Miller's Collectables Price Guides, available from Millers Publications.

Dolls Clothes

An antique dolls dress.
£45-50 *PAR*

A hand made couture dolls dress, made from old material.
£55-65 *PAR*

Two hand made dolls dresses, using antique materials and hand made lace.
£22-55 each *PAR*

A hand made dolls dress, made from antique materials and lace.
£45-50 *PAR*

A hand sewn dolls outfit, made from antique materials.
£50-60 *PAR*

A felt dolls coat and bonnet, 1930s.
£30-35 *PAR*

A dolls dress and jacket, 1930s.
£25-30 *PAR*

Dolls House Dolls

Seven German bisque headed dolls house dolls, 4 women and 3 men, c1880, 5.25 to 7.5in (13 to 19cm) high. **£1,300-1,500** *S*

A dolls house doll, c1880, 4.5in (11cm) high. **£40-60** *STK*

A French bisque headed dolls house doll, with set glass eyes, closed mouth, pin joined body, mohair wig, original costume, 3in (8cm) high. **£150-200** *STK*

Dolls House Furniture

A mid-Victorian mahogany miniature bureau, with false flap front and 3 long drawers and bracket feet, 8in (20cm) wide. **£150-250** *STK*

A brass fender and fire irons, fender 4in (10cm). **£100-150** *STK*

A pair of matching fabric lined dolls trunks, with assorted contents, hinges replaced, c1890, 12in (31cm) wide. **£250-350** *STK*

Cross Reference
Miniatures

A late Victorian wooden dolls cradle, 14in (36cm) long. **£70-150** *STK*

A tin fabric lined dolls trunk, with assorted contents, c1880, 14in (36cm) wide. **£150-250** *STK*

An early wickerwork dolls trunk, with assorted contents of dolls clothing, c1860, 11in (28cm) wide. **£150-250** *STK*

A child s toy tin scullery set, 'Alice in Kitchenland', with original box, 7in (18cm) high. **£15-18** *COL*

A miniature commode, base metal, 2in (5cm) high.
£15-20 *STK*

A tortoiseshell miniature toilet set.
£60-75 *PAR*

A pair of Victorian miniature chests, in rosewood and mahogany with boxwood stringing to the 2 long graduated drawers, with turned feet and shaped aprons, 7in (18cm) wide.
£200-250 *STK*

A group of painted metal, bone and wooden dolls house furniture and accessories, bisque and china miniature dolls, German and Anglo-Indian, some Rock and Graner, late 19thC.
£2,400-2,600 *S*

A Regency walnut and faux bamboo miniature dresser, with classical pediment above 2 shelves supported by 2 columns, base with one drawer and 2 doors, on turned feet, c1820, 15in (38cm) wide.
£300-400 *STK*

Dolls twin beds, 8in (20cm) long.
£65-75 *LB*

A selection of gilt metal dolls house chattels, including companion sets, a parrot cage and swing stand, a simulated bamboo framed picture, a clothes horse and magazine rack.
£850-900 *CSK*

A selection of tinplate dolls house furniture, c1950, dresser 4in (10cm) high, an Aga 2.25 by 3.25in (6 by 8cm) and a washing machine 3in (8cm) high.
£10-12 each *COL*

A group of dolls house miniatures and accessories, various dates.
£1,000-1,100 *S*

A dolls house bilboquet, c1880, 2in (5cm) high.
£30-45 *AMH*

A ceramic dolls house hip bath, 1920s, 3.5in (9cm) long.
£25-35 *STK*

A Victorian wickerwork cradle, 18in (46cm) long.
£50-60 *STK*

DRINKING

A Carlton Ware Flowers Brewery advertising ashtray, c1935, 9in (22.5cm) diam.
£35-55 *LIO*

A White Horse Whisky ceramic jug, with blue glaze and silver rim and handle, Shelley pottery mark, 5in (12.5cm) high.
£45-50 *BBR*

A Johnnie Walker character jug, by Ashtead Pottery, designed by Percy Metcalfe, 14in (35.5cm) high.
£250-350 *AOS*

Meredith's Whiskey bottle, white with turquoise transfer, 7.5in (19cm) high.
£45-50 *BBR*

A Truman's Ales & Stouts white glazed coaster, with Empire Works Stoke on Trent printed on base, 5.25in (13cm) diam.
£55-60 *BBR*

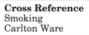

Cross Reference
Smoking
Carlton Ware

A Cruiskeen Lawn Old Irish Whisky bottle, with Port Dundas Pottery mark, 7.25in (18cm) high.
£40-45 *BBR*

A carved and painted wood bottle stopper, with a lever in the back to raise the hat.
£10-15 *ROW*

A double-ended wine rack.
£40-45 *WEL*

Corkscrews

A silver-mounted boar tusk handle corkscrew with surface, Walker bell cap lifter and wire cutter, centre worm.
£250-275 *C*

A French nickel plated single lever corkscrew, by Perille, c1880.
£120-150 *CS*

A Thomason corkscrew, with decorated fruiting vines barrel, turned bone barrel, and cyphered helix worm, inner thread mechanism faulty.
£280-300 *C*

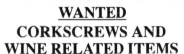

A souvenir key corkscrew, brass with antiqued verdigris finish.
£8-10 *CS*

A French Zig-Zag concertina corkscrew, c1920.
£25-35 *CS*

An all steel folding bow or harp corkscrew. **£10-15** *CS*

A Charles Hull's patent Royal Club corkscrew, 1864.
£750-800 *C*

An all steel four-pillar King's Screw, with turned bone handle, c1820.
£250-350 *CS*

A mechanical corkscrew known as a London Rack, turned rosewood handle with steel body, c1860. **£55-65** *CS*

A Saml. Cotterill Thomason corkscrew, with turned bone handle and brush, brass barrel and helix screw, 1802. **£230-250** *C*

A turned fruitwood handled T bar corkscrew, with dusting brush, c1830. **£15-25** *CS*

A turned walnut corkscrew, with T bar, brass stem and Henshall type button, c1840. **£35-45** *CS*

An English all steel seven tool pocket folding bow. **£90-100** *CS*

A King's Screw corkscrew, c1820. **£300-350** *CS*

A brass Farrow & Jackson type corkscrew, with wing-nut handle. **£65-75** *CS*

A corkscrew with patent ratchet mechanism, the barrel with applied gilt metal coat of arms, the turned bone handle fitted with a brush. **£230-250** *RBB*

A hinged lever corkscrew, with wooden handle, helix screw stamped J. B. & Sons on shaft for J. Burgess and A. Fenton, tip short, 1874. **£1,500-1,750** *C*

An English patent corkscrew combined Codd bottle marble ejector, marked Coney's Patent. **£35-45** *CS*

A Thomason type brass barrel corkscrew, with Gothic window embossed decoration, bone handle with dusting brush, c1818.
£400-600 *CS*

A King's Screw with four-pillar open frame, turned bone handle and brush, steel raising handle and narrow side rack, helix screw.
£275-300 *C*

The Columbus, a German corkscrew with sprung stem, 19thC. **£35-45** *CS*

A German sprung stem corkscrew, with bladed worm, c1890.
£30-40 *CS*

A combination corkscrew, with turned ash wood handle and Codd bottle marble ejector. **£10-15** *CS*

A two-part Lund's lever corkscrew, c1880.
£80-90 *CS*

A Rotary Eclipse brass mechanical cork drawer, c1880. **£400-500** *CS*

The circular base plate screws on to the top of a pub or coaching inn bar top.

A vintage barrel shaped brass corkscrew, with wooden handle.
£260-280 *GAK*

A turned barrel shaped handled corkscrew with dusting brush, an all steel Cellarmans type corkscrew, and an all steel Monopol corkscrew.
£10-30 each *CS*

A combination corkscrew, with scissor type wire cutters, c1890.
£35-45 *CS*

A Holborn Signet corkscrew, with finger-ring set under the turned rosewood handle, and bladed worm, c1880.
£15-20 *CS*

Two German Naughty Nineties corkscrews in celluloid and nickel silver, the ladies' legs flesh coloured with pink and white striped stockings.
£80-120 *CS*

Two corkscrews with turned rosewood handles, both fitted with dusting brush and hanging ring, *top:* turned steel stem with Henshall Button, c1830. **£45-55,** *bottom:* turned barrel shaped handle, c1820. **£30-40** *CS*

A cast steel combination corkscrew, with crown cap opener and hooked blade, c1900.
£10-15 *CS*

Guinness

A Guinness barometer, c1960.
£20-25 *COB*

A Carlton Ware penguin lamp for Arthur Guinness, with original revolving lampshade.
£150-175 *PAR*

A Carlton Ware Guinness advertising lamp, in the form of a seal balancing a revolving metal sphere upon its nose.
£150-200 *PAR*

A Guinness clock, c1970.
£10-12 *COB*

A graduated set of three Carlton Ware toucan wall plaques.
£250-300 *Bea*

A flower shaped 3 dimensional display with slots for bottles, inscribed 'Guinnessis Goodforia Andforallovus', c1950, 35.5in (90cm) high.
£120-130 *ONS*

A Carlton Ware Guinness advertising group, comprising: a man in an overall, a kangaroo in his pocket; a tortoise, a glass of Guinness on its back; a toucan; an ostrich; a sea- lion; and a kangaroo.
£400-500 the set *Bea*

Labels

Four Bacchanalian labels with mask, shell and vines border, die- stamped Claret, Sherry, Rum and Bucellas, c1825.
£280-300 *C*

Two escutcheon shaped labels, engraved Burgundy and Mountain, c1740, and 2 others.
£270-300 *C*

A Battersea enamel wine decanter label, inscribed Mountain, c1750.
£100-150 *CS*

A crescent shaped label, with pierced fretted edging, pierced Burgundy, Hester Bateman, c1770, and 3 others.
£350-375 *C*

Seven bisque pottery wine cellar bin labels, impressed on backs Wedgwood, Copeland Spode and Minton, c1850.
£20-70 each *CS*

A Sherry label by Peter and Anne Bateman, c1790, and 2 others.
£200-220 *C*

Egg Cups

A Victorian egg cup.
£15-20 *AA*

A porcelain egg cup, c1889.
£25-30 *AA*

A Worcester egg cup,
c1880. **£25-30** *AA*

A Mason's Ironstone egg
cup. **£18-22** *AA*

A sailor boy egg cup, 3.5in
(8.5cm) high.
£2-3 *ROS*

A set of 4 chrome Art Deco 'Style'
egg cups with covers, c1950.
£10-15 *COB*

A set of Shorter
Ware egg cups,
5in (12.5cm)
square.
£15-18 *COL*

A set of Doulton egg cups, c1920, 10in
(25cm) long. **£35-40** *AA*

A set of Crown Ducal egg cups.
£25-35 *AOS*

l. An egg cup, c1860, 2.5in
(6.5cm), **£25-30**
r. An egg cup, R. Hammersley &
Co., for T. Goode & Son, c1932,
2.5in (6.5cm) high, **£10-15** *AMH*

A set of porcelain egg cups, 19thC, 9in
(22.5cm) high. **£65-75** *AA*

EPHEMERA
Autographs

Henry Ford, signature on small card, VG. **£200-240** *VS*

George Bernard Shaw, signed piece, with one extra word in his hand, probably cut from the end of a letter, FR. **£55-60** *VS*

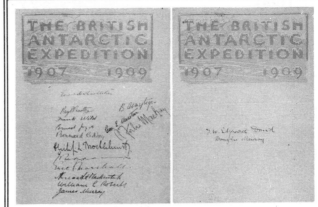

Ernest Shackleton, a set of 16 signatures of the members of the British Antarctic Expedition 1907-1909, on 2 sheets of headed notepaper.
£400-450 *VS*

Cartoonists

Barry Appleby, an original Gambols 3-panel cartoon strip in pen and ink, 1984, G.
£40-60 *VS*

Thomas Edison, signature on large album page, G.
£80-125 *VS*

Reg Smythe, an original 3-panel Andy Capp cartoon strip in pen and ink, 1990, VG.
£60-80 *VS*

Charles M. Schulz, an original 3- panel Peanuts cartoon strip in pen and ink, 1991.
£325-350 *VS*

Charles M. Schulz, 2 individual album pages signed and inscribed and bearing original pen and ink sketch, G to VG. **£425-475** *VS*

Hank Ketcham, an original 12- panel Dennis the Menace cartoon strip in pen and ink, 1985, G. **£80-120** *VS*

Political

David Lloyd George, signed and mounted photograph by Lewis, silvering to top edge of image, G.
£65-75 *VS*

Mikhail Gorbachev, signed colour photograph, 11.75 by 9.25in (30 by 23cm), VG.
£375-400 *VS*

Sir Winston S Churchill, signed typed letter to Malcolm Dunbar, one page, 9th May 1958, FR-VG.
£500-550 *VS*

Lyndon B Johnson, signed colour heavystock magazine photograph, G.   **£60-80** *VS*

Margaret Thatcher, signed photograph 8 by 6in (20 by 15cm), EX.
£80-100 *VS*

Sir Winston S Churchill, signed to mount, photograph by Walter Stoneman of London, extensive corner creasing, FR.
£725-775 *VS*

Ronald Reagan, signed photograph, inscribed 'To the Armed Service Directory Office in Hawaii', creased, 8 by 10in (20 by 25cm) VG.
£100-120 *VS*

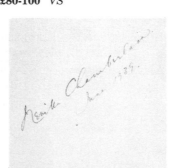

Neville Chamberlain, signed hardback edition of The Struggle for Peace, dated June 1939, previously belonged to Sir Arthur N. Rucker, Chamberlain's private secretary as Minister of Health.
£120-150 *VS*

Theodore Roosevelt, signed postcard, G.
£150-165 *VS*

Royalty

Queen Victoria, 2 pages, 8th November 1883, granting the lawyer Edward Clarke a Licence to plead in the trial of John Davis Walters, with embossed paper seal, VG.
£100-120 *VS*

Wallis, Duchess of Windsor, signed to mount, photograph by Dorothy Wilding also signed to mount, 7.5 by 5.25in (19 by 13cm), VG.
£280-320 *VS*

Queen Mary, Albert Duke of York (later King George VI) and Edward Prince of Wales (later King Edward VIII), one page given at the Court of Saint James's, 1st March 1929, granting the dignity of a Knight Grand Cross of the civil division of the Order of the British Empire to Sir Arthur Henry Crosfield, Baronet, G-VG.
£140-150 *VS*

Cross Reference
Royal Memorabilia

Queen Alexandra, autograph telegram, to Captain Patterson, in pencil, G.   **£40-55** *VS*

King George VI, 26th July 1941, a commission appointing Sir Wilfrid Edward Francis Jackson to be Governor and Commander-in-Chief of the Tanganyika Territory, VG.
£120-130 *VS*

EX	-	Excellent
FR	-	Fair
G	-	Good
MT	-	Mint
P	-	Poor
VG	-	Very Good

King George VI, 1st January 1943, signed document, granting the dignity of a Knight Grand Cross of the most Distinguished Order of Saint Michael and Saint George to Sir Wilfrid Edward Francis Jackson, VG.
£130-150 *VS*

Show Business

Enrico Caruso, signed
and inscribed postcard,
London 1907, FR-G.
£100-120 *VS*

Kathleen Ferrier, signed concert
programme, also signed by Gerald
Moore, 19th January 1952, VG.
£100-120 *VS*

Charles Chaplin, signed sepia
photograph, 11 by 14.5in (28 by
37cm), P to FR.
£200-220 *VS*

Harpo Marx, signed
photograph, 8 by 10in
(20 by 25cm), G.
£110-130 *VS*

Kirk Douglas and Barbara
Stanwyck, signed and inscribed
photograph, 8.5 by 6.5in (21 by
16cm).
£30-40 *VS*

Edith Piaf, signed French
programme, VG.
£120-130 *VS*

Alfred Hitchcock, signed
photograph in white crayon, 11.5
by 7.5in (29 by 19cm), P-FR.
£150-175 *VS*

Frank Sinatra, signed
photograph, 1991, 8 by 10in (20
by 25cm), VG.
£60-75 *VS*

Jim Henson, signed and inscribed
7 by 7.5in (18 by 19cm) piece, also
signed Frank Oz, VG.
£40-60 *VS*

Errol Flynn, signed
photograph, 5.75 by
9in (14 by 23cm), FR.
£90-100 *VS*

Laurence Olivier,
signed postcard,
G.
£40-60 *VS*

Laurel and Hardy, signed and
inscribed sepia, 8 by 10in (20 by
25cm), FR to G.
£400-450 *VS*

Marilyn Monroe, black and white
photograph, signed and inscribed
To Bob Couture, small creases,
9.5 by 7.5in (24 by 19cm).
£900-1,000 *CNY*

Rudolph Valentino, signed piece,
G to VG.
£200-220 *VS*

Lucille Ball, signed
photograph, 8.5 by
6.5in (21 by 16cm),
G-VG.
£40-60 *VS*

Richard Burton, in Roman
Costume, signed photograph , 6
by 9in (15 by 23cm), G.
£40-45 *VS*

Ghostbusters, signed by Dan
Ackroyd, Harold Ramis
and Rick Moranis, colour,
10.5 by 8.5in (26
by 21cm), VG.
£40-45 *VS*

Walt Disney, signed album page, slightly scratchy ink, VG. **£300-350** *VS*

Mel Blanc, signed and inscribed colour photograph, half length sat at desk surrounded by various cartoon characters including Bugs Bunny, 21st September 1981, 8 by 10in (20 by 25cm), VG. **£30-40** *VS*

Charles Laughton, signed photograph, 7.5 by 9.5in (19 by 24cm), VG. **£40-60** *VS*

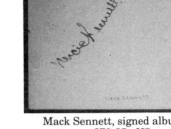

Mack Sennett, signed album page. **£70-85** *VS*

Elizabeth Taylor, signed photograph in costume from Beau Brummel inscribed to the photographer Fred Daniels, 10 by 7.5in (25 by 19cm), G. **£60-80** *VS*

Salvador Dali, signed colour magazine reproduction of one of his paintings featuring Gala, VG. **£65-70** *VS*

Maria Callas, signed album page, VG. **£80-120** *VS*

Ingrid Bergman, signed postcard, G. **£50-60** *VS*

Brigitte Bardot, signed postcard, Picturegoer No. D682, VG. **£20-30** *VS*

John Wayne, signed postcard, Picturegoer No. W477, VG. **£100-120** *VS*

Jayne Mansfield, signed postcard, 2nd October, 1957, VG. **£100-120** *VS*

A collection of autographs and photographs from the cast of The Wizard Of Oz, MGM, 1939, including Judy Garland, pen and ink on paper matted and framed with a photograph of the movie star. **£2,200-2,500** *S(NY)*

Jimi Hendrix, signed photograph, also partially signed by Noel Redding, 6 by 4in (15 by 10cm). **£300-325** *VS*

Freddie Mercury, signed colour photograph 8.5 by 12in (21 by 31cm), EX. **£150-175** *VS*

Cross Reference
Rock & Pop

The Rolling Stones, signed Decca EP to both sides of sleeve, FR-G. **£200-225** *VS*

The Beatles, all 4 signatures on 4.25 by 4.75in (10.5 by 12cm) piece, VG-EX. **£600-650** *VS*

Cigarette Cards

John Player & Sons, Straight
Line Caricatures, set of 50, 1926.
Grade 2 £20-25
Grade 1 £40-50 *ACC*

W.D & H.O. Wills, Arms of Oxford
& Cambridge Colleges, set of 42, 1922.
Grade 2 £40-50
Grade 1 £85-95 *ACC*

W.D. & H.O. Wills, Household
Hints, set of 50, 1927.
Grade 2 £8-12
Grade 1 £18-22 *ACC*

W.D. & H.O. Wills,
Romance of the
Heavans, set of 50,
1928.
Grade 2 £15-18
Grade 1 £30-35
ACC

W.D. & H.O. Wills, Arms of
Universities, set of 25, 1923.
Grade 2 £25-35
Grade 1 £55-65 *ACC*

W.D. & H.O. Wills, Household
Hints, set of 50, 1930.
Grade 2 £16-20
Grade 1 £35-40 *ACC*

F. & J. Smith, Famous Explorers,
set of 50, slight foxing and
scuffing to reverse, otherwise VG.
£220-250 *VS*

W.D. & H.O. Wills, Old Furniture,
set of 25, 1923.
Grade 2 £70-80
Grade 1 £140-160 *ACC*

W.D. & H.O. Wills, Household
Hints, set of 50, 1936.
Grade 2 £6-8
Grade 1 £10-12 *ACC*

Carreras Ltd., Tools, set of 50,
1925.
Grade 2 £32-38
Grade 1 £65-75 *ACC*

W.D. & H.O. Wills, Old Silver, set
of 25, 1924.
Grade 2 £55-65
Grade 1 £110-130 *ACC*

Ardath Tobacco Co. Ltd., Empire
Personalities, set of 50, 1937.
Grade 2 £28-32
Grade 1 £48-52 *ACC*

Cavenders Ltd., Ancient Egypt,
set of 25, 1928.
Grade 2 £12-18
Grade 1 £28-32 *ACC*

W.A. & A.C. Churchman,
Holidays in Britain, set of 48,
1937.
Grade 2 £8-10
Grade 1 £12-15 *ACC*

Carreras Ltd., Palmistry, set of
50, 1933.
Grade 2 £12-18
Grade 1 £22-28 *ACC*

W.D. & H.O. Wills, Gems of Russian Architecture, set
of 50, 1916.
Grade 2 £25-35
Grade 1 £55-65 *ACC*

Carreras Ltd., Notable M.Ps, set
of 50, 1929.
Grade 2 £32-38
Grade 1 £60-70

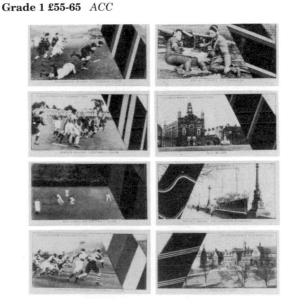

W.A. & A.C. Churchman,
Well Known Ties, Second
Series, set of 50, 1934.
Grade 2 £22-25
Grade 1 £38-42 *ACC*

Carreras Ltd., Happy Family,
set of 48, 1925.
Grade 2 £8-12
Grade 1 £20-22 *ACC*

Military

W.A. & A.C. Churchman, The
Navy at Work, set of 48, 1937.
Grade 2 £6-10
Grade 1 £12-16 *ACC*

Natural History

W.D. & H.O. Wills,
Animalloys,
set of 48, 1934.
Grade 2 £8-12
Grade 1 £18-22 *ACC*

Ogden's, Poultry, set of 25,
1916.
Grade 2 £55-65
Grade 1 £115-125 *ACC*

Gallaher Ltd., Army Badges, set
of 48, 1939.
Grade 2 £22-25
Grade 1 £35-38 *ACC*

W.A. & A.C. Churchman,
Warriors of all Nations, set of 25,
1929.
Grade 2 £55-65
Grade 1 £95-105 ACC

John Player & Sons, Animals of
the Countryside, set of 50, 1939.
Grade 2 £10-12
Grade 1 £18-20 *ACC*

W.D. & H.O. Wills, Flowering
Shrubs, set of 30, 1935.
Grade 2 £25-30
Grade 1 £55-60 ACC

W.D & H.O. Wills, Garden Flowers, set of 50, 1939.
Grade 2 £6-10   **Grade 1 £12-16** *ACC*

Show Business

Carreras Ltd., Glamour Girls, set
of 54, 1939.
Grade 2 £12-16
Grade 1 £18-24 *ACC*

Ardath Tobacco Co. Ltd., Famous
Film Stars, set of 50, 1934.
Grade 2 £32-38
Grade 1 £50-60 *ACC*

W.D. & H.O. Wills, Cinema Stars, set of 50, 1931.
Grade 2 £55-65
Grade 1 £110-130 *ACC*

Carreras Ltd., Film & Stage
Beauties, set of 54, 1939.
Grade 2 £10-14
Grade 1 £16-20 *ACC*

| **Grade 2** - Good Condition |
| **Grade 1** - Excellent to Mint |

Sport

W.A. & A.C. Churchman, Rugby
Internationals, set of 50, 1935.
Grade 2 £55-65
Grade 1 £110-130 *ACC*

John Player & Sons, Derby and
Grand National Winners, set of
50, 1933.
Grade 2 £75-80
Grade 1 £150-170 *ACC*

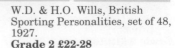

W.A. & A.C. Churchman,
Association Footballers, set of 50,
1938.
Grade 2 £15-20
Grade 1 £35-38 *ACC*

W.D. & H.O. Wills, British
Sporting Personalities, set of 48,
1927.
Grade 2 £22-28
Grade 1 £35-45 *ACC*

Transport

Gallaher Ltd., Trains of the
World, set of 48, 1937.
Grade 2 £28-32
Grade 1 £42-48 *ONS*

International Tobacco Co. Ltd.,
International Code of Signals, set
of 50, 1934.
Grade 2 £10-14
Grade 1 £20-25 *ACC*

W.D & H.O. Wills, Famous
British Liners, set of 30, 1935.
Grade 2 £70-75
Grade 1 £140-150 *ACC*

Continental Trade Cards

The following cards were issued
in OXO products all over Europe
in several languages, always using
the same artwork.

Liebig, Horse Drawn Vehicles, set of 6, 1897.
£50-75 *ACC*

Liebig, War Ships, Series 1, set of 6, 1897.
£20-30 *ACC*

Comics

If you are thinking of starting a collection of comics, a good rule is to focus on a particular company, character or artist and to concentrate on collecting everthing to do with that aspect before widening your scope.

It is important to remember that the price ranges shown in this book are just a guide and that the true value of a comic is what it is worth to you. However, do bear in mind two points: Firstly, British comics tend to be cheaper than American comics at present but given the astronomical price growth in recent years, this margin may soon narrow. Secondly, condition is vital so do steer away from damaged or brown, brittle comics. You will never be able to read the latter without bits falling off and in two years or so, you will be the proud owner of a bag of paper chips.

The last decade or two has seen the introduction of the comic speculator. Childhood memories can have a hard cash value. The only good to come from this is that at least comics are now appearing on the market instead of ending up in waste paper drives, which was the fate of millions of back issues!

Action, No. 27, D.C. Comics, 1940.
£180-200 *NOS*

All Select, No. 4, Timely, 1944.
£80-100 *NOS*

The Kinema, No. 312, Amalgamated Press, 1926. **£5-8** *NOS*

Crackers, No. 266, Amalgamated Press, 1934. **£8-10** *NOS*

Boys and Girls, Associated Newspapers, 1936.
£5-8 *NOS*

Superman, No. 12, D.C. Comics, 1941.
£200-225 *NOS*

Ally Sloper's Half Holiday, No. 1,
Ally Sloper Publications, 1949.
£3-5 *NOS*

Young Allies, No. 13,
Timely, 1944.
£70-80 *NOS*

The Champion, Volume III,
No. 21, 1895.
£8-10 *NOS*

Big Shot, No. 52, Columbia
Comic Corporation, 1945.
£8-12 *NOS*

The Rover, No. 1131,
D.C. Thompson, 1946.
£1-3 *NOS*

The Wizard, No. 1023, featuring Wilson, D.C.
Thompson, 1943.   **£3-5** *NOS*

Comet, No. 24, J.B. Allen,
1947.
£1.50-2.50 *NOS*

Sun, No. 1, J.B. Allen, 1947.
£7-10 *NOS*

The School
Friend, No. 1,
The first Bessie
Bunter story,
Fleetway
Publications,
1919.
£40-50 *NOS*

Ghost Rider, No. 11, M.E., 1953. **£18-22** *NOS*

Green Lantern, No. 24, D.C. Comics, 1960. **£100-125** *NOS*

Lion, No. 115, Amalgamated Press, 1954. **£1.50-2.50** *NOS*

The Hotspur, No. 786, D.C. Thompson, 1951. **£3-4** *NOS*

Girl, Volume VIII, No. 18, Hulton Press, 1959. **£1-2** *NOS*

Family Star, No. 542, D.C. Thompson, 1947. **£1-2** *NOS*

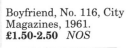

The Hornet, No. 369, D.C. Thompson, 1970. **£1-2** *NOS*

Boyfriend, No. 116, City Magazines, 1961. **£1.50-2.50** *NOS*

Pluck, No. 2, L. Miller, 1955. **£1.50-2.50** *NOS*

Romeo, D.C. Thompson, 1970. **50p-£1** *NOS*

Adventure, No. 174, D.C. Comics, 1952. **£40-50** *NOS*

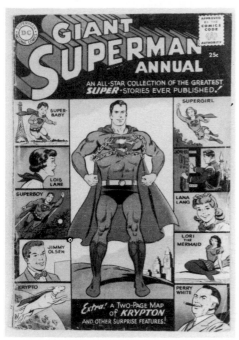

Giant Superman Annual, No. 1,
D.C. Comics, 1960.
£60-80 *NOS*

Al Capps Shmoo, No. 5,
Toby Press Inc., 1950.
£35-45 *NOS*

Toytown, No. 1, Williams
Pub. & Dist., 1972.
£2-3 *NOS*

The Hotspur, Nos. 792,
795 and 799, D.C.
Thompson, 1952.
£2.50-3.50 each *NOS*

Dandy and Nutty, No. 2292, D.C.
Thompson, 1985.
50p-£1 *NOS*

Ovaltiney's, No. 105, Target
Publications, 1937.
£5-8 *NOS*

Misty, Holiday Special,
1980.
£2-3 *NOS*

The Rover, Nos. 1134, 1136, 1143, 1145, 1146 and 1151, D.C. Thompson, 1946.
£1-3 each *NOS*

Princess, I.P.C., 1963.
£5-7.50 *NOS*

Jinty, No. 1, I.P.C., 1974.
£1-2 *NOS*

All Winners, No. 5, Timely, 1942.
£180-200 *NOS*

Diana for Girls, No. 19, D.C. Thompson, 1963.
50p-£1 *NOS*

Valiant and Lion, I.P.C., 1974.
£1-2 *NOS*

Sixties newcomer swallows up the fifties title.

Tarzan, No. 1, Byblos Productions, with free gift 'Survival Kit Bag', 1977.
£2-3 *NOS*

Battle, No. 1, I.P.C., 1975.
£1-2 *NOS*

Princess Tina, I.P.C., 1970.
50p-£1 *NOS*

Lindy, No. 1, I.P.C., 1975.
£1-2 *NOS*

The Victor, No. 503, D.C. Thompson, 1970.
£1-2 *NOS*

Princess, I.P.C., 1966.
£1-2 *NOS*

Solo, Nos. 3 and 14, City Magazines/Century 21, 1967.
£2-4 each *NOS*

Diana, No. 159, D.C. Thompson, 1966.
50p-£1 *NOS*

Greetings Cards

An early plastic card, with felt flowers, 6 by 3.5in (15 by 9cm).
£13-18 *LB*

A mechanical hand coloured lithographic card, by Dean & Son, and 4 others.
£160-180 *CSK*

Ten hand coloured engraved valentine cards, all with printed humorous verses, c1855.
£150-175 *CSK*

Magazines

The Aero, Volume I to VII, nos 1- 122, bound in 7 volumes with indices, May 25th 1909-May 1913.
£160-180 *ONS*

Cross Reference
Aeronautica

What To Do If It's Catching, c1930.
£1-1.50 *COL*

Two copies of Aero Modeller, 1957/58. **£1-3 each** *COL*

Flight, an illustrated weekly journal of aerial locomotion and transport, Volume I to VIII, bound in publisher's cloth with indices, January 1909-December 1916.
£575-600 *ONS*

Meccano Magazines, 1957-59.
£1-1.50 each *COL*

1930s manuals.
£50p-£1 each *COL*

The Wife's Handbook, 7in (18cm)
high.   **£3-5** *ROS*

Leach's Wool Embroidery
magazines, with transfers, c1929.
£2-3 each *COL*

Scraps

Beeton's Shilling Medical
Dictionary, c1930.
£5-8 *ROS*

A collection in modern photograph album, G.   **£100-120** *VS*

Fairgrounds

A Bayol prancing carousel horse, c1900, 56in (142cm) long.
£1,000-1,100 *REL*

A Chanvin fairground pig, c1905, 38in (96.5cm) long.
£400-500 *REL*

A Matthieu carousel camel, c1930, 39in (99cm) long.
£650-750 *REL*

A French papier mâché Revolution figure, 27in (69cm) high. **£180-220** *REL*

A Bayol fairground pig, 29in (74cm) long.
£500-600 *REL*

A wood motorcycle.
£80-100 *REL*

A Matthieu fairground duck, 37in (94cm) long.
£900-1,000 *REL*

A French carousel swan by Limonaire, 29in (74cm) long.
£350-400 *REL*

A Matthieu carousel ostrich, 42in (106.5cm) high.
£450-550 *REL*

A French fairground dog, c1930, 33in (84cm) long.
£700-800 *REL*

A French fairground nodding donkey, c1910, 38in (96.5cm) long.
£400-500 *REL*

A painted fairground sign, 40in (101.5cm) high.
£200-225 *REL*

A French carousel cat, 25in (64cm) long.
£400-500 *REL*

A French fairground pig, c1890, 31in (79cm) long.
£450-550 *REL*

A Devos fairground swan, 31in (79cm) long.
£500-600 *REL*

A French fairground poodle, c1910, 30in (76cm) long.
£450-550 *REL*

One of a pair of fairground horses. **£250-350** *REL*

An English fairground clown game.
£200-275 *REL*

A carved wood lady from centre of a carousel, 54in (137cm) high.
£800-900 *REL*

A Bayol fairground cat, c1890, 35in (89cm) long.
£700-800 *REL*

A Tunnel of Love boat.
£200-250 *REL*

A Mexican carousel horse, 37in
(94cm) long.
£450-550 *REL*

A French
fairground rabbit,
by Limonaire,
c1890, 37in (94cm)
long.
£500-600 *REL*

A French carousel rabbit, 34in
(86cm) long.
£500-600 *REL*

A French fairground goat,
c1890,
23in (59cm) long.
£550-600 *REL*

A pair of painted wood fairground
signs, 21 by 27in (53 by 69cm).
£300-350 *REL*

A Devos fairground
turkey, 35in (89cm)
long.
£700-800 *REL*

A French fairground swing boat,
with swans' heads, 67in (170cm)
long.
£300-400 *REL*

A carousel goat, by Cognereaux
Marèchal, with brass horns.
£450-500 *REL*

A French fairground
cat, by Limonaire,
c1890, 39in (99cm)
long.
£550-650 *REL*

A Devos carnival carved wood horse, 32in (81cm) long.
£450-550 *REL*

A French carousel donkey, with moving head, 29in (74cm) long.
£350-450 *REL*

A Spanish carousel bull, 54in (137cm) long.
£1,000-1,100 *REL*

Fans

A brisé fan painted with a cat and a border of mice, the verso with mice by a mousetrap, signed F. Lots, ribbon loose, c1900, 5in (13cm).
£400-450 *C*

A dismounted fan leaf, painted with a sage and musicians watching a waterfall, Japanese, Kano School, c1700, 19in (48cm) wide, framed and glazed.
£850-900 *C*

A fan illustrating Aix-les-Bains Les Hôtels Splendide Royal & Excelsior, 10in (25cm) high.
£110-125 *YV*

A Japanese ivory brisé fan, lacquered in gold with a landscape and volcano, the verso with quail, butterflies and flowers, late 19thC, 10.5in (26cm).
£2,600-2,800 *CSK*

A painted fan with an Assemblage of Gods, the verso with Roman soldiers in a landscape, with carved and pierced mother-of-pearl sticks, English or Flemish, c1765, 11in (28cm).
£925-975 *CSK*

Bought in Moscow in 1888.

A Japanese ivory brisé fan, gold
lacquered with cranes and other
birds, the guardsticks decorated
with Shibayama work birds and
flowers, c1880, 11.5in (29cm).
£3,250-3,500 *C*

A Dutch fan, the leaf
painted with an
allegory of Love, with
carved ivory sticks,
c1760, 11in (28cm).
£450-475 *C*

A painted fan depicting El Cid
defeating the Moors, the verso
with a distant view of the battle,
ivory sticks pierced and gilt with
the arms of Spain, 2 sticks
broken, c1750.
£500-550 *CSK*

A lithographic fan, printed with a
Turkish scene, the sticks of
Mauchline Ware, the guardsticks
with scenes of Loch Leven Castle
and Castle of Caldwall, some
damage, c1860, 11in (28cm).
£575-600 *C*

Le Chat Qui Crie, the silk
leaf painted with a cat
signed A. Thomasse,
embroidered with
sequins, horn sticks,
some wear, c1905, 9in
(23cm). **£1,250-1,350** *C*

A chicken skin fan painted
with a view of Rome, the verso
with a ruin in the Campagna,
ivory sticks, one repaired,
c1780, 10.5in (26cm), in
contemporary fan box labelled
Robt. Clarke, 26 Strand.
£1,750-1,950 *C*

A fan, the leaf painted with a classical
scene, the verso with lovers by a monument,
the pierced, silvered mother-of-pearl sticks
carved, and gilt, c1750, 19thC, 11.5in (29cm)
box by Rodien.
£1,400-1,500 *C*

A fan, the leaf painted with
figures in 18thC dress, signed E.
Chenneviere, tortoiseshell sticks
carved and pierced, c1890, 12in
(30.5cm), in Duvelleroy box.
£1,250-1,500 *C*

FISHING

A Victorian copper and brass maggot shute. **£90-100** *EP*

A still life, oil on canvas picture of various fish, dated 1897, 25 by 18in (64 by 46cm). **£400-600** *GHA*

Various novelty items shaped as fish, i.e. butter dishes, ashtrays, bottle openers, etc. **£10-30 each** *CPT*

A live bait can, 19thC, 7in (18cm) square. **£35-50** *GHA*

A japanned fly tin, with 6 trays holding 168 gut-eyed salmon flies, by C. Farlow & Co., 8.75 by 5in (22 by 13cm). **£500-600** *GHA*

A willow creel with brass fittings, by C. Farlow, 191 Strand, London, 10in (25.5cm) wide. **£165-185** *GHA*

A Hardy Weroda salmon fly box, with 30 flies, 6.25 by 8in (16 by 20cm) when open. **£80-100** *GHA*

A black japanned fly box, with extra section in the middle, to hold 100 flies, by Malloch of Perth. **£15-20** *JMG*

An antique shell fish scraper net **£50-60** and a galvanised live bait trap. **£70-80** *CPT*

A fishing net, 45in (114cm) long. **£40-60** *GHA*

A wicker creel, 11in (28cm) wide. **£65-85** *GHA*

A silver fish, made in India, c1930, 12in (31cm) long. **£40-50** *JMG*

A Scottish wicker and leather creel, 13in (33cm) wide. **£100-120** *GHA*

Two pigskin fly wallets, 7.5 by 5in (19 by 13cm). **£40-60 each** *GHA*

A Hardy wooden pear shaped landing net, with folding knuckle joint, fitted on Hardy extending Greenheart and bamboo shaft. **£175-195** *ND*

A Hardy rosewood box, No. 2, fitted with ivory leaves, 1911. **£200-225** *ND*

Two Victorian wooden tackle compendiums: *l.* A wood book type. **£40-45** *r.* Tubular design with detachable inner compartments. **£100-150** *CPT*

A fishing knife, made in Sheffield with silver outside finish, 3.5in (9cm). **£8-10** *JMG*

A fishing knife, made in Sheffield. **£8-12** *JMG*

An brass line drier, with wooden handle, 19thC, 17.5in (44cm) high. **£165-185** *GHA*

A brown trout mounted in bowfront case, with label 'Killed on Loch Beannoch June 1903', 40in (101.5cm) wide. **£500-600** *GHA*

An brass extending salmon gaff,
30in (76cm) extended.
£100-120 *GHA*

A line drier, with 4 brass arms
and spindle, with 3.5in (9cm)
brass crank stamped Hardy Bros,
Makers Alnwick, set in U-shaped
steel frame with affixed brass
clamp fitting, c1896.
£155-175 *EP*

A plaster cast salmon, J.M.V.
May 1907, Thurso, Caithness,
case 45.5in (115cm) long.
£800-1,200 *GHA*

Two wood priests, 8 and 9.5in (20
and 24cm) long.
£40-60 each *GHA*

A bamboo and brass fishing gaff,
43in (109cm) long.
£20-30 *GHA*

Three roach in bowfront gilt lined
case, by J. Cooper & Sons, 29in
(74cm) long.
£650-700 *ND*

A bowfront case, with gilt edging
and label 'Trout found dying
below Town Mill, Hungerford on
9th June 1914 - 8lb 14oz length
27in', J. Cooper & Sons, 32.5in
(82cm) long.
£500-550 *ND*

A fishing net, with brass fittings
and bamboo, 66in (167.5cm).
£75-100 *GHA*

A pair of Hardy half-moon spirit
flasks, with glass stoppers and SP
caps, 3.5in (9cm) diam., in
maker's leather case.
£225-250 *ND*

Reels
Hardy

A 2¾in Hardy Perfect reel, wide drum, ivorine handle, c1910. **£70-100** *JMG*

A 2⅛in Hardy Perfect reel, alloy with ivory handle, strap tension regulator, 1896 check. **£800-850** *ND*

A 2¾in Hardy Perfect brass faced trout fly reel. **£750-850** *ND*

A 2¾in Hardy Perfect all brass trout reel, with rod and shaded hand trademark, ivory handle, Pat. Nos. 18373 - 612, strapped tension screw, dished drum with central well and large and small perforations, nickel silver rim and pillars, brass ball bearings in open race. **£1,000-1,250** *EP*

A 6in Hardy Longstone Dorado reel, known as 'General Harrison Pattern', ratchet check action, brake indicator and dial, brass ribbed foot, stamped Pat. No. 272409. **£425-450** *ND*

FURTHER READING

Fishing Tackle, A Collectors Guide, Graham Turner, Ward Lock

A 2⅝in Hardy Perfect transitional brass reel. **£2,650-2,850** *ND*

A 3⅛in Hardy The Field reel, alloy with ivorine handle and smooth brass foot, c1900. **£180-200** *ND*

A 3in Hardy brass reel, with small Hardy name on face and Edinburgh, probably 1880s, **£80-100** *JMG*

A 5in Hardy Silex No. 2 brass sea fishing reel. **£200-300** *JMG*

Not shown in Hardy's catalogues.

A 3in Hardy Super Silex casting reel, with twin black handles, white indicator dial, ivorine check handle and grooved brass foot, in leather bag and maker's box. **£220-250** *EP*

The 3in Super Silex reel was discontinued c1939.

A 3⅜in Hardy Cascapedia reel, with ebonite front and backplates, nickel silver rims, the backplate having knurled check adjuster with 7 red marked settings with on and off ratchet control. **£4,000-4,500** *EP*

This reel was made for export between 1932 and 1939.

A 2⅝in Hardy 'Field' alloy trout fly reel, with fixed check, ivorine handle, brass drum, pillars and foot.
£360-400 *EP*

This is the smallest 'Field' reel made.

A 4⅞in Hardy Ebona sea reel, with central milled nut controlling brake pressure, twin horn handles and circular line guide attached to foot.
£175-200 *EP*

A 3⅝in Hardy Perfect early silent check trout fly reel, with ivorine handle, strapped tension screw, and brass foot, in maker's box.
£1,000-1,200 *EP*

The early silent Perfect reel was made from 1908 to 1910.

A 3¼in Hardy The Special Perfect reel.
£150-200 *JMG*

A 4in Hardy Perfect brass faced salmon fly reel, with rod and hand trademark, strapped tension screw with turks head locking nut, ivorine handle, brass foot and 1905 check.
£200-220 *EP*

A 3¾in Hardy Uniqua Spitfire model reel, from World War II, manufactured by Jimmy Smith.
£80-100 *JMG*

A 2⅞in Hardy Uniqua Pup Mark II telephone latch reel.
£65-75 *GHA*

A collection of 5 Bakelite centre pins, including a Gyrex, Allcocks Aerialite and Modernite Pixie.
£5-20 each *CPT*

A 4in Hardy Perfect brass faced reel with ivorine handle, hand trademark, 1896.
£500-600 *GHA*

A 3¾in Hardy Uniqua reel, with ivorine handle and wide drum, c1912.
£40-50 *JMG*

A 2⅞in Hardy Perfect duplicated MkII reel.
£80-90 *GHA*

A 4½in Hardy Megstone wood reel, 1920s. **£70-100** *JMG*

A Hardy The Jock-Scott spinning reel, possibly late 1940s. **£100-130** *JMG*

A Hardy 'The Altex' reel, first model with unusual curve at the bottom of the body. **£200-250** *JMG*

A 4½in Hardy Perfect brass faced salmon fly reel, with rod and hand trademark, nickel silver centre engraved 'Hardy's Patent Alnwick', strapped tension screw, inscribed 'W.H.S'. Cutler 2, ivorine handle, brass foot, 1905 check. **£425-450** *EP*

A Hardy Altex No. 2 MkIII reel. **£55-65** *GHA*

A 2½in Hardy Hercules all brass reel, with rod and hand trademark.
£300-400 *GHA*

General

A Howban Birmingham sidecasting alloy reel, twin handles and sliding line guide. **£160-180** *ND*

A 4⅛in Carter of London drum reel, by Walter Dingley. **£40-60** *JMG*

Dingley left Hardy's in 1910 and started his own business.

A 4⅛in G. Little of London reel, marked 'Makers to HRH Prince of Wales', 1880s. **£40-50** *JMG*

A 3¼in Ocean City Automatic reel, American, modern. **£20-30** *JMG*

Three freshwater spinning multipliers:
Top. Record 1550. **£85-95**
Bottom l. Youngs Gildex. **£20-25**
Bottom r. Hardy Elarex. **£25-30**
CPT

A 3in Chevalier Bowness & Bowness brass reel, with ivory handle, 1880s. **£40-60** *JMG*

A 3¼in Edward Vom Hofe of America reel, patented 1902. **£60-80** *JMG*

A Farlow Billiken multiplier reel, with counterbalanced crank, ivorine handle, in maker's oak box with compartment containing 5 spare vanes. **£700-720** *EP*

A 4in rosewood and brass plate reel, with ivory handle. **£200-220** *GHA*

A 4¾in Ogden Smith wide drum sea fishing reel. **£40-60** *JMG*

A 3¾in Malloch of Perth Sun & Planet fly reel, designed for use on the river Tay. **£60-80** *JMG*

Walt Disney, Fantasia, 1940,
9in (22.5cm) high.
£2,600-2,800 *CNY*

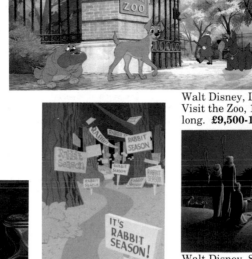

Walt Disney, Lady & The Tramp
Visit the Zoo, 1955, 29.5in (75cm)
long. **£9,500-10,000** *CNY*

Walt Disney, So Dear To My
Heart, The Nativity Scene, 1949.
£1,300-1,500 *CNY*

Walt Disney, Tinkerbelle, from Peter
Pan, 1953, 11in (28cm) wide.
£7,000-7,500 *CNY*

Walt Disney, The Pointer, 1939,
11in (28cm) long.
£3,000-3,500 *CNY*

l. Warner Bros, Rabbit Seasoning,
watercolour on paper, 1952, 32.5in
(82cm) long. **£5,700-5,900** *CNY*

Walt Disney, Make Mine Music:
Peter and the Wolf, 1946, 9.25in
(23cm) wide. **£2,000-2,500** *CNY*

Walt Disney, Fantasia,
1940, 9in (22.5cm) long.
£8,500-9,000 *CNY*

Walt Disney, 101 Dalmations,
1961, 18in (46cm) long.
£6,400-6,600 *CNY*

A poster by Jules Chéret, 2 sheets joined, linen backed, damp stain, worn on folds, repaired, 1894, 96in (243.5in) high. **£450-475** *BBA*

A poster by J. S. Anderson, Motorists Prefer Shell, 1935. **£1,750-1,950** *BBA*

A poster by Abram Games, c1941, fold marks, 30in (76cm) high. **£350-400** *BBA*

A Saville Lumley poster. **£550-575** *BBA*

A poster by E. Kealey, 29.5in (75cm) high. **£300-350** *BBA*

A poster by Eller, some damage, c1935. **£550-575** *BBA*

A poster by Jules Chéret, 2 sheets joined, backed, some damage and minor repairs, 1890, 90in (228in) high. **£450-470** *BBA*

A poster by Edward McKnight Kauffer, some damage, c1935. **£2,100-2,250** *BBA*

Italy For Your Holidays, by Austin Cooper, McCorquodale & Co., 1934. **£850-875** *BBA*

Travels in Space on your Doorstep, by Clifford and Rosemary Ellis, 1937. **£400-425** *BBA*

Norwich, It's Quicker By Rail, by Claude Muncaster, Gilmour & Dean, c1935. **£360-380** *BBA*

Frankfort O/M Via Harwich, by Fred Taylor, Vincent Brooks, Day & Son Ltd., c1935. **£230-250** *BBA*

Münchener Festsommer 1935, by Ludwig Hohlwein, 47.5in (121cm) high. **£200-225** *BBA*

Barbados, Outposts of Empire, Post Office. **£180-200** *BBA*

To The Far East, Canadian Pacific White Empress Route, c1936. **£275-295** *BBA*

Favorites, Business prizes go only to those who earn them. Let's Deserve, by Willard Frederick Elmes. **£300-325** *BBA*

Central Australia, Outposts of Empire, Post Office. **£120-130** *BBA*

The Adventures of ROBIN HOOD, Errol Flynn, Photographed in TECHNICOLOR. OLIVIA De HAVILLAND BASIL RATHBONE CLAUDE RAINS

Warner Bros., 1938, 81in (205.5cm)
£11,500-12,500 *CNY*

Son of Frankenstein, Universal, 1939,
41in (104cm). **£8,200-8,400** *CNY*

Double Indemnity,
Paramount, 1944.
£1,700-1,900 *CNY*

She Married Her Boss,
Columbia, 1935.
£1,900-2,100 *CNY*

Warner Brothers, 1941, 41in
(104cm). **£3,200-3,500** *CNY*

Universal, 1954, 41in (104cm).
£2,700-2,900 *CNY*

Gun Crazy, United Artists,
1950. **£2,700-2,900** *CNY*

Casablanca, Warner
Brothers, 1943, 11in
(28cm).
£2,900-3,100 *CNY*

King Kong, RKO, 1933, 81in
(205.5cm). **£33,000-35,000** *CNY*

The Virginian, Paramount, 1929, 41in (104cm). **£3,700-3,900** *CNY*

The Other Man, Triangle-Keystone, 1916, 41in (104cm). **£1,400-1,500** *CNY*

Citizen Kane, RKO, 1941, 41in (104cm). **£12,500-12,800** *CNY*

Out West, Paramount-Arbuckle, 1918, 41in (104cm) **£3,100-3,300** *CNY*

The Master of Mystery, Octagon Films, 1919, 41in (104cm). **£9,500-10,500** *CNY*

Dracula, Universal, 1931. **£19,000-20,000** *CNY*

The Devil Is A Woman, Paramount, 1935, 41in (104cm). **£9,500-9,700** *CNY*

The Wolf Man, Universal, 1941, 41in (104cm). **£11,000-12,000** *CNY*

Gentlemen Prefer Blondes, 20th Century Fox, 1953, 81in (205.5cm) **£820-850** *CNY*

Atom Man versus Superman, Columbia, 1950, 81in (205.5cm). **£4,800-5,000** *CNY*

The Wild One, Columbia, 1954, 41in (104cm) **£510-530** *CNY*

Rebel Without A Cause, Warner Brothers, 1955, 81in (205.5cm). **£2,250-2,500** *CNY*

An American In Paris, MGM, 1951, 81in (205.5cm) **£1,150-1,350** *CNY*

Werewolf of London, Universal, 1935, 36in (91.5cm). **£2,700-3,000** *CNY*

Jailhouse Rock, MGM, 1957, 81in (205.5cm). **£600-700** *CNY*

The War Of The Worlds, Paramount, 1953, 81in (205.5cm). **£3,100-3,300** *CNY*

Destry Rides Again, Universal, 1939, 41in (104cm). **£630-650** *CNY*

A $1,000 bond, for the
Marietta & North Georgia
Railway Company, 1887.
£55-65 *SCR*

Credit Athenien S.A., 1925.
£35-45 *SCR*

Banque Industrielle de Chine.
£30-40 *SCR*

Republic of Estonia, £100
Sterling bond.
£50-60 *SCR*

Compagnie des Installations
Maritime de Bruges, the
company formed to construct
the port at Bruges.
£165-185 *SCR*

Four unissued proofs for
Pioneers, W. & A. Churchman's
cigarettes, c1939.
£100-130 *VS*

Barcelona Traction Light &
Power, £20 bond, Waterlow
engraved.
£30-40 *SCR*

An American cigarette
card book, by W. Drake
& Sons, issued 1888.
£30-40 each *ACC*

Four unissued proofs,
Pioneers, W. & A.
Churchman's cigarettes,
c1939.
£80-120 *VS*

A B.O.A.C. advertising fan, c1950, 9in (23cm).
£25-30 *YV*

A Restaurant Frascati, London, advertising fan.
£65-75 *YV*

An Amer Picon advertising fan, 10in (25cm).
£75-85 *YV*

A Restaurant Toccardi, Paris, advertising fan, 9in (23cm).
£75-85 *YV*

An Amer Picon advertising fan, 9.5in (24cm).
£55-65 *YV*

A Tigre, Galeries Lafayette chromolitho advertising fan, 9.5in (24cm).
£55-65 *YV*

Reverse side of the Restaurant Frascati, London, advertising fan, *top right*.

A Marie Bryard, Art Deco advertising fan, 9.5in (24cm) **£65-75** *YV*

A Carlton Hotel & Restaurant, London, advertising fan, signed George Redan, 10in (25cm). **£75-85** *YV*

A Galeries Lafayette advertising fan, 8.5in (21cm). **£55-65** *YV*

Two onion shaped carafes, c1840, 8.5 and 9in (21 and 22.5cm). **£250-275 each** *Som*

A spirit decanter, c1810. **£1,800-1,900** *Som*

A decanter, c1815. **£85-95** *Som*

A set of 3 spirit bottles, in a silver plated stand, c1860. **£860-885** *Som*

A decanter with lozenge stopper, c1780. **£240-260** *Som*

Two flagons, with cork and metal stoppers, c1830. **£180-250 each** *Som*

Three flagons, with compressed sides and loop handles, c1830. **£160-200** *Som*
r. A pair of spirit bottles, c1800. **£500-550** *Som*

A triple twist wine glass, the round funnel bowl on a stem with a canary coloured central cable, an inner spiralling opaque white thread and an outer laminated ply, c1770, 6in (15cm).
£8,000-8,500 *Som*

A green faceted glass wine glass, with gilded decoration, 5.75in (14cm).
£400-500 *CB*

A pair of roemer type wine glasses, 1830, 4in (10cm).
£180-190 and a single roemer type wine glass, with heavy milled prunted knop and hollow ribbed foot, c1800, 5.25in (13cm). **£180-190** *Som*

Four green wine glasses, c1830, 4 to 5.25in (10 to 13cm). **£60-85 each** *Som*

An engraved roemer, c1680, 5.5in (14cm).
£600-700 *CB*

A wine glass, with bell bowl on a plain stem and plain folded conical foot, c1750, 7in (17.5cm).
£320-350 *Som*

A wine glass, with incised twist stem, c1760, 5.25in (13.5cm).
£850-900 *Som*

An export type wine glass, c1760, 5.5in (14cm).
£600-650 *Som*

A light green export type wine glass, with double ogee bowl, c1760.
£950-1,000 *Som*

A Baccarat garlanded pompom weight, star cut base, bruised, mid-19thC. **£2,000-2,250** *C*

A Baccarat butterfly weight, on star cut base, mid-19thC. **£1,250-1,500** *C*

A Baccarat millefiori weight, mid-19thC, 3in (8cm) diam. **£850-950** *C*

A Clichy fruit weight, mid-19thC, 2.75in (7cm) diam. **£1,500-1,750** *C*

A Clichy garlanded patterned millefiori weight, mid-19thC, 3in (8cm) diam. **£850-900** *C*

A St. Louis red pelargonium weight, mid-19thC, 2.75in (6.7cm) diam. **£1,400-1,600** *C*

A Clichy close millefiori weight, bruised and chipped, mid-19thC. **£1,250-1,500** *C*

A Clichy faceted patterned millefiori weight, mid-19thC. **£2,300-2,500** *C*

A St. Louis pink dahlia weight, mid-19thC. **£1,250-1,500** *C*

l. A St. Louis faceted upright bouquet weight, cut with a window and 3 rows of printies, mid-19thC, 3in (8cm) diam. **£1,000-1,250** *C*

l. A St. Louis weight, set in a white ground, with 4 radiating panels, mid-19thC, 3in (8cm) diam. **£6,000-6,500** *C*

Three scent bottles: *l.* c1830, *c.* c1780, *r.* c1840. **£150-400 each** *Som*

A cut glass scent bottle, c1850, 5in (12.5cm). **£100-200** *CB*

A 'Wrockwardine' jug, with marvered decoration, c1810, 8.5in (22cm). **£650-680** *Som*

A clear scent bottle, with cut green overlay, embossed silver mount, c1860. **£275-300** *Som*

l. A splatter type, clear cased, scent bottle, c1830. **£850-900** *r.* A double ended scent bottle, c1880. **£180-200** *Som*

A blue dish with flat diamond cutting, unmarked silver rim, c1780, 3.5in (9cm). **£600-620** *Som*

An early 'Nailsea' crown glass inkwell, c1820, 2.5in (6cm) high. **£60-70** *Som*

Three clear glass scent bottles, c1820, *l.* with silver mount, *c & r.* with gold mounts. **£450-500 each** *Som*

A glass vase, possibly French, c1800. **£120-140** *Som*

An amethyst cream jug and sugar basin, probably North Country, c1810, jug 4.5in (11.5cm). **£400-430** *Som*

l. A green scent bottle, c1880. **£100-120** *r.* A flat blue scent bottle, with gilt decoration, c1780, 4.5in (11.5cm). **£750-800** *Som*

A sugar comport and cover, c1800, 5.5in (13.5cm). **£600-620** *Som*

A cased glass biscuit barrel, possibly Boulton & Mills, c1900. **£265-285** *CB*

A pair of Victorian vaseline glass vases. **£60-90** *CB*

A cranberry glass posy vase, c1880, 3in (8cm). **£30-50** *CB*

Two opaque flasks, with enamelled decoration, c1760. **£650-680 each** *Som*

A French opaline glass vase, c1850. **£1,000-1,200** *CB*

An opaque glass flask, c1760. **£800-1,000** *Som*

A Victorian vaseline glass vase. **£80-120** *CB*

A pair of cornucopia vases, on marble and alabaster bases, c1840. **£950-980** *CB*

Cranberry glass oil bottles. **£70-80** *PCh*

A cranberry glass celery vase, c1880. **£100-150** *AMH*

A pair of glass tazzas, c1900. **£550-600** *CB*

A Stourbridge night light, c1900. **£80-100** *CB*

An opalescent wrythen glass jug and bowl, c1890, jug 4in (10cm) high. **£100-160** *CB*

A carnival glass vase, in ripple pattern, 10in (25cm) high.
£65-70 *TS*

A Mary Gregory glass box, 3in (7.5cm) diam.
£100-200 *CB*

A hand painted glass ashtray. **£40-45** *HEW*

Three hyacinth vases. **£20-40 each** *CB*

Wax fruit/still life arrangements under glass, English, c1870. **£50-150 each** *CB*

A pressed glass bowl, c1894. **£35-40** *AMH*

A selection of hyacinth vases, 4 to 7.5in (10 to 19cm).
£20-50 each *CB*

Below: A Murano glass vase, 8in (20cm) high.
£30-35 *ROW*

A carnival glass bowl with grapes, 7.25in (19cm) diam. **£45-50** *TS*

A selection of hyacinth vases, c1870, 5 to 8.5in (13 to 21cm) high.
£40-50 each *CB*

r. An Orange Tree carnival glass bowl, 8.5in (21cm) diam.
£65-70 *TS*

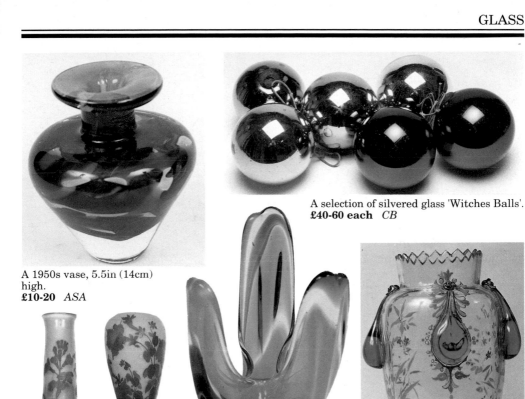

A selection of silvered glass 'Witches Balls'. **£40-60 each** *CB*

A 1950s vase, 5.5in (14cm) high. **£10-20** *ASA*

A Gallé cameo glass vase, c1900, marked **£2,000-2,500** *S(AM)*

A Gallé cameo glass vase, marked, c1910. **£1,500-1,750** *S(AM)*

Λ 1960s glass vase, 11.5in (29cm) high. **£20-30** *ASA*

A Continental glass vase, with enamelled decoration, 10.25in (26cm) high. **£90-100** *ING*

A selection of 'Witches Balls', 3 to 18in (8 to 46cm) diam. **£40-300 each** *CB*

r. An Austrian streaked glass lemonade set, with 5 glasses, c1900, jug 10in (25cm) high. **£150-200** *ASA*

A Scottish silver and agate brooch, with citrine centre, c1850, 2in (5cm) diam.
£250-280 *BWA*

A gold oval pavé set half pearl locket pendant, 19thC.
£1,100-1,200 *CSK*

A gold and diamond oval locket, with central diamonds, 19thC.
£700-800 *Bea*

A 15ct gold, peridot and seed pearl pendant brooch.
£450-500 *Bea*

A gold, silver and diamond pavé set brooch, 19thC.
£2,200-2,500 *Bea*

A Scottish silver and agate brooch, with Cairngorm centre, c1850, 2in (5cm) diam.
£225-275 *BWA*

A gold mounted agate and diamond pendant, 19thC. **£850-900** *CSK*

A carved coral bull's head brooch, 19thC. **£350-400** *CSK*

A gold, silver and diamond brooch, 19thC.
£850-950 *Bea*

A gold and emerald pendant.
£300-350 *CSK*

A Scottish silver and agate brooch, with Cairngorm centre, c1860.
£125-150 *BWA*

GLASS

A hand blown blue eye glass, English, c1840, 2.75in (7cm).
£60-80 *CB*

A Victorian opaline hand painted glass vase, 10.5in (26cm).
£30-35 *ING*

A spiral vaseline specimen vase, c1880, 7.75in (19cm).
£25-30 *WAC*

Two dwarf ales, the conical bowls engraved with hops and barley, c1800, 4.5 and 5in (12.5 and 13cm).
£65-70 each *Som*

A Bohemian cased glass egg cup set, mid-19thC, 6.5in (16cm) diam.
£55-65 *WAC*

Two toddy lifters, c1820, 5.5 and 7.5in (14 and 18.5cm).
£85-95 *Som*

l. & r. A pair of cut jelly glasses, the trumpet bowls with flute and diamond cut notched rims, c1820, 4in (10cm).
£70-80
c. A syllabub glass, with pan top and notched rim, facet cut foot, c1820, 4in (10cm).
£25-35 *Som*

l. A jelly glass, c1800, 4.5in (11cm).
£30-35
c. A bonnet glass, c1750, 3in (8cm).
£40-50
r. A rib moulded jelly glass, c1750, 3.75in (9cm).
£40-50 *Som*

Two rummers, c1820.
£60-75 *Som*

l. A dry mustard pot, with loose
hollow lid, c1800, 6in (15cm).
£65-75
c. A toddy lifter, c1830, 7in
(18cm).
£85-95
r. A pepper, with rib moulded
body, on square lemon squeezer
foot, brass cap, c1810, 4in (10cm).
£65-75 *Som*

Two Victorian crackle glass jugs,
3.75in (9cm). **£10-15**
6in (15cm). **£25-30** *FMN*

A water jug, with prism cut neck,
notched rim and strap handle,
c1840, 7in (17.5cm).
£150-170 *Som*

A Stourbridge double overlay
cruet, c1880, 2.5in (6cm).
£40-50 *WAC*

A Bristol blown blue drinking
glass, c1840, 4.75in (12cm).
£80-100 *CB*

A glass boot, 3in (8cm).
£50-80 *CB*

A glass trumpet,
c1900, 8in
(20.5cm).
£40-45 *TS*

A Victorian sardine dish, with silver plated stand. **£30-40** *TRU*

An English opaque glass vase, 6in (15cm).
£25-30 *WAC*

A pink opaline vase, 10.5in (26cm).
£25-35 *WAC*

A pair of cut salts, the oval bodies with slice cutting and crenellated rims, on moulded diamond lemon squeezer feet, c1800, 3in (7.5cm).
£180-200 *Som*

Two Victorian custard cups, 2.5 and 3.5in (7 and 9cm).
£10-15 *Som*

A Mary Gregory blue hyacinth vase, 6in (15cm).
£55-65 *WAC*

A cut glass wig stand, early 19thC, 7in (17cm).
£35-45 *WAC*

An English opaline mug, c1830, 3in (8cm).
£150-200 *CB*

Two Victorian green glass jugs, with lily of the valley pattern and gilt rims, 5.5in (14cm). **£45-50 each** *TS*

A hand blown specimen vase, c1910, 3in (8cm). **£10-15** *TS*

A Stourbridge cased jug, 6in (15cm). c1880, **£55-65** *WAC*

A pair of Victorian opaline glass vases, with gilding and jewelled decoration. **£25-30** TS

A Victorian glass vase, small chips, 3.5in (9cm). **£20-30** *WAC*

Two Victorian crackle glass vases, 4.5 and 7in (11 and 18cm). **£20-25 each** *FMN*

A pair of hand painted green glass tankards, 6in (15cm). **£15-20** *TS*

A pair of glass door knobs, with glitter inside, 3in (8cm).
£20-25 *TS*

l. An ovoid bowl rummer, with short stem and conical foot, c1810, 4.5in (11.5cm).
£45-55
r. An ovoid bowl rummer, engraved 'S. Marrion', with floral decoration and a bird in flight, c1820, 5in (12.5cm).
£85-95 *Som*

A Thomas Webb cameo glass scent bottle, the stopper with embossed silver outer cover, moulded mark, assay mark for Birmingham 1888, 6in (15cm).
£650-680 *Bea*

A pressed glass commemorative bowl, Queen Victoria's silver jubilee, 7in (18cm).
£20-25 *TS*

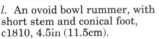

A green glass lamp reservoir.
£25-30 *TS*

> **Cross Reference**
> Commemorative
> Ceramics
> Royal Memorabilia

A Victorian blue glass posy bowl.
£30-35 *TS*

A gilded 'frigger', 'I Love a Sailor', 14in (36cm) long.
£100-180 *CB*

A red glass cornucopia, with gilding, c1880, 7in (18cm).
£20-25 *TS*

Cranberry Glass

A Victorian cranberry cut glass decanter, 10.75in (27cm) high. **£75-95** *AA*

An early Victorian heavy cranberry glass perfume bottle, 4in (10cm). **£60-70** *AA*

A late Victorian cranberry bowl, with silver plated stand, 6.5in (16cm) high. **£60-70** *AA*

A Victorian flower vase épergne, on original mirror back, 12in (31cm) high. **£150-200** *AA*

A cranberry glass ice plate, c1860, 6.5in (16cm) diam. **£50-55** *AMH*

A cranberry glass powder bowl, c1880, 4in (10cm) diam. **£100-135** *AMH*

A Mary Gregory cranberry glass vase, 4in (10cm). **£75-85** *FMN*

A cranberry glass stein, with pewter hinged lid, decorated in Mary Gregory style with a Norseman warrior, with 3 beakers, late 19thC. **£400-450** *GAK*

A shaded cranberry glass beaker, in silver holder, hallmarked Birmingham 1928, 4in (10cm). **£35-45** *AA*

Decanters

Four decanters, c1810, 6.5 to 8in (17 to 20.5cm).
£80-90 each *Som*

A Victorian cut
glass decanter,
9in (23cm).
£35-40 *TS*

A tapered decanter, the body
engraved with leaf pattern and
alternate birds and springs in
between loops and bows, bevelled
lozenge stopper, c1780, 9in
(23cm).
£250-280 *Som*

An emerald green decanter, with
lily of the valley pattern in white,
c1885, 13in (33cm).
£85-90 *TS*

A three bottle silver plated
tantalus. **£150-160** *LF*

A pair of vase shaped decanters,
with diamond and slice cut
bodies, foot rings star cut
underneath, pouring lips and
spire stoppers, c1880, 10.5in
(26.5cm).
£100-110 *Som*

l. & r. Two Victorian Stourbridge claret jugs.
c. A claret jug, 19thC, 12in (31cm).
£200-225 each *P(S)*

Paperweights

A French glass sulphide portrait paperweight, with crystallo ceramic bust of Queen Victoria, set on a blue and white spiral cushion, 3in (7.5cm). **£625-650** *Bea*

For a further selection of paperweights, please refer to Miller's Collectables Price Guide, Volume IV.

Pressed Glass

A John Northwood thread glass bowl, c1880, 5.5in (14cm) diam. **£45-50** *TS*

John Northwood invented the machine that does this threading.

Cross Reference
Colour Section

A brown cloud glass vase-on-stand, 5in (12.5cm) high. **£45-50** *TS*

A Davidson's amethyst cloud glass tray, c1922, 14in (36cm) wide. **£45-60** *TS*

A pressed glass sugar bowl, 5.5in (14cm) diam. **£8-10** *TS*

A Davidson's jet glass match striker, 3in (7.5cm). **£10-15** *TS*

A celery vase, 6.5in (16cm). **£15-20** *TS*

A Sowerby blue glass bowl, marked, 13in (33cm) wide. **£25-30** *TS*

Art Nouveau

A pair of Daum enamelled perfume bottles, with applied silver mounts. **£1,000-1,200** *ABS*

A Daum cameo glass vase, with applied decoration, c1900. **£5,500-6,000** *ABS*

A cream hand painted vase, c1900, 14in (35.5cm). **£85-90** *TS*

A Müller cameo glass lamp, c1910. **£5,000-6,000** *ABS*

Cross Reference
Lighting

A Daum cameo and enamelled vase, c1900. **£2,000-2,500** *ABS*

A Gallé triple overlay cameo glass vase. **£1,500-2,000** *ABS*

A miniature Daum cameo and enamelled vase. **£850-900** *ABS*

A blue glass vase, with raised decoration, slight damage, c1900, 10.75in (27cm). **£55-65** *TS*

A Loetz vase, with applied handles, Austrian, c1900. **£900-1,000** *ABS*

Lalique

Two René Lalique opalescent bowls:
Top. 'Ondines Ouverte', wheel cut mark, and stencilled No.380, after 1921, 8in (20.5cm) diam.
£660-700
Bottom. Stencilled mark, 14.5in (37cm) diam.
£1,900-2,000 *S*

A René Lalique perfume bottle, 'Pan'.
£800-1,000 *ABS*

A René Lalique lamp, 'Gros Poissons Vagues', the bronze base fitted for electricity, engraved mark, after 1922, 15.5in (39.5cm).
£2,400-2,500 *S*

Cross Reference
Automobilia

A René Lalique mascot, 'Tête d'Aigle', moulded mark, after 1928, 4.5in (11cm).
£800-825 *S*

A René Lalique figure, 'Suzanne', engraved and moulded mark, c1925, 9in (23cm).
£9,000-9,500 *S*

Carnival Glass

An Imperial Art Glass bowl, 6.25in (16cm) diam.
£45-50 *TS*

A commemorative plate, 'Independence Hall', 1950s, 8in (20.5cm) diam.
£25-30 *TS*

A comport, 7in (17.5cm) high.
£35-45 *TS*

A Davidson marigold basket,
c1930, 7in (17.5cm) diam.
£15-20 *TS*

A Northwood amethyst basket
weave comport, with plain
interior, 5in (12.5cm) high.
£60-70 *TS*

A marigold glass bowl, 8.75in
(22cm) diam.
£25-35 *WAC*

A Northwood strawberry and
basket weave comport, with
twisted stem, 7in (17.5cm).
£45-50 *TS*

An amethyst glass bowl, 7.5in
(19cm) diam.
£30-40 *WAC*

A green glass bowl, 8.5in (21cm)
diam.
£45-55 WAC

A Northwood
green Good
Luck bowl,
9in (23cm)
diam.
£85-95 *TS*

A marigold sugar bowl, 5.25in
(13cm) diam.
£15-20 *TS*

A blue peacock
and grape bowl,
with bearded
berry back,
8.75in (22cm)
diam.
£75-85 *TS*

20th Century Glass

A Wiener Werkstätte hand painted beaker, c1908.
£250-300 *ABS*

A Wilhelm Wagenfeld for Vereinigte Lausitzer Glaswerke A.G., 'Kubus-Geschirr', storage containers with two-handled tray, marked, 1938, tray 16.5in (42cm) wide. **£2,000-2,250** *S*

A glass tazza, on a chrome base, c1930, 9in (23cm). **£75-80** *TS*

A toothpick holder, hand painted with a snipe, 3.5in (9cm) high.
£18-20 *AMH*

A Venetian glass clown, slight damage, 14in (36cm) high.
£40-45 *WAC*

An Art Deco amber glass dressing table set, c1930, 13in (33cm).
£30-35 *TS*

An Italian glass vase, 1960s, 6.5in (16cm) high. **£20-30** *ASA*

A Kosta vase, designed by Vicke Lindstrand, c1959, 4.5in (11cm) high.
£150-170 *KAC*

An American glass bowl, with amethyst rim, c1930, 6in (15cm) diam. **£15-20** *TS*

Gramophones

A Columbia early open works phonograph, with 3 cylinders, 14in (36cm) long. **£160 185** *DWA*

An HMV mahogany table gramophone, records and needles, spring guaranteed, c1935, 18.5 by 15.75in (47 by 40cm). **£125-155** *BWA*

A Decca gramophone and needles, 16 by 12in (41 by 31cm). **£60-75** *BWA*

A gramophone, by The Standard Talking Machine Co., of Chicago, original condition, c1900, 19in (48cm) long. **£450-475** *BWA*

The first models had Finch turntables and no tone arm, i.e. the soundbox connected directly to the horn. The winding handle was removed before playing and 78 rpm records could be played, but the centre hole had to be enlarged - 10in records had not been invented.

A portable Academy 'Nippy' gramophone, 13 by 9in (33 by 23cm). **£45-55** *BWA*

Gramophone Needle Tins

A Filmophone
needle tin.
£12-14 *NF*

Gramophone needles were in use in the
UK from about 1900 until the 1950s,
but they continued to be made and
used overseas. The most sought after
needles are pre-WWI.

Gramophone needle tins are principally
collected for their rarity of design and,
as ever, condition is of paramount
importance. Slight differences in
design and wording on seemingly
identical tins are also of interest to the
collector.

Aero-Needles.
£45-55 *NF*

Rifanco Elephant needles.
£18-20 *NF*

An HMV aluminium needle tin.
£15-20 *NF*

The 4 most common needle tins,
Embassy, Columbia, Songster and
HMV.
£4-6 each *NF*

Golden Pyramid needle tin.
£18-22 *NF*

A Columbia Duragold
needle tin. **£4-6** *NF*

> **Cross Reference**
> Tins
> Signs & Advertising

A needle tin for Disc Talking
Machine.
£25-30 *NF*

Hatpins & Hatpin Holders

A Victorian elephant hatpin, 9in (23cm).
£15-20 *AA*

A Bakelite and paste Art Deco hatpin, 7in (18cm).
£20-25 *AA*

A silver and amber glass golf club hatpin, c1905, 10in (25cm) long.
£35-40 *AA*

In 1914 the length of hatpins was restricted. They had been made up to 24in long and were considered to be dangerous.

Inkstands

An Edwardian hatpin holder, 4.75in (12cm) high. £30-40 Hatpins £5-30 each *AA*

An Art Nouveau porcelain hatpin holder, 4.5in (11cm) high.
£35-40 *AA*

A silver inkstand, inscribed 'South Leeds General Election 1906 to Dr & Mrs Hawkyard, A Souvenir from Sir John & Lady Walton', Chester 1904, maker James Jay, 9.5 by 6.75in (24 by 17cm).
£600-800 *AMH*

A silver plated golfing inkstand, English, late 19thC, 8in (20cm) wide.
£450-475 *S*

A boat shaped silver inkwell, with single faceted glass bottle, hinged silver lid, Sheffield 1906.
£175-185 *GAK*

Cross Reference
Golf

An agate and ormolu inkwell, in the form of an oil lamp, 19thC, 6in (15cm) wide.
£180-220 *BWA*

A silver plated ram's horn desk stand, fitted with 2 lidded ink pots modelled as mesh patterned golf balls, 21in (53cm) wide.
£350-370 *C(S)*

A silver capstan inkwell, with reed and tie decoration to base and lid, Sheffield 1905.
£130-140 *GAK*

A silver capstan inkwell, Birmingham 1926, base 3in (8cm) diam.
£55-65 *TRU*

JEWELLERY

A Bohemian gilded brass filigree necklace, with green glass stones, c1920. **£30-40** *AA*

An Edwardian coral necklace, 16in (41cm) long.
£20-25 *AA*

A white metal and enamel pendant, c1930.
£10-20 *ASA*

l. An early Victorian 15ct gold, ruby, diamond and pearl ring.
£250-275
c. A Victorian 18ct gold, ruby and diamond gypsy set ring.
£295-325
r. An Edwardian 18ct gold, pearl and tourmaline ring, Birmingham 1912.
£150-165 *FMN*

A gold bangle, set with 11 graduated opals and 20 diamonds, one opal replaced.
£1,200-1,300 *SWO*

A Victorian rope chain necklace.
£70-100 *ASA*

A simulated pearl and paste baguette necklace, c1935. **£30-40** *AA*

A 9ct gold, amethyst and seed pearl pendant, 1in (2.5cm) diam. **£90-110** *FMN*

An Edwardian silver, seed pearl and paste pendant, 3in (8cm). **£90-120** *FMN*

A Victorian 9ct gold, peridot and pearl Art Nouveau style pendant, 1.5in (4cm). **£150-165** *FMN*

An Edwardian 9ct rose gold bracelet, Chester 1907. **£190-225** *FMN*

A Victorian 9ct gold, peridot and pearl Art Nouveau style pendant, 1.5in (4cm). **£185-200** *FMN*

An opaline glass and crystal necklace, c1940, 28in (71cm) long. **£25-35** *AA*

A Victorian filigree gilded brass necklace, with pink paste stones. **£35-40** *AA*

An Art Deco frosted amber glass necklace, c1920. **£25-35** *AA*

An Edwardian paste necklace, with faceted glass stones in brass setting. **£25-30** *AA*

A gold bracelet set with semi-precious stones. **£120-180** *ASA*

Brooches

A Victorian 18ct gold bar brooch, set with seed pearls.
£80-90 *TRU*

A Victorian 15ct gold, pearl and aquamarine brooch, 1in (2.5cm) high.
£295-350 *FMN*

A Victorian mosaic on silver brooch, 1in (2.5cm) diam.
£40-45 *FMN*

A Victorian mosaic brooch, with carved mother-of-pearl centre, 1.25in (3cm) wide.
£40-45 *FMN*

An O.B.E. enamel brooch.
£70-75 *PAR*

An Edwardian mosaic brooch, 1.75in (5cm) wide. **£30-40** *FMN*

A Victorian silver brooch, engraved with Skipton Castle, Birmingham 1892, 1.5in (4cm) wide.
£35-40 *FMN*

A silver mounted agate brooch.
£30-40 *ASA*

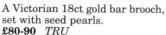

Cross Reference
Militaria

A North Devon Hussars tortoiseshell and silver brooch.
£50-55 *PAR*

A gilt metal brooch. **£30-50** *ASA*

A 15ct gold brooch, the dove of Peace carrying a branch set with 3 seed pearls.
£140-150 *HSS*

An Arts & Crafts brooch, set with shell, c1920, 4in (10cm).
£150-175 *DID*

An aquamarine and seed pearl bar brooch, 1920s, 2in (5cm) long.
£130-140 *FMN*

Art Nouveau Jewellery

A French 18ct gold brooch, by Emile Vernier, c1900, 1.5in (4cm).
£275-300 *DID*

A Murrle Bennet & Co. enamel and sterling silver bracelet, c1900. **£225-250** *DID*

A Murrle Bennet & Co. silver long guard.
£245-275
DID

Mexican Jewellery

A silver pendant.
£50-80 *ASA*

An enamel necklace, c1950.
£235-250 *DID*

A white metal and onyx square panel and link bracelet, Antonia Pineda, 1940s. **£100-150** *CSK*

A silver pendant, set with a semi-precious stone, c1900.
£70-100 *ASA*

A metal and enamel buckle.
£15-30 *ASA*

Cross Reference
Buckles

A Danish brooch, c1900, 4in (10cm). **£225-250** *DID*

A 9ct gold pendant, with mother-of-pearl centre and fresh water pearl drop, 2in (5cm) long. **£75-95** *AA*

A silver and enamel necklace.
£120-200 *ASA*

A Murrle Bennet & Co. silver and enamel pendant, 2.25in (6cm).
£250-275 *DID*

A 15ct gold and opal brooch, English, c1900.
£200-225 *DID*

A Murrle Bennet & Co.18ct gold opal ring, c1900.
£180-200 *DID*

A silver, enamel and mother-of-pearl brooch.
£50-80 *ASA*

A Murrle Bennet & Co. gold locket, c1900.
£375-400 *DID*

Liberty

A buckle, by A. Knox for Liberty & Co., c1900.
£300-350 *DID*

A silver and pearl brooch, by Oliver Baker for Liberty & Co., 1in (3cm). **£200-250** *DID*

An enamel butterfly locket, by A. Knox for Liberty & Co., c1900.
£380-400 *DID*

An Arts & Crafts pearl and turquoise brooch, 2.75in (7cm).
£135-150 *DID*

A Liberty & Co. ruby and enamel on silver pendant, c1900, 1.5in (4cm).
£200-250 *DID*

A silver and enamel Liberty & Co. brooch, c1900, 1in (3cm).
£140-175 *DID*

Art Deco Jewellery

A pair of base metal ear clips, 1.25in (3cm). **£5-7** *COL*

A simulated jade bracelet, c1930.
£15-20 *ASA*

A silver ring, set with turquoise and mother-of-pearl.
£50-80 *ASA*

A three-sectional white metal buckle, with central green glass feature. **£25-45** *ASA*

A silver and turquoise bracelet. **£120-180** *ASA*

An amber leaf shaped brooch.
£5-15 *ASA*

A silver chain necklace, with green stone pendant, c1920.
£25-30 *AA*

Bog Oak Jewellery

Cuff Links

A pair of 9ct gold cuff links, Birmingham 1939.
£65-70 *FMN*

A pair of enamel and mother-of-pearl cuff links.
£40-45 *JBB*

A pair of Connemara marble cuff links.
£25-32 *JBB*

A pair of earrings, with 9ct gold wires.   **£40-45** *PR*

A pair of Edwardian gold plated on brass cuff links, engraved with swallows.
£25-30 *FMN*

A pair of earrings, with 9ct gold wires.   **£40-45** *PR*

A pair of Edinburgh silver cuff links.   **£40-45** *JBB*

A pair of Oriental silver gilt cuff
links. **£50-55** *JBB*

A pair of enamel on brass cuff
links, c1930. **£30-35** *FMN*

A pair of dyed mother-of-pearl in
metal cuff links.
£30-40 *JBB*

A pair of 9ct gold engraved cuff links,
c1960. **£60-70** *FMN*

A pair of Art Deco enamel cuff
links. **£25-30** *JBB*

A pair of silver cuff links,
Birmingham 1902.
£35-40 *JBB*

A pair of silver and enamel rose
shaped cuff links.
£35-40 *JBB*

A pair of agate cuff links.
£30-35 *JBB*

A pair of 9ct gold cuff links,
Birmingham 1944.
£60-65 *FMN*

A pair of 18ct white gold with
diamonds cuff links.
£400-425 *JBB*

Two pairs of gold plated
on brass cuff links, with
horses and Scottie dogs,
c1940.
£12-14 each pair *FMN*

A pair of silver cuff links, c1930.
£25-30 *FMN*

Costume Jewellery

A selection of costume jewellery.
£18-70 each *JBB*

A cabochon and pearl on gilt
parrot's head brooch, from Oscar
de la Renta's Fashion Show.
£225-250 *MAS*

A Trifari eagle's head
brooch, with white and
blue paste decoration
and marquise red
paste eye.
£150-160 *CSK*

A cut glass and gilt leaf design
bracelet, by Schiaparelli, 1940s.
£150-175 *MAS*

A silver and agate bracelet, made
by Napier, 1950s.
£100-125 *MAS*

A Trifari ballerina white paste
brooch, with imitation moonstone
face, and a Boucheron imitation
cabochon, amethyst and white
paste star brooch.
£110-120 *CSK*

A Pennino coppered white metal spray brooch,
with central imitation aquamarine cluster, and
a gilt white metal ribbon scroll brooch, with
circular purple, red and white paste decoration.
£175-185 *CSK*

A silver and enamel butterfly
brooch.
£50-80 *ASA*

A pair of metal ear clips, 1930.
£3-5 *COL*

A silver dancing couple brooch,
1940s.
£30-35 *TRU*

A French heart shaped paste and
pearl brooch, c1940.
£65-75 *MAS*

A silver ballerina brooch,
1940s. £25-30 *TRU*

A silver and enamel butterfly
brooch.
£40-80 *ASA*

American Costume Jewellery

A gilt and paste mask brooch, 1940s.
£80-90 *MAS*

A gilt swirl brooch, 1940s.
£70-80 *MAS*

A gilt and paste bird brooch, designed by Schlumberger for Trifari, 1940s.
£240-250 *MAS*

A rhodium plated paste and pearl peacock brooch. **£75-95** *MAS*

A silver gilt brooch, marked Jomaz, 1940s. **£170-180** *MAS*

An enamel and paste on gilt spray brooch, by Coro, 1940s.
£140-150 *MAS*

A rhodium plated lantern brooch, unsigned, 1940s.
£90-100 *MAS*

A gilt and paste rooster brooch, by Napier, 1940s. **£140-150** *MAS*

Jet Jewellery

A Whitby jet necklace with turquoise pendant drop.
£40-45 *PR*

A Whitby jet bracelet, with gold relief. **£45-55** *PR*

A Whitby jet bracelet.
£40-45 *PR*

A Whitby jet necklace, with diamanté clasp, 14.5in (37cm) long.
£80-90 *PR*

A Whitby jet short necklace, with cross, 10in (25cm) long. **£45-50** *PR*

A pair of Whitby jet earrings, on 9ct gold drop wires.
£40-45 *PR*

A Whitby jet necklace, with bird pendant, 9in (23cm) long.
£45-55 *PR*

A pair of Whitby jet earrings.
£25-30 *PR*

A Whitby jet serpent bracelet.
£45-50 *PR*

A pair of Whitby jet long drop earrings, on gold wires.
£45-50 *PR*

A Victorian jet necklace. **£90-100** with matching bracelet. **£60-65** and earrings. **£30-35** *PR*

A Whitby jet bead necklace, with original clasp, 13in (33cm) long. **£80-90** *PR*

A Victorian necklace, possibly vulcanite, with Whitby jet cross, 16.5in (42cm) long. **£65-75** *PR*

A Whitby jet long rope of beads with cross. **£55-70** *PR*

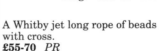

A Whitby jet link necklace, with original clasp, 11in (28cm) long. **£30-36** *PR*

Name Brooches

A silver Mizpah brooch, Chester 1889, 1in (2.5cm) diam. **£45-55** *FMN*

A silver buckle name brooch, Alice, W.J.H. registered design, Birmingham 1897, 1.5in (4cm) long. **£60-65** *FMN*

A silver name brooch, Matilda, with raised heart, Chester 1897, 1.5in (4cm) long. **£60-65** *FMN*

A silver name brooch, Mercy Ellen, CD & FD Birmingham 1896, 1.5in (4cm) long. **£50-55** *FMN*

A silver name brooch, Lydia, Chester 1898, 1.75in (5cm) long. **£60-65** *FMN*

A silver name brooch with gold edges, Sarah, Chester 1893, 1.75in (5cm) long. **£60-65** *FMN*

Scottish Jewellery

A double heart brooch, the centre symbol has romantic association with Mary Queen of Scots, c1860, 2.75in (7cm) wide. **£80-100** *BWA*

A silver and grey agate brooch, c1860. **£150-175** *BWA*

A silver brooch, set with agate and citrine star centre, c1850, 1.75in (4cm) diam. **£120-150** *BWA*

A Victorian Luckenbooth brooch, set with Perthshire agates, the centre symbol has romantic association with Mary Queen of Scots, 2.25in (6cm) high. **£150-175** *BWA*

A Celtic style silver brooch, c1930, 1.75in (5cm) diam. **£12-15** *TRU*

A Luckenbooth silver double heart brooch, c1850, 2.5in (6cm). **£70-80** *BWA*

Luckenbooth brooches were given as good luck and betrothal presents and 18thC examples often have inscriptions.

A silver and agate fouled anchor brooch, 3in (8cm) high. **£125-130** *BWA*

A Luckenbooth double heart engraved brooch, c1850, 2.75in (7cm) high. **£70-80** *BWA*

Jukeboxes & Slot Machines

● Jukeboxes from the 1940s (the 'Golden Age') have remained static in price during the past year.

● Jukeboxes from the 1950s (the 'Silver Age') have shown a steady 10-20% increase in value over the last 12 months.

The Wurlitzer model 2000 was introduced in 1956 to celebrate the company's centennial year. It was the first 200 selection model from the Wurlitzer factory.

A Wurlitzer model 2000 jukebox, with 200 selections of 45rpm records and rotary turning pages, fully restored, 55.5in (140cm) high. **£5,500-6,500** *CSC*

A Wurlitzer 1080 jukebox, with 24 selections of 78rpm records, c1947, fully restored, 59in (150cm) high. **£9,500-9,800** *CJS*

A Wurlitzer model 1100, with 24 selections of 78rpm records, fully restored, 58in (147cm) high. **£7,500-8,500** *CSC*

Model 1100 was most colourful of all Wurlitzer jukeboxes. The use of facet cut clear plastic pilasters over revolving multi-coloured cylinders caused it to be more vivid. The Gothic shaped dome offered clear visibility to the mechanism. This was the last jukebox that Paul Fuller designed for the company.

A Chantal Meteor 200 jukebox, with 200 selections of 45rpm records, c1959, restored, 59in (150cm) high. **£6,000-6,500** *CJS*

The Chantal was the only jukebox made in England.

A Seeburg KD200 jukebox, with 200 selections, rotating selection drum and automobile like fins, c1957, fully restored, 56.5in (143cm). **£3,000-3,500** *CJS*

The Seeburg model KD200 was produced in 1957.

A Rock-Ola Commando jukebox, with bird's-eye maple veneers and illuminated red and yellow front glasses, with 20 selections of 78rpm records, fully restored, 1942, 72.25in (183cm) high. **£14,000-16,000** *CSC*

An AMI Continental jukebox, with domed glass porthole revealing the record changer, c1962, fully restored, 65in (165cm). **£3,000-3,250** *CJS*

An AMI Continental II jukebox, fully restored, 65in (165cm) high. **£3,250-3,850** *CSC*

The AMI Continental II of 1962 was the last of the classics from AMI. Available as either a 100 or 200 selection 45rpm machine it was once found in many English coffee bars.

A Rock-Ola 1446 Comet jukebox, fully restored, 53in (135cm) high. **£3,500-4,250** *CSC*

The Rock-Ola model 1446 Comet was the 45rpm model for 1954. The capacity of 120 selections are housed within a carousel and the corresponding titles are hidden away on a rotary selection drum.

A Seeburg model V200 jukebox, 45rpm, fully restored, 56.5in (143cm) high. **£5,400-6,300** *CSC*

A Wurlitzer model 600 jukebox, with 20 selections of 78rpm records, fully restored, 54in (137cm) high. **£5,000-6,000** *CSC*

The Wurlitzer model 600 was introduced in August 1938 and was one of the early models that incorporated illuminated plastics.

Slot Machines

A Bryans 'Elevenses' penny play 'Allwin' machine, c1965, 18 by 14in (46 by 36cm). **£195-395** *CJS*

A Watlings 'Rol-A-Top' one-arm bandit Bird of Paradise machine, c1920. **£850-1,000** *CJS*

A Mills 'High Top' one-arm bandit, with escalator and jackpot, c1960. **£275-475** *CJS*

A Circle Skill cigarette vending machine, 1928. **£250-350** *CJS*

A Mills 'Black Cherry' one-arm bandit, c1920. **£650-850** *CJS*

A National brass till. **£275-300** *MR*

A Jennings 'The Governor' Indian head one-arm bandit, c1960. **£350-750** *CJS*

A William IV officer's gilt shoulder belt plate of the Grenadier Guards.
£300-325 *WAL*

A Victorian officer's gilt and silver helmet plate of The Prince of Wales's Volunteers, in very good condition.
£110-120 *WAL*

An officer's 1869 pattern gilt and silver plated shako plate of the 4th Royal Lancashire Light Infantry Militia.
£130-150 *WAL*

An officer's silver plated copper shoulder belt plate, East Lothian Yeomanry Cavalry, c1795. **£300-325** *WAL*

A Georgian officer's gilt and silver plated shoulder belt plate of The 3rd Foot Guards.
£525-575 *WAL*

An Irish officer's silver coloured shoulder belt plate of the Dublin Volunteers, c1795.
£450-485 *WAL*

A Georgian officer's gilt and silver plated shoulder belt plate of the Coldstream Regiment of Foot Guards, c1795.
£350-375 *WAL*

An officer's 1812 pattern diestruck copper gilt shako plate of the Yorkshire Militia.
£235-250 *WAL*

An Irish officer's copper gilt shoulder belt plate, c1795.
£350-375 *WAL*

An officer's gilt and silver plated shoulder belt plate of The Highland Light Infantry, post-1902.
£260-280 *WAL*

An Irish officer's silver plated copper shoulder belt plate of the Walworth Infantry, c1795.
£450-485 *WAL*

l. An officer's gilt and silver plated shoulder belt plate of The First Regiment of Foot Guards, c1795.
£750-775 *WAL*

l. An officer's gilt and silver plated shoulder belt plate of the Coldstream Guards, c1835.
£450-475 *WAL*

265

A Victorian officer's blue cloth shabraque of the Second Life Guards. **£900-1,000** *WAL*

A painted wood bass drum of the Royal Horse Guards, bearing Royal Arms with George V Cypher, maker's plate George Potter & Co., Aldershot. **£300-350** *WAL*

An officer's sabretache of the 11th Hussars, c1850. **£2,500-2,750** *CSK*

A post-1902 Household Cavalry trooper's plated cuirass. **£425-475** *WAL*

An officer's steel cuirass of the Household Cavalry, steel with leather and velvet, early 19thC. **£1,600-1,750** *WAL*

l. A Georgian Lieutenant General's scarlet coatee, with embroidery and gilt buttons, c1825. **£900-1,000** *WAL*

r. A Victorian officer's scarlet cloth shabraque of the Royal Horse Guards, with embroidery. **£450-500** *WAL*

l. A copper powder flask embossed as entwined dolphins. **£300-350** *WAL*

A Victorian officer's blue cloth shabraque of the 1st (Royal) Dragoons, with embroidery. **£600-675** *WAL*

r. An officer's sabretache flap of the 9th Queen's Royal Lancers, c1840 **£1,500-1,750** *CSK*

A Victorian officer's full dress sabretache of the 7th Queen's Own Hussars, 11.75in (30cm) high. **£1,000-1,100** *CSK*

A pair of 36 bore travelling flintlock pistols by Hole of Bristol, c1815, 8in (20.5cm). **£825-875** *WAL*

A 6 shot .36 Colt Navy revolver, 13in (33.5cm). **£1,200-1,300** *WAL*

A pair of 40 bore flintlock pistols, by E. Jordan, c1740, 12.5in (32cm). **£850-900** *WAL*

A flintlock blunderbuss pistol with bayonet, by Waters, c1790. **£925-975** *WAL*

A double barrelled flintlock pistol, c1820. **£375-425** *WAL*

A 16 bore New Land pattern flintlock holster pistol, 15in (38cm). **£600-650** *WAL*

A 16 bore Military Yeomanry flintlock pistol, c1820. **£425-460** *WAL*

A 6 shot .44in Remington Army revolver, 14in (35.5cm). **£800-875** *WAL*

A 16 bore double barrelled back action pistol by J. W. Edge, c1840, 11in (28cm). **£460-485** *WAL*

A flintlock pocket pistol, by T. Ketland & Co., c1820, 7in (17.5cm). **£225-260** *WAL*

A pair of 20 bore percussion pistols, by T. K. Baker, 13.5in (34.5cm). **£750-775** *WAL*

A 24 bore Tower Heavy Dragoon flintlock pistol of 3rd Dragoon Guards, 18.5in (47cm). **£900-975** *WAL*

A pair of 28 bore Irish pistols, by Skelton of Omagh, c1840, 7.5in (19cm). **£450-480** *WAL*

A Victorian officer's silver plated helmet of the Royal Horse Guards.
£2,300-2,500 *WAL*

An officer's bearskin of the Irish Guards, with St. Patrick's blue hackle feather plume on right.
£450-475 *WAL*

An officer's bearskin of the Grenadier Guards, with hair plume on left.
£600-650 *WAL*

An officer's helmet of the East Devon Volunteer Cavalry, 1812 pattern black leather with horsehair mane, c1820.
£2,100-2,200 *CSK*

A Victorian officer's silver plated helmet of the 1st Royal Dragoons.
£1,200-1,300 *WAL*

An 1843 pattern officer's helmet of the 3rd Dragoon Guards, burnished gilt skull, lined with leather.
£3,300-3,500 *CSK*

An officer's bearskin of the Coldstream Guards, with scarlet hackle feather plume on right.
£450-475 *WAL*

An Elizabeth II officer's silver plated helmet of The Life Guards, with white hair falling plume.
£1,100-1,250 *WAL*

A post-1902 officer's silver plated helmet of The Life Guards, with white hair falling plume.
£1,850-2,000 *WAL*

An Indian helmet Khula Khud, the one piece bowl chiselled overall with flowering foliage, twin plume sockets, sliding nasal bar, and tall top spike, c1800.
£780-950 *WAL*

A Scottish officer's dress dirk set, carved wood hilt, gilt metal mounts and companion knife and fork, blade 10in (25cm). **£500-550** *WAL*

l. A Georgian officer's dress dirk of The 1st Regiment, with double edge tapering blade, gilt hilt, fluted ivory grip with central band and oval cartouche engraved with thistles and crown, in its leather sheath with engraved gilt locket and chape, slight damage, blade 13.5in (34cm). **£275-300** *WAL*

r. A Cromwellian basket hilted mortuary backsword, with 32.75in (83cm) straight single edge blade. **£850-950** *WAL*

An officer's special pattern full dress brown leather pouch of The 11th Prince Albert's Own Hussars, with gilt mounts, c1830. **£800-900** *WAL*

An Elizabeth II 1865 pattern Scottish officer's military broadsword, by Wilkinson Sword, 32in (81cm) blade. **£550-600** *WAL*

A Victorian officer's full dress embroidered blue cloth pouch of the Royal Regiment of Artillery, with gilt lace border. **£100-120** *WAL*

r. An officer's sword of the Royal Horse Guards, blade with hatchet tip, by Prosser, c1832, blade 38in (97cm). **£925-1,000** *WAL*

A Victorian Rifle Volunteer officer's silver mounted presentation sword, by Pillin, etched '38th Middlesex (The Artists) Rifle Voltrs', 32in (82cm) blade, in its German silver scabbard. **£1,600-1,750** *WAL*

r. An Edward VII officer's mameluke sabre of 11th Prince Albert's Own Hussars. **£2,000-2,250** *WAL*

l. A Georgian Naval officer's dirk, curved blade 11in (28cm). **£180-200** *WAL*

r. An Edward VII 1897 pattern curved blade officer's sword of the West Riding Territorial Engineers, straight fullered blade, by Hobson & Sons, blade 32.5in (83cm). **£150-165** *WAL*

l. A Scots Guards piper's dirk Mk II, scallop backed blade, by Robt. Mole & Sons, in leather covered sheath, 11.5in (29cm). **£220-250** *WAL*

A Canton plate, depicting 'The Drunken Poet', c1830, 10in (25cm) diam. **£100-120** *BOW*

Sumida figures, Meiji period, Japanese, c1900, largest 8in (20cm) high. **£60-70 each** *BOW*

A Kutani vase, Meiji period, c1880, 8.75in (22cm) high. **£70-80** *BOW*

An Arita dish, from the Fukagawa factory, Orchid mark, Japanese, c1870, 8.5in (21cm) diam. **£60-70** *BOW*

A Satsuma Imperial style vase, Edo period, c1830. **£120-140** *BOW*

A pair of Japanese Imari vases, Edo period, c1820, 10.75in (27cm) high. **£450-500** *BOW*

l. A set of 6 Japanese porcelain plates, Showa period, 7in (17.5cm). **£100-120** *BOW*

A Satsuma 15 piece tea set, Tai-Sho period, c1915, teapot 6in (15cm) high. **£250-280** *BOW*

A Satsuma vase, mid-19thC, 12in (30.5cm) high. **£150-160** *BOW*

An Excelda gramophone, Swiss, 1931. **£140-180** *NF*

A Nirona gramophone, German, 1924. **£250-300** *NF*

A Mikiphone, Swiss, 1924. **£250-300** *NF*

A Bing Kiddyphone, German, 1930. **£180-220** *NF*

A Peter Pan gramophone, British, c1926. **£200-250** *NF*

A Pixie Grippa, by Perephone, London, 1924. **£150-200** *NF*

A Peter Pan gramophone with telescopic horn, British, 1923. **£200-250** *NF*

A Bing Pygmyphone, German, 1924. **£100-150** *NF*

An Acme miniature portable, by Nissan, c1950. **£220-280** *NF*

A Gamanette tinplate gramophone, German, 1930. **£200-250** *NF*

A tinplate gramophone, German, c1925. **£200-250** *NF*

A Chad Valley gramophone, c1950. **£100-150** *NF*

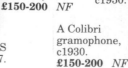

A Bingola gramophone, German, 1928. **£150-200** *NF*

A Pixiephone, from US Zone, Germany, c1947. **£150-200** *NF*

A Colibri gramophone, c1930. **£150-200** *NF*

200 Winner gramophone needles. **£12-15** *NF*

Kosmos Extra gramophone needles. **£20-25** *NF*

200 Tournaphone needles. **£18-22** *NF*

'Embassy' Radiogram gilded needles. **£14-18** *NF*

The four most common gramophone needle tins. **£4-6 each** *NF*

A circular tin of Columbia gramophone needles. **£35-40** *NF*

A tin of Submarine gramophone needles. **£45-50** *NF*

A tin of Tudor gramophone needles. **£10-12** *NF*

200 Decca gramophone needles. **£8-10** *NF*

HMV Tungstyle gramophone needles. **£18-20** *NF*

A circular tin of Dominion gramophone needles. **£30-35** *NF*

HMV Triple-tone needles. **£30-35** *NF*

A tin of Verona gramophone needles. **£18-22** *NF*

A Wurlitzer 1700, 104 selections of 45rpm, 1954, fully restored, 55.5in (141cm) high. **£4,500-5,500** *CSC*

A Seeburg 148, 20 selections of 78rpm, restored, 57in (144.5cm). **£4,000-4,500** *CSC*

A Wurlitzer 2000 Centennial model, 200 selections, restored, c1956, 56in (142cm) high. **£5,500-6,000** *CJS*

A Rock-Ola 464, c1976, 46in (116.5cm) high. **£900-1,200** *CJS*

A Wurlitzer 1015, c1946, 60in (152cm) high. **£10,500-12,000** *CSC*

A Seeburg 8800 Hitone, 1941, 63in (160cm) high. **£5,000-6,000** *CSC*

A Wurlitzer 1050 Nostalgia model, limited edition, the last 'American' Wurlitzer made, 58in (147cm) high. **£5,000-5,500** *CJS*

A Wurlitzer 750, 24 selections of 78rpm, 1941, 56in (142cm) high. **£10,000-11,000** *CSC*

A Rock-Ola 1422, 20 selections of 78rpm, fully restored, 1946, 58in (147cm) high.
£5,500-6,250 *CSC*

A Wurlitzer 1800, 104 selections of 45rpm, c1955, 55in (139.5cm) high. **£3,000-4,000** *CJS*

A Wurlitzer 10 cassette jukebox, c1974, 42in (106.5cm) high.
£1,200-1,800 *CJS*

A Rock-Ola 1428, 20 selections of 78rpm, c1948, 58in (147cm) high. **£5,500-6,000** *CJS*

An AMI model I, with curved glass windscreen, fully restored, c1958.
£3,250-3,750 *CJS*

A Seeburg V200, 200 selections of 45rpm, c1955, 56.5in (143cm) high.
£5,200-5,800 *CJS*

An AMI model A, 40 selections of 78rpm, restored, 1946, 68in (172.5cm) high.
£5,000-6,000 *CSC*

A Rock-Ola Tempo I, c1959, 60in (152cm) high.
£3,000-3,500 *CJS*
This machine featured on T.V. 'Jukebox Jury' programme

An illustrated record, 'Mademoiselle' by Chris Denver, c1930. **£30-40** *HEW*

A Mura Phone wall telephone, by G.E.C., c1950, 9in (23cm) high. **£225-275** *NOW*

An illustrated record, playing a selection from 'A Bedtime Story'. **£30-40** *HEW*

A green Ericsson 300 Series telephone, with drawer. **£250-300** *NOW*

A selection of Coronet Midget cameras, 2.5in (6.5cm) high, black **£40-50**, coloured **£80-120 each** *NOW*

A Binatone Canberra radio, c1960, 10in (25cm) high. **£22-25** *COL*

An illustrated record, playing 'Don't Blame Me', by Betty Bolton, c1930. **£30-40** *HEW*

A Neo Phone, with drawer, c1945. **£300-500** *NOW*

An illustrated record, playing 'Unless', by the Odonians Dance Orchestra. **£30-40** *HEW*

An illustrated record, 'Hold Your Man', c1930. **£30-40** *HEW*

An illustrated record, playing 'Pardon Madame', c1930. **£30-40** *HEW*

A telephone in working order, c1930. **£40-60** *WAC*

A devil's costume, comprising a catsuit and horned helmet, worn by Alice Cooper on stage c1970.
£1,400-1,500 *CSK*

A military style stage jacket, worn by Michael Jackson during the 1984 Victory tour.
£3,300-3,500 *CSK*

Madonna's crucifix pendant, Virgin Tour brochure, 1985, 3 photographs and a letter of authenticity.
£3,900-4,000 *CSK*

Derek and the Dominos D-35 Martin acoustic guitar, serial No. 263874.
Est. £5,700-8,500 *S(NY)*

Prince's custom-made perspex cane filled with translucent fluid and various shaped pieces of glitter, used on stage during the Purple Rain World Tour, 1984-85.
£1,200-1,300 *CSK*

Jimi Hendrix's Gibson Les Paul electric guitar, Serial No. 56043.
Est. £17,000-19,000 *S(NY)*

A piece of a guitar smashed by Jimi Hendrix at the Monterey Pop Festival, c1967.
£5,000-5,500 *S(NY)*

Jimi Hendrix's Hagstrom 8-string electric bass guitar, 1967.
Est. £3,500-4,500 *S(NY)*

Derek and the Dominos electric guitar, 1966.
Est. £2,800-4,000 *S(NY)*

Elton John's racoon coat, worn on his 1984 World Tour. **£3,100-3,250** *CSK*

John Lennon's Hofner Compensator steel string acoustic guitar, 1960s.
£19,000-20,000 *S(NY)*

A 1960s PVC vanity case, 10in (25.5cm) wide.
£8-10 *FAB*

A group of Dam trolls, 1961-65, 6 to 12in (15 to 30.5cm).
£10-30 each *FAB*

A psychedelic table lamp, 1960s, 10in (25cm) high.
£20-25 *FAB*

The first Rave magazine, 1964. **£15-20** *FAB*

A 1928 Mercedes Benz barometer, 1960s. **£8-12** *FAB*

A pair of platform sole shoes, 1970s.
£6-8 *FAB*

A 1960s paperweight, 3.25in (8cm) diam.
£5-8 *FAB*

A nest of 3 tables, made in U.K. **£40-50**
Four melamine cups and saucers. **£8-10** *FAB*

A copy of Vogue, September 1964.
£8-10 *FAB*

A Japanese musical cocktail set, 10in (25cm) high.
£60-70 *FAB*

A melamine dish, Harry Shaw Coaches, c1960, 5in (12.5cm) long.
£5-7 *FAB*

An enamel sign, 18in (45.5cm) high.
£100-150 *K*

A Bovril chromolithograph die-cut show card, 19in (48.5cm). **£60-80** *ACh*

A Hudson's Dry Soap chromo-lithograph, c1900, 18in (45.5cm). **£150-200** *ACh*

A Fry's Chocolate Cream Egg box label, c1930, 8.5in (21cm) square. **£25-35** *ACh*

A Phillips's Tea enamel sign, c1900, 48in (122cm) high. **£300-400** *ACh*

A Pelaw Metal Polish transfer printed tinplate sign.
£180-250 *K*

A Cadbury's paper window bill and wrapper, c1938.
£20-25 *ACh*

A tinplate advertisement for Pritchard's Health Salt Headache Drink.
£100-150 *K*

A large advertisement for Cooper's Powder Dip.
£175-200 *K*

A chromolithograph die-cut show card, c1920s. **£60-70** *ACh*

A transfer printed tinplate finger plate. **£150-200** *K*

A dummy paper wrapped biscuit tin, 1917-1920, 9.5in (24cm) square. **£30-40** *ACh*

A Spa Chocolates Squirrel Brand box, c1930, 12.5in (32cm) wide. **£20-30** *ACh*

A McVitie & Price's sample biscuit tin, 3.25in (8cm) diam. **£20-25** *ACh*

A chromolithograph dummy salmon package, c1920, 13.5in (35cm) high. **£40-60** *ACh*

A Coleman's shop size toffee tin, 8in (20.5cm). **£30-40** *ACh*

An unopened packet of Rinso, c1930, 5.5in (14cm) high. **£10-15** *ACh*

A Terry's chocolate show card, c1950, 8in (20cm) high. **£18-20** *ACh*

Kitchenalia

An early copper traveller's kettle, with fold-over handle, 5in (13cm) diam.
£30-35 *PAR*

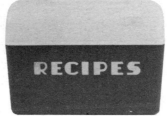

A red and white plastic recipe box.
£5-6 *AAM*

A string cutter, c1930, 7in (18cm) wide.
£35-40 *COL*

Menu Holders, 1920s, 4in (10cm) long.
£15-20 each *HEW*

A marmalade cutter, by Follows & Bate Ltd., Manchester, c1900.
£25-30 *ING*

A set of 6 painted plywood napkin holders, 1930s.
£15-20 *CSA*

A copper kettle, 11in (28cm) high.
£65-70 *COL*

A pair of old bellows, leather renewed.
£90-95 *AL*

A 'Star' vacuum cleaner, 51in (130cm) long.
£20-28 *TRU*

A pair of thistle pickle forks, Birmingham 1946, 4.5in (11cm) long.
£30-40 *TVA*

A copper pan, with brass handles, 15in (38cm) diam.
£260-270 *PAR*

A 'Black Mama' plaster kitchen notepad holder, 1930s, 10.5in (26cm) high. **£2-4** *TRU*

A copper and wrought iron stand, 34in (86cm) high. **£80-90** *AL*

A Rippingille's oil stove, c1890, 18.5in (47cm) wide.
£185-200 *AL*

A copper grog bucket, with swing top handle and fixed side handle, 19thC, 10in (25cm) diam. **£250-275** *PAR*

A copper pan and cover, with brass handles, 9in (23cm) diam. **£45-50** *PAR*

A spherical clear glass bowl fly catcher, on 3 feet, with applied ring round lip damaged. **£30-35** *BBR*

A copper stove cover, c1880, 36in (92cm) high. **£250-300** *AL*

Gas Cookers

A 'Puritan' No. 502 double hot plate, by the Florence Co., USA, the front tap rail with 2 brass taps, c1890. **£75-150** *CSK*

A brass nursery gas wall light bracket with boiling ring, c1885. **£110-150** *CSK*

The boiling ring would have been used for heating the baby's milk.

A grey enamel No. 1 'Bungalow' cooker on cast iron stand, by The Foundry Co. Ltd., Elmscott Warwick, with cast iron sides and back, 3 brass taps for 2 boiling rings and grill, c1912. **£35-100** *CSK*

A 'Talbot' hot plate, by Fletcher Russell & Co., with front tap rail for 2 burners and turnover grill, drop-in bar-type grid and white enamel base plate, c1897.
£270-300 *CSK*

Formerly in the Segas Museum, Old Kent Road Depot.

The 'Great Duck' portable deflector cooker, of sheet steel with 4 cast iron cabriole feet, 3 boiling rings, the oven, deflector oven and hotplate, c1915, 32.5in (82cm).
£155-255 *CSK*

A French blue enamel table gas cooker, 'Le Standard No. 3', by Et. Brachet & Richard, drop-down door with porcelain handle, 4 brass taps for 3 boiling rings, grill and top boiler, side tap for oven, boiling rings missing, c1900.
£110-150 *CSK*

A 'Davis Wee Cooker', by the Davis Gas Stove Co., London, with 4 brass butterfly taps for 2 boiling rings, one grill and oven, on original stand, c1898.
£660-760 *CSK*

A Main cooker, No.52, with removable burners and cast one-piece grid, c1905, 28.75in (73cm) high.
£110-200 *CSK*

Originally hired out by the Gas Light & Coke Company at 1/9d per quarter.

A 'Metropolitan' No. 211 double gas range, by the Davis Gas Stove Co., London, with 8 taps and cast plate rack, burners and grill plates missing.
£210-250 *CSK*

Two gas cookers by John Wright & Co.:
l. No. 552, with loose white enamel crown plate and cast iron oven, c1910. **£155-255**
r. A 'Eureka' No. 405, with front tap rail for 2 rack type boiling burners and grill, fixed white enamel crown plate and enamel back and sides to oven, c1907, 21.5in (54cm) high.
£385-450 *CSK*

A French amber enamel table gas cooker, 'Le Vatel' type 400, by Lilor Paris, with 6 brass taps to feed oven burner, 2 grill burners and 3 boiling burners, door to oven and oven spit, c1915. **£825-900** *CSK*

A gas range, Model 140 New Pattern, by Richmond & Co., Warrington & London, with original copper hot water urn and gas attachment, side tap rail with 6 brass taps for 5 boiling burners and grill and brass side tap for oven, 1897. **£1,100-1,500** *CSK*

Installed from new at the cost of £12 13s 6d in 1897 at G. Austin & Sons cow keepers and dairymen, 39 Brayard Road, Peckham SE15, in their milk processing room. Taken out of service Oct. 26 1989.

A circular gas cooker, by Hare & Co., with single wrought iron boiling ring on top and another in oven base, 38in (97cm) high. **£1,100-1,500** *CSK*

Formerly in the Segas Museum, Old Kent Road Depot.

A Fletcher Russell 'Celebrity' copper disc hot water heater with bracket, c1905. **£70-100** *CSK*

Keys

A 'Kater' cooker on stand, by The British Gas Appliance Co., 3 brass taps feeding the side boiling ring, grill and oven burners and turnover grill, c1907. **£105-150** *CSK*

Two Art Nouveau style pedestal table boiling burners, c1905. **£125-150** *CSK*

A selection of keys, 2 to 4.25in (5 to 11cm) long. **£8-18 each** *OD*

A selection of keys, 3.25 to 5.5in 8 to 14cm) long. **£6-22 each** *OD*

Lighting

A frosted wall light, possibly Lalique, 6 by 11in (15 by 28cm). **£80-150** *ASA*

A Victorian oil lamp with marble stand, 29in (74cm) high. **£200-300** *ASA*

An English coral satin glass oil lamp, c1880, 20in (51cm) high. **£400-500** *CB*

A copper table lamp, 1960s, 16.75in (42cm) high. **£18-22** *COL*

An Art Nouveau brass and bronze lamp, 29in (74cm) high. **£150-200** *ASA*

A cream marbled with gold Anglepoise lamp, made by Herbert Terry & Sons Ltd., Redditch, c1940. **£20-30** *ROW*

A brass lamp with a globe shade, 24in (61cm) high. **£150-200** *ASA*

A pair of gilt metal wall lights. **£250-300** *ASH*

A chinoiserie lamp, with replacement shade, 1930s, 60in (152cm) high.
£275-295 *ROW*

A domed octagonal hanging ceiling shade, decorated with pink and blue hydrangeas on green foliage, by Löys Lucha, c1929, 23in (59cm) diam, with triple silk suspension cords.
£950-1,000 *RID*

A pair of Venetian and overlaid glass lustres, hung with prism drops, one repaired, 9.5in (24cm).
£200-250 *GAK*

A crystal glass table lamp, 15in (38cm) high.
£100-200 *ASA*

A pair of Victorian red painted metal oil filled Christmas candles, with green painted holly pattern, 8in (20cm) high.
£28-32 *ROW*

A Venini clown lamp, 23.5in (60cm) high.
£100-200 *ASA*

A domed octagonal hanging ceiling shade, decorated with yellow, blue and white flowers with peacock centres, by Löys Lucha, 1930s, 23in (59cm) diam, with triple silk suspension cords.
£1,000-1,100 *RID*

A copper table lamp, filled with oil and wax, heat from bulb melts wax to give volcanic effect, 1960s, 16.25in (41cm) high.
£15-18 *COL*

An Art Nouveau spelter figure table lamp, signed at base, 'Ch Perron', Verde Antico base, 26in (66cm). **£240-260** *GAK*

A silver plated Corinthian column oil lamp, with cut glass font, 32in (81cm). **£285-300** *GAK*

An Art Nouveau wrought iron and glass ceiling light. **£300-400** *ASA*

Luggage

A Coracle four-person picnic set, the leathercloth case with fitted interior holding kettle and burner, cups, glasses, plates, cutlery, food boxes and other accessories, 1920s-30s, 22.5in (57cm) wide. **£1,320-1,500** *S*

A Drew & Sons leather cased four-person picnic set, with wicker lined interior holding kettle, pan and burner, cups, saucers, food boxes, glasses, 2 enamel plates, sugar jar, cream or milk jar and wicker covered bottle, 1910s-1920s, 22in (56cm) wide. **£360-400** *S*

A lady's trunk, covered in LV material, bound in wood, brass and leather, labelled Louis Vuitton, Paris, London 143954, lock no. 019412, monogrammed L.LL, 40in (101.5cm) long. **£1,250-1,400** *CSK*

A leather covered trunk, with card and leather fittings, mid-19thC, 31in (79cm) wide. **£100-120** *TRU*

METALWARE

Arts & Crafts and Art Nouveau

A Tudric pewter tray, for Liberty & Co.,
No. 025, c1902, 18 by 13in (46 by 33cm).
£90-100 *ROW*

A copper vase, by Roycroft, USA,
9.5in (24cm) high.
£250-280 *NCA*

A Liberty Tudric pewter tumbler
holder, designed by Archibald
Knox, 2.5in (6cm) high, with
glass. **£50-60** *HEW*

An Art Nouveau copper plant
holder, 12.5in (31cm) long.
£30-35 *OD*

A pair of copper and brass wall
vases, 9in (23cm) high.
£15-20 *OD*

An Art Nouveau initialled
silver plate hand mirror,
10.5in (26cm) long.
£75-85 *HEW*

A WMF pin tray, 4.5in (11cm)
diam.
£70-80 *NCA*

A pewter jardinière, 4.25in
(11cm) high.
£50-60 *HEW*

A Cymric matchbox holder,
2.5in (6cm) long.
£80-100 *NCA*

A Newlyn copper tray,
5.5in (14cm) diam.
£30-40 *NCA*

An Arts & Crafts
copper framed
mirror, 21 by
17in (53 by 43cm).
£70-75 *ROW*

A Newlyn copper
tray, 5.25in
(13cm) square.
£40-45 *NCA*

A Newlyn copper tray,
4.25in (11cm) diam.
£40-45 *NCA*

An Art Nouveau pewter
smoking lady wall
plaque, 7in (18cm) wide.
£40-45 *HEW*

Brass

A Victorian brass crumb scoop,
with ebony handle.
£25-30 *TRU*

A Victorian brass shoe horn, 9in
(23cm) high.
£30-35 *OD*

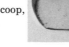

> **Cross Reference**
> Candlesticks

A brass trivet,
6in (15cm)
diam.
£18-20 *ROW*

Four brass candlesticks:
l. A French domed cylindrical
base and tall slender stem, c1600,
8in (20cm). **£475-500**
c. Dutch bell shaped base with
mid-drip pan and baluster stem,
17thC, 5.5in (14cm). **£475-500**
r. A pair of candlesticks, each
with petal base and knopped
stem, c1750, 7.25in (18.5cm).
£250-275 *S(S)*

Two brass vestas:
l. An eagle's head, 2.25in (5cm)
£70-75
r. An owl wearing a top hat, 2in (5cm).
£60-65 *GAK*

Cross Reference
Smoking

A selection of brass door knockers, Victorian Dartmoor pixie, the others 1920s, 3 to 5in (8 to 13cm) long.
£18-22 each *ML*

A pair of painted brass bookends depicting the Cutty Sark. **£40-50** *TRU*

A brass adjustable book rest, 15in (38cm) high.
£35-45 *AMH*

A solid brass backplate from a cash register, 13 by 8.5in (33 by 21cm). **£10-15** *ROW*

Bronze

Two bronze mortars:
l. Decorated in relief with 2 beaded lugs, twin handles, initialled 'T.I.', 'A.I.' and a cross, 17thC, 5.5in (14cm). **£375-400**
r. With 4 loop handles, late 16thC, 6.5in (16cm).
£225-250 *S(S)*

Copper

A bronze urn and cover by Moigney, 8.5in (21cm) high.
£120-130 *TRU*

An Edwardian coal box, with brass finial, handles and feet, 18in (46cm) high. **£90-100** *ROW*

Door Stops

Ally Sloper and Mrs Sloper, 11.75in (30cm) high. **£250-350** *PC*

Characters from a comic strip which appeared in a weekly humorous magazine Judy, in August 1867.

Mr Punch, c1870, 12.5in (32cm) high. **£100-150** *PC*

An early cast iron door stop, 16in (41cm). **£40-50** *PAR*

A cast iron lion, 6in (15cm) high. **£25-30** *ROW*

A cast iron lion, 9.25in (23cm) long. **£35-40** *ROW*

Jesus and the Woman of Samaria, c1865, 10in (25cm) high. **£100-150** *PC*

Pewter

A Queen Anne tavern pot, by William Hux, William III capacity mark, ownership initials H.I. to handle, touch in base O.P. 2498, restored, c1705, 5in (13cm).
£3,500-3,750 *S(S)*

A Sheffield pewter musical tankard, plays Marching through Georgia, 6in (15cm) high. **£50-100** *PC*

A pair of chalices, with engraved inscription dated 1736, 6.25in (16cm).
£950-1,000 *S(S)*

A William III beaded tazza, c1690, 8.75in (22cm) diam.
£300-325 *S(S)*

Two broad rim plates:
l. Continental, by Claude Morant, 9in (23cm), **£275-295**
r. By George Smith, initialled IM, touch adverso O.P. 4347, c1681, 12in (31cm).
£500-550 *S(S)*

A pair of baluster stem candlesticks, each with canted rectangular dished base, early 18thC, 6.25in (16cm).
£350-375 *S(S)*

A porringer with anchor mark flanked by initials to base, inscribed John Archer died 1740, c1680, 5in (13cm) diam.
£410-440 *S(S)*

A Queen Anne tavern pot, ownership initials EH to handle, and later engraved cartouche, c1705, 5in (13cm).
£1,500-1,600 *S(S)*

Two reeded rim bowls, both c1690, 14 and 15in (36 and 38cm) diam. **£300-350 each** *S(S)*

A Jersey lidded measure, by John De St Croix, with touch under lid and ownership SDC to handle, c1780, 10.75in (27cm).
£300-325 *S(S)*

Silver

A bosuns whistle, London 1798, T. Streeter, 4.5in (11cm) long.
£500-600 *AMH*

An Edwardian silver mounted prayer book, London 1904, 5.5 by 2.75in (14 by 7cm).
£80-90 *TRU*

A silver and ivory cucumber slicer, made by Phipps & Robinson, London 1795, 8.5in (21cm) long.
£1,200-1,400 *AMH*

A tea infuser frame, London c1830, 3in (8cm) diam.
£80-100 *AMH*

The muslin bag was fixed into the holes around the ring.

A snuff box, Birmingham 1873.
£210-230 *TRU*

A gentleman's hair brush, with engine turned silver back.
£12-15 *TRU*

A pair of boxed napkin rings, Birmingham 1926.
£50-60 *TRU*

An apple corer and fruit knife, Birmingham 1831, 6.5in (16cm) long. **£550-650** *AMH*

Two baby's rattles:
l. Birmingham 1894, 2.5in (6cm).
r. Birmingham 1902, 3.5in (9cm)
long.
£50-60 each *HOW*

A George III toast rack, Sheffield
1819, 6.5in (16cm) long.
£225-275 *TRU*

A cigar case,
5.5in (14cm) long.
£60-70 *TRU*

Cross Reference
Smoking

A pair of chased sugar tongs,
Sheffield 1906, 6in (15cm).
£20-25 *ROW*

A George III oval teapot, with
ivory handle, by James Young,
1790, with contemporary plain
oval stand, by Elizabeth Jones,
1791, 21oz together.
£500-525 *GAK*

A set of 12 Edwardian dessert
knives and forks, with ivory
handles, Sheffield 1903.
£250-270 *TRU*

A set of 6 silver and enamel
teaspoons, Birmingham 1934.
£80-90 *TRU*

A silver topped jar, Birmingham
1913.
£25-30 *TRU*

Four Victorian oval salts, with pierced sides, complete with liners, Chester 1896.
£30-35 *GAK*

An oval pap boat, with off set pourer, by Andrew Fogelberg, London 1798. **£125-150** *GAK*

A Victorian toast rack of 7 hoop design, with central ringlet carrying handle, London 1874, 9oz. **£120-140** *GAK*

A pair of cast silver salt frames complete with blue glass liners, Sheffield 1892, 5oz.
£225-250 *GAK*

A Victorian two-handled octagonal tea tray, with presentation inscription, made by Elkington & Co. Ltd., London 1890, 154oz, complete with original oak case.
£1,500-1,600 *RBB*

A 4-piece tea service, by Mappin & Webb, Sheffield 1933, 55oz.
£660-700 *GAK*

An Edwardian cream jug, with hammered finish, Birmingham 1902.
£70-80 *TRU*

An Edwardian 3-piece silver tea set, the sugar bowl and cream jug internally gilded, London 1911/13, approx. 30oz together.
£500-550 *GAK*

A Victorian presentation trowel, engraved with an inscription dated 1894, ivory handle, Sheffield 1893.
£140-160 *GAK*

A pair of sugar tongs, Sheffield 1905, 6.5in (16cm).
£20-25 *ROW*

A silver plated cocktail shaker.
£25-30 *TRU*

A George II two-handled porringer with hollow handles, marked for London 1755, maker Henry Brind, 5in (13cm) high, 16oz.
£825-850 *GAK*

Cross Reference
Drinking

A pair of George III silver goblets, bearing a crest, London c1773, 16oz.
£550-575 *GAK*

A stud box, hallmarked Birmingham 1912.
£900-1,000 *S*

Originally belonged to Harry Vardo, together with 2 postcards, one depicting Harry Vardon with trophy, the other depicting trophies.

A Charles II two-handled porringer, with maker's mark A.R. Mullet, engraved with initials, 2.75in (7cm) high, 3.75oz.
£500-550 *P(L)*

A silver mounted hip flask, Sheffield 1932, 4.5in (11cm) high.
£90-100 *TRU*

A sauceboat, Birmingham 1934.
£70-80 *TRU*

Silver Plate

Two pairs of grape scissors,
c1870.   **£30-40 each**   *CS*

A Continental electro plated
centrepiece, early 20thC.
£500-525   *DaD*

A locket containing butterfly seal.
£5-15   *ASA*

A sugar basin and shovel,
design attributed to Christopher
Dresser, 6in (15cm).
£150-200   *ZEI*

Spelter

A mirror with alabaster base,
1930s, 12in (31cm) high.
£180-200   *HEW*

A bronzed spelter figure
clock ornament with
mariner and ship's
wheel, 27in (69cm).
£175-200   *GAK*

A pair of figures,
labelled 'L'Orage'
par Bruchon,
19in (48cm) high.
£100-125   *ROW*

A pair of figurines depicting seated
Roman warriors on horseback
escorting slaves, on rectangular
matching plinths, 19thC, 17in (43cm) high.
£185-200   *GH*

A figure by Lorenzl, 8.25in (21cm)
high.
£200-250   *HEW*

MILITARIA
General

A framed advertising display of
Eley's Sporting Ammunition, 25
by 31in (64 by 79cm).
£850-875 *WAL*

A French officer's iron campaign
bed, mounted in ormolu, signed
Desouches, late 18thC, 68in
(172.5cm) long.
£7,600-8,600 *S(NY)*

*According to Harding Collection
records, this bed was used by
Napoleon Bonaparte during the
Egyptian Campaign of 1798.*

An English percussion eprouvette,
signed S. Nock, minor damage,
c1825, 5.5in (14cm).
£300-350 *ASB*

A flintlock eprouvette, measuring
wheel with 15 divisions, walnut
stock, brass trigger guard and
pommel, 18thC, damaged, 14in
(36cm) long. **£450-475** *HSS*

A German sporting crossbow for a
child, late 18thC, fitted with later
string and woollen tassels, 17.5in
(44cm). **£650-700** *S(NY)*

A model of a field gun and limber,
with bronze barrel, minor
restorations, 19thC, 24.25in
(62cm). **£1,100-1,500** *S(NY)*

Richard Simkin, Officers and Men of the 15th (King's) Hussars, 1768-1884, signed, watercolour heightened with white, unframed, 18.75 by 13.25in (48 by 34cm). **£450-475** *S*

The 15th Light Dragoons raised in 1759 and first commanded by Colonel George Augustus Eliott became known as the 15th (or the King's) Regiment of (Light) Dragoons in 1766. In 1807, in common with other light dragoons, they were called hussars. The title was simplified in 1861 to the 15th (The King's) Hussars. In 1920 they amalgamated with the 19th Hussars (Queen Alexandra's Own) and in 1933 the regiment became the 15th/19th King's Royal Hussars.

A square car pennant of the Commander-in-Chief of the Luftwaffe Reichsmarschall Göring, minor stains. **£225-250** *WAL*

No provenance, probably good post-war copy.

A brass powder and shot measure, scales to 2oz and 5 drams, c1800, 6in (15cm). **£160-180** *WAL*

Richard Simkin, The Royal Irish Fusiliers at Dublin Castle, signed watercolour, 14.5 by 21.5in (37 by 54cm). **£750-800** *S*

A framed display of Eley sporting and military cartridges. **£2,000-2,400** *S(S)*

Richard Simkin, Officers and Men of the 2nd Dragoon Guards Queen's Bays, 1687-1914, signed, watercolour heightened with white, unframed, 21.25 by 14.25in (54 by 36cm).
£500-550 *S*

A German horseman's hammer, grip replaced, early 17thC, 21in (53cm).
£1,100-1,500 *S(NY)*

A framed advertising display of Eley's sporting cartridges, 24.5 by 30.5in (62 by 77cm). **£950-1,000** *WAL*

Badges

A pre-1922 cast pouch or belt badge of the 3rd Skinner's Horse.
£80-90 *WAL*

A Victorian officer's gilt and silver plated glengarry badge of The Gloucestershire Regt., with original velvet, some wear, c1895.
£90-100 *WAL*

An other rank's brass glengarry badge of the R Anglesey Light Infantry Militia.
£60-70 *WAL*

An other rank's white metal cap badge of the 1st Voluntary Battalion The Lancashire Fusiliers. **£70-80** *WAL*

A Boer War brass slouch hat badge of Marshall's horse.
£100-110 *WAL*

A Victorian officer's embroidered forage cap badge of the Essex Regt, some wear to velvet.
£90-100 *WAL*

A pre-1922 other rank's die struck cap badge of the 119th Infantry (The Mooltan Regt).
£170-190 *WAL*

A pre-1947 officer's silver cap badge of the 16th Light Cavalry, London 1926.
£140-150 *WAL*

A pre-1922 other rank's die struck brass puggaree badge of the 1st Brahmans, brooch pin.
£65-75 *WAL*

An officer's cap badge of The Oxfordshire Light Infantry, hallmarked Birmingham 1903.
£85-95 *WAL*

A pre-1903 officer's silver plated cap badge of the 2nd Bengal Lancers and a cast brass 2 BL title.
£110-120 *WAL*

A silver cap badge of the Liverpool Pals, hallmarked London 1914.
£85-95 *WAL*

As given by the Earl of Derby to each recruit joining before 16.10.1914.

A pre-1922 silver cap badge of the 4th Rajputs, hallmarked Birmingham 1916.
£210-225 *WAL*

A cap badge of The King's Shropshire Light Infantry, gilt initials.
£60-70 *WAL*

A gilt cap badge of the Westminster Dragoons IY, brooch pin.
£70-80 *WAL*

An officer's cap badge of the Prince Albert Volunteers, by Scully, Montreal.
£95-100 *WAL*

A pre-1922 other rank's cast white metal puggaree badge of the 84th Punjabis, brooch pin.
£100-110 *WAL*

A pre-1947 officer's silver cap badge of the 1st Madras Pioneers, Birmingham 1926.
£170-180 *WAL*

An officer's cap badge of The
Royal Armoured Corps,
hallmarked Birmingham 1942.
£95-110 *WAL*

An officer's cap badge of The
South Wales Borderers,
hallmarked Birmingham 1942.
£110-120 *WAL*

A silver cap badge of the
Somersetshire Light Infantry,
Birmingham 1906.
£110-125 *WAL*

An officer's cap badge of the
90th Punjabis, hallmarked
Birmingham 1907.
£110-125 *WAL*

A Victorian officer's Maltese
Cross puggaree badge of the 31st
Punjab Infantry, hallmarked
Birmingham 1892.
£290-310 *WAL*

An officer's puggaree badge of the
16th Punjab Regt., Birmingham
1925.
£110-125 *WAL*

An officer's cap badge of the Kings
Own Royal Lancaster Regt.,
Birmingham 1935.
£130-150 *WAL*

A pre-1903 other rank's cast brass
badge of the 9th Bengal Artillery,
slide fastening.
£150-170 *WAL*

Gorgets

A Georgian officer's universal
pattern gilt gorget.
£130-150 *WAL*

A Georgian officer's copper gorget
of the Omagh Corps, retaining
traces of gilt.
£140-160 *WAL*

Helmet Plates

A Dragoon Guards officer's 1834 pattern gilt helmet plate, slight damage.
£110-125 *WAL*

A Victorian officer's helmet plate of the Ordnance Stores Department.
£170-180 *WAL*

A Victorian cadet's gilt helmet plate of the Royal Military College.
£75-85 *WAL*

A post 1902 officer's gilt helmet plate of The Royal Artillery.
£60-75 *WAL*

A Victorian officer's gilt and silver plated helmet plate of The Hampshire Regiment.
£140-150 *WAL*

A post 1902 other rank's white metal helmet plate of the 13th (Kensington) County of London Regiment.
£60-70 *WAL*

A Victorian officer's blackened white metal helmet plate of a Voluntary Battalion The Royal Irish Rifles.
£250-270 *WAL*

Shoulder Belt Plates

Bayonets

An Austrian M 1849 Augustin rifle sword socket bayonet, blade 23in (59cm).
£120-140 *WAL*

A George III officer's silver gilt rectangular shoulder belt plate of The 25th (Kings Own Borderers) Regiment.
£575-600 *WAL*

This pattern is not mentioned by Parkyn and was evidently worn about the Waterloo period and preceded the better known special scrolled pattern with slide.

A Georgian officer's die struck copper gilt oval shoulder belt plate of the St Martin's Loyal Volunteers, gilt rubbed.
£150-170 *WAL*

A second pattern sword bayonet 1843 pattern, for the Sappers & Miners carbine, socket marked '15.C.92', blade 24.5in (62cm),.
£120-130 *WAL*

A Georgian other rank's rectangular brass shoulder belt plate of The 58th (Rutland) Regiment.
£225-250 *WAL*

Daggers

A Soviet army officer's dagger, blade 7.5in (19cm).
£80-90 *WAL*

An officer's gilt and silver plated rectangular shoulder belt plate of The 96th Regiment, with original leather liner.
£225-250 *WAL*

A pre-1855 officer's gilt rectangular shoulder belt plate of The Royal Artillery.
£240-260 *WAL*

A Nazi land customs officer's dagger, by Paul Weyersberg.
£375-400 *WAL*

Dirks

Oriental

A German left hand dagger, late 16th/early 17thC, 18.75in (48cm). **£880-950** *S(NY)*

A Spanish dagger stiletto, blade deeply etched 'Fabrica de Toledo, Ano De 1880', 6.25in (16cm). **£85-95** *WAL*

A Victorian Scottish dirk set, plain blade 11.5in (29cm). **£160-170** *WAL*

A Spanish main gauche dagger, 18thC, 12.5in (32cm). **£320-350** *WAL*

A left hand dagger, early 17thC, 16.25in (41cm). **£950-1,000** *S(NY)*

A Victorian Scottish officer's dirk set of the Seaforth Highlanders, scallop back blade 10in (25cm), retaining all original polish, etched with crown, V.R. thistles, foliage, crown, 'L' elephant 'Assaye' and 'Cuidich'n Righ'. **£1,200-1,400** *WAL*

A 1st pattern commando field service fighting knife, with tapering blade of diamond section, contemporary scratched inscription 'R. Wright (E) Troop 12th Commando', blade 6.5in (16cm). **£240-280** *WAL*

A silver mounted Sumbawa executioner's kris, 19thC, blade 18.5in (47cm). **£170-190** *WAL*

A Cossack shashqa, hilt and scabbard encased in silver, blade 30in (76cm).
£1,250-1,300
S(NY)

A silver mounted Sumatran kris, with carved wood Garuda hilt, in wood sheath, 19thC, blade 12.5in (31cm).
£110-130 *WAL*

An Ngala executioner's sword, with iron wound grip, blade 20.5in (52cm).
£80-100 *WAL*

A katar from Southern India, 17thC, blade 14in (36cm).
£250-270
WAL

An Indian scissors dagger katar, 16in (41cm), with twin blades 7.5in (19cm) which open when grip bars are squeezed to reveal an inner blade.
£150-170 *WAL*

Swords

An Elizabeth II Royal Horse Guards officer's State sword, by Wilkinson Sword No. 84347, etched with 'R.H.G.', blade 37in (94cm). **£500-550** *WAL*

A George VI Household Cavalry trooper's 1892 pattern sword, by W.S.C., issue marks for 1947, blade 34in (86cm). **£170-190** *WAL*

A silver hilted smallsword, mid-18thC, blade 32in (81cm). **£650-850** *S(NY)*

A 1912 pattern cavalry officer's sword, fullered blade etched 'V.R. Pochin 2/1 Leic Yeo', 34in (86cm). **£250-275** *WAL*

A general officer's mameluke pattern sword, 1831, blade 33.5in (85cm). **£210-230** *HSS*

A French M 1822 light company trooper's sabre, engraved 'Mre D'Armes de Chatt Obre 1878 Cavrie Lre Mle 1822', curved blade 36in (92cm). **£170-190** *WAL*

An English cavalry officer's brass hilted broadsword, c1670, blade 32in (81cm). **£440-480** *WAL*

A heavy cavalry sword, c1812, straight single edge blade, 36in (92cm). **£725-750** *WAL*

A gilt brass hilted smallsword, subsequently used for mourning, c1750, colichemarde blade 31.5in (80cm). **£330-350** *WAL*

An 1821 pattern RA officer's levée sword. **£160-180** *WAL*

A German hunting hanger, mid-19thC, straight fullered blade 22.5in (57cm). **£220-250** *WAL*

An officer's 1821 pattern sword of the Victoria Rifles, blade 33in (84cm). **£95-110** *WAL*

An Indian artillery trooper's sword, issued 1915, blade 30in (76cm) with Enfield inspector's stamps. **£440-480** *WAL*

A Georgian military basket hilted sidearm, slightly curved blade, c1780, 25in (64cm).
£310-330 *WAL*

A Georgian naval officer's spadroon, retailed by Knubley, 11 Charing Cross, London, c1800, blade 27.75in (70cm).
£580-620 *ASB*

A brass hilted 1856 pioneer sidearm, saw backed blade 22in (56cm).
£140-150 *WAL*

A George VI copper gilt mounted court sword, straight blade 32in (81cm).
£170-190 *WAL*

A French Napoleonic officer's sword, c1800, straight single edged blade 32in (81cm).
£270-290 *WAL*

A German smallsword, late 18thC, with diamond section blade 35in (89cm).
£310-330 *WAL*

A Nazi era forestry official's dress hunting sword, straight single edged blade, by P.D. Luneschloss, etched 'Werwaidmannisch Jagt Wie Sichis Gehort Den Schopfer Im Geschopfe Ehrt', 12in (31cm).
£190-210 *WAL*

A George V R.A.F. officer's sword, by Burberry's Haymarket, blade 31.5in (80cm).
£400-450 *WAL*

A French AN XIII cuirassiers sword, engraved on backstrap 'Manufre Rle Du Klingenthal Obre' 1814, blade 37.5in (95cm).
£450-475 *WAL*

Medals

A naval general service medal 1793-1840, dated 1848, with one bar 'Java', awarded to Amos Batron.
£275-295 *HSS*

An RAF cross and bar group for World War II and Korea.
£1,500-1,750 *CAA*

Awarded to a Squadron Leader, complete with pilot's wings and minatures.

A World War I C.G.M. pair, awarded to Able Seaman E.J. Moore, R.N., Conspicuous Gallantry Medal, Geo. V (A.B., English Channel, 19 Feb. 1918), British War Medal, 1914-1918 (A.B., R.N.). **£1,100-1,500** *S*

Approximately 110 Conspicuous Gallantry Medals were awarded to Naval and Royal Marine Personnel for W.W.I.

A Shackleton Expedition Polar Medal pair, awarded to an Albert Medallist Petty Officer 1st Class H.E. Wild, R.N., Polar Medal 1904, 1 clasp, Antarctic 1914-16, in silver (H.E.Wild, In Charge of Stores, Aurora), Messina Earthquake, 1908, small silver medal.
£4,250-4,750 *S*

Approximately 32 such Polar Medals for Shackleton's Trans-Antarctic Expedition, 1914-1916, the Messina Earthquake Medal was for services aboard H.M.S. Lancaster.

A World War II C.G.M. group for operation agreement, Sergeant J. Povall, Royal Marines, C.G.M. Geo. VI (T./Cpl., R.M.), impressed naming, fixed suspension, 1939-45 Star, Africa Star, War Medal, Royal Marine Meritorious Service Medal, Geo. VI (Sgt., C.G.M., 28.2.1951), R.N. Long Service and Good Conduct Medal, Geo.VI (Mne., R.M.), this one stamped 'replacement'.
£5,500-6,000 *S*

A George Cross (exchange E.G.M.) group, awarded to Able Seaman G.W. Harrison, Royal Navy, George Cross, 1914-15 Star (A.B., R.N.), British War Medal, Victory Medal, 1939-45 Star, Atlantic Star, Africa Star, Defence Medal, War Medal, R.N. Long Service and Good Conduct Medal, Geo. V.
£3,000-3,500 *S*

Approximately 112 Empire Gallantry Medal recipients were entitled to an exchange George Cross at the time of the latter award's institution in 1940.

An Egypt Campaign C.G.M. group, awarded to Sergeant H. Henry, Royal Marine Light Infantry, Conspicuous Gallantry Medal, Vic., second type (Corporal, R.M.L.I.) officially impressed in large block capitals, Egypt Campaign, 1882, rev. dated, 1 clasp, Tel-el-Kebir (Corpl., R.M.L.I.), Royal Naval L.S. & G.C., Vic., 1.25ins. type (Sergt., R.M.L.I.), Khedive's Star, dated 1882.
£3,750-4,250 *S*

Approximately 250 Conspicuous Gallantry Medals have been won by Naval or Royal Marine Personnel since the award's institution in 1855, but only about 40 of these to the latter body, 10 of them for the Egyptian operations of 1882-85.

A Davison's pewter medal for Trafalgar, 1805, as struck for crew members of H.M.S. Victory.
£1,300-1,400 *S*

An O.B.E., Military Cross group, awarded to a Lt. Colonel who was Deputy Director of Supply and Transport for India. **£500-650** *CAA*

A World War II Distinguished Service Order group. **£700-800** *CAA*

Awarded to a naval Commander for sinking 3 enemy submarines.

A Boulton's medal for Trafalgar, 1805, specimen striking. **£600-650** *S*

A Waterloo June 18th 1815 medal, awarded to George Cooper, 3rd Batallion of Grenadier Guards, with ribbon and a note of the family provenance. **£250-275** *HSS*

A Royal National Institution for the Preservation of Life from Shipwreck (R.N.L.I.), awarded to Mr Richard Eddy, voted 19 March 1834, Silver Medal, Bust of George IV, reverse Lifesaving Scene, with second award boat, with integral loop and ring suspension. **£800-900** *S*

An early K.C.B., K.H. group awarded to Admiral Sir Robert Smart, R.N., The Most Honourable Order of the Bath (K.C.B.), Military Division, The Royal Guelphic Order of Hanover (K.H.) Military Division, Naval General Service, 1793, 2 clasps, Algiers (1328), Navarino (1142) (Lieut., R.N.), Germany, Prussia, Order of the Red Eagle, Knight's breast badge in gold and enamels. **£5,000-5,500** *S*

A Zulu War and Arctic Exploration pair, awarded to Abl Seaman J. Pearson, R.N., South Africa 1877, 1 clasp, 1879 (A.B., H.M.S. Shah), a later impressed issue, c1890, Arctic Discoveries, 1875-76 (A.B., H.M.S. Alert). **£1,500-1,750** *S*

Approximately 170 such Arctic Medals issued, 63 of these to H.M.S. Alert.

Uniforms

A Victorian goat hair sporran, with silver mounts, 20in (51cm) long.
£350-450 *BWA*

A Victorian officer's brown leather Voluntary Rifles. pouch of the Isle of Man
£110-130 *WAL*

A Victorian Volunteer Artillery officer's full dress shoulder belt and embroidered pouch.
£65-85 *WAL*

An officer's brown leather shoulder belt and pouch of the 27th Punjab Infantry.
£400-440 *WAL*

A Captain's full dress blue tunic, with scarlet facings of a Bengal Lancers Regiment.
£260-280 *WAL*

Headdress

A Victorian officer's blue cloth spike helmet of The Bedfordshire Regiment.
£370-390 *WAL*

A Victorian officer's full dress embroidered pouch of the Queen's Own Glasgow Yeomanry, blue cloth.
£300-350 *WAL*

A 1902-8 other rank's busby grey cloth of the Queen's Westminster Rifle Volunteers.
£220-250 *WAL*

A post 1902 officer's silver plated helmet of the 1st Royal Dragoons.
£950-975 *WAL*

A Royal Horse Artillery other rank's busby.
£150-175 *WAL*

A Victorian officer's silver plated helmet of the Second Life Guards.
£1,750-1,950 *WAL*

A post 1902 officer's blue cloth spike helmet of The Worcestershire Regiment.
£420-450 *WAL*

An Italian Marines shako, label inscribed 'Chaco Italian Army', c1910.
£150-170 *WAL*

A German Gothic sallet, c1480, 8.75in (22cm) high.
£2,350-2,750 *S(NY)*

An officer's bearskin of the Scots Guards.
£425-450 *WAL*

A comb morion, single piece construction, brass rivets restored, plume holder lacking, late 16thC.
£800-900 *S*

Pistols

A pair of flintlock turn-over pistols, unsigned, English or Flemish, c1825, 12in (31cm).
£1,600-2,000 *S(NY)*

A pair of Italian silver mounted ebony stocked flintlock pistols, late 18thC, barrels and locks refinished, 9in (22cm).
£2,500-3,000 *S(NY)*

The decoration on the barrels is probably the work of Tortiglione, c1835.

A 16 bore British New Land Pattern flintlock pistol, c1810, barrel 9in (23cm).
£380-420 *ASB*

A Queen Anne style cannon barrelled boxlock flintlock pocket pistol, by Collis of Oxford, barrel 7.25in (18cm).
£375-400 *WAL*

A 16 bore Light Dragoon flintlock holster pistol, Tower proofs, barrel 9in (23cm) . **£580-620** *WAL*

A pair of English flintlock boxlock over-and-under tap action pocket pistols, by Mortimer, London, Birmingham proof marks, c1820, 6in (15cm).
£1,400-1,800 *S(NY)*

A Queen Anne type brass flintlock travelling pistol, boxlock action, by Parkes of London, c1775, .56 brass barrel proof marked London, 12in (31cm). **£525-550** *L*

A pair of English silver mounted flintlock turn-off pistols, by Stanton, London proof marks and foreigner's mark, London silver hallmark and maker's mark of Jeremiah Ashley, c1750.
£2,000-2,500 *S(NY)*

Jonathan Stanton was apprenticed to his uncle William Turvey in 1739 and elected Master of the Gunmaker's Company in 1765.

An English cased pair of flintlock officer's pistols, by Blissett, London proof marks, c1820, 13.5in (34cm).
£1,750-2,200 *S(NY)*

A boxlock flintlock pistol, 18thC, 5in (13cm) steel turn-off barrel.
£550-580 *HSS*

A Persian flintlock blunderbuss pistol, c1860, barrel 8.5in (21cm).
£240-260 *WAL*

A .56 sea service flintlock belt pistol, Tower proved, barrel 12in (31cm). **£775-825** *WAL*

A pair of 16 bore officer's percussion travelling pistols, by Hamburger & Co. London, c1830.   **£900-950** *HSS*

An English cased pair of flintlock coat pistols, by H.W. Mortimer & Son, Gunmakers to His Majesty, 89 Fleet Street, c1810, 8.5in (21cm).
£2,000-2,500 *S(NY)*

A brass framed and barrelled boxlock flintlock pocket pistol, 6.75in (17cm), barrel 2in (5cm).
£175-185 *WAL*

A 22 bore percussion holster pistol by Harvey of Plymouth, 11in (28cm), octagonal twist barrel 6.25in (16cm).
£300-330 *WAL*

A 6-shot .28 E Whitney patent single action percussion pocket revolver, No. 1421, 7.5in (19cm), barrel 3.5in (9cm).
£400-425 *WAL*

An English 70 bore Cooper's patent 6-shot self cocking bar hammer percussion pepperbox revolver, by Reilly, London, c1855, barrel 3.5in (9cm).
£1,200-1,400 *ASB*

A 24 bore percussion travelling pistol, by Wood of Worcester, converted from flintlock, 9.5in (24cm), octagonal barrel 5in (13cm).
£290-320 *WAL*

A British Lancer style percussion pistol, Lovell's Pattern 1842 lock with crowned VR and Tower 1854 markings, barrel 9in (23cm).
£325-375 *ASB*

A 6-shot .44 Remington Army single action percussion revolver, No. 73082, 13.5in (34cm), octagonal barrel 8in (20cm).
£550-600 *WAL*

A gold plated pinfire revolver, 12mm 6-shot, 10.75in (27cm) long.
£775-800 *L*

Believed to be the property of Napoleon III.

A Wm Moore & Grey .450/.455/.476 Tranters patent double action revolver, No. 5023, 6-shot fluted cylinder, 6in (15cm) barrel, original finish, in fitted oak case. **£900-950** *S(S)*

A pair of Irish 15 bore percussion pocket pistols, signed Harris, Dublin, c1840, barrels 4in (10cm). **£1,500-1,700** *ASB*

A 4-shot self cocking Mariette patent percussion pepperbox pistol, grip strap stamped 'Mariette Brevete', 7in (18cm), turn off barrels 2.5in (6cm). **£340-380** *WAL*

A boxlock flintlock pocket pistol, 7.5in (19cm), barrel 2.5in (6cm). **£110-130** *WAL*

A cased English Colt navy, 36 calibre, No. 35761, barrel has London address, some tools. **£525-575** *L*

A 30 bore English percussion pocket pistol, retailed by Field, Oxford, c1840. **£300-350** *ASB*

A cased 12-shot pinfire 7mm revolver, serial No. 39602, in original condition. **£400-450** *L*

A cased pair of miniature percussion pistols, small paper label inscribed in script 'Pistols used in the duel between Count Swaggeras and M Bomastis', c1840, barrel .5in (2cm) long, 4mm bore. **£2,250-2,500** *S*

Rifles, Muskets & Shotguns

An India pattern flintlock musket and bayonet, c1800, musket 55in (140cm), bayonet 21.5in (54cm).
£800-850 *S*

A flintlock double barrelled fowling piece, by Charles Moore, with 30in (76cm) browned damascus barrels.
£800-900 *EP*

A 16 bore British flintlock cavalry carbine, guard with regimental marking RC CH E41, dated 1797, barrel 20.25in (51cm).
£580-600 *ASB*

Three blunderbusses:
Top. An English H.E.I.C. flintlock, c1800, 25in (64cm).
£1,100-1,200
Centre. A brass barrelled flintlock with spring bayonet, by Twigg, London, late 18thC, 30in (76cm). **£850-900**
Bottom. An Irish iron barrelled flintlock with spring bayonet, by McDermot, Dublin, c1800, 31.5in (80cm).
£850-900 *S*

A cased percussion double barrelled 2-groove game rifle, serial No.6092, 39 bore, the rib inscribed J. Purdey, Oxford Street, London, 30in (76cm) browned and sighted twist barrels, case 34in (86cm) long. **£5,750-6,000** *S*

A percussion muzzle loading shotgun, by J. Purdey, with 29.5in (65cm) browned damascus barrels.
£2,200-2,400 *EP*

A cased pair of percussion double barrelled sporting guns, 16 bore with ribs inscribed W. Dooley 11 Ranelagh Street, Liverpool, c1849, 30in (76cm) browned twist barrels, case 33in (84cm) long.
£5,500-6,000 *S*

An Alexander Henry .500 black powder express double rifle, with 28in (71cm) barrels. **£800-900** *EP*

A full stock flintlock swivel gun, signed Columbell on lock and barrel, 72in (183cm) overall, barrel 54in (137cm), **£700-750** *L*

Columbell was a gunmaker to the Ordnance, 1756, also EIC 1716, capp to Garrett Johnson 1712, trading from Parliament Street West 1763.

Trench Art

● Refers to all those domestic items produced by the armed forces during periods of inactivity, to pass the time and to give away as keepsakes.

● Made from whatever materials were to hand, often spent brass shell cases or bullets.

● Shell cases turn up as ingenious containers which often had intricate, hand worked patterns on the sides.

● Others were made into curios, such as miniature brass peaked caps or miniature coal buckets.

● Another example of trench art is seen where soldiers cut out a rectangle from a khaki shirt and inked in a scene or a rhyme. These would serve as personal greeting 'cards' at Christmas or on birthdays.

A brass container and cover, embossed with blank shield, bow and floral swags, WWI, 6in (15cm) high. **£80-90** *PAR*

A hand punched pattern container, made from shell casing, WWI. **£30-35** *PAR*

Miniature Furniture

An inlaid mahogany linen press, mid-19thC, 15in (38cm) wide.
£3,000-3,500 *S(NY)*

A rosewood bookcase cabinet, late 19thC, 17in (43cm) wide.
£2,200-2,500 *S(NY)*

A chinoiserie gilt decorated black japanned bowfront cabinet, early 19thC, 10.25in (26cm) wide.
£700-900 *S(NY)*

Cross Reference
Dolls House Furniture
& Accessories

An inlaid walnut chest of drawers, 18thC, 13in (33cm) wide.
£760-850 *S(NY)*

A George II style inlaid walnut bureau, with fitted interior, 19thC, 10in (25cm) wide.
£2,800-3,200 *S(NY)*

A Victorian tip-up table, 3in (8cm) high.
£40-45 *TRU*

An inlaid mahogany bowfront chest of drawers, early 19thC, 14.25in (36cm) wide.
£950-1,200 *S(NY)*

Money Boxes

A cast iron 'Trick Pony' mechanical bank, coin retainer missing, by Shepard Hardware Company, c1885, 7in (18cm) long.
£570-600 *S(NY)*

A 'Dentist' mechanical bank, by J. & E. Stevens Company, spring broken, c1885, 9.5in (24cm) long.
£7,000-7,500 *S(NY)*

Place coin in the dentist's pocket, press lever at his feet, the dentist extracts a tooth and the patient falls backwards depositing the coin in the gas bag. The patient falls backwards in the chair throwing his arms up.

A 'Mason Bank' mechanical bank, by Shepard Hardware Company, c1887, 7.25in (18cm) long.
£5,700-8,500 *S(NY)*

A 6d money box which when full contains £1 for a wireless licence, 2.25in (6cm) high.
£3-4 *TRU*

A treacle glaze money box in the form of a lady's head, mid-19thC, 4.25in (11cm) high.
£40-45 *OD*

A cast iron 'New Creedmore Bank' mechanical bank, by J. & E. Stevens Company, c1877, 10in (25cm) long.
£200-250 *S(NY)*

A 'Boy Scout' mechanical bank, by J. & E. Stevens Company, c1912.
£8,200-9,000 *S(NY)*

A cast iron 'Mule Entering Barn' mechanical bank, by J. & E. Stevens Company, c1880, 8.5in (21cm) long.
£1,200-1,500 *S(NY)*

Lock the mule into position and place coin between the hind legs, pushing lever activates the mule to kick the coin into the barn and a dog appears simultaneously.

A brass and mahogany money box, c1880, 10.5in (26cm) long.
£200-300 *AMH*

A 'Called Out Bank' mechanical bank, by J. & E. Stevens Company, c1900, 9in (23cm) high.
£5,200-5,500 *S(NY)*

'Paddy and the Pig' mechanical bank. by J. & E. Stevens Company, c1882, 8.5in (21cm) high.
£1,900-2,200 *S(NY)*

A 'Professor Pug Frog's Great Bicycle Feat' mechanical bank, by J. & E. Stevens Company, c1892.
£6,300-7,000 *S(NY)*

Place the coin over rear bicycle wheel, turning the centre crank makes the frog spin, depositing the coin.

A 'Santa Claus at Chimney' cast iron mechanical bank, by Shepard Hardware Company.
£650-750 *CNY*

Musical

An 'Aslanian' bird's-eye maple concert harp, 72in (182.5cm).
£1,300-1,500 *ALL*

An 'Odeon' piano accordion, c1940, 16in (41cm) wide.
£40-50 *TRU*

A giltwood and painted harp, by Sebastian Erard, London.
£1,700-1,900 *DA*

A mandolin, inlaid with a butterfly in tortoiseshell, mother-of-pearl and ivory, with case.
£80-90 *TRU*

A Gallanti Super Dominator accordion, in black and white chrome mounted Art Deco case, with rexine carrying case.
£340-380 *DA*

Mechanical Music

A French musical automaton of a girl holding a tray, Leopald Lambert, Jumeau head stamped in red Deposé, Tête Jumeau, Bte S.G.D.G., 14, late 19thC, with original tune sheet, 18in (46cm) high.
£1,700-2,200 *S(NY)*

An HMV portable gramophone in black rexine suitcase style case.
£60-70 *PAR*

> **Cross Reference**
> Gramophones

Night Lights

Two night lights:
l. A ceramic turret, with Greener base, badly matched,
r. A Spode lighthouse, 5in (12.5cm).
£25-30 each PC

A cobalt blue Queen Mary head figural night light, base embossed Eclipse Lamp, Rd No 566724, British Made, 4.25in (11cm) high.
£170-180 *BBR*

A porcelain night light holder, 8.75in (22cm) high.
£40-50 *PC*

Oriental

A carved hardwood bear, 6.25in (16cm) high.
£65-75 *TRU*

A Mongolian style coconut and white metal mounted snuff bottle, the stopper inset with coral and malachite, 3.25in (8cm) high.
£250-300 *CSK*

A Japanese jubako (picnic box) in Arita blue and white porcelain, c1900, 11in (28cm) high.
£100-120 *BOW*

These are still used particularly during celebrations.

A Chinese ivory carving of a locust and bunch of cherries on a lettuce, 9.75in (24cm) long, with plush box.
£600-650 *CSK*

A carved hardwood lion, chipped, 13in (33cm) long.
£40-50 *TRU*

Cross Reference
Militaria

A Japanese court sword or tachi, signed Seki No Ju Kani Tono Hira Kumi Tsokuru, c1890.
£1,200-1,500 *CAA*

A Korean rectangular box, decorated in mother-of-pearl, damaged, 17th/18thC, 9.75in (24cm) long.
£225-250 *CSK*

A Japanese articulated bronze model of a crayfish, 6 claws missing, 17in (43cm) long with antennae.
£220-250 *CSK*

For a further selection of snuff bottles see Miller's Collectables Volume IV pages 334-336

A Chinese crocidolite (blue tiger's eye) snuff bottle and stopper, carved as a turtle, 3.25in (8cm) long.
£190-210 *CSK*

A Chinese bamboo cylindrical brushpot, chipped, 6.25in (16cm) high.
£1,300-1,400 *CSK*

A Japanese black lacquer circular dish, inlaid in ivory, mother-of-pearl and bone, 21in (53cm) diam.
£450-475 *CSK*

Oriental Ceramics

A Japanese hors d'oeuvre set, 12in (31cm) diam, with hand painted box.
£85-95 *RFA*

A pair of Japanese Kutani figures, decorated in green, gold, black and red, mid-19thC.
£180-220 *BOW*

A Chinese blue and white meat platter, made for export to Europe, Chien Lung period, 1770, 16in (41cm) wide.
£250-280 *BOW*

An Arita soup bowl and cover, in blue, white, red and gold pattern, c1900, 5.5in (14cm) diam.
£30-35 *BOW*

A Chinese blue and white planter, depicting precious objects, mid-19thC, 7.25in (18cm) wide.
£70-80 *BOW*

Two Chinese blue and white wine cups, depicting Li Tai Po, the drunken poet with children, marked Yung Cheng, late 18thC, 2.5in (6cm) high.
£70-80 *BOW*

A Chinese blue and white plate, made for export to Europe, Chien Lung period, c1770, 9in (23cm) diam. **£40-50** *BOW*

A Chinese porcelain tea caddy, Chien Lung period, c1780, 4in (10cm) high.
£80-90 *BOW*

A Chinese soup bowl, famille rose colours, early 1900, 4.5in (11cm) diam. **£30-40** *BOW*

A Cantonese blue and white moon or pilgrim flask, c1875, 24in (62cm) high.
£500-550 *BOW*

A copy of a Ming design, used for keeping water.

Oriental Metalware

A Chinese silver dish, with dollar in base, c1930, 3.5in (9cm) diam.
£12-14 *BOW*

A Chinese silver mug, with good luck character, c1900, 2.5in (6cm) high.
£45-50 *BOW*

A Japanese silver temple gate pepper, c1920, 2.5in (6cm) high.
£30-35 *BOW*

A Japanese silver maple leaf dish, c1920, 8in (20cm) wide.   **£45-50** *BOW*

A set of Chinese silver teaspoons, c1900, 5in (13cm) long.   **£50-60** *BOW*

Osbornes & Wax Pictures

The Weavers, Canterbury, 8 by 6in (20 by 15cm).
£12-18 *FMN*

A Georgian wax portrait of a gentleman, in gilt frame with circular mount.
£170-180 *DA*

For a further selection of waxed pictures see Miller's Collectables Volume IV pages 469-472

Andrew Lumisden Esq., a profile portrait on a black oval ground, inscribed, signed and dated Tassie F 1784, gilt metal frame, 3 by 2.5in (8 by 6cm).
£325-350 *MCA*

Andrew Lumisden (1720-1801), a prominent Jacobite, became private secretary to Prince Charles Edward Stuart and was present at Culloden

Llanberis Pass, 5.75 by 7.75in (14 by 19cm).
£20-25 *JMC*

Paperweights

A granite paperweight with silver and citrine handle, 5.5in (14cm) wide.
£120-150 *BWA*

For a further selection of paperweights please see the Glass Section

Papier Mâché

A pair of red dishes, with gold stars, 6.5in (16cm) diam. **£25-30 each** *AI*

Cross Reference
Writing

A shell dish, 12in (31cm) wide.
£25-30 *AI*

A tray, 12.5 by 10in (32 by 25cm).
£20-28 *AI*

A pin tray, 5.75in (14cm) diam.
£10-12 *AI*

A tray, 10in (25cm) diam.
£20-26 *AI*

A papier mâché mirror, 9in (23cm) high.
£60-70 *AI*

A papier mâché on copper bowl, 10in (25cm) diam.
£60-70 *AI*

Patch Boxes

Patch boxes are tiny ornate containers used to hold beauty patches or beauty spots. These patches, as well as being fashionable in the 18thC, were often used to cover pox marks and scars.

A silver and agate patch box with the word EDINA, short for Edinburgh, on the lid, 1.5in (4cm) high. **£180-200** *BWA*

Photograph Frames

An English silver photograph frame, with blue velvet easel back, modern, 11.75in (30cm) high. **£180-190** *CNY*

An English silver photograph frame, with blue velvet easel back, modern, 12in (31cm) high. **£285-300** *CNY*

An English silver double photograph frame, with blue velvet easel back, modern, 12.25in (31cm) wide. **£165-175** *CNY*

Photographic Pictures

These photographic pictures are glass photographic negatives that have been hand coloured or painted on the reverse.
This method of producing very attractive and colourful pictures was popular between 1840 and 1870.

Roman potters, 14.25 by 12in (36 by 31cm). **£95-115** *AA*

These pieces illustrate how these paintings on glass negatives are produced. Once broken they are irreparable.

The figure of a girl, 21 by 16.75in (53.5 by 43cm). **£110-125** *AA*

A portrait of a lady, 9.5 by 8.5in (24 by 22cm). **£90-95** *AA*

Playing Cards

A double pack of Aircraft playing cards, 1950s. **£5-6** *COB*

For a further selection of playing cards see Miller's Collectables Price Guide Volume IV, pages 349-350.

Police

A Metropolitan Special Constabulary hat, 1936. **£28-30** *COL*

A silver Metropolitan Special Constabulary First Aid Competition badge, Birmingham 1938. **£20-22** *COL*

A Metropolitan Police, Driving School, Hendon, Certificate, 1949, 10.25 by 12.25in (26 by 31cm). **£10-12** *COL*

A silver Metropolitan Special Constabulary medal, Beckenham, c1935, in original box. **£15-18** *COL*

A Victorian brass tipstaff, with 2-piece crown soldered to body and turned ebony handle, 9.5in (24cm). **£100-150** *WAL*

Portrait Miniatures

A young gentleman wearing a blue coat over a white waistcoat and stock, by Savinien-Edome Dubourjal, signed and dated 1829, 3.5in (8.5cm) high. **£820-860** *C(G)*

Two ladies, after Plimer, in décolleté dresses, 19thC, 2.75in (7cm) high. **£375-400** *CSK*

Posy Holders

A Russian cornet shaped posy holder, engraved with a presentation inscription and name in German enclosed by flowers and foliage, with chain attached, c1900, 6.5in (16cm). **£325-375** *CSK*

For a further selection of posy holders see Miller's Collectables Price Guide, Volume I, page 305.

A lady in a white dress with forget-me-nots in her hair, with a bright-cut gilt metal mount, after François Hall, 19thC, 2in (5cm) high. **£725-775** *CSK*

A lady in a blue dress and lace bonnet with blue ribbons, German School, 19thC, 2.5in (6cm) high. **£150-175** *CSK*

An officer with grey hair and a red coat, in a gilt wood frame, mid-18thC, 3 by 2.25in (7.5 by 5.25cm). **£340-360** *P(S)*

A lady, set in the lid of a tortoiseshell box, French School, 19thC, 2.5in (6.5cm) diam. **£440-480** *CSK*

Postcards

Raphael Tuck, In the Forest, 9336 complete, a set of 6, G. **£28-32** *VS*

Raphael Tuck, Educational Series, embossed, butterflies, No. 8 complete, set of 12, VG. **£45-50** *VS*

Bridlington Lifeboat with Motor Tractor, by Photochrome, corner crease, G. **£30-35** *VS*

Raphael Tuck, Empire, 243-254 complete, Battleships, set of 12, VR. **£60-65** *VS*

Ellam, Russo-Japanese War, comedy, Hildesheimer 5243 complete, set of 6, VG. **£50-55** *VS*

H. Willebeek Le Mair, Children's Pieces of Schumann, complete, published by Augener, set of 12, VG-EX. **£65-70** *VS*

Cats, C.W.F., 793 complete, slight album corner, marks, set of 6, G. **£55-60** *VS*

Cross Reference
Ephemera
Autographs

Dogs, chromos, series 53, published by Misch & Stock, set of 3, G-VG. **£22-25** *VS*

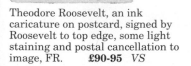

Theodore Roosevelt, an ink caricature on postcard, signed by Roosevelt to top edge, some light staining and postal cancellation to image, FR. **£90-95** *VS*

Tenterden Station, Kent, slight album corner marks, VG-EX. **£20-25** *VS*

Southend-on-Sea, Steam Lifeboat, set of 3, G. **£28-30** *VS*

Margaret Tarrant, Months of the Year, complete, some with album corner marks, set of 12, G. **£40-60** *VS*

Japan, Imperial Government Railways, views with embossed Art Nouveau surrounds, set of 3, VG. **£18-20** *VS*

The Elizabeth Simson lifeboat and Crew at Gorleston, VG. **£15-18** *VS*

New Zealand Railway Stations, black and white and coloured, set of 6, G-VG **£28-30** *VS*

Cameroons, German Period, set of 4, G. **£18-22** *VS*

London Suburbs, Stations by Spalding, G-VG, set of 7. **£65-70** *VS*

Billericay Station by Spalding, set of 3, G-VG. **£25-30** *VS*

Advertisements, a scarce set of Aviation/Balloons, from Au Bon Marché, Aviation in the Year 2000, slight scuffing, set of 8, G. **£65-70** *VS*

Crete, an unusual selection, including the 1911 Deputies, all sepia, set of 13, G-EX. **£38-42** *VS*

'CHIEF QUANAH'
Last of the Comanches

QUANAH ACME & PACIFIC RAILWAY COMPANY

USA, Quanah, Acme & Pacific Railway Co., including Red Indian, trains, etc., set of 8, VG. **£40-45** *VS*

Paddle Steamer Adverts for Cosens, set of 6, G. **£60-65** *VS*

Political, Gruss von der Maifeier, 'Freedom, Equality, Brotherhood', workers and interior of blacksmith's shop, EX. **£15-18** *VS*

Great Yarmouth Lifeboat, black and white return of Lifeboat after Skylark Disaster, set of 4, G-VG. **£30-35** *VS*

First Train in Tickhill Station, 1908, slight corner knock, VG. **£25-30** *VS*

Titanic, by Batchelder Bros., signed to reverse by B. V. Dean, survivor, VG. **£28-30** *VS* **£40-70** **unsigned** *VS*

Lifeboats at the SS Lugano Fire, by Judges, postally used 1906, VG. **£22-25** *VS*

Louis Wain

Tucks, Mascot, Series 3, 3553, The Contented Mascot, VG.
£40-70 *VS*

Tucks, Mascot, Series 3, 3553, The Meal-time Mascot, VG.
£40-70 *VS*

Tucks, Mascot, Series 3, 3553, The Skipping Mascot, VG.
£40-70 *VS*

C.W.F. Series 598, cats heads, complete, postally used, set of 6, G-VG.
£120-130 *VS*

C.W.F., 453 complete, set of 6, VG.
£110-120 *VS*

Tucks Mascot, Series 3, 3553, The Runner's Mascot, VG.
£40-70 *VS*

C.W.F. 484 complete, 2 postally used, set of 6, G-VG. **£80-85** *VS*

Tucks, Stripes to the Front, 8716, EX.
£30-35 *VS*

Tucks, Cheer Up, 8826, postally used, G-VG.
£16-18 *VS*

Tucks, Theatre Cats, 3896 complete, nos. 3885- set of 12, G.
£250-260 *VS*

Advertisement, Jacksons Hats and Boots, Cricket Game, postally used 1912, corner crease, G.
£130-140 *VS*

Write-Aways, green back, including Cricketer, Bathing, Fishing, set of 11, VR. **£130-140** *VS*

Advertisement for Jackson Boots, postally used 1908, corner crease, G.
£48-52 *VS*

Posters

Motoring

Edwin Calligan, Plas Newydd, 1936.
£170-180 *BBA*

Cross Reference
Railway Posters
Shipping Posters

Tristram Hillier, Tourists Prefer Shell, 1936. **£550-575** *BBA*

Wartime

Britian Needs You At Once, WW1, 29.5 by 19.5in (75 by 49.5cm).
£65-75 *BBA*

Abram Games, Danger, Don't Touch, J. Weiner Ltd., for H.M.S.O., c1941, 40 by 25in (101.5 by 63.5cm).
£170-180 *BBA*

Your Country's Call, Isn't This Worth Fighting For, 29.5 by 19.5in (75 by 49.5cm). **£425-450** *BBA*

Lewitt-Him, Think Twice Before Making Any Trunk Call, 1943, 28 by 36in (71 by 91.5cm).
£140-150 *BBA*

Baron Low, Everyone Should Do His Bit, Enlist Now, WW1, 29.5 by 19.5in (75 by 49.5cm).
£130-150 *BBA*

Radios & Televisions

A Mullard Master 3 radio, c1928,
21in (53cm) wide.
£75-80 *HEG*

A Pye mains radio, c1931,
18.5in (47cm) high.
£150-170 *HEG*

A G.E.C. BC3235 all electric
AC model radio, with wood
case and Bakelite grill,
c1931, 18in (46cm) high.
£150-170 *HEG*

A B.T.H. loudspeaker, 15in
(38cm) high, c1931.
£50-60 *HEG*

A McMichael super range
portable 4 radio, 1931.
£100-120 *HEG*

A Decca battery radio, c1940,
12.5in (31cm) wide.
£25-30 *COL*

A Marconiphone Model P20B
portable radio, c1948, 6.5in
(16cm) wide.   **£20-30** *HEG*

A B.T.H. speaker, c1928, 23in
(53cm) high.
£40-60 *HEG*

A Sobell cream Bakelite
portable radio, c1948, 8.5in
(21cm) high.   **£60-70** *HEG*

An Ekco U75 Consort Bakelite
radio, c1948, 14in (36cm) wide.
£60-80 *HEG*

A G.E.C. BC4750 radio, c1945, 22in (56cm) wide. **£70-80** *HEG*

This model was also produced with a TV screen in the centre.

A Premier Bakelite radio, made from a kit, c1948, 11.5in (29cm) wide. **£50-60** *HEG*

A Pye 200 Bakelite electric radio, 1948, 13in (33cm) wide. **£60-80** *HEG*

A Braun portable valve radio, c1955, 8.5in (21cm) wide. **£40-50** *HEG*

EARLY WIRELESS & TELEVISION SETS WANTED
SOME EXAMPLES OF TYPES AND PRICES PAID

MARCONI MULTIPLE TUNER
£2,000

W.W.I. TRENCH RECEIVER
£700

GEC° PHONE 2 VALVE

£400

HMV MARCONI TELEVISION

£300

BAIRD TELEVISOR
£1,500

ERICSSON 4 VALVE
£800

ALL OTHER EARLY WIRELESS/TELEVISION SETS WANTED.
ALSO HORN GRAMOPHONES, PHONOGRAPHS, TELEPHONES ETC.
MR. YATES, THE HEWARTHS, SANDIACRE, NOTTM. NG10 5NQ 0602 393139

A wartime civilian radio, made from cheapest materials, available, 1944.
£75-85 *HEG*

An Ever Ready portable painted perspex case, c1946, 14in (36cm) high.
£50-60 *HEG*

A Philco Model 527 People's Set Bakelite radio, c1936, 16.5in (42cm) high.
£250-300 *HEG*

An Ekco A22 radio, c1945, 14in (36cm) high.
£250-300 *HEG*

An Ekco transistor battery radio, 1950s, 8in (20cm) wide.
£12-15 *COL*

An Ultra Model R906 snakeskin covered radio, c1952, 14.5in (37cm) wide.
£60-80 *HEG*

A KB Model FB10 cream Bakelite 'toaster' radio, 1950, 9.5in (24cm) wide.
£80-90 *HEG*

A French Reela L'Empereur radio, green and gold metal, c1955, 21.5in (54cm) wide.
£100-120 *HEG*

An Ultra Coronation Twin Bakelite portable radio, battery and mains, 1953, 11.5in (29cm) wide.
£50-60 *HEG*

A Pye personal transistor radio, with original box and instructions, c1958, 6in (15cm) wide. **£30-40** *HEG*

A Philips Philetta gold plastic electric radio, c1955.
£50-60 *HEG*

Novelty Radios

A Keiller of Dundee tin, in the shape of a radio, 7.5in (19cm) wide. **£10-15** *HEG*

A Bambi portable radio, c1960, 5in (13cm) wide. **£20-30** *HEG*

A Minifon wire recorder, with watch microphone, West German, c1955.
£100-150 *HEG*

A boat radio, c1970, 11in (28cm) wide.
£30-40 *HEG*

An Adam & Eve radio, made in Hong Kong, c1972, 8in (20cm) high.
£30-40 *HEG*

A Radio Rex novelty toy, with original box and instructions, c1935, 6.5in (16cm) high.
£50-60 *HEG*

When you call 'Rex' the dog jumps out of the kennel.

A microphone radio, made in Hong Kong, c1989, 10.5in (27cm) high.
£15-20 *HEG*

Television

A Bush 22in (56cm) TV, c1950, 15in (38cm) high.
£200-250 *HEG*

A Bush Model TV12B, BBC Birmingham only, 1949.
£180-200 *RR*

A Bush Model T18, 12in (31cm) TV/Radio, 1938.
£500-600 *RR*

A Marconiphone Model 707, 7in (18cm) TV/Radio, 1937.
£900-1,200 *RR*

A Bush Model TV85 BBC/ITV 17in (43cm) table model TV, with Belling Lee 'Golden V' antenna aerial.
£30-50 *RR*

A Pye Model VT4, BBC/ITV 12in (31cm) table model TV, 1954. **£75-95** *RR*

A Baird Televisor, 30-line electro-mechanical television, 1930.
£1,500-1,700 *RR*

TV Related Toys

A Pye Model T102, 9in (23cm) table model TV, 1947. **£100-130** *RR*

A set of BBC Television Toys, 1959, a mobile control room, extending mast and roving eye vehicles.
£250-300 *RR*

An ivory box, depicting Leda and the Swan, 2.5in (6cm) diam. **£420-450** *CSK*

A German papier mâché tobacco box, 19thC, 5.25in (13cm). **£2,100-2,300** *CSK*

A Stobwasser papier mâché tobacco box, early 19thC, 5.5in (14cm) diam. **£3,000-3,250** *CSK*

A papier mâché snuff box, 19thC, 4in (10cm) diam. **£200-250** *CSK*

A papier mâché snuff box, with painted lid, 3.25in (8cm) long. **£60-70** *PC*

A German papier mâché snuff box, 19thC, 3.75in (9cm) diam. **£2,400-2,600** *CSK*

A tortoiseshell lined papier mâché snuff box, 3.5in (9cm) diam. **£950-1,000** *CSK*

A silver snuff box, London 1881, 4in (10.5cm) long, 6oz 15dwt. **£1,100-1,250** *S*

A silver snuff box, by Rawlings & Summers, London 1843, 3.75in (9.5cm) long. **£400-450** *S*

A George I silver tobacco box, 3.75in (10cm) long. **£2,000-2,500** *S*

A German papier mâché snuff box, the cover printed and painted, mid-19thC, 3.5in (9cm) wide. **£180-200** *CSK*

A papier mâché snuff box, early 19thC, 4in (10cm) diam. **£450-500** *CSK*

l. A papier mâché snuff box, early 19thC, 3.5in (9cm) wide. **£2,100-2,300** *CSK*

A pair of circular salts, by R. & S. Garrard, London 1907, 14oz. **£240-260** *AAR*

Two wine labels, London 1821 and 1834. **£250-280** *S*

Two George II wine labels, c1740. **£220-230** *S*

A pair of George III wine labels, London 1812. **£125-150** *S*

A silver gilt etui, c1720, 7.75in (19cm) long. **£1,200-1,400** *S*

A Victorian silver sugar basket, London, 1877, 8oz. **£240-260** *AAR*

A silver punch bowl, by William Comyns & Sons, London 1896, 10in (25cm) diam, 64oz. **£1,500-1,700** *AAR*

A pair of George III silver gilt wine labels, London 1811. **£1,500-1,600** *S*

A vinaigrette, Birmingham 1843, 1.5in (3.5cm) long. **£1,500-1,600** *S*

Companion silver gilt wine label to 'Port' label *above right*.

Three William IV wine labels, c1835. **£225-250** *S*

A pair of pierced silver salts, by E. J. & W. Barnard, London 1842, 5.5oz. **£280-300** *AAR*

A selection of Shropshire clay pipes, c1900.
£150-200 each *ACh*

A Wedgwood match striker, 3.75in (9.5cm).
£45-55 *PC*

A boot match striker, 2.25in (6cm) high.
£15-30 *PC*

A brass vesta box, decorated with a bird print, 1.75in (4.5cm) high.
£25-30 *PC*

A silver mounted Meerschaum and amber cheroot holder, 19thC.
£2,300-2,500 *S*

l. A ceramic match striker, 3.5in (9cm) high.
£25-30 *OD*

A Russian cigarette and vesta case, gilt lined, 4in (10cm) high.
£475-500 *CSK*

A mother-of-pearl vesta box, 2in (5cm) high.
£40-50 *PC*

r. A German papier mâché cigar case, painted with a portrait of Prince Albert of Saxe Coburg, c1840, 5.25in (13cm) high.
£1,400-1,500 *CSK*

An agate and silver plated vesta box, 2in (5cm) high.
£35-40 *PC*

A complete set of 176 Cracker Jack baseball cards, 1915.
£56,000-60,000 *S(NY)*

Joe Di Maggio's auto-graphed game used bat, 1941.
£10,000-11,000 *S(NY)*

1887 Detroit Baseball Club Team cabinet. **£3,200-3,500** *S(NY)*

A complete set of 66 Topps Super Baseball cards, mint condition, 1969.
£2,500-3,000 *S(NY)*

Roger Maris' 1961 All-Star base-ball bat, and his personal bat.
£14,000-16,000 *S(NY)*

59 '144 Series' Cracker Jack cards, 1914. **£3,000-3,500** *S(NY)*

1951 Bowman, No.253 Mickey Mantle, mint condition.
£8,000-8,500 *S(NY)*

Honus Wagner, Sweet Caporal Cigarettes, c1910.
£125,000+ *S(NY)*

Eddie Plank, Sweet Caporal Cigarettes, c1910.
£11,000-12,000 *S(NY)*

A complete set of 340 Topps baseball cards, near mint condition, 1956.
£3,500-4,500 *S(NY)*

Willie Mays' San Francisco Giants jersey, 1965.
£12,000-12,500 *S(NY)*

Joe Di Maggio's game worn spikes, 1941.
£4,000-4,500 *S(NY)*

The Syracuse Stars Imperial Team cabinet, 1888.
£6,000-6,500 *S(NY)*

Don Drysdale's Dodgers flannel jersey, 1958. **£2,000-2,500** *S(NY)*

1963 New York Yankees World Series ring.
£5,000-6,000 *S(NY)*

Madonna's baseball uniform.
£4,000-4,500 *S(NY)*

Ty Cobb's game worn jersey, c1922. **£47,000-50,000** *S(NY)*

 Joe Di Maggio's New York Yankees uniform, 1941.
£58,000-60,000 *S(NY)*

Sandy Koufax' Los Angeles Dodgers jersey, 1963.
£8,000-9,000 *S(NY)*

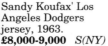

Ted Williams' Boston Red Sox jersey, 1966. **£6,000-6,500** *S(NY)*

Chicago Baseball Club, 1888, features Cap Anson.
£7,000-7,500 *S(NY)*

An unused 'Cormorant' golf ball, by G. Brodie Breeze. **£475-525** *C(S)*

An unused gutta ball, by Andrew Patrick, c1860. **£7,800-8,000** *C(S)*

A smooth gutta golf ball, c1850. **£1,750-1,850** *C(S)*

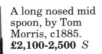

A long nosed mid spoon, by Tom Morris, c1885. **£2,100-2,500** *S*

A Wm. Park long transitional driver, with beech head and hickory shaft, c1890. **£575-625** *S*

A track iron, stamped Kilrymont, c1860. **£1,500-1,600** *C(S)*

A black-smith made track iron, c1790. **£21,000-22,000** *C(S)*

A long nosed driver, by McEwan, c1870. **£1,800-1,900** *C(S)*

A baffing spoon, by McEwan, c1870. **£3,100-3,300** *C(S)*

A feathery golf ball, by J. Gourlay, c1835. **£5,500-6,000** *S*

A feathery golf ball, 1845, 1.6in (4cm) diam. **£2,500-2,750** *S*

A Ludwig Sandison (Aberdeen) long nosed putter, c1885. **£1,600-1,800** *S*

A feathery golf ball, mid-19thC. **£1,700-1,800** *S*

A large feathery golf ball, 19thC. **£2,100-2,250** *S*

A long nosed spoon, by Tom Morris, c1885. **£3,500-3,750** *S*

An R. Forgan & Son driver, with Prince of Wales feathers stamp, c1885. **£1,250-1,350** *S*

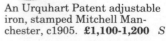

An Urquhart Patent adjustable iron, stamped Mitchell Manchester, c1905. **£1,100-1,200** *S*

A Gourlay feathery golf
ball, c1840.
£2,600-2,750 *S*

A feathery golf ball,
mid-19thC.
£1,500-1,600 *S*

A 'hoe' design putter, with
shortened hickory shaft,
stamped R. Forgan & Son,
St. Andrews, c1900.
£1,600-1,750 *S*

An Anderson patent
cross head crescent
shaped iron, c1895.
£1,000-1,100 *S*

A feather filled golf ball,
c1840.
£2,100-2,250 *C(S)*

A red painted feather
filled golf ball, c1840.
£2,750-2,950 *C(S)*

A T. Alexander feather ball,
c1830, 2in (4.6cm) diam.
£8,900-9,500 *S*

A Sir W. H. Dalrymple
hammer cross head
patent golf club,
c1892, and 2 other
20thC clubs.
£2,500-2,750 *S*

A Coste Jeu de Mail
hardwood iron bound club,
French, mid-18thC.
£10,500-11,500 *S*

Six Jeu de Mail hardwood
balls, French, mid-18thC,
various sizes.
£1,600-1,750 *S*

A Robert
Simpson driver,
c1885.
£1,000-1,100 *S*

A Thomas Dunn
short spoon,
c1875.
£2,100-2,300 *S*

A Doulton Burslem wall plaque, painted with a panel of a golfer and his caddy, 14in (36cm).
£3,600-3,800   *C(S)*

A bronze figure of The Rt. Hon. A. J. Balfour, c1894, 16.5in (42cm).
£3,000-3,300   *S*

A red playing coat, the brass buttons engraved L.G.C., for Leicestershire Golf Club, c1890.   **£950-1,000**   *C(S)*

A Royal Doulton Crombie Series Ware bowl, c1925.
£1,200-1,300   *S*

A Foley miniature crested china golfing jug, early 20thC, 1.5in (4cm).
£140-150   *S*

l. A Lenox silver mounted three-handled cup, c1900.
£4,000-4,500   *S*

A Copeland Spode stoneware decanter, 18in (46cm).
£1,500-1,600   *C(S)*

A Lenox silver mounted golfing jug, American, signed E. A. Delan, hallmarked silver rim and spout, some damage, c1898, 14.5in (37cm).
£2,400-2,600   *S*

A Burntsfield Links West End Golfing Club silver medal, c1850, uninscribed.
£1,200-1,300   *S*

A boxed putting set, c1900.
£1,800-2,000   *S*

Railways

A British Railways 'totem' station sign.
£100-150   *SRA*

An early number plate.
£300-400   *SRA*

A Great Eastern Railway station lamp top, 32.5in (82cm) high.
£250-275   *ONS*

A Pullman pen holder.
£10-15   *COB*

A selection of oval engraved free passes for the Great Northern Railway, 19thC.
£85-95 each   *DN*

An early 'Trespassers Will Be Prosecuted' sign.
£100-150   *SRA*

A cast iron Sheffield & Midland Railway sign.
£500-600   *SRA*

l. An LMS Railway lamp, c1930.
£30-35
r. A SR Railway lamp, c1930.
£20-25   *COB*

A 5in gauge live steam locomotive.
£4,500-5,000   *SRA*

A Great Eastern Railway mahogany mantel clock, inscribed Beaven London. **£485-500** *ONS*

A selection of early railway timetables. **£60-80** *SRA*

Nameplates

Bonnie Dundee, No. 2059, finished in blue, 66in (167cm) long. **£5,200-5,500** *ONS*

A Great Western Railway nameplate. **£4,500-5,000** *SRA*

A London & North Western Railway nameplate, 1904. **£2,500-3,000** *SRA*

A LMSR Jubilee Class cast brass nameplate No 5571, together with a photograph of locomotive, 20in (50cm) long. **£4,000-5,000** *ONS*

Osprey, No. 2031, finished in red, slight damage, 41in (104cm) long. **£4,500-5,000** *ONS*

A London Midland & Scottish Railway nameplate. **£13,500-14,000** *SRA*

Scottish Union No. 2025, finished in blue, 71.5in (181cm) long. **£5,000-5,500** *ONS*

Sea Eagle, No. 2039, finished in red, slight damage. 58in (147cm) long. **£4,800-5,000** *ONS*

Kestrel, No. 2030, finished in red, 43.5in (110cm) long. **£4,500-4,800** *ONS*

A London & North Eastern Railway nameplate. **£12,000-14,000** *SRA*

Railway Posters

Scot Passes Scot, LMS poster.
£350-400 *SRA*

First in the Field, New West Country Engines, by Leslie Carr, published by Southern Railway, 1945.
£225-250 *ONS*

Winter Sunshine Southern Electric, McCorquodale & Co. Ltd. for Southern Railway, 1935, 40 by 25in (102 by 64cm).
£190-210 *BBA*

A Great Western Railway poster.
£400-450 *SRA*

Dresden via Harwich, by Fred Taylor, John Waddington Ltd. for LNER, c1930, 50in (127cm) long.
£240-260 *BBA*

An LMS poster of Loch Awe.
£200-250 *SRA*

A Highland Railway poster of Strathpeffer Spa.
£250-300 *SRA*

C.W. Taylor, Explore East Anglia, Vincent Brooks, Day & Son Ltd. for L.N.E.R., c1935, 40 by 25in (102 by 64cm).
£120-130 *BBA*

Austin Cooper, Paris for the Weekend, Waterlow & Sons Ltd. for Southern Railway, 1934, 40 by 25in (102 by 64cm).
£750-800 *BBA*

Rojan, Kew Gardens, The Baynard Press for Southern Railway, 1937, 40 by 25in (102 by 64cm). **£320-340** *BBA*

British Railways Locomotives, by A. N. Wolsternholme, published by the British Transport Commission, views of 21 various locomotives of early BR period including electric, turbine, diesel and steam engines, 51in (129.5cm) wide.
£330-350 *CSK*

George Massiot Brown, While you Sleep, London-Paris by Train-Ferry, The Baynard Press for Southern Railway, 1937, 40 by 25in (102 by 64cm).
£275-300 *BBA*

Scarborough, by Fred Taylor.
£225-250 *ONS*

SKEGNESS

IS SO BRACING

Skegness Is So Bracing, by John Hassall for GNR, 1908, 80in (201cm) high.
£480-520 *ONS*

ST. JOHN'S BRIDGE
CAMBRIDGE
IT'S QUICKER BY RAIL
Full information from any L·N·E·R Office or Agency

Gwen Raverat, St. John's Bridge, Cambridge, Vincent Brooks, Day & Son Ltd. for L.N.E.R., c1935, 40 by 25in (102 by 64cm).
£180-200 *BBA*

Viola Gardner, Trunks In Advance, Waterlow & Sons Ltd. for Southern Railway, 1934, 40 by 25in (102 by 64cm).
£125-145 *BBA*

A Great Western Railway poster of Cornwall. **£400-450** *SRA*

London Transport

KENWOOD

UNDERGROUND
to GOLDERS GREEN
or HIGHGATE STATION
thence by bus 210
to "The Spaniards"
Daily every 7½ minutes

TRAM
3, 5 to HAMPSTEAD
7, 15 to HIGHGATE Rd
11 to HIGHGATE VILLAGE
from Moorgate or Holborn
Daily every 5 minutes

Margaret Calkin James, Kenwood, Dangerfield Printing Co. Ltd., 1935, 40 by 25in (102 by 64cm).
£165-185 *BBA*

TOUCHING
THE RICHES OF LONDON
BY
LONDON'S
UNDERGROUND

Frederick Charles Herrick, The Riches of London: Touching, The Baynard Press, 1927, 40 by 25in (102 by 64cm).
£165-185 *BBA*

LONDON TRANSPORT SERVICES

Public Enquiries
55 Broadway
S.W.1.

ABB
1234

FOR ALL INFORMATION CALL, WRITE OR PHONE

Tom Eckersley, London Transport Services, Public Enquiries, J. Weiner Ltd., 1945, 25 by 18.5in (64 by 47cm).
£85-90 *BBA*

GT. PORTLAND STREET OR
BAKER STREET STATION

SEE THE SHOWS OF DAHLIAS
NEAR CLARENCE GATE & ST. ANDREW'S GATE

REGENT'S PARK

Edward Bawden, Regent's Park, Curwen Press, 1936, 40 by 25in (102 by 64cm).
£320-350 *BBA*

Rock & Pop

A Columbia Records album, Born To Run, signed by Bruce Springsteen and The E Street Band in black felt pen, c1984.
£400-425 *CSK*

An original 3-sheet poster from the 1957 film 'Rock, Rock, Rock'.
£630-680 *S(NY)*

The Animals pen and ink autographs, on The Hotel George Washington stationery, 1965.
£630-680 *S(NY)*

The Animals signed the stationery at the hotel where they were staying at the time of the concert.

An advertising poster for Jerry Lee Lewis at the Tower Ballroom, New Brighton, May 1962, 30 by 20in (76 by 51cm).
£775-800 *S*

Prince's black matador style stage jacket.
£1,600-1,700 *CSK*

Accompanied by a letter from the vendor stating that Prince wore the jacket in Holland during his Parade Tour and that he threw it into the crowd during the song Kiss at the Rotterdam, Ahoy, August 19th 1986.

A Premier chrome plated snare drum, snare missing, with autographed letter signed Rick Buckler of The Jam.
£585-625 *CSK*

A concert poster for The Supremes at the Lincoln Center, Diana Ross, Florence Ballard and Mary Wilson, 1965, 37.5 by 24.5in (95 by 62cm) framed.
£2,000-2,500 *S(NY)*

A Fender Pro-Amp amplifier, serial no. 57118, the valve combo with one speaker 15in (38cm) diam., brown rexine covering and beige cloth grille, 2 Normal/Vibrato inputs.
£7,500-7,750 *S*

It is a matter for conjecture as to whether this particular amplifier may have been used by the Beatles: they were certainly using Fender equipment in the late 60s and John Lennon is pictured with a similar amplifier.

A BTR 2.A/M recording console from the Abbey Road Studios, serial no. 4465, 1950s, 31.5in (80cm) wide.
£575-600 *S*

A British Record Industry Award, Stand and Deliver, inscribed Best Selling Single 1981, Second Place Awarded to Adam and The Ants, 13 by 9in (33 by 23cm) framed.
£70-80 *CSK*

A harmonica, M. Hohner, Marine Band harp, used by Bob Dylan in his first appearance at Gerdis Folk City, and throughout the summer of 1961.
£2,200-2,500 *S(NY)*

A black and white photograph of a German group signed on the reverse by the Jimi Hendrix Experience, in black felt tip pen, creased, 8 by 10in (20 by 25cm).
£575-600 *S*

The signatures were obtained when the Experience played at the Jaguar Club, Scala, Herford on 28th May, 1967, the vendor was a member of the Other Fire and played regularly at the club from 1963-67.

A pair of Keith Moon's bass drumskins, as used in the film 'Tommy', 1974.
£2,200-2,300 *S*

A pair of Eric Clapton's shoes: turquoise leather stage shoes, by Terry de Havillard, London.
£1,200-1,300 *CSK*

Boy George's clown costume, in purple and silver lamé, 1980s.
£600-650 *S*

Donated by Boy George to raise money for the charity Shelter.

Guitars

A Gretsch Chet Atkins 6120 archtop electric guitar, serial no. 35400 in an orange finish, with hardshell case, 1960.
£1,650-1,850 *CSK*

A new Fender Squier Telecaster solidbody electric guitar, serial no. M2124601, in a cream finish, signed and inscribed 'Love God' Prince, in blue felt pen.
£2,600-2,800 *CSK*

A Kramer Axe solidbody electric guitar, serial number A5145, with black finish, signed and numbered 118/1000 by Gene Simmons, in hardshell case, 1980.
£3,500-3,700 *CSK*

A Mexican guitar, signed by all 4 Beatles, strings missing, with case, c1965.
£6,300-6,800 *S(NY)*

The Beatles

A Rickenbacker 335 semi-acoustic electric guitar, serial no. 2V237, in a sunburst finish, 1958.
£1,100-1,200 *CSK*

Two customised flight bags:
l. A B.E.A. black canvas bag, 1964, 9.5 by 13.75in (24 by 35cm).
£1,200-1300
r. A T.W.A. red plastic bag, 1965, 12in (31cm) high.
£1,800-2,000 *S*

A wood bass promotional drum, from Sgt Peppers Lonely Hearts Club Band, 28in (71cm) diam.
£1,800-2,200 *S(NY)*

A John Lennon autograph and caricature, blue felt tip pen on paper, inscribed 'Give Peace A Chance' love John Lennon 69, 3.25 by 4.75in (8 by 12cm).
£1,800-2,200 *S(NY)*

An advertising poster proof, September 16, 1964, for a City Park Stadium, New Orleans, La., Beatles concert, 22 by 13.75in (56 by 35cm).
£1,250-1,450 *S(NY)*

Elvis Presley

A 14ct gold ring with oval tiger's eye in a Florentine finish.
£5,100-5,300 *S(NY)*

A biography from a programme book, inscribed 'To Bill my respect Elvis Presley', matted and framed. **£760-800** *S(NY)*

A concert poster proof, August 9, 1956, for Pontchartrain Beach, New Orleans, LA., 22 by 13.75in (56 by 35cm).
£1,800-2,200 *S(NY)*

Queen

A black wet-look two-piece stage suit, with maker's printed label Fred Spurr stitched inside, worn by Freddie Mercury on stage, c1979. **£2,800-2,900** *CSK*

A presentation 'gold' disc, 'We Are The Champions', signed on the reverse by Peter Brown, 14.25 by 10.25in (36 by 26cm), framed.
£650-675 *CSK*

Rolling Stones

A German tour poster for Hamburg, Ernst-Merck-Halle, April 1st, 1967, 23 by 32.75in (59 by 83cm), together with 2 other tour programmes.
£3,000-3,100 *CSK*

A purple plush velvet suit, worn by Keith Richards c1972.
£800-825 *CSK*

Film Memorabilia

Charleton Heston's shirt from
Ben Hur, oatmeal coloured cotton
blouse with light blue embroidery,
Western Costume Co., Hollywood,
MGM, 1959.
£450-550 *S(NY)*

A Universal Studios, Paul
Newman's costume from Butch
Cassidy and the Sundance Kid,
label inscribed 2471//P. Newman,
mounted in a display case, , 1969.
£4,800-5,000 *S(NY)*

Sets of lobby cards:
Top: Three The Adventures of
Robin Hood, First National Re-
issue, Errol Flynn, Basil
Rathbone, Olivia de Havilland.
£150-175
Bottom: Eight The Fighting
69th, Warner Bros., 1940,
James Cagney, Pat O'Brien,
George Brent.
£250-275 *Bon*

> **Cross Reference**
> Colour Review

A Wizard of Oz costume,
emerald green felt jacket
with cream coloured
appliqué and blue/green
brocade, MGM, 1938.
£2,000-2,200 *S(NY)*

*Worn by one of the inhabitants
of Emerald City.*

A Hanna-Barbera Studios
gouache on multi-cel setup
applied to a watercolour
production background, The
Flintstones, A Night on the Town,
1960s, 7.5 by 9.5in (19 by 24cm).
£570-600 *CNY*

A Walt Disney
Studios gouache on
full celluloid applied
to a watercolour
production
background, Pooh
Gets Ready for Bed,
9 by 12in (23 by
31cm).
£1,100-1,300 *CNY*

A Walt Disney Studios, gouache
on partial celluloid applied to a
Courvoisier airbrush background,
Jiminy Cricket, Pinocchio, 1940,
9.5 by 8in (24 by 20cm).
£1,800-2,200 *CNY*

E.T.

Two plastic and metal key rings, 1.75 and 2.5in (4 and 6cm) high. **30-40p each** *PC*

Two E.T. Hugglets vinyl lapel clip-ons, 3.5 and 4in (9 and 10cm) high. **£1-2 each** *PC*

An E.T. Spaceship board game, 17 by 9in (43 by 23cm). **£10-15** *PC*

A grey pottery E.T. money box, 5in (13cm) high. **£3-5** *PC*

A battery operated grey E.T. vinyl Bendy Toy, his finger lights up red, 6in (15cm) high. **£10-15** *PC*

A talking E.T. figure, c1984, 10in (25cm) high. **£10-15** *PC*

A grey pottery E.T. figure, 5in (13cm) high. **£4-6** *PC*

A grey pottery E.T. jug, with hand painted black features, 4.25in (11cm) high. **£4-6** *PC*

A grey E.T. mug, 4.25in (12cm) high. **£4-6** *PC*

Royal Memorabilia

A silver Jubilee holder, with pull-out photographs of King George V and Queen Mary, 1935, 1.25in (3cm) square.
£12-15 *ROS*

A Davenport blue and white plate, with George III in the centre surrounded by agricultural implements.
£400-425 *SCW*

An Edward VIII unused carved foundation stone, 11.5 by 8.5in (29 by 21cm).
£40-45 *OD*

A tin tray to commemorate the marriage of H.R.H. Prince Charles and Princess Diana, 1981. **£2-3** *WAC*

> **Cross Reference**
> Ceramics
> Commemorative Ware

A bronze King Edward VIII wall plaque, 9in (23cm) diam. **£90-110** *COB*

A Paragon mug with a portrait of Prince Charles aged 4 years, produced at the time of his mother's Coronation, 1953.
£100-110 *SCW*

A Berwickshire Railway presentation ceremonial spade, dated 1862, 36in (92cm) long.
£720-750 *S*

The first turf of the Berwickshire Railway was cut with this spade by Lady Campbell, Tuesday 14th October, 1862.

A Mayer's cyclamen pink loving cup, with multi-colour underglaze print of Edward and Alexandra to commemorate their wedding in 1863, 5in (13cm) high. **£700-725** *SCW*

Ten chromo plated illustrations from a Wills hard back book to commemorate Queen Victoria's Diamond Jubilee, June 22nd 1897. **£160-180** *VS*

Scales, Balances & Weights

A Royal Copenhagen plate, commemorating the 40th Jubilee of King Christian IX, the father of Queen Alexandra. **£150-160** *SCW*

A set of 10 brass bell weights, stamped Oxon, 19thC, 14lb-1oz. **£450-475** *CSK*

A black enamelled and lacquered brass electric balance, signed Lord Kelvins' Patents Electric Balance No. 694, James White Glasgow and London, 22in (56cm) wide. **£240-260** *CSK*

A beam balance jockey scale, by W. & T. Avery & Co., Birmingham, with leather covered wood seat, c1900, base 71.5in (180cm) wide. **£3,000-3,250** *CSK*

A set of 6 Wedgwood china weights. **£660-720** *SUF*

A set of 5 Burmese bronze 'chicken' weights, and a companion set of 6 'duck' weights. **£275-300** *CSK*

Scientific Instruments

A boxwood nocturnal dial, index arm and rotating disc stamped with lunar and solar scales, with two projecting lugs inscribed 'G' and 'L' for Great and Little Bear, the reverse with points of the compass, 18thC, 10in (25cm) high.
£1,500-1,700 *HSS*

An oxidised and lacquered brass aneroid barometer, signed J. Goldschmid à Zurich No. 445, in fitted leather covered case, 6in (15cm) wide.
£420-450 *CSK*

A Thatcher's rotary calculator, by Keuffel & Esser, New York, No. 4012, with instructions on baseboard and mahogany case with label in lid, 24in (61cm) wide.
£575-600 *CSK*

A lacquered brass barograph, unsigned, in a glazed mahogany case with chart drawer, 15in (38cm) wide.
£600-625 *CSK*

A pocket barometer with case, by Negretti & Zambra, with inches, millibars and feet, c1880, 3in (7.5cm) diam.
£80-100 *BWA*

A child's Magic Lantern, German, made for Gamages, with coloured strips and slipping slides, in original box.
£100-120 *HEG*

A Palmer's Computing Scale, revolving printed card dial, with gilt tooled leather border, 11in (28cm) square.
£135-150 *CSK*

A Curta Type 1 calculator, sectioned for display with separate components, in fitted case, by Contina, Liechtenstein.
£650-700 *CSK*

A lacquered brass diamond frame sextant, by Troughton & Simms London Platina 3523, in fitted mahogany case, 13.5in (34.5cm) wide. **£550-575** *CSK*

A Slater's Improved Armillary Sphere, late 19thC, overall height 13in (33cm). **£650-675** *C*

A Persian Celestial globe, unsigned, 19thC, stand probably later, overall height 12in (30cm). **£1,900-2,200** *C*

The inclusion of planetary positions makes this sphere unique among Islamic celestial globes.

Globes

A metal celestial globe, probably Indo-Persian, unsigned and undated, overall height 11in (28cm). **£2,250-2,500** *C*

A miniature terrestrial globe in English, by Rand McNaley & Co., 5in (13cm) high. **£110-130** *CSK*

A terrestrial pocket globe, by Jacob and Halse, London, 1809, 3in (7cm) diam. **£1,600-1,800** *C*

A Geographic Educator terrestrial globe, American, with track of the trans-Atlantic flights of Lindbergh and Chamberlain dividing into 7 sections containing jig-saw puzzles of the Continents, one piece missing, 11in (28cm) high. **£225-250** *CSK*

A 'sphere terrestre' children's game, by R. Barbot, published for the Ministère de l'Instruction Publique, the globe on a Paris prime meridian, decorated with the paper flags of 24 nations and tracks of the principal steamship routes, in original box with instruction sheet, overall height 11in (28cm). **£1,200-1,400** *C*

A New Portable Terrestrial Globe, by John Betts, London, collapsing globe, c1860, 15in (38cm) diam. **£400-440** *C*

The first issue of the Betts umbrella globe; Betts died c1863, and the publication of the globe was taken up by George Philip & Son in 1880.

Microscopes

A mahogany slide cabinet of 21 drawers with bone handles, with many slide preparations, 19thC, 14.5in (37cm) high. **£1,100-1,200** *CSK*

An oxidised and lacquered brass microscope, signed W. Watson & Son, 313 High Holborn, London, No. 6641, with accessories, c1900, 13in (33cm) high. **£500-550** *CSK*

A lacquered brass compound binocular microscope, signed on the stand J. B. Dancer, optician, Manchester, No. 407, 19thC, in mahogany case, 18in (45.5cm) high. **£950-1,100** *C*

Surveying

A brass surveying compass, signed S. Thaxter & Sons, Boston, with maker's trade label, in fitted mahogany case, 19thC, 15.5in (39.5cm) wide, with tripod. **£220-240** *CSK*

A lacquered brass theodolite, signed Cary London, in fitted mahogany case with accessories, late 18th/early 19thC, 9in (22.5cm) wide. **£1,100-1,250** *CSK*

A lacquered brass surveyor's cross, signed W. & T. Gilbert, London, in mahogany case, 19thC, 5in (12cm) wide. **£480-520** *CSK*

A lacquered brass surveying compass, signed W. & L. E. Gurley, Troy, N.Y., in fitted mahogany case with maker's trade label, 16.5in (42cm) wide. **£275-295** *CSK*

Telescopes

A four draw telescope, unsigned, object glass 1in diam., shagreen covered outer body tube cover, 18thC, 12.5in (32cm) long closed. **£850-900** *C*

A lacquered brass 3in refracting telescope, signed Newton & Co., 41.25in (105cm) long body tube, in fitted mahogany case with accessories, 19thC. **£1,750-1,850** *C*

A lacquered brass 2.25in refracting portable telescope, signed Cary London Francis E. James from A.H.H. 1903, 29in (74cm) body, in fitted mahogany case. **£1,500-1,600** *C*

A 3in reflecting telescope, signed on the back plate, James Short London, c1747, in mahogany veneered oak carrying case. **£1,850-1,950** *CSK*

A brass 2in reflecting telescope, unsigned, simulated fishskin covered, 14in (35.5cm) long body tube, late 18thC, in oak case. **£775-825** *CSK*

Stereoscopes

A Brewster pattern walnut stereoscope. **£150-160** *HEG*

A wood Sunscope, folds down to fit into card box, with boxed views, 1920. **£140-160** *HEG*

A Jules Rickard stereoscopic slide projector, contained in a fitted case together with slides, spectacles and spare bulbs. **£220-240** *HSS*

A stereoscopic viewer and cards, c1860. **£250-300** *LBL*

A collection of stereo cards of South Africa, 1900.
£50-60 *BBA*

A Holmes viewer, with wood body,
and 12 cards, 1895. **£35-45** *HEG*

A Holmes viewer, with aluminium body, and
12 cards, 1905. **£35-45** *HEG*

A talking View-
Master stereoscope,
with Flipper story
and music, c1960.
£10-12 *HEG*

A boxed set of 100 Boar War
stereograms, 1901.
£100-120 *HEG*

A Camerascope,
the cards given
with Army Club
cigarettes, c1920s.
£20-30
Cards 40p a pair
HEG

A Stitz Auto illuminated viewer,
1960s.
£45-55 *HEG*

A novelty
Vistascreen
stereoscope,
with boxed
stereograms,
c1950.
£15-20 *HEG*

A View-Master
stereoscope, with
3 picture reels,
1954. **£8-10** *HEG*

Medical Instruments

A Millikin & Lawley half-disarticulated human skeleton.
£75-85 *HCH*

A pharmacist's brass table for folding powder papers, 19thC, 2.75in (7cm) wide.
£20-30 *MRT*

A burnished steel tooth key, with claw and chequer grip ivory handle, and 2 shaped elevators with chequer grip bone handles.
£220-240 *CSK*

A hearing trumpet.
£100-110 *BWA*

A pharmacist's boxwood pill rounder, 19thC, 3in (8cm) diam.
£25-35 *MRT*

A porcelain phrenological bust, impressed mark by F. Bridges Phrenologist, 19thC, 5.5in (14cm) high.
£650-675 *CSK*

A hearing trumpet, 11.5in (29.5cm) long.
£100-140 *BWA*

A 13 second glass pulse taker, in boxwood case, 19thC, 7in (18cm) long.
£35-45 *MRT*

A surgeon's amputation set, signed Laundy, in fitted velvet lined mahogany case, large bone saw missing, c1800, 16in (41cm) wide. **£675-725** *CSK*

A glass syringe, in boxwood case, 19thC, 9in (23cm) long.
£35-45 *MRT*

A surgeon's silver plated bullet prober, mid-19thC, 9.5in (24cm) long. **£40-50** *BWA*

A male contraceptive device, of animal membrane, with printed satirical scene, inscription 'Voila mon choix', and thread and silk tie, French, early 19thC, 8in (20cm) long. **£3,500-4,000** *CSK*

Male contraceptives were first alluded to in the 11thC by a Greek writer Antoninus Liberalis. In the 16thC Gabriel Fallope suggested the use of a 'fine linen bag' and a preparation of astringent herbs. Colonel Cundum is said to have invented the dried gut of sheep worn by men in the act of coition to prevent venereal infection c1700.

A brass adjustable leg splint, with foot support, with locking screw, 19thC, 20in (51cm) high. **£125-150** *CSK*

A Dr. Nelson inhaler, 9.5in (24cm) high. **£25-30** *ROS*

A hanging lifesize instructional print of a human skeleton, flanked by sectional illustrations, on paper, some tears, 76in (193cm) long. **£150-175** *CSK*

A pharmacist's rosewood handled poultice iron, 19thC, 11.5in (29.5cm) long. **£20-30** *MRT*

A pharmacist's turned boxwood double-ended powder measure, late 19thC, 3.5in (9cm) high. **£35-45** *MRT*

Spectacles

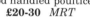

A pair of Chinese lacquered frame spectacles, brass cased folding bridge, possibly 18thC, 4.5in (11.5cm) wide. **£720-750** *CSK*

A pair of Golding spectacles, with a tortoiseshell case, 19thC, 7.5in (19cm) long. **£100-140** *BWA*

A pair of ring-sided spectacles, c1750. **£160-180** *BWA*

A pair of surgeon's binocular glasses. **£40-45** *BWA*

A pair of silver sunglasses, c1824. **£80-95** *BWA*

Scripophily

A bearer share in S. A. André Citroën, with cars round the border, c1936. **£32-35** *SCR*

A gold mining share in Mines D'Or de Kilo Moto, a Belgian Congo company, nationalised without compensation, red and black, 1944. **£5-6** *SCR*

A share certificate of the Mediterranean Electric Telegraph Company, which linked Sardinia with the European mainland, black and white, 1854. **£110-120** *SCR*

These companies achieved their objectives by laying cable under the sea. John Brett, who signed the share, was one of the most successful engineers in this field, having laid the Dover-Calais cable and later, using Brunel's SS Great Eastern, the Atlantic cable.

A Chinese Government loan reorganisation certificate, engraved by Waterlow, 1913. Brown **£12-15** Blue **£32-35** *SCR*

A £100 bond for the Kingdom of Roumania, with vignette of the castle on which Dracula stories are based, engraved by Waterlow, blue and black, 1929. **£32-35** *SCR*

Akcionarsky Pivovar Na Smichove, a share in Czech brewer of Pils, multi-coloured, 1937. **£145-150** *SCR*

The buildings still exist but are now almost derelict.

A $1000 bond for the Kingdom of Bulgaria, issued under the 1928 Stabilisation Loan, engraved by Bradbury Wilkinson. **£72-75** *SCR*

A share certificate for The London & New Zealand Exploration Company, formed to invest in and raise capital for New Zealand mining companies, English and French text, green and beige, 1896. **£32-35** *SCR*

A Certificate of Education, 1907, 11.5in (29.5cm) wide. **£2-3** *COL*

America

A $1,000 bond issued by the State of Ohio, for Cleveland Short Line Railway Company, brown, 1911.
£10-12 *SCR*

A Cincinnati Indianapolis St Louis & Chicago Railway Company $1,000 bond, one of only 7,500 issued, green and black, 1880.
£38-40 *SCR*

A $10,000 registered bond for New York Central Rail Road Company, blue, 1913.
£10-12 *SCR*

A Providence & Worcester Railroad Company share, green and black with orange printed 'seal', c1957. **£8-10** *SCR*

A California Diamond Oil Company, share issued in San Francisco incorporated under the laws of Arizona, green and black, 1905. **£12-15** *SCR*

A Chicago, Burlington & Quincy Railroad share, red and black, c1900. **£23-25** *SCR*

A Beech Creek Railroad Company bond, brown and black, 1892. **£28-30** *SCR*

A State of Kansas bond, issued by the Osage City Bank on behalf of the State, repayable in gold, One of 750 issued, engraved by the St Louis Banknote Company, brown, 1882.
£28-30 *SCR*

A $1,000 West Shore Railroad Company bond, red and black, c1918. **£8-10** *SCR*

Canada

A Canadian Collieries (Dunsmuir) Ltd. share certificate, registered in Toronto, green and black, c1913.   **£10-12** *SCR*

Great Britain

A Liverpool Sewage Utilization Company certificate, black and white, c1868.   **£23-25** *SCR*

A share certificate of West Canadian Oil & Gas Ltd., registered in Calgary, blue and black, 1959. **£6-8** *SCR*

A British Gas Light Co., share certificate, 1825.   **£270-275** *SCR*

A General Screw Steam Shipping Company share certificate, 1852.
£32-35 *SCR*

A Claridge's Hotels share certificate, orange, yellow and black, 1921. **£68-70** *SCR*

India

An Rs500 India General Navigation & Railway Company Ltd. debenture, engraved by Waterlow, green and black, 1915.
£15-18 *SCR*

Mexico

A Compania Mexicana de Petroleo 'El Tigre' bearer share with coupons attached, green and black with printed revenue stamps, 1929.
£16-18 *SCR*

A Negociacion Agricola 'La Sautena' share in Mexican hacienda located on the Texas border, green, red and black, 1907.
£52-55 *SCR*

A Savana Industrial and Financial Company, Pondichery, India certificate, brown, 1952.
£12-15 *SCR*

South Africa

A share certificate of The South African Irrigation & Investment Co., black and white with red overprint, 1863.
£32-35 *SCR*

Russia

A St Petersburg Land & Mortgage Co. Ltd. £100 debenture, engraved by Waterlow.
£62-65 *SCR*

A New Russia Company Ltd. First Mortgage Debenture, engraved by Waterlow, blue, 1910.
£23-25 *SCR*

The company formed in 1869 by John Hughes, a Welsh expatriate recruited by the Tsar to recreate the steel town of Merthyr Tydfil in Russia. The result was Donetz, originally known as Hughesovska.

Spain

A SA Minas Del Tesorero bearer share, issued in Madrid, green and black, 1907. **£38-40** *SCR*

A certificate of La España Industrial textile company, black, 1854. **£16-18** *SCR*

Insurance Policies

A Law Accident Insurance Society Ltd. employers' indemnity policy, damaged, 1909, 21in (53cm) long.
£4-6 *COL*

An Atlas Assurance Company Ltd. insurance policy, 1908, 20in (51cm) long.
£8-11 *COL*

A Royal Exchange Assurance insurance policy, 1911, 20in (51cm) long.
£10-14 *COL*

Sewing

A brass thimble.
£3-5 *AA*

A Regency mahogany and foliate inlaid sewing box, with tray, sewing implements and small ivory dishes, 9.25in (23cm) wide.
£450-500 *CSK*

A Naumann sewing machine, without cover, 20 by 10.5in (51 by 26cm).
£12-14 *AL*

An advertising box for Coats threads.
£100-115 *LBL*

A Winselmann Titan sewing machine, without cover, 16 by 9in (41 by 23cm). **£20-25** *AL*

A tin sewing box, painted jade green, with internal brass lift-out section, divided as illustrated on the lid, early 20thC.
£50-60 *ROW*

Two silver thimbles:
r. Chester 1918.
l. London 1927.
£17-20 each *AA*

A sewing machine inside its box, 19 by 9.25in (48 by 23cm).
£25-30 *AL*

A Victorian novelty pin cushion, applied with various coloured agates, Birmingham, 3.5in (9cm).
£200-250 *CSK*

A Singer sewing machine, with cover.
£25-30 *AL*

A metal tape measure, early 20thC, 2in (5cm) high.
£80-98 *AMH*

Shipping

A brass ship's bell, 'Commodore', English, inscribed on one side, c1880, 15in (38cm) diam.
£350-375 *S*

A Siebe Gorman & Company diver's helmet, early 20thC, 18in (46cm) high.
£1,050-1,150 *S*

An oak brass bound ship's wheel, 30in (76cm) diam.
£150-175 *PCh*

A ship's oil can, c1930, 5in (13cm) high.
£8-10 *COL*

The diameter measures the same as height so that when filled it cannot fall over.

A wood casket encrusted with a wide variety of sea shells, English, mid-19thC, 11.5in (29cm) wide.　**£250-275** *S*

A Merchant Navy pennant, 1940s, 24in (62cm) long.
£25-30 *COB*

Two sailors' arm badges, pre-WWII.　**£5-8** *COB*

A Royal Navy sailors' document case, c1840.　**£30-35** *COB*

A white canvas covered circular lifebuoy, R.M.S. Titanic, Liverpool.
£1,800-2,000 *ONS*

A pair of Barbadian shell pictures, mid-19thC, 8.25 and 9in (21 and 23cm) wide each.
£1,850-1,950 *S*

A Norwegian pattern rotary foghorn, in stained pine case, French and English instructions, late 19thC, 23in (59cm) long.
£450-480 *S*

A carved mahogany tiller, in the form of a knotted length of rope, chipped, 27.5in (70cm) long.
£900-950 *S*

Lanterns

A Russian ship's lamp, c1960.
£50-60 *DHO*

Two ship's lanterns, Port and Starboard, 24.5in (62cm) high.
£100-155 *GRF*

A Sestrel ship's binnacle compass, on mahogany and oak base, English, 1930s, 56in (142cm) high.
£1,000-1,100 *S*

A Griffin & George Ltd., Kew pattern marine barometer, with brass cased mercury thermometer, English, 1920s, 36.5in (93cm) long.
£850-900 *S*

A copper ship's lamp, c1850, 23in (59cm) high.
£100-120 *DHO*

A ship's Port lamp, c1940, 21.5in (54cm) high.
£50-60 *DHO*

Shipping Ephemera

A passenger list for a Cunard Cruise, 1933.
£7-8 *COB*

A selection of shipping companies sailing lists, 1930s-60s.
£10-15 each *COB*

A Cunard brochure, 1950s.
£5-6 *COB*

An advertising booklet, The World's Wonder Ships. **£4-5** *COB*

Two photographs of the SS Titanic, 8 by 10in (20 by 25cm) each.
£5-6 each *COB*

An Admiralty book of lost or damaged vessels during WWII, 1947.
£15-20 *COB*

A selection of shipping companies matchboxes. **£1-2 each** *COB*

A publicity brochure for the Orient Line, 1948.
£6-7 *COB*

An advertising brochure for the Orient Line, 1950s. **£5-6** *COB*

A sailing list for the White Star Line, 1928.
£8-10 *COB*

Menus

A Canadian Pacific Line menu,
1935.   £6-7   COB

A Cunard Line menu, 1930s.
£4-5   COB

A Union-Castle Line menu,
1950s.   £5-6   COB

Posters

A black and white advertising
poster for John Brown &
Company, Ltd., 1915.
£10-15   COB

A Richard Beck poster for Orient
Line Cruises, The Baynard Press,
1937, 40 by 25in (101.5 by 64cm).
£160-180   BBA

A Charles
Dixon poster,
Union-
Australasian
Line to New
Zealand and
Australia.
£100-120
ONS

An advertising
poster for
Cook's, The
Wise Traveller
Has Friends
Everywhere.
£110-130
ONS

A broadsheet for an early Isle of
Wight Regatta, 1835.
£35-40   COB

Cross Reference
Posters
Railway Posters

A P Irwin Brown poster for LMS
Express & Cunard Liner, Royal
Scot alongside Aquitania, 1924.
£3,250-3,500   ONS

*This is believed to be the first
poster published by the LMS after
the grouping in 1924.*

Sixties & Seventies

A 'donkey' cruet set, made in Hong Kong, 1960s.
£2-3 *FAB*

A 'Babycham' cruet set, 1960, 6.5in (16cm) high.
£2-4 *FAB*

Two Melamine dishes, 1960, larger advertising 5in (13cm) long, **£3-5** and small **£2-3** *FAB*

A black and yellow cruet set, 1960s, 1.5in (4cm) high.
£3-5 *FAB*

A liqueur bottle and box, decorated by Dali, c1971, 12.5in (32cm) high.
£100-120 *KAC*

A tin, 1960s, 7in (18cm) high.
£3-5 *FAB*

A plastic cruet set, made in Hong Kong, 1960, 2.5in (6cm) high, with box.
£3-5 *FAB*

A pair of blue and grey Permaware ashtrays, 4.25in (11cm) wide.
£3-5 *FAB*

Two plastic clothes brushes, shaped as a dog and cat, 1960s, 8 and 9in (20 and 23cm) high.
£3-5 each *FAB*

A 'Fuzz Puppy' tissue box cover, with original tissues, American, 1970s, 8in (20cm) high.
£5-8 *FAB*

A pair of red and black Permaware ashtrays, c1960, 4.25in (11cm) long.
£3-5 *FAB*

A green and orange 'Gonk', 1960s, 14in (36cm) high.
£8-10 *PC*

A set of coasters, with cocktail recipes, early 1960s.
£3-5 *FAB*

A Pifco electric foot massager, shown at 1961 Ideal Home Exhibition.
£8-10 *FAB*

A Morphy-Richards hair dryer, in original box, 1960s.
£8-10 *FAB*

A G Plan red plastic clock, c1970, 10.5in (26cm) high.
£6-8 *FAB*

A Sparklets soda syphon, with original box, c1970.
£6-8 *FAB*

Mary Quant knitting patterns.
£1-2 each *FAB*

Lambretta touch up paint and stand, early 1960s, 19in (48cm) high.
£200-250 *FAB*

Three Lord Nelson's pottery containers, 5 to 7.5in (13 to 19cm) high.
£3-5 each *FAB*

A copy of Vogue, April 1964.
£8-10 *FAB*

An ornamental wrought iron guitar, 1960s, 29.5in (75cm) long. **£8-10** *FAB*

A Crossroads Special book, autographed by the cast, c1970. **£10-12** *FAB*

A set of different coloured egg cups, 1960s. **£4-5 the set** *FAB*

A Royal Copenhagen bottle vase, 1960s, 11in (28cm) high. **£70-90** *KAC*

A plastic Britvic pineapple ice bucket, 1960s, 12in (31cm) high. **£12-15** *FAB*

A pair of kitchen storage tins, 1970s, 5.5in (14cm) high. **£2-3** *FAB*

An Armitage Shanks ceramic advertising ashtray, to mark 150 year anniversary. **£4-6** *FAB*

Three kitchen storage tins, 1970s, 5.5in (14cm) high. **£3-4** *FAB*

A smoker's stand, 1970s, 21in (53cm) high. **£8-10** *FAB*

60s & 70s Ceramics

A chalk hyacinth vase, 1960s, 9in (23cm) high. **£4-5** *FAB*

A Crown Devon ceramic jug, black, red and grey on a mottled ground, 1960, 7in (18cm) high. **£10-15** *FAB*

A Piazza ware ceramic jug, black and red on white ground, by M.J. Wood, 1960s, 9in (23cm) high. **£8-10** *FAB*

A Crown Devon vase, Memphis, designed by Colin Melbourne, 1960s, 6in (15cm) high. **£40-50** *FAB*

Two Beswick ceramic items, black and white with yellow interior, vase 7in (18cm) high. **£12-15**
dish 6.25in (16cm) wide. **£8-10** *FAB*

A brown and white jug, by Arthur Wood, 1960s, 9.5in (24cm) high. **£8-10** *FAB*

A foreign ceramic vase, 1960s, 8in (20cm) high. **£6-8** *FAB*

A Midwinter plate, Cannes, designed by Hugh Casson, 7.5in (19cm) diam. **£3-4** *FAB*

A Midwinter cup and plate set, Cannes, designed by Hugh Casson, 9.25in (23cm) wide. **£5-8** *FAB*

A Midwinter plate, Flower Mint, designed by Jessie Tait, c1960. **£5-6** *FAB*

A Homemaker plate, Woolworths from 1957-61, 9in (23cm) diam. **£6-8** *FAB*

Three items of Hornsea ware, black and white with yellow interiors, 1960s, 2.25 to 5.5in (6 to 14cm) high. **£3-5 each** *FAB*

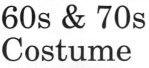

A cat jug, 1960s, 8in (20cm) high. **£6-8** *FAB*

A ceramic bowl, coloured grey and yellow, late 1950s, 11in (28cm) wide. **£12-15** *FAB*

A Troika pottery cylinder vase, 1960s, 14.5in (37cm) high. **£60-80** *KAC*

A ceramic cat, 1960s, 14in (36cm) high. **£6-8** *FAB*

60s & 70s Costume

A Carnaby Street Mina smock, coloured red, white and blue, 1960s. **£10-12** *FAB*

A Mary Quant designed Alligator blue check raincoat, 1960s. **£50-60** *FAB*

A Delamare PVC raincoat, 1960s. **£30-40** *FAB*

Cross Reference
Textiles

A jacket, The Jam pop group, could be bought by mail order from the Musical Express, late 1970s.
£40-50 *FAB*

A pair of Levi flared jeans, c1960.
£35-40 *FAB*

A psychedelic coat, 1960s.
£25-35 *FAB*

A kaftan, coloured pink, black, turquoise and blue, 1960s.
£8-10 *FAB*

A pair of cork soled sandals, 1960s.   **£4-8** *FAB*

Two pairs of stockings, Lucky Charm and Strümpfe, 1960s.
£8-12 *FAB*

A turquoise suede synthetic fur trimmed coat.   **£20-25** *FAB*

A Donovan cap, in blue and green Welsh tweed, 1960s.
£6-8 *FAB*

A suede mesh bag, with metal handles, 1960s, 18in (46cm) long.
£2-3 *FAB*

Two leather belts, 1960s.
£2-3 each *FAB*

A brown and beige leather tie belt, 1960s.
£2-3 *FAB*

60s & 70s Furniture

A green Habitat chair of Swedish design, early 1970s.
£15-25 *FAB*

An occasional table, 1960s, 13.5in (34cm) diam. **£5-8** *FAB*

A psychedelic magazine rack, c1960, 12in (31cm) wide.
£5-8 *FAB*

A metal and coloured plastic coat rack, 1960s, 18in (46cm) wide. **£5-6** *FAB*

A daisy shaped compressed cardboard table, with purple top and green base, 1960s, 52in (132cm) diam.
£85-100 *FAB*

60s & 70s Glass

An art glass vase, c1960, 12in (30.5cm) high.
£20-30 *FAB*

Cross Reference
Glass

A yellow cased glass vase, 1960s, 20in (51cm) high.
£10-15 *FAB*

Three red, yellow and blue Murano cased glass pieces, largest 9in (22.5cm) high **£10-15**, small 3.5in (9cm) wide **£4-6** *FAB*

A green glass fish, c1960, 7in (17.5cm) high.
£3-5 *FAB*

A blue and green Murano glass bowl, c1960, 6in (15cm) diam.
£10-12 *FAB*

60s & 70s Jewellery

A pewter brooch by Caret, c1960
£10-12 *FAB*

A silver pendant, 1960s.
£15-20 *FAB*

Three stainless steel pendants, 1960s, 2 to 3in (5 to 7cm) long. **£3-8 each** *FAB*

A 'Top of the Pops' pendant, 1970. **£3-5** *FAB*

A selection of silver brooches, c1960, 1.75 to 2.5in (4 to 6.5cm) long. **£15-20 each** *FAB*

A filigree metal bangle, c1960s, 2in (5cm) diam. **£3-5** *FAB*

60s & 70s Lamps

Cross Reference
Lighting

A set of 3 purple hanging lamps, c1970.
£10-15 *FAB*

An orange plastic lampshade, c1970, 9in (23cm) high.
£3-5 *FAB*

A Lamperti lamp, by Casati and Ponzio, 1960s, 13in (33cm) high.
£100-120 *KAC*

A lava lamp, c1960, 17in (43cm) high.
£25-30 *FAB*

60s & 70s Stainless Steel

Two pairs of stainless steel candle holders, 1960, 2 and 3in (5 and 8cm) diam.
£3-5 a pair *FAB*

A group of Viners stainless steel goblet and bowls, 1960. **£4-6 each** *FAB*

A set of Viners stainless steel spoons in a box and a 3-piece cutlery set, 1960.
£5-6 each set *FAB*

A 7-piece stainless steel party set, 3.5in (9cm) diam., with box.
£4-6 *FAB*

A set of Trentway stainless steel napkin rings, in box, made exclusively for Boots, 1960.
£4-5 *FAB*

A chrome Ronson table lighter, lined in blue, 1960s, 3in (8cm) high.
£10-12 *FAB*

A satin steel dish, 1960, 20in (51cm) long.
£6-8 *FAB*

60s & 70s Toys

A three-dimensional executive toy, as seen on TV in 'Blake's Seven', 1970s, 8in (20cm) high.
£10-15 *FAB*

Two Chad Valley kaleidoscopes, 7.5 and 13.5in (19 and 34cm) long.
£2-6 each *FAB*

A Sexy Anna, The Beach Girl, with box, 1960, 6in (15cm) high.
£5-10 *FAB*

Cross Reference
Toys

Smoking

A cigar cabinet, for restoration, 19thC, 16.5in (42cm) wide.
£60-65 *TRU*

A Craven 'A' cork tipped Virginia cigarette tin, 'Made specially to prevent sore throats'.
£4-5 *ROW*

A tobacco rasp, with maker's mark J.M. in script, dated 1703, 2.75in (7cm) long.
£750-800 *S*

Cross Reference
Ceramics

A cast iron match holder, in the form of a Turk, 6in (15cm) high.
£400-500 *BWA*

A Staffordshire pottery tobacco jar, 19thC, 5in (13cm) high.
£50-55 *TRU*

A late Victorian cigarette holder, mouthpiece cracked, with case.   **£55-65** *WW*

A silver match holder, c1930.
£20-30 *ASA*

A Bryant and May taper case, 12.25in (31cm) long.
£4-5 *TRU*

An Art Deco silver and enamel extending cigarette holder.   **£30-60** *ASA*

Cigarette Cases

A chromium plated petrol fuelled table cigarette lighter, in the form of a jet fighter aeroplane, 1950s, 9.5in (23.5cm) long.
£60-80 *HSS*

A silver cigarette case, c1930.
£30-50 *ASA*

A commemorative silver and enamel cigarette case, base inscribed R.M.S. 'Empress of China' (H.M. Armed Cruiser) Launched By Lady Northcote Barrow in Furness, 25th March 1891, scratched and chipped, hallmarked Chester 1890, 3.25 by 4.25in (8 by 10.5cm).
£825-975 *S*

A gilt metal combination compact and cigarette case, c1940.
£15-30 *ASA*

A highly decorated silver cigarette case. **£20-40** *ASA*

A Bakelite cigarette container, the doors swing open to reveal cigarettes, 7in (18cm) high.
£18-20 *COL*

A simulated tortoiseshell cigarette case, with watch set into the lid. **£30-50** *ASA*

A white metal and enamel cigarette case, c1930.
£15-25 *ASA*

Pipes

A Meerschaum clay pipe, the bowl carved in the form of the Devil, 19thC, 5in (13cm) long.
£140-150 *TRU*

A silver mounted Meerschaum pipe, with amber stem, 7in (18cm) long.
£150-160 *TRU*

A Meerschaum pipe in the form of a bird's head, the stem forming the beak, 19thC, 6in (15cm) long.
£175-185 *TRU*

A Bavarian carved stained horn and wood pipe base, 19thC, 20in (51cm).
£80-100 *MJB*

Vesta Cases

A silver line engraved vesta case, Birmingham 1912, 1.75in (5cm) wide. **£25-30** *TRU*

An engraved silver vesta case, Birmingham 1920, 1.75in (5cm) wide. **£35-40** *TRU*

An engraved silver vesta case, Birmingham 1915, 1in (3cm) wide. **£20-22** *TRU*

A silver vesta case set with agate thistles, c1880, 1.75in (5cm) long. **£80-90** *BWA*

A fluted silver vesta case, with taper case to side, London 1890, 1.5in (4cm) wide. **£55-60** *TRU*

A silver vesta case, Birmingham 1919, 1.75in (5cm) wide. **£30-35** *TRU*

Snuff Boxes

A leather vesta case, c1890, 2.5in (6cm) long. **£60-75** *AMH*

A carved wood Scottish snuff figure, early 19thC, 29in (74cm) high. **£1,750-1,850** *B*

A nickel plated snuff box, the lid engraved 'Hugh Bennett', 3in (8cm) wide. **£18-20** *TRU*

A plain silver vesta case, Birmingham 1873, 1.25in (3cm) wide. **£35-40** *TRU*

A selection of Scottish snuff mulls, in wood, ivory and horn, with silver mounts and dedications, 2.25 and 2.5in (5 and 6cm). **£300-500 each** *BWA*

Spoons

A pair of Georgian engraved gold plated serving spoons, London 1810.
£125-150 *AA*

A pair of thread pattern salt spoons, moulded with shells and armorial engraved, Toulouse c1770, 6.75in (16.5cm) long, 50gr.
£1,110-1,150 *S(Mon)*

A pair of French salt spoons, with reeded borders and armorial engraved, 18thC, 6.25in (15.5cm) long, 36gr.
£420-450 *S(Mon)*

Caddy Spoons

A caddy spoon, Hester Bateman, London 1787, 2.5in (6cm) long.
£250-300 *AMH*

A silver caddy spoon, London 1820, 3.5in (9cm) long.
£60-70 *AMH*

Three caddy spoons, by Hilliard & Thompson, Birmingham c1860.   **£200-260** *AMH*

A caddy spoon, by E. Morley, London c1795, 3in (8cm).
£180-225 *AMH*

A caddy spoon, maker G.F., London 1878.
£100-135 *AMH*

A silver caddy spoon by Lias & Wakely, London 1878, 4in (10cm) long.
£100-125 *AMH*

A filigree silver caddy spoon, c1795, 2.5in (6cm) long.
£200-225 *AMH*

A caddy spoon, by H. Hyams, London 1866, 3.5in (9cm) long.
£200-230 *AMH*

A caddy spoon, maker W.M., Edinburgh 1878, 4in (10cm) long.
£200-225 *AMH*

Sport

A set of 50 cards Parkhurst Ice Hockey, 1957/58, featuring players from Montreal and Toronto. **£1,000-1,200** *S(NY)*

A game of Parlour Croquet, in original mahogany box, 14.5in (37cm) long. **£330-360** *CSK*

A pair of lignum vitae bowling balls, the inset ivory disc with owner's initials and number of ball. **£30-40** *PAR*

An Eton Royal Football Club cap, 1913-14. **£60-65** *COB*

American Football

A group of 4 football programmes of matches all played in New York, 1929-1931. **£350-400** *S(NY)*

A complete run of 24 Superbowl programmes, 1967-1990. **£1,150-1,250** *S(NY)*

A jersey worn by Joe Namath, New York Jets, c1967. **£2,850-3,000** *S(NY)*

A jersey worn by Merlin Olsen, L.A. Rams, early 1970s. **£775-875** *S(NY)*

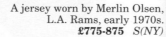

Twenty Seven unused football matchbooks, in mint condition, 1930s-1940s. **£220-250** *S(NY)*

Baseball

A 1927 Pirates
World's Series
Press Pin.
£820-850 *S(NY)*

A 1955 World Series Phantom
Press Pin at Comiskey Park.
£820-850 *S(NY)*

A piece of Joe DiMaggio's wedding
cake, wedding and reception
invitations and a newspaper
cutting, November 19, 1939.
£700-750 *S(NY)*

*At the wedding of Joe DiMaggio
and actress Dorothy Arnold in
San Francisco, guests were given
wedding cake wrapped in
cellophane to take home. This
piece is exactly as it was given in
1939, with 2 bisque columns and
a rose from the cake.*

Who's Who in Baseball magazine,
published by Baseball Magazine,
soft cover, 1916.
£200-240 *S(NY)*

An Adirondack bat
used by Mike Schmidt
during his first MVP
season in 1980, 170A,
No.20 on knob.
£450-500 *S(NY)*

A Brooklyn Dodgers autographed
baseball, with 28 signatures on an
official National League ball,
1947.
£820-850 *S(NY)*

An Adirondack bat used by Willie
Mays, No.302.
£1,800-2,200 *S(NY)*

*Willie Mays hit 660 home runs
during his career.*

A 1912 World's Series ticket stub,
for New York vs Boston Game 3,
at Fenway Park in Boston.
£450-550 *S(NY)*

A sterling silver season pass for
Cincinnati Ball Park, 1902.
£2,500-3,000 *S(NY)*

An Al Simmons cigar box,
c1930.
£630-680 *S(NY)*

Basketball

A set of 72 Bowman basketball cards and memorabilia, 1948.
£2,900-3,100 *S(NY)*

A Scott's Potato Chips basketball card of George Mikan, 1950, 4in (10cm) high.
£2,750-3,000 *S(NY)*

These regionally issued basketball cards are extemely rare, very few are known and the Mikan card may well be the rarest of all basketball cards.

A Topps basketball poster ruler, a complete set of 23, c1969.
£475-500 *S(NY)*

No.5 was not issued.

Boxing

A Jake Kilrain, 'Champion Pugilist of the World' silk boxing scarf. **£1,800-2,000** *S(NY)*

A brass snuff box depicting John Heenan and Thomas Sayers in their famous bout for the boxing championship of the world, 1860.
£500-700 *S(NY)*

Cross Reference
Snuff Boxes

A poster for the Louis/Schmeling fight, 1936, 22in (56cm) high.
£700-900 *S(NY)*

Cricket

Yorkshire Cricket (Lord Hawke), a chromolithograph by Spy, 1892, 12 by 7in (31 by 18cm), mounted.
£280-320 *CSK*

Gubby Allen's photograph album, chiefly of sporting teams and fixtures during his time at Eton (1915-21) and Cambridge (1922-23), containing 51 photographs.
£2,800-3,200 *DN*

The Australians 1888, a commemorative printed silk handkerchief, depicting the Australian IX of 1888, 16in (41cm) sq.
£260-280 *CSK*

Curling

Bonnor Stood Still at the
Crease, Lord Sherman
Keeping Wicket, by Lucien
Davis, RI, signed, 9 by 6in
(23 by 15cm).
£225-250 *Bon*

A curling stone, with an iron ring,
c1830, 8.5in (21.5cm) high.
£70-80 *LBL*

A box of curling stones, stamped
J. C. Forgan, with removable
handles. **£350-450** *LBL*

A pair of
presentation
curling stones,
with ivory handles,
c1895.
£250-300 *LBL*

Golfing

An Elkington bronze trophy
figure of Harry Vardon after
Ludlow, early 20thC.
£1,250-1,500 *S*

A Doulton Lambeth
stoneware golfing jug,
relief moulded showing
Lost Ball, Putting and
Driving scenes, c1905,
7.5in (19cm) high.
£750-775 *S*

A brass gutty golf ball mould for
the Trophy dimple pattern golf
ball, stamped John White & Co.,
Edinburgh, numbered 1917/3657,
3in (8cm) diam. **£800-850** *C(S)*

Twelve unused Cestrian gutty
balls, mostly wrapped, made by
the Telegraph Manufacturing Co.
Ltd., Helsby, Cheshire, in original
cardboard box, c1898.
£3,250-3,500 *S*

A silver plated golfing desk piece,
late 19thC, 6in (15cm) high.
£480-500 *S*

A Verulam Golf Club brass
captain's prize, presented to
Samuel Ryder, depicting Abe
Mitchell in the centre of a circular
tray, 1927, 5.75in (14.5cm) diam.
£475-500 *S*

A boxed set of dress buttons, depicting golfers in various positions, together with a spelter figure of a golfer, and a Doulton Lambeth ceramic golf ball matchstriker, c1900.
£650-675 *S*

A metal golf ball marking machine, stamped Chamber's patent No. 18712-10.
£375-400 *C(S)*

A silver plated golfing inkwell, c1890, 11in (28cm) wide.   **£700-750** *S*

An unused silver score book, originally belonged to Harry Vardon, engraved H.V., hallmarked Birmingham 1906, 4.5in (11cm) high.
£1,600-1,700 *S*

Three boxes of the Colonel patented Blue Ring cardboard tees.   **£550-575** *C(S)*

Golf Clubs

A McEwan long nosed putter, with beech head and hickory shaft, c1880.
£550-580 *S*

A Dalrymple's Patent brass and wood dual lofted club, stamped Sir W. Dalrymple's Patent, 34.
£2,750-3,000 *C(S)*

A rut iron head, shaft missing, c1865, hosel 5in (12.5in).
£600-625 *S*

A mammoth niblick, by Cochrane of Edinburgh, stamped Fortnum & Mason, Piccadilly, London. **£725-750** *C(S)*

A Transitional scared head play club, by Robert Forgan.
£550-580 *C(S)*

A scared head long nosed putter, the head stamped T. Morris, the shaft reduced.
£350-380 *C(S)*

A blacksmith-made lofter, with dished hand hammered face, c1870.
£975-1,025 *C(S)*

A patented putter, with short socket and hand punched face, the sole plate stamped Legh 9941.
£875-925 *C(S)*

A mid-iron with pierced and sparred face, the head stamped 4, the shaft inscribed 'W', stamped W. Wilson, Maker, St Andrews.
£3,750-4,000 *C(S)*

A Sterling silver Walter Hagen putter, inscribed Silver Putters Sweepstakes, with ebonised shaft.
£450-480 *C(S)*

A brass headed Centro putter by Gibson of Kinghorn, head stamped John Henry Patent No. 1559.
£425-450 *C(S)*

Golfing Ephemera

The Royal and Ancient Game of Golf, by H. H. Hilton, numbered 239/900.
£850-875 *S*

Rules of the Royal and Ancient Golf Club St Andrews with alphabetical list of members, 1888.
£350-375 *S*

Three golf books and a letter from A. G. Tait, comprising: Hutchinson British Golf Links, numbered 169/250, Taylor on Golf, 1902, and F. G. Tait a Record, by J.L. Low, 1900.
£1,300-1,400 *S*

The Banff Golf Club Bazaar, Edinburgh 1895, by J. P. Grant.
£680-720 *S*

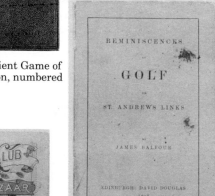

Reminiscences of Golf on St Andrews Links, by James Balfour, printed by David Douglas, Edinburgh, 1887.
£1,600-1,800 *S*

A cartoon, How To Get A Good Tip Out Of The Golfer, 1913, 18 by 14.5in (46 by 37.5cm).
£50-55 *AMH*

Stanhopes

Stanhopes are small trinkets or souvenir items made from a variety of materials such as bone, metal, wood, plastic or plaster. Each contains a tiny microscope lens invented in the latter half of the 18thC by the 3rd Earl Stanhope, after whom Stanhopes were named. Mounted within each lens is a minute early 'transparency' usually depicting from one to a dozen different views of a popular tourist resort or other place of interest. Others commemorate important events such as exhibitions, or contain a portrait of a famous person. It was in 1853, not long after the invention of photography, that David Brewster first had the idea of placing one of these micro-photographs within a piece of jewellery, thus producing the first Stanhope.

From the 1860s until well into the 20thC a great variety of objects were manufactured, mainly in the UK and France, the earliest examples being rings and brooches. Those most commonly found today date from the 1890s and later, and include pens, pencils, paper knives, crosses, sewing aids, miniature binoculars and a variety of gold and silver charms. More scarce, but still available to the diligent searcher, are such items as smokers' requisites, perfume bottles, bookmarks and whistles. The early pieces of jewellery and any object containing more than one Stanhope are much harder to find.

The most interesting images are views of any place outside the UK or France, royalty, maps, nudes and marriage vows. The number of views shown on any one Stanhope is normally 1, 5, 6 or 8, but up to 12 can be found. Quite scarce and worth looking for are hand tinted images. Those seen are often of English seaside resorts tinted blue, pink or lilac with varying degrees of skill.

Although Stanhopes were still being produced as late as the 1960s their popularity died out after WWI, owing probably to the general loss of interest suffered by any novelty with the passing of time.

A needle case with a view of Exposition de 1867, 3.5in (9cm) long.
£40-50 *AMH*

An American advertising penknife, with a horse picture, 3.25in (8.5cm) long.
£40-60 *PC*

An étui, with memory of Andover, incomplete, 4.25in (11cm) long.
£25-35 *PC*

A red cut glass scent bottle, with a silver metal top, and a view of Birchington-on-Sea, 2in (5cm) high. **£45-60** *PC*

A vesta vase, with compass and views of walks, memory of Knighton.
£55-65 *PC*

A thimble, with a view of Shakespeare, 1in (2.5cm) high.
£35-45 *PC*

A watch, .75in (2cm) diam.
£35-45 *PC*

A rifle pencil, 6in (15cm) long.
£35-45 *PC*

Three acorn thimble holders, 2.5 to 2.75in (6 to 7cm) high.
£35-45 each *PC*

Two Napoleon paper knives, longest mother-of-pearl, 6in (15cm) long.
£25-35 each *PC*

An Indian head, with view of Niagara Falls, 3in (7.5cm) high.
£35-45 *PC*

A prayer book, with a view of The Marine Parade, Lowestoft, 1in (2.5cm) high. **£30-40** *PC*

A bellows pencil, 2in (5.5cm) long.
£35-45 *PC*

A selection of Stanhope pencils, 2 to 5in (5 to 13cm) long.
£25-35 each *PC*

A pair of scissors, with views of London, with case 2in (5cm) long. **£45-55** *PC*

A selection of bone parasols, 4 to 5.25in (10 to 13cm) long. **£30-35 each** *PC*

Four binocular Stanhopes: Eiffel Tower, .75in (2cm), Brighton, 1in (2.5cm), Dumfries, 1in (2.5cm), Linton & Lynmouth, 1in (2.5cm) long. **£15-20 each** *PC*

A thimble holder in a nutshell case, with '2002' view, 2in (5cm) long. **£45-55** *PC*

A metal ring with a naughty picture. **£80-90** *PC*

A bottle/pipe with dice, made for the Franco British Exhibition, London, 1908, with a view of Edinburgh, 5.5in (14cm) long. **£40-50** *PC*

A needlework box with 2 drawers, 4in (10cm) wide. **£85-100** *PC*

A silver metal bracelet. **£50-60** *PC*

Two needle holders and tape measures, 4.25 to 4.5in (11 to 12cm) long. **£35-40 each** *PC*

A miniature pipe, 2in (5cm) long. **£35-45** *PC*

An egg cup, with a view of Rheinfall, 3in (7.5cm) high. **£35-45** *PC*

A selection of Stanhope pens, 3.75 to 6in (9 to 15cm) long.
£15-25 each *PC*

A selection of paper knives, 4.5 to 9in (11.5 to 23cm) long.
£15-25 each *PC*

A brass letter opener with magnifying glass, 6.5in (16.5cm). **£50-60** *PC*

Two German pipes, 4.5in (11.5cm) and 3.25in (8cm) long.
£35-45 each *PC*

A Cinematographe prayer book with views of clothed figures, when squeezed the clothes are removed, .75in (2cm) high.
£75-85 *PC*

A penknife with 6 views of Clacton-on-Sea, 2.25in (6cm) long.
£35-45 *PC*

A bottle/pipe for the Franco British Exhibition, London, 1908. **£20-25** *BWA*

Two shakers, probably sand to blot ink, with views of Jerusalem in Arabic, 4in (10cm) high.
£35-45 each *PC*

A selection of Stanhope pens with paper knives, 7 and 8in (18 and 20cm) long.
£15-25 each *PC*

A bottle/pipe, for the Imperial International Exhibition, London, 1908 and 1909, 5.5in (14cm) long.
£40-50 *PC*

A Foto Kino, with different views when handle is turned. **£75-85** *PC*

A bone rolling pin, The Guildhall, 4in (10cm) long.
£35-45 *PC*

Taxidermy

A badger's head.
£85-95 *EB*

Two pheasants in a glass case,
37in (94cm) wide.
£150-200 *GHA*

Two kingfishers,
mounted in a flat
fronted case, 10.5in
(26cm) high.
£80-120 *GHA*

A pike's head, 20lb weight.
£70-80 *EB*

A fox with a partridge, mounted
in a flat fronted cabinet, 19thC,
42in (106.5cm) wide.
£250-300 *GHA*

A pike, caught at Tring,
Hertfordshire, by L. H. Holmes,
on 11 March 1908, 9lbs 8oz,
mounted in a bow fronted case,
40in (101.5cm). **£600-800** *GHA*

Cross Reference
Fishing

A vixen in a flat fronted case,
probably by Hutchinson,
Aberystwyth.
£250-270 *ND*

A grouse in a glass case.
£100-110 *EB*

A monkey's skull.
£18-20 *EB*

A monkey's head made into a
paperweight.
£60-65 *EB*

A squirrel on a log.
£55-65 *EB*

Tea Caddies

An inlaid mahogany and cross-banded tea caddy, mid-19thC, 11.75in (30cm) wide.
£100-120 *PCh*

A Victorian oval tea caddy, with hinged half lid and small ivory handle.
£80-90 *LF*

A Regency rosewood crossbanded and brass inlaid tea caddy, with fitted interior, 13.5in (34.5cm) wide. **£100-120** *PCh*

A Regency mahogany tea caddy, c1810. **£400-600** *WA*

Teapots

A Victorian black glazed teapot, restored, c1880, 10in (25cm) wide.
£20-25 *OD*

A Gibson's black and gold teapot, 7in (17.5cm) high.
£30-35 *OD*

Tea Making

A tea blender's tasting jug, c1900, 2.5in (6.5cm) high. **£10-12** *OD*

A treacle glazed stoneware Toby teapot, c1820, 8in (20cm) high. **£70-80** *OD*

An Aylesford Priory teapot, c1960, 10.5in (26.5cm) high.
£25-30 *OD*

A Hobb's infuser, by R. H. Plant & Co., design reg. 1885, 4in (10cm) diam. **£10-12** *OD*

An Etruscan style teapot, 7.5in (19cm) high.
£12-18 *OD*

An underglaze brown printed
teapot, c1840, 12.5in (31cm) high.
£70-75 *OD*

A black and gilt teapot, 6.25in
(16cm) high. **£20-25** *OD*

A puce yellow lustre teapot and
lid, with blue transfer print,
c1840, 6.5in (16.5cm) high.
£30-35 *OD*

A miniature drab coloured
stoneware teapot, with moulded
decoration, c1840. **£30-35** *OD*

A Cyples teapot, damaged,
c1810, 5.5in (14cm) high.
£60-65 *OD*

A Royal Worcester brown teapot,
c1965, 4.5in (11.5cm) high.
£8-10 *OD*

Cross Reference
Ceramics

A yellow glaze teapot, William
Fishley-Holland, c1930.
£20-22 *OD*

A Staffordshire Pottery limited
edition Batman teapot and cover,
8in (20cm) high. **£50-60** *PC*

A Wade green teapot, with
purple, pink and yellow
decoration, 6.5in(16.5cm) high.
£5-8 *OD*

A Lovatt's Potteries Ltd. green
teapot, 5.5in (13.5cm) high.
£10-12 *OD*

A Tudric pewter teapot with fibre
handle, Liberty & Co., c1905, 4in
(10cm) high. **£45-50** *OD*

A Festival of Britain tea caddy,
1951, 4in (10cm) high.
£5-6
An Elizabeth II Coronation
commemoration teapot, by Swan
Cromalin, 3in (8cm) high.
£6-8 *OD*

An Art Deco copper teapot, with
a ceramic lining, 6in (15cm)
high. **£30-35** *OD*

A transfer printed anti-tannic tea
infuser pot, by Marshalls Patent,
c1910, 5.5in (14cm) high.
£30-35 *OD*

Telephones

A Neophone on a bell box, c1940.
£100-130 *NOW*

An Ericsson ivory telephone,
c1940s.
£180-240 *NOW*

A Neophone 200 Series, with
drawer and small ringer,
restored, c1930-50.
£75-115 *NOW*

A Bakelite red telephone, c1945.
£350-500 *BHE*

A royal blue telephone, 1938, in
working order.
£75-85 *BGA*

An Ericsson 300 Series
telephone, with drawer, and
a call exchange button.
£70-90 *NOW*

A double-sided Public Telephone
sign, c1930.
£150-200 *BHE*

An ATM Monophone, as used on
the Hull Corporation telephone
system.
£125-175 *NOW*

An Ericsson 300 Series telephone,
c1937-59.
£60-85 *NOW*

A Bakelite ivory telephone, c1945.
£250-375 *BHE*

A K6 telephone kiosk, c1935.
Restored. **£1,250-1,500**
Unrestored. **£425-475**
BHE

An Ericsson 'cobra' phone, ringer missing, 1950s.
£10-35
NOW

A City of London Police Public Call Post telephone, c1930.
£5,000-6,500
BHE

A Metropolitan Police Public Call Post telephone, c1935.
£4,000-5,000 *BHE*

A Bakelite green 300 Series telephone, c1945. **£350-500** *BHE*

Toy Telephones

A toy telephone bank, 13in (33cm) high.
£30-35 *NOW*

A toy candlestick telephone, 6in (15cm) high.
£20-35 *NOW*

A toy telephone and money box, with slot under the handle, 3.5in (9cm) high.
£15-20 *NOW*

A toy coin box telephone money bank, 7in (18cm) high.
£35-40 *NOW*

A toy candlestick telephone, 9.5in (24cm) high.
£25-45 *NOW*

Miniature 300 Series telephones, available in blue, red and cream 1.5in (4cm) high.
£5-10 each *NOW*

A red toy telephone, with clockwork ringer, operated by handset cradle, 7in (18cm) wide.
£25-30 *NOW*

TEXTILES

A woolwork picture, after George Morland, early 19thC, 22 by 15in(55 by 37.5cm).
£175-185 *DN*

A wool printed Paisley pattern shawl, predominantly cream and red, slight damage, 19thC.
£120-130 *PAR*

An early Welsh checked wool blanket, purple and blue on cream ground, hand cut and blanket stitched.
£50-60 *CHA*

Large rolls of this material were made then cut in lengths.

An orange ostrich feather fan, with diamante handle, 1920s, 28in (71cm) long.
£40-50 *LB*

A set of 5 lace edged mats, painted with music hall dancers, 19thC.   **£80-100** *TVA*

A pair of pictures, silk work on metal.
£140-150
AI

Babywear

A hand painted moiré silk cover for Baby Book, unused, c1930.
£12-16 *AA*

A young girl's dress and jacket of tartan silk, labelled Spécialité pour Enfant, Mme Fontaine Duclos, 4 rue Mondovi, 4 Paris, c1865.
£225-250 *CSK*

A very fine lawn baby's dress.
£30-40 *PAR*

An antique silk toddler's dress, with hand made lace.
£55-65 *PAR*

A very fine lawn toddler's dress.
£25-35 *PAR*

A Victorian silk baby's gown, with hand made lace.
£90-100 *PAR*

A pair of Oriental baby's shoes.
£15-25 *PAR*

A Victorian fine lawn baby gown.
£30-40 *PAR*

A pair of Victorian baby's shoes.
£40-45 *PAR*

A French silk hand made baby's dress. **£40-45** *PAR*

A cotton lawn christening robe, with lace trimming, 44in (112cm) long.
£60-80 *LB*

Beadwork

A beaded handbag, c1925, 8in (20cm) wide. **£8-12** *COL*

A beaded pin cushion, a WWI sweetheart gift, 7.5in (19cm) long. **£28-30** *TS*

A beaded pin cushion, 3.75in (9cm) square. **£15-20** *LB*

A beaded bag, with handles, c1925, 8in (20cm) wide. **£8-10** *COL*

A pair of Regency wrist bracelets, finely beaded on silk in flower designs, with ormolu and chalcedony clasps, 7in (18cm) long. **£150-250** *TOR*

Costume

A late Victorian burgundy velvet gown, with bustled skirt, 56in (142cm) long. **£200-250** *LB*

An ivory satin evening dress, the back trained with bows, c1870. **£85-95** *CSK*

A gentleman's cotton dressing gown, c1815. **£2,250-2,350** *CSK*

A pair of kid gloves, English, c1610. **£1,600-1,700** *CSK*

A folding top hat, with original box. **£50-60** *AL*

Head Scarves

A black and white crepe scarf. **£4-6** *LB*

A floral silk crepe head scarf. **£6-8** *LB*

Dressmaking Patterns Handbags & Purses

Vogue patterns for evening wear, 1950s. **£4-6 each** *COL*

A sequinned evening bag, c1930, 5.5 by 6.5in (14 by 16cm). **£8-10** *BGA*

A Simplicity pattern, 1950s. **£4-6** *COL*

A black beaded bag, c1920, 8.5in (21cm) wide. **£8-12** *COL*

A silver mesh evening purse, Birmingham 1913, 6oz. **£30-40** *TRU*

Rug Fragment Covers

A Kurdish rug fragment cushion, 19thC, 19in (48cm) wide. **£60-75** *SAM*

A mahogany stool, with antique Shahsavan jajim fragment top, 25in (64cm) wide. **£350-450** *SAM*

An amboyna wood stool, inlaid with ebony, maple and burr yew, with Qashqai tribal bag face South West Persian top, 24in (61cm) wide. **£800-1,200** *SAM*

Two cushions of Shahsavan Tribal kelim fragments, c1900, 16in (41cm) square. **£45-55 each** *SAM*

A Qashqai tribal produce bag, filled with down to provide a bolster cushion, 19thC, 41in (104cm) long. **£250-350** *SAM*

A Shahsavan bedding bag, turned upside down and used as either a seat or table, c1900, 39in (99cm) long. **£400-600** *SAM*

Samplers

A finely worked Continental sampler, by Anna Pagand, showing animals, birds and plants, 19thC, 15.5 by 10in (39 by 25cm), unframed.
£150-175 *PAR*

A needlework sampler, by Alison Clunie, in Birmingham frame, 1830, 22 by 23in (56 by 59cm).
£450-500 *LBL*

A woolwork sampler, by Margaret Kearton, 1853, 24 by 23in (62 by 59cm). **£475-500** *DN*

Tiles

A display of fireplace tiles.
£30-40 *GRF*

A set of 12 tiles, stamped De Morgan, Merton Abbey, turquoise ground with daisy pattern.
£1,200-1,300 *LRG*

A Mintons ship tile, by Moyr Smith, 6in (15cm) square.
£25-28 *NCA*

A Mintons tile, Oranges, 6in (15cm) square.
£25-30 *NCA*

> **Cross Reference**
> Art Nouveau

A set of 6 C.H. Brannam tiles, depicting fish, each 6in (15cm) square. **£480-500** *NCA*

A selection of fireplace tiles.
£8-10 each *GRF*

A Wedgwood tile, 1890s, 9in (23cm) square.
£30-35 *COB*

Sets of 6 fireplace tiles.
£40-60 the set *GRF*

A Belgian brass theodolite, signed Brand Frères Opticiens du Roı, Bruxelles, 19thC, 13in (33cm) high. **£775-800** *C*

A lacquered brass binocular microscope, 19thC. **£675-700** *C*

A bone woman paper knife figurine, 19thC, 5in (12.5cm). **£500-550** *CSK*

A pair of Nuremburg nose spectacles. **£2,750-3,000** *CSK*

A Dutch brass and fruitwood Cuff-type monocular microscrope, 18thC, 22in (56cm) high. **£2,750-3,000** *C*

A 4in lacquered brass telescope, by Nairne & Blunt, 19thC, 25.5in (65cm) long. **£900-950** *C*

An electric dental drill, with Edison motor, c1880, 11in (28cm) long. **£750-850** *BWA*

An ivory cane handle, 19thC, 2.5in (6.5cm). **£1,400-1,600** *CSK*

A brass monocular microscope, 19thC. **£1,400-1,600** *C*

A Cuff-type microscope, mid-18thC, 17in (43.5cm) high. **£3,400-3,600** *C*

A pair of Nuremburg single wire nose spectacles, German, 17thC, in original wooden case. **£4,200-4,400** *CSK*

l. A brass No. 1 monocular microscope, by Powell & Lealand, 1877, 19in (49cm) high. **£6,500-7,000** *C*

A terrestrial globe, by Charles Smith & Son, c1834, 3.75in (9.5cm) diam. **£2,400-2,600** *C*

A selection of miniature lacquered brass sextants, 19thC, largest 6in (15cm) wide. **£1,000-1,800 each** *C*

A boxwood and mahogany octant, American, 1778, 19.5in (49.5cm) wide. **£2,200-2,500** CSK

A pocket globe, by Newton & Son, c1831, 3in (8cm) diam. **£1,600-1,700** *C*

A lignum and boxwood backstaff, English, late 18thC, 25in (64cm) long. **£2,200-2,500** *S*

An ebony and brass octant, 12in (30.5cm). **£550-600** *CSK*

A brass and ebony octant, 14.5in (37cm). **£650-700** *CSK*

A 'Davis' backstaff, by F. Blow, London, 18thC, 23.5in (60cm) wide. **£2,900-3,100** *C*

An 'A' frame sextant, 19thC, 6.5in (16.5cm) wide. **£550-600** *CSK*

A pocket globe, by N. Lane, c1833, 3in (7.5cm) diam. **£1,800-1,900** *C*

A J.H. Dallmeyer 2 by 4in box camera, with lens. **£2,750-3,000** *CSK*

A Marion & Co., half-plate tropical reflex camera, No. M907, with a Ross, London Homocentric 8.5in f6.3 lens No. 140661. **£3,000-3,400** *CSK*

A London Stereoscopic Co., quarter plate camera, with Black Band lens, No. 17147 and maker's plaque. **£825-875** *CSK*

A London Stereoscopic Co., with Goerz Dagor lens. **£1,100-1,250** *CSK*

A Thornton-Pickard quarter plate Folding Ruby camera, with a Dallmeyer Stigmatic f6 6.4in lens No. 137707. **£1,250-1,350** *CSK*

A Stereoscopic Co., Parvex De Luxe camera. **£1,250-1,400** *CSK*

A London Stereoscopic Co. quarter plate Artists Reflex camera No. S132. **£3,100-3,300** *CSK*

A Nouvel Appareil Gaudin daguerreotype camera outfit, signed A. Gaudin, Rue Montmartre, 76, Paris, contained in a wood box with brass handle, hinged lid and side panels. **£18,000-20,000** *CSK*

A Simons & Co. 35mm Sico camera, No. 52. **£4,500-5,000** *CSK*

419

A 6.5 by 3in mahogany body and brass bound stereoscopic hand and stand camera, A. Adams & Co., London, with a pair of Ross Homocentric f6.3 5in lenses, and plate.
£2,500-2,750
CSK

A 45 by 107mm mahogany body Royal Mail Stereolette camera, W. Butcher & Sons. **£1,000-1,100**   *CSK*

r. A 35mm walnut body cinematographic camera/projector, Lumiére, France.
£12,750-13,250
CSK

A 9 by 12cm boxform Anschütz camera, C. P. Goerz. **£3,500-3,750**   *CSK*

l. A quarter plate mahogany body patent Optimus detective camera, Perken, Son & Rayment.
£1,100-1,250   *CSK*

A 6 by 9cm boxform patent Anschütz camera, C. P. Goerz.
£3,250-3,750   *CSK*

A floor standing Sapho stereoscope, Royal Novelty Co. **£3,000-3,300**   *CSK*

A 6 by 13cm Stereo Sigriste camera, S. O. L./J.G. Sigriste, Paris.
£6,750-7,250   *CSK*

A 2.5 by 2.5in Ford's Tom Thumb camera, Max Jurnick, U.S.A.
£8,250-8,750   *CSK*

r. A 6 x 9cm collapsable Spido strut camera, Gaumont, Paris.
£500-550   *CSK*

A wood and aluminium 'Perfecscope', made in the U.S.A., c1895.
£50-70 *BBA*

A collection of stereoscopes and stereo cards.
£50-70 each *BBA*

A Napier coffee maker, c1850, 10.5in (26.5cm) high.
£400-450 *BWA*

A Senior Monarch gramophone, c1908.
£1,200-1,450 *BWA*

A praxinoscope and musical box, E. Reyauld, Paris, 8.5in (21.5cm) drum. **£7,800-8,500** *CSK*

l. An early type wood stereoscope, possibly mahogany, c1885.
£90-135 *BBA*

r. An all aluminium stereoscope, made in the U.S.A.
£50-70 *BBA*

A wood and brass stereoscope, with magnifying glass, c1865.
£300-350 *BBA*

A MacFarlane box containing playing cards, c1890, 3.5in (9cm) high. **£150-200** *LBL*

A Mauchline family photograph album, c1885, 8.5in (21.5cm) long. **£300-350** *LBL*

A Tartan ware card case, 4.5in (11.5cm) long. **£100-125** *LBL*

Two novels with McKenzie and Drummond Tartan ware covers. **£600-700 each** *LBL*

A plaid box, c1885, 3.5in (9cm) long. **£90-100** *LBL*

A Mauchline ware money box, 4in (10cm) long. **£65-75** *LBL*

A darning mushroom, c1885, 3.5in (9cm) high. **£40-50** *LBL*

Four Tartan ware napkin rings. **£20-25 each** *LBL*

A book mark, 9in (22.5cm) long. **£80-110** *LBL*

A tub/pot, 3in (7.5cm) high. **£30-35** *LBL*

A Stuart stamp box with drawer, c1850, 1.25in (3cm) wide. **£100-120** *LBL*

A Stuart string holder, c1845, 4in (10cm) high. **£300-400** *LBL*

A Mauchline ware jewellery box, 6in (15cm) wide. **£100-125** *LBL*

Four large napkin rings, 2in (5cm) diam. **£35-45 each** *LBL*

A Maclean spectacle case, 5.5in (14cm) long. **£100-110** *LBL*

A quilt, probably Durham. **£100-125** *AI*

A beaded bag, 7in
(17.5cm) long.
£30-40 *LB*

A beaded bag, c1925,
£35-40 *HEW*

A Regency beadwork wrist bracelet,
6in (15cm) long. **£25-75** *TOR*

Two late Victorian beadwork cushions,
18in (45.5cm) long. **£100-120** *LBL*

A patchwork quilt, c1840, 72in
(182.5cm). **£550-600** *LBL*

A pair of Regency beaded bracelets,
7in (17.5cm) long. **£150-350** *TOR*

An Art Nouveau panel,
c1890, 37in (94cm) long.
£45-60 *STK*

A Regency embroidered velvet wrist
bracelet, with ormolu clasp, 7in
(17.5cm) long. **£25-65** *TOR*

A glass beadwork
embroidered cushion,
c1880. **£80-120** *STK*

A sampler in a rosewood frame,
c1820, 21in (53.5cm) long.
£650-700 *LBL*

l. An American style
Durham quilt.
£400-500 *LB*

An Edwardian broderie anglaise and lace christening gown. **£75-100** *LB*

A 1920s gold and bronze lace dress. **£120-130** *ACL*

A nurse's uniform, with pinafore, c1915. **£50-60** *ACL*

A 1960s mini dress, 37in (94cm) long. **£45-50** *CLA*

A 1950s boned corselette **£20-25** and a net petticoat. **£12-15** *CLA*

A crepe dress, with braid trim and utility label, c1940, 45in (114cm) long. **£50-60** *CLA*

A 1940s red Cross uniform, 42in (107cm) long. **£40-50** *ACL*

An Ayrtia worked baby gown and cap, c1870. **£250-300** *LB*

A baby's christening gown, hand tucked and trimmed with ribbon and lace, c1870. **£200-250** *LB*

r. A Mary Quant mini dress, 32in (81cm) long. **£30-40** *CLA*

A builder's half model of The SS Duke of Fife, by the
Ailsa Ship Building Co., Troon, in original glazed case,
76in (194.5cm) long. **£4,250-4,500** *CSK*

A detailed builder's half model of the barque
Torridon, built by Paul Hall & Co., Aberdeen, 1865,
81.5in (206cm) long. **£7,250-7,500** *CSK*

A builder's model of The SS St. Magnus, built for the
North of Scotland, Orkney & Shetland Steam
Navigation Co. Ltd., by Paul Russell & Co.,
Aberdeen, 63in (160cm) long. **£12,500-13,500** *CSK*

A French
prisoner-of-war
boxwood model
of a 100-gun
man-of-war, 13in
(33cm) long, on
original oval
rosewood base
and later domed
cover.
£13,500-14,000
CSK

Embessage of Newcastle, built for Hall Brothers
Steam Ship Co., by Joseph Thompson & Sons
Ltd., Sunderland, 1935, 54in (137cm) long.
£4,500-5,000 *CSK*

A model of the motor 'Pair' fishing vessel Lirana
of San Sebastian, built by Paul Russell & Co.,
Aberdeen, 21.5in (54.5cm) long, in contemporary
glazed mahogany case. **£5,750-6,250** *CSK*

A boxwood ·
model of HMS
Victory, c1806,
18in (46cm)
long.
£12,500-13,500
S

A Bassett Lowke one-eighth inch scale model
of the steam ship Great Britain, 48in (122cm)
long, in presentation glazed display case.
£5,000-5,500 *S*

A Märklin tinplate circus set, controlled by gyroscopic action. **£10,250-10,500** *CNY*

An airship musical roundabout, possibly French, c1915. **£1,800-2,000** *CNY*

An American National wood, tin and brass pedal car, c1910. **£5,700-5,900** *CNY*

A biplane circling a hangar, by Cardini, Italy, c1925, 14in (35.5cm) high. **£1,100-1,300** *CNY*

A Nomura Toys tinplate Fokker tri-motor plane, Japanese, c1930. **£3,250-3,500** *S*

A Doll and Cie ferris wheel ride, 13.5in (34cm) high. **£2,500-2,700** *CNY*

A Märklin tinplate carousel, c1910, 16in (41cm) diam. **£48,000-50,000** *S*

An acrobat, German, c1905, 15in (38cm) high. **£3,250-3,500** *S*

A Bing De Dion tinplate car, German, c1907, 8.25in (21cm) long. **£1,400-1,600** *CSK*

A tinplate saloon car, German, c1910, 10in (25cm) long. **£2,000-2,250** *S*

A Fischer Bleriot monoplane, German, c1910, 9.5in (24cm) long. **£2,000-2,500** *S*

A Radiguet tinplate and copper steam battleship, 'Inflexible', French, c1895. **£6,300-6,700** *CNY*

A Märklin tinplate phaeton, German, c1910, 11.5in (29cm) long. **£10,000-11,000** *S*

A Carette tinplate landaulette, with clockwork motor, c1910, 12.5in (32cm) long. **£6,000-6,500** *S*

A lithographed tinplate roadster, with clockwork motor, German, c1925, 10in (25cm) long. **£775-850** *S*

A French tinplate horse-drawn open double decker tram, c1890. **£41,000-43,000** *CNY*

A Bing tinplate racing car, with clockwork motor some restoration, c1904, 11.5in (29cm) long. **£8,750-9,000** *S*

A tinplate phaeton, c1885, 20in (51cm) long. **£13,000-14,000** *CNY*

A Märklin tinplate motor car, German, c1910, 8.5in (21.5cm) long. **£4,500-5,000** *S*

A Carette lithographed tinplate French double deck motor omnibus, German, c1910, 11.5in (29cm) long. **£12,500-13,500** *S*

A 5in gauge model of the
London, Chatham & Dover
Railway 2-4-0 locomotive
and tender 'Asia', by E. V. Fry,
52in (132cm) long.
£2,300-2,500 *C*

A Märklin Gauge III steam
4-4-0 locomotive and tender,
with 2 carriages, 'The Tsar's
Train', some damage, c1905,
28in (71cm) long.
£15,500-16,500 *S*

A 2.25:12in scale 5in gauge
model of the Fowler 0-6-0 side
tank locomotive, 'The Wild
Fowler', built from drawings by
W. Fidler, c1964, 47in (119.5cm)
long.
£2,250-2,500 *C*

A Bing gauge I 4-6-2
Pacific clockwork
locomotive and
tender, control
leavers to cab, c1920,
27.25in (69cm) long.
£1,250-1,500 *S*

A Märklin Gauge I 4-6-0
clockwork experiment
locomotive, G 1021, with a
six-wheeled tender, c1925,
23in (59cm) long.
£1,800-2,000 *S*

An exhibition standard
gauge O two rail electric
model of the LNER Class
VI 2-6-2 side tank
locomotive, No. 2908, built
by J. S. Beeson, fitted with
Westinghouse vacuum
pump, 11.25in (28.5cm)
long, showtrack and glazed
case.
£2,250-2,500 *C*

A scale model of a Burrell single cylinder 2-speed, 3 shaft, 10 ton road roller of 1922, built by G.D. McLeman, 14.25in (36cm) long. **£6,800-7,000** *C*

A Märklin painted tinplate refreshment trolley, 9in (23cm) long. **£2,000-2,500** *CNY*

A detailed scale model of the twin cylinder Foden steam wagon of 1912, Reg. No. M4441, built by G.D. McLeman, 16in (41cm) long, with display base and glazed cover. **£6,750-7,000** *C*

A detailed 7mm fine scale 2-rail electric model of GWR Castle Class 4-6-0 locomotive and tender, built by J.S. Beeson. **£7,250-7,500** *CSK*

r. A detailed model of the LNER Ivatt Class C1 4-4-2 Atlantic locomotive and tender, built by J.S. Beeson. **£5,500-6,000** *CSK*

l. A 7mm fine scale 2-rail electric model of the LMS Rebuilt Royal Scot 4-6-0 locomotive and tender, built by J. Brierley, 17.75in (45cm) long. **£3,500-3,750** *CSK*

r. A French Trix diecast 'Nord' 4-4-0 locomotive No. 68374 and 8-wheel bogie tender, **£1,500-1,600** a Trix 'Nord' bogie coach, **£350-400** and a Trix 'Nord' baggage car, all items 1936. **£550-600** *CSK*

A Märklin clockwork tinplate
'District Railway' bogie, c1906,
£6,050-6,500 and
Station, Cat. Ref. 2023, c1910.
£2,400-2,600 *CSK*

A brass and wrought iron model of a
twin oscillating cylinder condensing
paddle engine. **£4,750-5,000** *C*

A Märklin hand painted
railway station, c1910.
£12,000-13,000 *CNY*

r. A Dessin tinplate floor train, with
paper label DE.S. **£7,000-7,500** *S*

A Märklin 3-rail electric 2-8-2 LNER locomotive,
No. 2001, and matching 8-wheel tender, Cat. Ref.
L70/12920, c1938. **£8,500-9,000** *CSK*

A Hornby clockwork type 51
locomotive, tender, 2 passenger and
one brake coach and track, c1940.
£100-150 *STK*

A Märklin hand painted 4-4-2
locomotive and 6-wheel tender, with
reverse, brake and speed control,
c1904.
£1,750-2,000 *CSK*

r. A Bing gauge 1 4-6-0 clockwork
locomotive, 'Sir Sam Fry', No. 423, together
with 6-wheel tender, 24in (61cm) long.
£2,000-2,250 *S*

A Coronation Street jigsaw, c1960.
£10-15 *COB*

Toy tractor, 5.5in (14cm) high,
c1950, **£100-120**, and small
Matchbox tractor. **£8-10** *NOW*

A centaur carousel, by Anderson,
41in (104cm) long. **£900-1,000** *REL*

A Mickey Mouse speaking
toy, 5in (13cm) high.
£15-20 *COL*

A celluloid Mickey Mouse
riding Pluto toy, Japanese,
c1932, 7.75in (19cm) long.
£4,800-5,000 *CNY*

A Minnie Mouse carousel figure,
37in (94cm) high. **£450-500** *REL*

Fantasia poster, 1940, 41in
(104cm) high.
£3,200-3,400 *CNY*

A Märklin automaton, c1910,
11in (28cm) high.
£5,500-6,000 *CNY*

A Lincoln pedal car, restored, c1935,
45in (114cm) long.
£5,200-5,500 *CNY*

A Mickey Mouse watch, by
Ingersoll, c1930, hands
missing. **£50-60** *COB*

A tinplate castle, probably German, 42in (106.5cm) long. **£2,600-3,000** *CNY*

A Marusan Ford Sedan, Japanese, c1950, good condition, 13in (33cm) long. **£1,900-2,100** *S*

A boxed set of German bisque head aviator figures, c1920. **£3,200-3,500** *CNY*

A Märklin castle, with revolving moat, 13in (33cm) high. **£2,200-2,500** *CNY*

A Toschi Ferrari Grand Prix racing car, Italian, c1959, 22in (56cm) long. **£2,400-2,600** *S*

A Märklin hand painted kitchen, c1900, 37in (94cm) long. **£5,800-6,200** *CNY*

A Märklin pull-along water tanker, c1912, 22.5in (57.5cm) long. **£11,500-12,000** *CNY*

A Chad Valley double deck Carr's biscuit tin bus, 10in (25cm) long. **£1,100-1,300** *S*

A Spanish boxed tinplate toy, c1964, 8.5in (21cm) high. **£50-60** *ACh*

A Märklin pond, c1900, 16in (41cm) diam. **£1,100-1,500** *CNY*

Boxed sets of Meccano aeroplane construction kits. **£300-500 each** *CNY*

A Mettoy musical jack-in-the-box, c1960, 6in (15cm). **£100-120** *ACh*

Tins, Signs & Advertising

Advertising

An O-Cedar Mop advertisement, c1940, 6.5in (16.5cm) diam.
£4-6 *COL*

A Wrigley's PK Chewing Gum machine.
£80-90 *WEL*

An Atora chromolithographed die cut show card, 15in (38cm) wide.
£20-30 *ACh*

A U.S. Royal Cord Balloon advertisement blotter card, 6.5in (16.5cm) wide.
£6-8 *AAM*

A Gold Flake Cigarettes shop advertising pack, pre-war, 12in (30.5cm) high.
£8-10 *COB*

A Be-Ro Self Raising Flour advertising card, drawing signed VH, c1950, 12in (30.5cm) high.
£20-25 *ACh*

An Ever Ready Alldry Radio shaped standing display, with hinged platform for radio, 38.5in (97cm) wide.
£65-70 *ONS*

A cigarette cabinet, c1900, 33in (84cm) high.
£145-160 *BBR*

Cross Reference
Golf

Two Penfold plaster advertising figures, late 1930s, 20.5in (52cm) high.
With Pipe. **£500-550**
Without Pipe. **£265-285** *S*

A Mitchell's Gold Medal
Cigarettes display cabinet.
£400-450 *SRA*

A Dewar's Perth Whisky 'classic'
coaster, W.T. Copeland & Sons,
Stoke-on-Trent, 6.25in (16cm)
diam.
£210-240 *BBR*

A Dunville's Old Irish
Whisky card advertisement,
white lettering on orange
background, 20.5in
(52.5cm) wide.
£28-32 *BBR*

A Compo advertising card.
£100-120 *SRA*

> **Cross Reference**
> Drinking

An optician's wall hanging
shop front clock, 50in
(127cm) high.
£90-125 *REL*

Packaging

A Capstan hardboard
advertisement and stand for
outside a shop, c1950, 32in (81cm)
high.
£40-50 *ACh*

An Ever Ready standing three
dimensional four-section display,
40in (101cm) high.
£55-60 *ONS*

A plaster display cow from a
butcher's shop, 60in (152cm) long.
£400-500 *REL*

A Persil box made from
recycled paper, c1940.
£10-15 *ACh*

A Monkey Brand soap packet, c1920,
5in (14cm) wide. **£5-6** *ACh*

A cardboard
matchbox sized
chocolate box,
c1890.
£10-12
COB

Paper Bags

A Chiesmans' paper bag, c1955.
50p-70p *COL*

A paper bag advertising Ibcol,
c1955, 7in (18cm) wide.
50p-70p *COL*

A Borax packet,
c1930, 5.5in
(14cm) wide.
£3-4 *ACh*

A confectionery
bag from
Sheerness,
c1950.
50p-70p *COL*

An Oxydol soap powder packet,
c1940, 6.5in (16.5cm) wide. **£10-15** *ACh*

A selection of soap powder boxes, 1920-30,
largest 5.5in (14cm) high.
£3-12 each *ACh*

Signs

A Melox enamel sign, c1930.
£15-25 *COB*

An Angus F. Gunn Ltd. sign from
a taxi cab. **£10-12** *COL*

An enamel sign for Wincarnis
Wine Tonic, 73in (185cm) high.
£450-500 *REL*

A Budweiser metal advertising
sign, 1970s. **£25-30** *COB*

A metal sign from a taxi cab,
9.5in (24cm) wide.
£12-14 *COL*

A Fry's Chocolate enamel
advertising sign.
£300-350 *SRA*

A Ogston's Toilet Soaps celluloid
coated chromolithographed sign,
framed and glazed, c1890, 23.5in
(60.5cm) high.
£70-100 *ACh*

A Jenner Bros Ltd. sign from
a taxi cab, 9.5in (24cm) wide.
£8-10 *COL*

An Oxo window poster, framed
and glazed, c1930, 12.5in (32cm)
high.
£35-45 *ACh*

A Grosvenor Studio sign
from a taxicab.
£15-16 *COL*

Prices are affected by condition.

A brass firescreen,
c1930.
£25-30 *COB*

Cross Reference
Drinking

Pub Signs

A painted iron pub sign, 42in (106.5cm) high.
£35-40 *REL*

A painted wood pub sign, 36in (92cm) high.
£50-60 *REL*

A glass sign from an Irish pub, 66in (167.5cm) high.
£900-1,000 *REL*

A painted iron pub sign, 42in (106.5cm) high.
£40-45 *REL*

A painted wood pub sign, 36in (92cm) high.
£40-45 *REL*

Tins

A Carters Seidlitz Powders tin, c1920, 5in (12.5cm) high.
£20-25 *ACh*

A McVitie & Price biscuit tin, decorated with Victoria Cross Episodes, 5.5in (14cm) wide.
£85-95 *Bea*

Toiletries

A silver gilt and red glass double-ended scent bottle, 5in (13cm) long, in fitted case.
£200-250 *BWA*

Two silver topped and blue glass double-ended scent bottles, 4in (10cm) long.
£125-150 each *BWA*

A silver powder brush holder, made for Selfridges, Birmingham 1937, 2.5in (6cm) long.
£40-50 *AMH*

A Bilston blue enamel etui, c1780, 3.75in (9cm) long.
£900-1,200 *RdeR*

A baby's brush and comb set, Birmingham silver hallmark, 1927, in original box, 3 by 4in (8 by 10cm).
£35-40 *AA*

A silver comb case, with engine turned decoration, c1930. **£10-20** *ASA*

Powder Compacts

A silver and enamel compact, c1930.
£30-45 *ASA*

An Art Deco white metal and enamel compact.
£5-15 *ASA*

A black enamel and silver powder compact. **£30-50** *ASA*

A combination compact and lipstick holder.
£10-20 *ASA*

An Art Deco white metal and enamel compact.
£10-20 *ASA*

A Continental silver enamel compact, with gilded interior and back, c1920.
£250-325 *AA*

Razors

A Rolls Autostrop razor, with case, 6in (15cm) long.
£6-7 *TRU*

A box of 7 'Days of the Week' razors.
£60-75 *PAR*

A razor case, 3.5in (9cm) long.
£3-4 *ROS*

A Valet razor, without box.
£1-2 *TRU*

Tools & Farm Implements

A set of 12 piano adjuster's tools, late 19thC.
£45-55 *MRT*

A selection of Silversmith's burnishers, 19thC.
£1-3 each *MRT*

Two ebony and brass levels, 19thC, plain 10in (25cm) long. **£18-22** and fancy 12in (31cm).
£30-40 *MRT*

Blacksmith's Tools

A blacksmith's swage. **£5-10** *PLO*

A blacksmith's plater. **£5-10** *PLO*

A horse tooth rasp, 25in (64cm) long.
£12-15 *PLO*

A box of English nickel silver drawing instruments, the lift-out tray with ivory rules, late 19thC, 6.5 by 11in (16 by 28cm).
£150-200 *MRT*

A blacksmith's hot set.
£5-10 *PLO*

A pair of blacksmith's tongs.
£6-10 *PLO*

Two hot sets. **£10-15** *PLO*

Irons for firing tendons on horses, 14 to 17in (36 to 43cm) long.
£15-20 each *PLO*

This practise is now illegal in England.

A blacksmith's hammer.
£5-10 *PLO*

Bookbinder's Tools

Two bookbinder's centre tools, 19thC, 1 and 2.5in (2.5 and 6cm) wide.
£10-20 each *MRT*

A brass decorative pallet, used to apply gilt decoration to leather bindings, 19thC, 3in (8cm).
£20-30 *MRT*

Two ornamental rolls, 19thC, 2 and 3.5in (5 and 9cm) diam.
£30-50 each *MRT*

A bookbinder's beech plough, 19thC, 18in (46cm).
£35-45 *MRT*

Farm Implements

Three drainage ladles, 87in (221cm) long.
£15-20 each *PLO*

Three dyke spades and handles, 97in (246cm) long.
£35-40 each *PLO*

A clay spade, 43in (109cm) long.
£20-30 *PLO*

A thatcher's eaves knife, 62in (157cm) long.
£20-30 *PLO*

A post hole digger 36in (92cm) long.
£15-20 *PLO*

A hayrick knife, 58in (147cm) long.
£12-20 *PLO*

Two cast iron seats for farm machinery.
£40-50 each *PLO*

A thatcher's comb or rake, 40in (102cm) long.
£12-20 *PLO*

A land drain pipe cleaner, 68in (173cm) long.
£12-15 *PLO*

A rabbiting spade with hook for lead on ferret, 90in (229cm) long.
£30-40 *PLO*

A shearing hook, used for thatching hay and straw.
£5-10 *PLO*

Two cross cut saws, 65in (165cm) long.
£15-20 each *PLO*

A pair of wood and leather clogs.
£15-20 *PLO*

A ditching spade, c1920, 42in (107cm) long.
£35-50 *PLO*

Two pitchforks, the large one for loading hay onto a wagon, 69in (175cm) long, the small one for stable use, with more blunted ends. **£12-15 each** *PLO*

A shepherd's crook, c1900.
£35-50 *PLO*

A short handled turfing spade,
56in (142cm) long.
£15-20 *PLO*

A dab fork for
fishing, 47in
(119cm) long.
£30-40 *PLO*

A turf spade, c1900,
83in (211cm) long.
£20-30 *PLO*

A Hampshire hay rake, 72in
(183cm). **£25-30** *PLO*

*The shape of the handle tells the
area of its origin.*

A selection of garden and sheep
shears, 12in (31cm) long.
£4-5 each *PLO*

*The difference between garden
and sheep shears is that the ends
of the blades on the garden shears
have sharp points; sheep shears
more blunted ends.*

A wooden cart jack, late 19thC,
30in (76cm) long.
£40-50 *PLO*

A digging iron, 5in (13cm) long.
£6-10 a pair *PLO*

*This iron was strapped to the boot
to protect the foot when digging.*

A cast iron cart jack, 32in
(81cm) long. **£40-50** *PLO*

Three billhooks of various
makes, c1900, 13 to 18in
(33 to 46cm) long.
£10-20 each *MRT*

A cast iron bridle rack.
£20-30 *PLO*

A large dock or thistle fork.
£5-15 *PLO*

A weeding tool, 47in (119cm) long.
£30-40 *PLO*

A gin trap, 12in (31cm) long.
£4-5 *PLO*

Rules

An ivory proof slide rule, for calculating the strength of, and duty payable on, alcoholic drink, c1900, 6in (15cm).
£40-50 *MRT*

A folding boxwood barrel measuring rule, c1900, 24in (61cm). **£30-40** *MRT*
This rule gives a direct reading of barrel contents and is intended only for small barrels, pins, firkins etc.

An ivory folding rule, 19thC, 12in (31cm). **£40-50** *TRU*

A Rabone four-fold boxwood rule with level, c1920, 36in (92cm).
£25-35 *MRT*

Woodworking Tools

A mitre plane, by Buck, c1850, 9in (23cm) long.
£230-250 *MRT*

A small size lock mortice chisel, early 20thC, 16in (41cm) long.
£20-25 *MRT*

A selection of carving tools, various dates, 8 to 11in (20 to 28cm) long.
£4-8 each *MRT*

A cast iron, rosewood filled 1.5in (29cm) wide shoulder plane, c1870, 8in (20cm) long.
£35-45 *MRT*

Two joiner's ebony and brass squares, mitre 13.5in (34cm).
£25-35 and square, 7.5in (19cm).
£6-8 *MRT*

A rosewood handled timber scribe, 19thC, 9in (23cm) long.
£25-35 *MRT*

Two large brass carpenter's trammel heads, 19thC, 7in (18cm) long.
£30-40 *MRT*

443

Two small brass carpenter's trammel heads, 19thC, 4in (10cm) long.
£25-35 *MRT*

Two craftsman made bow saws, beech 21in (53cm) long. **£25-35** boxwood, 12in (31cm) long.
£60-70 *MRT*

An Ultimatum brace, by William Marples, c1880, 14in (36cm) long.
£125-175 *MRT*

Three router planes: mahogany, 18thC, 8in (20cm). **£80-100**, mahogany, 19thC, 8in (20cm). **£55-65**, and ebony, 19thC, 3in (8cm). **£45-55** *MRT*

A beech rounding plane, by Varvill & Son, c1850, 9in (23cm) long.
£35-45 *MRT*

A brass and ebony mortice gauge, c1910, 8in (20cm) long.
£25-35 *MRT*

Two rosewood and brass boat levels, by Edward Preston, Birmingham, 19thC, 6 and 9in (15 and 23cm) long.
£15-35 each *MRT*

Three boxwood thumb planes: c1880, 2in (5cm) long, **£50-60**, compassed, 3.5in (9cm) long, **£30-40**, and compassed, 5in (13cm) long. **£20-30** *MRT*

Two mahogany trammel heads, with iron points and screws, c1860, 11.5in (29cm) long.
£80-100 *MRT*

A boxwood carver's maul, 19thC, 4in (10cm) diam.
£35-45 *MRT*

Two moulding planes:
l. mid-19thC, by Moseley, 9.5in (24cm) long. **£10-15**
r. by Loveage, London, c1745, 10in (25cm) long. **£55-65** *MRT*

An octagon box-handled paring chisel, 19thC, 11.5in (29cm) long.
£18-22 *MRT*

A boxwood cutting gauge, late 19thC, 10in (25cm) long.
£10-15 *MRT*

Three turnscrews, 19thC, 21 to
25in (53 to 64cm) long.
£10-35 each   *MRT*

Three beechwood moulding
planes, 19thC, 9.5in (24cm) long,
4-irons. **£300-350**,
3-irons. **£125-175**, and
2-irons. **£35-45**   *MRT*

Three mortice chisels, late 19thC,
10.5 to 14in (26 to 36cm) long.
£5-12 each   *MRT*

Tortoiseshell

An early Victorian impressed
tortoiseshell veneered card case,
with a view of Abbotsford.
£125-135   *WW*

Japanese gold lacquer on
tortoiseshell napkin rings,
c1900.
£25-45   *TOR*

A celluloid tortoiseshell comb,
c1905, 5in (13cm) long.
£15-20   *AA*

A tortoiseshell, gold and silver
brooch, 1855.
£50-175   *TOR*

A papier mâché snuff box with
simulated tortoiseshell top, c1835.
£25-65   *TOR*

A Victorian tortoiseshell
veneered card case, with
printed glass picture.
£140-150   *WW*

A Neapolitan
tortoiseshell
veneered guitar,
with ivory pegs and
mother-of-pearl
inlay, 5.5in (14cm).
£20-50   *TOR*

TOYS

A French speaking picture book, c1910, in boxed cover, 12 by 9.5in (31 by 24cm).
£750-800 *S*

A German static electricity 'Humoristic Mystic Box' toy, box applied with print of circus with celluloid cover and 4 balsa wood clown figures that dance when cover is rubbed, 11.75in (29cm), and a Blondin acrobat sand toy, in a wooden case, c1910, 10in (25.5cm) high.
£525-550 *S*

A paster hanging Bonzo, 3in (7.5cm) high.
£5-6 *HEG*

A Spider-Man toy camera for 126 cartridges, c1978, 5.25in (13cm) wide. **£10-15** *HEG*

A Panorama 'London to Paris', with wooden stage, cloth curtain, and folding card side flaps, depicting a long train and boat journey between London and Paris in watercolours on paper, hand operated on 2 rolls, late 19thC, 12in (31cm) wide, in original wooden box.
£625-650 *S*

A tinplate wind-up Punch and Judy show, 7 by 7.5in (18 by 19cm).
£25-30 *HEG*

A William Britains mechanical footrace toy, in original wooden box with Milliken & Lawley retailer's label, English, late 19thC.
£5,500-6,000 *S*

An American painted wood-jointed Bimbo cat figure, c1935, 9in (22.5cm) high.
£270-300 *CNY*

A Mr McGregor battery operated toy, in original box, 11in (28cm) high. **£40-60** *NOW*

A French 'Jeu d'Ovide' metamorphic toy, with details of head profile altered by series of turned wooden knobs mounted alongside the image, in a card case, early 20thC, 16in (41cm) wide.
£600-650 *S*

A celluloid pull toy, stamped 'Germany' under trolley, c1900, 10in (25cm) wide.
£150-250 *STK*

Diecast Toys

A Mighty Mouse Home Movie, Mother Goose's Birthday Party, in original box, 5.25in (13cm) wide.
£10-12 *COL*

A child's sit-on toy, c1960.
£10-15 *COB*

A Dinky Paris Autobus, in original box, 5.5in (12.5cm) long.
£40-45 *HEG*

Four Corgi Mini Cooper rally cars, c1960, in original boxes.
£600-650 *N*

Three Corgi toy cars: Chitty-Chitty Bang Bang, James Bond's Aston Martin, and Pcpeye's Paddle Wagon.
£100-125 the set *PCh*

A Meccano Dinky Toys French aeroplane set, 61Z, c1930, lacking box lid. **£825-875** *S*

A Corgi Batman set, No. 40, including Batmobile, figures, Bat- boat and trailer and Batcopter, in original display box. **£160-180** *WAL*

A Dinky Thunderbird 2, No.101, in original display box. **£200-225** *WAL*

Two Dinky Trojan vans.
£100-120 *SWO*

Disney

A Mickey Mouse battery powered car, c1960.
£10-15 *COB*

Two Mickey Mouse finger puppets, 3.75in (9cm) high.
£3-4 each *COL*

Two Mickey and Minnie Mouse figures, c1930, 9 and 10in (22.5 and 25cm) high. **£70-100 each** *NOW*

Meccano

A French Mickey Mouse balance toy, lithographed paper on metal figure, the tail used as a counter weight, 11.5in (29.5cm) high. **£130-150** *S(NY)*

A painted wooden Emerson Mickey Mouse radio, c1935, 7.5in (18.5cm) high. **£700-750** *CNY*

A Meccano Aeroplane No 0 Constructor Set, finished in Service Grey, in original blue wartime packing box, with instructions, propeller broken, 1941. **£385-400** *CSK*

A Meccano tinplate Aeroplane Constructor kit, Outfit No. 0, in green and cream, in box, with instructions, incomplete, c1934. **£160-180** *DN*

Rocking Horses

● J (Jervis) Collinson has always been a small family business in the city of Liverpool. Started in 1836, they produced a variety of coloured horses until 1850 when Queen Victoria visited the factory riding a dapple grey horse after which they only produced grey rocking horses. Collinson horses were unmarked until 1981, since when a gold plate has been applied to the front of the stand base.

● Baby Carriages Ltd. was founded by members of the Collinson family in about 1884 in Liverpool. They produced a variety of rocking horses, toy horses and carts until 1958.

● G. & J. Lines produced rocking horses from their factory in the Caledonian Road between 1850 and 1931 and claimed to be the largest toy factory in Britain. Their trademark was a metal disc stamped with a thistle.

● F. H. Ayres were located at Aldersgate in London and produced high quality toys and sports goods as well as rocking horses from 1864. If Ayres horses are marked, there is a stamped plate under the belly or a small plaque on the swing top. They had ceased production of these high quality horses by 1940.

● Patterson Edwards were established in 1892 in the Old Kent Road by H.S. Jarvis. In 1955 the trademark LEEWAY was adopted for all their rocking horses and prams.

A Victorian carved pine rocking horse, with original paint, on turned supports and stand. **£450-500** *LRG*

A rocking horse, on a carriage spring safety stand, by F. H. Ayres, c1907, 54in (137cm) long. **£1,800-2,000 when restored** *STE*

A rocking horse, by F. H. Ayres,
c1900, 72in (182.5cm) long.
**£1,900-2,100 in good condition
with original paint
£1,200-1,300 in poor condition
or badly restored** *STE*

A rocking horse by G. & J. Lines,
c1911, 31in (79cm) long.
**£1,500-1,600 in good condition,
£400-500 in poor condition or
badly restored** *STE*

A Victorian dapple grey rocking
horse, on a safety stand, with
replacement real horsehair mane
and tail and hand made hand
dyed tack, paintwork restored and
reglazed.
£1,200-2,500 *WA*

FURTHER READING
*The Rocking Horse, A History of
Toy Horses,* by Patricia
Mullins, New Cavendish Books

A rocking horse, by G. & J. Lines, not original paint, c1910, 81in (205.5cm) long.
£1,600-1,700 if original or well restored
£1,000-1,100 in poor condition   *STE*

A rocking horse, by F. H. Ayres, made for Gamages, London, c1900, 52in (132cm) long.
£1,800-2,000   *STE*

A Bauer Krause rocking horse, German, fully restored, 46in (116.5cm) long. c1920
£800-900 in good condition
£100-200 in poor condition
STE

A rocking horse, by Leeway, London, c1955, 35in (89cm) long.
£300-400 in original condition, £500-600 if larger   *STE*

A rocking horse, by Collinson, original paint, c1940, 50in (127cm) long.
£700-800 restored
£100-200 in poor condition   *STE*

A rocking horse, by Baby Carriages of Liverpool, original paint, c1910, 37in (94cm) long.
£900-1,000 in good condition or restored larger £1,300-1,400   £300-400 in poor condition or badly restored *STE*

Not to be confused with Collinsons of Liverpool, which are inferior quality and have studs for eyes. Baby Carriage horses are very well made with glass eyes and some have a transfer on the centre of the stand, 'B.C.C. Rambler Liverpool'.

A Triang rocking horse, on a light varnished beech stand, with identification marks, round disc on front, triangle on rear of base, Triang written in red, original paint, new saddle blanket, c1939, 34in (86cm) long.
£1,100-1,300 in good condition, £300-400 in poor condition *STE*

Soldiers & Figures

A Johillco Silver Jubilee Set, in original presentation box, some damage, 1935. **£185-200** *CSK*

A Britain's No. 44F Country Cottage, with a Greenhouse, cold frame, lawn mower, swing, trellis and trees, in original box. **£540-560** *S(S)*

A selection of Rose Miniatures, Military figures: *l*: Indian Army, Queen's Own Corps of Guides. **£100-110** *r*: Indian Army, Sikhs. **£90-110** *WAL*

A Britain's for CFE or Charterhouse CIV Supply Wagon. **£550-575** *CSK*

A Pre-War set No. 7, The Royal Fusiliers, City of London Regiment. **£90-100**
A Set No. 74, Royal Welsh Fusiliers, 23rd Foot with mascot ram. **£100-110**
A pre-war Set No. 212, The Royal Scots/The Royal Regiment. **£160-180**
A pre-war Set No. 114, The Queen's Own Cameron Highlanders, in kilted tropical dress. **£140-160**
A pre-war Set No. 205, The Coldstream Guards, at the salute. **£120-140**
A pre-war set No. 240, The Royal Air Force. **£350-375** *WAL*

A collection of figures formed as a Circus Display and Big Top, 'Reynolds's Model Circus', by various makers, probably 1950s. **£1,600-1,700** *CSK*

Cinema Favourites, 3 Felix the Cats, in original box, and 2 'Pets Stores' toy grocery shops, some parts missing. **£325-350** *CSK*

Stuffed Toys

A Dean's rag book Dismal Desmond, c1920, 4.75in (12cm) high. **£40-50** *NOW*

A Chad Valley articulated Bonzo, c1920, 9.5in (24cm) high. **£100-150** *NOW*

A Steiff black mohair and plush poodle on wheels, c1910, 17.25in (44cm) long. **£750-775** *S*

Teddy Bears

A Stevenson growler bear, with glass eyes, stuffed with wood shavings, limited edition of 100, 23in (59cm) high. **£150-200** *STE*

A well loved teddy bear, c1930, 16in (41cm) high. **£100-125** *PAR*

A Merrythought Golly, c1950, tear on trousers, 35.5in (90cm) high. **£375-400** *S(S)*

An articulated Felix The Cat, c1920, 11in (28cm) high. **£75-100** *NOW*

A Merrythought Cheeky teddy bear, label on one foot. **£60-75** *PAR*

A hand sewn teddy bear, by Anita Oliver, 1in (2.5cm) high. **£30-35** *CD*

A Chiltern bear, 14in (35.5cm) high. **£130-150** *PAR*

A Chad Valley teddy bear, with label on one foot, 10in (25cm) high.
£60-75 *PAR*

'Lukas' an English pale golden plush covered teddy bear, with brown glass eyes, and a photograph of him with Miss Rebecca Ridgway preparing for the British Cape Horn Kayak Expedition, 1992, 10in (25cm) high. **£25-30** *CSK*

A Chad Valley teddy bear, pads replaced, 13in (33cm) high.
£120-130 *PAR*

A pair of early German teddy bears, pre-1920, 8in (20cm) high.
£180-200 each *PAR*

A straw-filled teddy bear, possibly Herman, 1950s, 14in (36cm) high.
£200-240 *PAR*

A Chad Valley straw-filled teddy bear, with button in ear and label on foot, a small hump on the back, c1930, 27in (68.5cm) high.
£500-550 *PAR*

A German cream mohair teddy bear, 'Wispa', maker unknown, 10in (25cm) high.
£300-400 *TEM*

A Steiff cone nose bear, 'Mr Chump', apricot colour, with blank ear button, c1905, 28in (71cm) high.
£3,000-3,500 *TEM*

A teddy bear with a waistcoat, 1930s, 20in (51cm) high.
£120-145 *PAR*

'Jed', a teddy bear, origin unknown, with boot button eyes, 12in (31cm) high.
£100-120 *TEM*

An English teddy bear, 'Big Brother', gold with black leather pads, c1950, 24in (61cm) high.
£100-150 *TEM*

Two Steiff teddy bears, c1910: A large golden plush covered, with growler and button in ear, pads recovered, 13in (33cm) high.
£925-950
A small white plush bear with brown glass eyes, button in ear and rattle in tummy, wear to plush, c1910, 5in (13cm) high.
£400-425 *CSK*

An English straw-filled teddy bear, late 1930s, 10in (25cm) high. **£80-95** *PAR*

A Chad Valley straw-filled teddy bear, with button under the chin, 25in (64cm) high.
£300-350 *PAR*

A Steiff 'Edward' silver blonde bear, pre-1907, 24in (61cm) high.
£1,200-1,800 *TEM*

Tinplate

An articulated tinplate fish, 8in
(20cm) long.
£15-20 *HEG*

A Superman tinplate lunch box,
1978, 8in (20cm) wide.
£20-25 *HEG*

A green tinplate trunk, 2.75in
(7cm) wide. **£4-7** *HEG*

A Märklin hand painted tinplate
steam driven water trough, in
yellow and brown with a green
base, c1904, 12.5in (31cm) long.
£950-1,200 *S(NY)*

*A similar toy is illustrated in the
1904 Märklin catalogue no. 4231.*

A Wills's football game, c1930, 6
by 4in (15 by 25cm).
£12-15 *HEG*

A German lithographed tinplate
mechanical fairground ride toy,
'The Whip', 1920s, 8.75in (22cm)
wide, in original lithographed box.
£1,700-1,800 *S*

A tinplate monkey on a
stick, 19in (48cm) long.
£15-18 *COL*

A Chad Valley tinplate money
box, 5.5in (14cm) high.
£15-20 *HEG*

Cross Reference
Money Boxes

A tinplate toy tambourine, hand painted, c1920, 8.5in (21cm) diam.
£20-25 *PSA*

A Japanese electric tinplate car, 12.5in (32cm) long.
£65-70 *COL*

A Burnett tinplate armoured car, lithographed in grey, with clockwork motor driving rear wheels, c1915, 7.5in (19cm) long.
£500-550 *S*

A Paya tinplate motorcyclist, with HP monogram, numberplate I-804 and chrome exhaust which emits sparks as the bike moves, small rust patch, c1930, 11in (28cm).
£1,650-1,750 *S*

A Marusan electric tinplate Cadillac sedan, c1951, 12.5in (32cm) long.
£1,850-2,000 *S*

A Marusan friction drive tinplate Ford sedan, finished in yellow and white, 13in (33cm) long.
£6,200-6,500 *S*

A German tinplate motorcycling family, by Tipp & Co., lacking headlamp, c1930, 9.5in (24cm).
£1,500-1,650 *S*

A tinplate and clockwork racing car, by Tipp & Co., probably based on the Alfa-Romeo P2, in silver and grey, driver missing, 19.25in (49cm).
£380-400 *S(S)*

A Wells grandfather clock, 8in (20cm) high.
£40-50 *HEG*

A Günthermann lithographed tinplate 'Captain Campbell's Blue Bird' record car, in sea green, c1930, 20in (51cm) long, in original worn box.
£1,550-1,650 *S*

A Shuco painted tinplate 6080 construction turntable fire escape, with 4-section extending ladder, firemen and 1 wheel nut missing, 1950s, 10.5in (26cm) long.
£625-650 *CSK*

A green tinplate 'Clikka' frog, 3in (8cm) wide.
£1-2 *HEG*

Two somersaulting tinplate boys, 4in (10cm) wide.
£4-5 *HEG*

A Mettoy Minor tinplate typewriter, c1950, in original box, 10.5in (26cm) wide.
£20-22 *COL*

A clockwork tinplate tractor, in working order, c1950, 8.5in (21cm) long.
£30-40 *BGA*

A tinplate musical box, 7.5in (19cm) high.
£8-10 *HEG*

A sand bucket, 4.5in (11cm) high.
£6-7 *COL*

A boxed matchbox Jumbo, c1940, 4.25in (11cm) long.
£150-200 *NOW*

A group of Märklin constructor car toys, 1930s, chassis 14in (36cm) long.
£4,750-5,000 *S*

A tinplate pecking bird, 2.75in (7cm) wide.
£10-12 *HEG*

A tinplate globe, 1.5in (4cm) diam.
£2-3 *HEG*

A Chad Valley tinplate double deck Greenline bus, lithographed green, with yellow roof, as a No.721 Aldgate and Brentwood service, 10in (25cm) long.
£1,100-1,250 *S*

Trains

A display model of a 3.5in (9cm) gauge 2-4-2 tank locomotive No.112, powered by an electric motor to all wheels, finished in MR green livery, in glazed case.
£1,100-1,200 *S(S)*

A 3.5in (9cm) gauge model of the SR King Arthur Class 4-6-0 locomotive and tender No.777 'Sir Lamiel', built by J M Proud, with carrying boxes, instructions, firing irons, boiler certificate valid to 10.10.86, 10 by 50.25in (25 by 128cm). **£2,400-2,600** *CSK*

A French Hornby brake van, 6in (15cm) long.
£80-85 *NOW*

A Hornby Series LNER Special electric Pullman train set, c1935, all in original box.
£2,800-3,000 *CSK*

A Hornby Paris Lyons Marseilles engine, 0-4-0 gauge, 6.75in (17cm) long. **£135-170** *NOW*

A Bing gauge I 'Sydney' 4-4-0 clockwork locomotive and tender, in Great Western green, restored, 22.75in (58cm) long.
£820-850 *S*

A Bing gauge III spirit fired live steam model 4-4-0 locomotive and tender, No. 7093, 'King Edward' repainted black, 27in (69cm) overall.
£475-500 *Bca*

A Hornby clockwork train set, with tank engine, LMS, 1930s.
£150-250 *STK*

A Trix portable train set, in original fitted wooden case with special inserts, apparently unused, case 21in (54cm) long.
£550-575 *CSK*

A Märklin 'Disaster' hut, 'exploding' when door is pushed or fired on, with spring mechanism and cap detonator, c1905. **£840-860** *CSK*

Treen

A clerk of works lignum vitae coring ball, for rolling through drains to test, 6in (15cm) diam.
£40-50 *MRT*

A selection of plumber's lignum vitae turnpins, 1 to 4in (3 to 10cm) diam.
£1-15 each *MRT*

A selection of plumber's lignum vitae bobbins, .75 to 2.5in (4 to 6cm) diam. **£1-8 each** *MRT*

A boxwood cartridge crimper, 19thC, 6.5in (16cm) long.
£40-50 *MRT*

Two boxwood cartridge filling devices, 19thC, 7.25 and 8.5in (18 and 21cm) long.
£75-95 each *MRT*

Mauchline Ware

Mauchline (pronounced Mochlin) is a small Scottish town near Ayr, which gave its name to this very collectable range of decorative Scottish souvenir ware.

The industry was it is peak during the 1860s and continued until 1933 when the box works burnt down, effectively ending production.

A vast array of goods were produced, sent to all corners of the U.K. and the Commonwealth, providing a rich area for today's collectors.

A luggie, a drinking vessel, with print of Burns Monument, 3.5in (9cm) diam. **£55-65** *LBL*

A razor hone, 10in (25cm) long.
£70-80 *LBL*

A rolling pin with print of Sea View Isle of Wight, 6.5in (16cm) long. **£25-35** *LBL*

Three napkin rings.
£25-30 each *LBL*

A Mauchline ware and papier mâché card box, 4.5in (11cm) long.
£80-90 *LBL*

A string holder with print of Holyrood Palace, 3.5in (9cm) high. **£45-55** *LBL*

A table/money box, with print of Edinburgh From The Calton Hill, 4.75in (12cm) long. **£55-65** *LBL*

A snuff box, with hidden hinge, 3.5in (9cm) long. **£45-55** *LBL*

Tartan Ware

A card case with cards, 'Miss Florence Danby', 4.25 by 3in (11 by 8cm). **£65-70** *AI*

A cannister with lid, 3.25in (8cm) high. **£22-28** *AI*

A box, 5 by 3in (13 by 8cm). **£55-60** *AI*

A napkin ring, 2in (5cm) diam. **£22-25** *AI*

A rolling pin, for sealing letters, 6.75in (17cm) long. **£25-30** *AI*

A counter, 3 by 2in (8 by 5cm). **£70-75** *LBL*

A Stuart Tartan ware pin cushion, 2in (5cm) wide. **£80-100** *LBL*

A Caledonian Tartan ware stamp box, 1.75in (5cm) diam. **£70-80** *LBL*

A cribbage box, 4.75 by 3in (12 by 8cm). **£28-32** *AI*

Typewriters

A Corona portable typewriter, the case finished in green enamel.
£25-30 *TRU*

An Oliver portable typewriter, in black crackle finish case.
£12-14 *TRU*

A Blickensderfer No. 5 portable typewriter.
£75-85 *HCH*

Walking Sticks

A convertible steel walking/shooting stick, with leather covered handle.
£25-30 *ROW*

A carved bone cudgel, 25in (64cm) long.
£175-200 *PCh*

A mechanical donkey's head walking stick, probably German, the collar engraved 'Brigg London', on knotted wood shaft, late 19thC.
£1,100-1,200 *S*

The spelter head with button eyes drops its jaw and pricks its long ears at the touch of a button on the gilt collar.

A hammered copper umbrella stand, c1900, 16.5in (42cm) high.
£45-50 *ROW*

An ivory handled silver mounted ebony cane, Birmingham 1918.
£120-130 *ROW*

A wooden stick with silver tip, Birmingham 1923.
£35-40 *ROW*

Watches

An American nickel cased pocket watch, by Elgin.
£50-60 *TRU*

A gentleman's silver cased pocket watch, with English fusee lever movement by J.C. Heselton, Beverley, London, 1857.
£60-70 *TRU*

A small 14ct gold fob watch, with Swiss cylinder movement, c1890.
£80-100 *TRU*

A nickel cased pocket watch, with Swiss lever movement, the dial signed Kay & Co.
£50-60 *TRU*

A gentleman's brass cased pocket watch, with pin pallet lever escapement, 1920s.
£15-25 *TRU*

A silver cased fob watch, with silvered dial and Swiss cylinder movement.
£30-40 *TRU*

A brass cased key wound fob watch, with cylinder escapement, 19thC.
£25-30 *TRU*

A nickel cased 8-day Goliath pocket watch, 3in (8cm) diam.
£80-90 *TRU*

A silver cased fusee lever pocket watch, with silvered dial, by William Gray, Mid Calder, case hallmarked London 1865.
£75-80 *TRU*

A lady's keyless fob watch, with engine turned silver case and Swiss lever movement. **£40-50** *TRU*

A brass hunter cased pocket watch, with pin pallet lever escapement, made for the Turkish market, 19thC. **£30-40** *TRU*

A pocket watch, with square pillar movement, lacking outer case, signed Taylor, London, early 18thC. **£140-160** *TRU*

A leather covered gilt metal (5cm) long. **£250-275** *L*

A silver and gold Movado purse watch, with import mark for 1928, and case, maker G.S. **£225-250** *L*

A 9ct gold half hunter pocket watch, with Swiss movement, finished by Benson, Birmingham 1926, 2in (5cm) diam. **£240-280** *TRU*

A silver pair cased verge pocket watch, by Turner & Son, Cliffe, Lewes, London 1875, 2.25in (7cm) diam. **£145-155** *TRU*

A silver pair cased verge pocket watch, by John Lewis, Chalford, Nr Stroud, case hallmarked London 1821, 2.25in (6cm) diam. **£150-200** *TRU*

An 800 standard silver cased hunter pocket watch, jewelled Swiss lever movement, made for the Turkish market, 1.75in (4cm) diam. **£70-80** *TRU*

Wristwatches

A Boucheron white gold wristwatch, 2.5cm square. **£1,500-1,700** *C*

A WWII German airman's wristwatch, by A. Lange & Sohne, 5.5cm diam. **£925-950** *C*

An International Watch Co. pink gold wristwatch, 3.5cm diam. **£1,000-1,100** *C*

A chrome cased rotary wristwatch, in waterproof case, with silvered dial and Arabic numerals, 1930s. **£35-40** *TRU*

A gentleman's silver wristwatch, 1920s. **£65-70** *TRU*

A lady's silver wristwatch, with enamel dial and silver expanding bracelet. **£25-30** *TRU*

A lady's 9ct gold wristwatch, with Swiss 15 jewel lever movement and 9ct gold expanding bracelet. **£50-55** *TRU*

A gentleman's Swiss chronograph wristwatch, with 18ct gold case. **£240-250** *TRU*

A Tourneau gold calendar and moonphase chronograph wristwatch, 3.5cm diam. **£950-975** *C*

A silver wristwatch, with black enamel dial, 1920s. **£55-60** *TRU*

A steel cased wristwatch, with pin pallet movement, 1920s. **£35-40** *TRU*

Omega

A lady's 9ct gold Omega wristwatch, in original Bakelite box, 1930s.
£85-95 *TRU*

A modern 18ct gold calendar quartz Constellation wristwatch, in original presentation case, 3.2cm diam.
£950-975 *L*

An automatic wristwatch, with centre seconds and date aperture, in gold plated case, c1960.
£90-100 *TRU*

An automatic Seamaster 600, professional diver's steel wristwatch.
£225-250 *CSK*

Patek Philippe

An 18ct pink gold Calatrava wristwatch, with original black leather strap and pink gold buckle, certificate of origin dated March 1992 and original packaging, 3cm diam.
£4,500-5,500 *C*

A gentleman's gold automatic Genève date wristwatch.
£225-250 *CSK*

A gentleman's gold wristwatch, 1.5in (3.5cm) diam.
£1,800-2,200 *C*

Piaget

A gold wristwatch, 1950s, 3 by 3.6cm.
£3,250-3,350 *C*

A modern platinum perpetual calendar automatic wristwatch, with original black leather strap and platinum buckle, presentation box with date change tool, certificate of origin, red leather wallet and outer packaging, 3.5cm diam.
£24,000-25,000 *C*

An 18ct gold wristwatch, with gold flexible bracelet and clasp, 2.5cm square.
£1,250-1,500 *C*

An 18ct gold rectangular wristwatch, with cabouchon winder, 2.5cm square.
£875-925 *C*

Rolex

A lady's gold and diamond set Oyster Perpetual Date-Just chronometer wristwatch, with flexible gold bracelet and deployant clasp, 1in (2.5cm) diam.
£3,500-3,750 *C*

A Prince wristwatch, with vertical rectangular dial, 1920s.
£1,900-2,100 *HSS*

A 9ct yellow gold scientific wristwatch, 3cm diam.
£2,750-3,000 *C*

Swatch Art Collection, Keith Haring, Models avec Personnages GZ100, Mille Pattes GZ103, Serpent GZ102 and Blanc sur Noir GZ104.
£1,750-1,950 *C*

Keith Haring was already known as a graffiti artist when, in 1985, he was asked to design a Special for Swatch USA. Modele avec personnages was followed by 3 more in autumn 1985. Each piece was produced in a limited edition of 9,999 pieces. The artist died recently in New York.

Swatch Watches

A jelly fish 1985, created by the artist Andrew Logan and produced in a limited edition of 30 pieces.
£1,750-1,950 *C*

A jelly fish 1985, created by Andrew Logan and produced in a limited edition of 30 pieces.
£1,650-1,850 *C*

These models were commissioned by Swatch for the 1985 Alternative Miss World Contest. Each piece is unique and signed by the artist and was given exclusively to notable guests at this event.

Two USA Specials, velvet undergrounds, No. GZ999.
£8,000-8,500 *C*

Each model produced as one of 500 only in 1985.

Watch Chains

An American gold plated watch chain, 19thC.
£25-30 *TRU*

Two gold plated single albert watch chains.
£18-25 each *TRU*

Two silver curb link watch chains, c1900, 12 and 16in (31 and 41cm) long. **£25-30 each** *TRU*

A Continental silver albertine watch chain.
£12-18 *TRU*

A curb link watch chain, c1900.
£25-30 *TRU*

A Victorian brass watch chain, bar missing.
£5-8 *TRU*

A Continental silver plated albertine watch chain.
£10-15 *TRU*

Writing Accessories

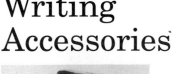

A boxwood pen wiper in the form of a coal scuttle, c1870, 3.5in (8.5cm) wide.
£90-110 *AMH*

An imitation pearl, amber and paste propelling pencil, gold plated end, c1930, 4in (10cm) long.
£20-30 *FMN*

A combined travelling inkwell, vesta case, and 'go-to-bed' taper, c1880, 2in (5cm) high.
£80-110 *AMH*

Cross Reference
Inkstands

Fountain Pens

A Dunhill Namiki gold dust and painted floral decoration lever fill pen, with yellow metal lever and Dunhill Namiki nib.
£450-475 *CSK*

A chased plunger fill pen, with metal band and Onoto nib, by De La Rue Co.
£60-70 *CSK*

Mont Blanc

A Spider's Web white metal overlaid safety pen, with No.O nib, nib damaged, c1920.
£825-850 *Bon*

Mabie Todd

A chased barrel eyedropper fill pen, the cap marked 4500, with Swan clip and nib.
£90-100 *CSK*

Parker

A Duofold Special red pen, with Duofold Canada C nib, c1927.
£100-120 *Bon*

A red Streamline Duofold Special, with twin cap bands and Duofold nib, c1929.
£75-85 *Bon*

Sheaffer

A black/pearl Lifetime pen, with Lifetime Serial Number nib, cap lip cracked, c1928.
£80-90 *Bon*

A black/pearl long Ladies Balance Lifetime pen, with Lifetime nib, c1930.
£70-80 *Bon*

A red veined grey Balance JR pen and pencil set, with feather touch nib, c1930.
£125-145 *Bon*

Wahl-Eversharp

A coral red Gold Seal Junior pen and pencil set, with high rollerball clips and Gold Seal flexible nib, c1929, with box.
£300-325 *Bon*

Waterman

A white metal Pansy 452½V Panel pen, with No. 2 nib.
£80-100 *Bon*

A white metal 452½ Gothic pen, with No. 2 nib, c1925.
£100-125 *Bon*

A plain black lever-fill No. 52 pen, with three 9ct gold bands, in maker's box.
£75-85 *CSK*

DIRECTORY OF SPECIALISTS

(A&A) Arms & Armour, (A&C) Arts & Crafts, (A&M) Arms & Militaria, (AD) Art Deco, (ADC) Art Deco Ceramics, (ADJ) Art Deco Jewellery, (Ae) Aeronautica, (AN) Art Nouveau, (Au) Automobilia, (B) Boxes, (Ba) Barometers, (BH) Button Hooks, (Bk) Books, (BM) Beer Mats, (Bot) Bottles, (BP) Baxter Prints, (Bu) Buttons, (C) Costume, (Ca) Cameras, (CaC) Card Cases, (CC) Cigarette Cards, (Ce) Ceramics, (Co) Comics, (Cns) Coins, (Col) Collectables, (Com) Commemorative, (Cor) Corkscrews, (D) Doulton, (DHF) Dolls House Furniture, (Do) Dolls, (DS) Display Stands, (E) Ephemera, (F) Fishing, (Fa) Fans, (G&CC) Goss & Crested China, (G) Glass, (Ga) Games, (GC) Greeting Cards, (Go) Golfing, (Gr) Gramophones, (H/HP) Hairdressing & Hat Pins, (I) Inkwells, (J) Jewellery, (Ju) Jukeboxes, (K), Kitchenalia, (L&K) Locks & Keys, (L&L) Linen & Lace, (LB) Le Blond Prints, (M) Metalware, (Ma) Matchboxes, (MB) Money Boxes, (O) Oriental, (OAM) Old Amusement Machines, (P) Pottery, (PB) Perfume Bottles, (PL) Pot Lids, (PM) Papier Mâché, (PMem) Police Memorabilia, (Po) Postcards, (R) Radios, (R&C) Rugs & Carpets, (Ra) Railwayana, (RH) Rocking Horses, (S) Silver, (S&MI) Scientific & Medical Instruments, (SC) Scottish Collectables, (Scr) Scripophily), (Sew) Sewing, (Sh) Shipping, (SP) Staffordshire Pottery, (St) Stereoscopes, (T&MS) Tins & Metal Signs, (T) Textiles, (Ta) Tartanware, (TB) Teddy Bears, (Te) Telephones, (Ti) Tiles, (To) Toys, (TP) Torquay Pottery, (Tr) Treen, (TW) Tunbridge Ware, (TV) Televisions, (W) Watches, (Wr) Writing, (WS) Walking Sticks

LONDON

A. J. Partners (Shelley), J28 Gray's-in-the-Mews, 1-7 Davies Mews, W1. Tel: 071-629 7034/723 5363 (ADC)

Abstract, Kensington Church Street Antique Centre, 58-60 Kensington Church Street, W8. Tel: 071-376 2652 (ADJ)

Academy Costumes Ltd. (Hire only), 25 Murphy Street, SE1. Tel: 071-620 0771 (T, C)

Act One Hire Ltd., 2a Scampston Mews, Cambridge Gardens, W10. Tel: 081-960 1456/1494 (T, C)

Andrews, Frank, 10 Vincent Road, N22. Tel: 081-881 0658 (home) (G)

Antique Textile Company, 100 Portland Road, Holland Park, W11. Tel: 071-221 7730 (T, C)

Anything American, 33-35 Duddenhill Lane, NW10. Tel: 081-451 0320 (Ju)

Baddiel, Colin, Gray's Mews, 1-7 Davies Mews, W1. Tel: 071-408 1239/081-452 7243 (T)

Baddiel, Sarah, The Book Gallery, B12 Gray's Mews, 1-7 Davies Mews, W1. Tel: 071-408 1239/081-452 7243 (Go)

Bangs, Christopher, SW11. Tel: 071-223 5676 (M)

Barham Antiques, 83 Portobello Road, W11. Tel: 071-727 3845 (B)

Barometer Fair, at Cartographia Ltd., Pied Bull Yard, Bury Place, Bloomsbury, WC1. Tel: 071-404 4521/4050 (Ba)

Beverley & Beth, 30 Church Street, NW8. Tel: 071-262 1576 (AD, G)

Blanchard, Sophia, Alfie's Antique Market, Church Street, NW8. Tel: 071-723 5731 (T)

Boston, Nicolaus, Kensington Church Street Antiques Centre, 58-60 Kensington Church Street, W8. Tel: 071-376 0425 (P)

Bridge, Christine, 78 Castelnau, SW13. Tel: 081-741 5501 (G)

British Commemoratives, 1st Floor, Georgian Village, Camden Passage, N1. Tel: 071-359 4560 (Com, G&CC)

Brittania, Stand 101, Gray's Antique Market, 58 Davies Street, W1. Tel: 071-629 6772 (D)

Button Queen, 19 Marylebone Lane, W1. Tel: 071-935 1505 (Bu)

Cameron, Jasmin, Stand J6, Antiquarius, 131-141 King's Road, SW3. Tel: 071-351 4154 (Wr)

Capon, Patrick, 350 Upper Street, Islington, N1. Tel: 071-354 0487/081-467 5722 (Ba)

Casimir, Jack, Ltd., The Brass Shop, 23 Pembridge Road, W11. Tel: 071-727 8643 (M)

Cekay Antiques, Gray's Antique Market, 58 Davies Street, W1. Tel: 071-629 5130 (WS)

Chelsea Lion, Chenil Galleries, 181-183 King's Road, SW3. Tel: 071-351 9338 (Do, To)

Chenil Galleries, Enigma Z2, Pamela Haywood Z3, Persifage Z5, Forthergill Crowley D11-12, 181-183 King's Road, SW3. Tel: 071-351 5353 (T, C)

Childhood Memories, Teapot Arcade, Portobello Road, W11. (Do)

Clark, Gerald, Antiques, 1 High Street, Mill Hill Village, NW7 Tel: 081-906 0342 (SP)

Classic Collection, Pied Bull Yard, Bury Place, WC1. Tel: 071-831 6000 (Ca)

Classic Costumes Ltd..
Tel: 081-764 8858/071-620 0771
(T, C)

Collector's Shop, The,
9 Church Street, NW8.
Tel: 071-706 4586
(D)

Cropper, Stuart, Gray's Mews, 1-7 Davies Mews, W1.
Tel: 071-629 7034
(To)

Dauphin Display Cabinet Co., 118 Holland Park Avenue, W11.
Tel: 071-727 0715
(DS)

David, 141 Gray's Antique Market, Davies Street, W1.
Tel: 071-493 0208
(Cor, K, PMem)

De Fresne, Pierre,
'Beaux Bijoux', Q9/10 Antiquarius, 135 King's Road, SW3.
Tel: 071-352 8882
(ADJ)

Decodence (Bakelite) (Gad Sassower), Shop 13, The Mall, Camden Passage, N1.
Tel: 071-354 4473
(AD)

Dollyland, 864 Green Lanes, Winchmore Hill, N21.
Tel: 081-360 1053
(Do)

Donay, 35 Camden Passage, N1.
Tel: 071-359 1880
(Ga)

Donohoe, L25/7, M10/12 Gray's Mews, 1-7 Davies Mews, W1.
Tel: 071-629 5633/081-455 5507
(S)

East Gates Antiques, Stand G006, Alfie's Antique Market, 13-25 Church Street, NW8.
Tel: 071-724 5650
(G)

Eureka Antiques, Geoffrey Vanns Arcade, 105 Portobello Road, W11.
(Saturdays)
(Ta, CaC, J)

Field, Audrey, Alfie's Antique Market, 13-25 Church Street, NW8.
Tel: 071-723 6066
(L&L)

Fobbister, Rosemary, Stand 28, The Chelsea Antique Market, 245-263 King's Road, SW3.
Tel: 071-352 5581
(PM)

Gallery of Antique Costume & Textiles, 2 Church Street, Marylebone, NW8.
Tel: 071-723 9981
(T, C)

Gee, Rob, Flea Market, Camden Passage, N1.
Tel: 071-226 6627
(Bot, PL)

Georgian Village, 1st Floor, Islington Green, N1.
Tel: 071-226 1571/5393
(Bot)

German, Michael, 38B Kensington Church Street, W8.
Tel: 071-937 2771
(A&A, WS)

Gerwat-Clark, Brenda, Alfie's Antique Market, 13 25 Church Street, NW8.
Tel: 071-706 4699
(Do)

Goldsmith & Perris, Stand 327, Alfie's Antique Market, 13-25 Church Street, NW8.
Tel: 071-724 7051
(S)

Gosh Comics, 39 Great Russell Street, WC1.
Tel: 071-636 1011
(Co)

Harbottle, Patricia, Geoffrey Vann Arcade, 107 Portobello Road, W11.
(Saturdays)
Tel: 071-731 1972
(Cor)

Harrington Bros., The Chelsea Antique Market, 253 King's Road, SW3.
Tel: 071-352 1720
(Bk)

Heather's Teddys, World Famous Arcade, 177 Portobello Road, W11.
Tel: 081-204 0106
(TB)

Hebbs, Pam,
5 The Annexe, Camden Passage, N1.
(TB)

Hogg, David, S141, Gray's Antique Market, Davies St., W1.
Tel: 071-493 0208
(BH)

Horne, Jonathan, 66B & C Kensington Church Street, W8.
Tel: 071-221 5658
(SP)

Howard, Derek, Chelsea Antique Market, 245-253 King's Road, SW3.
Tel: 071-352 4113
(S&MI)

Howard, Valerie
131E Kensington Church Street, W8
Tel: 071-792 9702
(P)

Ilse Antiques, 30-32 The Vaults, The Georgian Village, Islington, N1.
(Ti)

Jaertelius, Monica, The Mall, Camden Passage, N1.
Tel: 081-546 2807
(Bu)

Jag, Unit 6, Kensington Church Street Antiques Centre, 58-60, Kensington Church Street, W8.
Tel: 071-938 4404
(ADC)

Jessops, 65 Great Russell Street, WC1.
Tel: 071-831 3640
(Ca)

Keith, Old Advertising, Unit 14, 155a Northcote Road, Battersea, SW11.
Tel: 071-228 0741/6850
(T&MS)

King & Country, Unit 46, Alfie's Antique Market, 13-25 Church Street, NW8.
Tel: 071-724 3439
(Go)

Lassalle, Judith, 7 Pierrepont Arcade, Camden Passage, N1.
Tel: 071-607 7121
(Wed & Sat)
(RH)

Latford, Cliff, Photography, G006, Alfie's Antique Market, 13-25 Church Street, NW8.
Tel: 071-724 5650, and at Colchester
Tel: 0206 564474
(Ca)

London Silver Vaults, Chancery House, 53-65 Chancery Lane, WC2.
Tel: 071-242 3844
(S)

Maskerade, Antique Centre, Kensington Church Street, W8.
Tel: 071-937 8974
(J)

Memories, 18 Bell Lane, Hendon, NW4.
Tel: 081-203 1772/202 9080
(Po)

Miller, Jess, PO Box 1461, W6.
Tel: 081-748 9314
(F)

Moderne, Stand 5, Georgian Village, Camden Passage, N1.
(Bu)

Murray Cards (International) Ltd., 51 Watford Way, Hendon Central, NW4.
Tel: 081-202 5688
(E, CC)

New Century, Art Pottery, 69 Kensington Church Street, W8.
Tel: 071-376 2810
(ADC)

Noelle Antiques, S26 Chelsea Antiques Market, 253 King's Road, SW3.
Tel: 071-352 5581
(BH)

Norman, Sue, Stand L4 Antiquarius, 135 King's Road, SW3.
Tel: 071-352 7217
(C)

Old Amusement Machines,.
Tel: 081-889 2213/0782 680667
(OAM)

Oosthuizen, Jacqueline 1st Floor, Georgian Village,
Camden Passage, N1.
Tel: 071-226 5393/352 5581 and
23 Cale Street, SW3.
Tel: 071-352 6071
(SP, TP)

Oosthuizen, Pieter G. K., 16 Britten Street, SW3
Tel: 071-352 1094/1493
(A&M)

Ormonde Gallery, 156 Portobello Road, W11.
Tel: 071-229 9800/042482 226
(O)

Past and Present Toys, 862 Green Lanes, Winchmore Hill, N21.
Tel: 081-364 1370
(TB, To)

Past and Present, York Arcade, Unit 5, Camden Passage, N1.
Tel: 071-833 2640
(ADC)

Patrician, 1st Floor, Georgian Village, Camden Passage, N1.
Tel: 071-359 4560/435 3159
(ADC, I, PB)

Pieces of Time, Gray's Mews, 1-7 Davies Street, W1.
Tel: 071-629 2422
(W)

Pinchin, Doug, Dixon's Antique Centre, 471 Upper Richmond Road West, East Sheen, SW14
Tel: 081-878 6788/948 1029
(D)

Powell, Sylvia, Decorative Arts, 18 The Mall, Camden Passage, N1.
Tel: 071-354 2977
(Ce)

Pleasures of Past Times, 11 Cecil Court, Charing Cross Road, WC2.
Tel: 071-836 1142
(Bk, GC)

Relic Antiques, 248 Camden High Street, NW1.
Tel: 071-485 8072
(K)

Reubens, 44 Honor Oak Park, Brockley, SE23.
Tel: 081-291 1786
(S&MI)

Rotation Antiques, Pierrepont Row Fleamarket, Camden Passage, N1.
Tel: 071-226 8211
(ADC)

Scripophily Shop, Britannia Hotel, Grosvenor Square, W1.
Tel: 071-495 0580
(Scr)

Stateside Comics plc, 125 East Barnet Road, N4
Tel: 081-449 5535
(Co)

Thimble Society of London, The Bees, S134 Gray's Antique Market, 58 Davies Street, W1.
Tel: 071-493 0560
(Sew)

Top Ten Comics, 9-12 St Anne's Court, Soho, W1.
Tel: 071-734 7388
(Co)

Trio (Theresa Clayton). Gray's Mews, 1-7 Davies Mews, W1.
Tel: 071-629 1184
(PB)

Ursula, P16, 15 & 14, Antiquarius, 135 King's Road, SW3.
Tel: 071-352 2203
(H/HP)

Vintage Cameras Ltd., 254 & 256 Kirkdale, Sydenham, SE26.
Tel: 081-778 5416/5841
(Ca)

Walker, Pat, Georgian Village, Camden Passage, N1
Tel: 071-359 4560/435 3159
(Do)

West, Mark J., Cobb Antiques, 39B High Street, Wimbledon Village, SW19.
Tel: 081-946 2811/540 7982
(G)

Weston, David, Ltd. 44 Duke Street St James, SW1.
Tel: 071-839 1051/2/3
(S&MI)

White, John, Alfie's Antique Market, 13-25 Church Street, NW8.
Tel: 071-723 0449
(ADC)

Wilcox, Norman, Alfie's Antique Market, 13-25 Church Street, NW8.
Tel: 071-724 5650
(R)

Wynyards Antiques, 5 Ladbroke Road, W11.
Tel: 071-221 7936
(Tr)

Yesterday Child, Angel Arcade, 118 Islington High Street, N1.
Tel: 071-354 1601/0908 583403
(Do)

Young, Robert, Antiques, 68 Battersea Bridge Road, SW11.
Tel: 071-228 7847
(P)

Yvonne, K3 Chenil Galleries, 183 King's Road, SW3.
Tel: 071-352 7384
(Fa)

Zeitgeist, 58 Kensington Church Street, W8.
Tel: 071-938 4817
(A&C, AN)

Avon

Barometer Shop, 3 Lower Park Row, Bristol.
Tel: 0272 272565
(Ba)

Bath Dolls' Hospital & Teddy Bear Clinic, 2 Grosvenor Place, London Road, Bath.
Tel: 0225 319668
(Do)

Bristol Dolls' Hospital, 50-52 Alpha Road, Southville, Bristol.
Tel: 0272 664368
(Do)

China Doll, The, 31 Walcot Street, Bath.
Tel: 0225 465849
(Do, DHF)

Dando, Andrew, 4 Wood Street, Bath.
Tel: 0225 422702
(P)

Gibson, Gloria, 2 Beaufort West, London Road, Bath BA1 6QB.
Tel: 0225 446646
(B)

Great Western Toys, Great Western Antique Centre, Bartlett Street, Bath.
(To)

Jessie's Button Box, Great Western Antique Centre, Bartlett Street, Bath.
Tel: 0272 299065
(Bu)

Linford, Carr, 10-11 Walcot Buildings, London Road, Bath.
Tel: 0225 317516
(CaC)

Marchant, Nick, 13 Orwell Drive, Keynsham, Bristol.
Tel: 0272 865182
(M)

Pugh, Robert & Carol, Bath.
Tel: 0225 314713
(P)

Saffell, Michael & Jo, 3 Walcot Buildings, London Road, Bath.
Tel: 0225 315857
(T&MS)

Scott's, Bartlett Street Antiques Centre, Bartlett Street, Bath.
Tel: 0225 625335
(Ce)

Somervale Antiques, 6 Radstock Road, Midsomer Norton, Bath.
Tel: 0761 412686
(G, PB)

Winstone Stamp Company, S82 Great Western Antiques Centre, Bartlett Street, Bath.
Tel: 0225 310388
(CC, Ra)

Bedfordshire

Sykes Christopher Antiques, The Old Parsonage, Woburn.
Tel: 0525 290259
(Cor, S&MI, M)

Berkshire

Asquiths of Windsor, 10 George V Place, Thames Avenue, Windsor.
Tel: 0753 854954/831200
(TB)

Below Stairs, 103 High Street, Hungerford.
Tel: 0488 682317
(K)

Boxes From Derek McIntosh, 10 Wickham Road, Stockcross, Newbury.
Tel: 0488 38295
(B)

Mostly Boxes, 92 & 52b High Street, Eton,Windsor.
Tel: 0753 858470
(B, I, TW)

Buckinghamshire Cars Only, 4 Granville Square, Willen Local Centre, Willen, Milton Keynes.
Tel: 0908 690024
(To)

Foster, A. & E., Little Heysham, Forge Road, Naphill.
Tel: 024 024 2024
(Tr)

Neale, Gillian A., The Old Post Office, Wendover.
Tel: 0296 625335
(Ce)

Cambridgeshire

Cambridge Fine Art Ltd., Priest House, 33 Church Street, Little Shelford.
Tel: 0223 842866/843537
(BP)

Cheshire

Avalon, 1 City Walls, Northgate Street, Chester.
Tel: 0244 318406
(Po)

Dé Jà Vu Antiques, Hatters Row, Horsemarket Street, Warrington.
Tel: 0925 232677
(Te)

Dollectable, 53 Lower Bridge Street, Chester. Tel: 0244 44888/679195 (Do)

Eureka Antiques, 7a Church Brow, Bowdon. Tel: 061-926 9722 (CaC, J, Ta)

Nantwich Art Deco & Decorative Arts, 87 Welsh Row, Nantwich. Tel: 0270 624876 (AD)

Rayment, Derek, Antiques, Orchard House, Barton Road, Barton, Nr Malpas. Tel: 0829 270429 (Ba)

Cornwall
Millcraft Rocking Horse Co., Lower Trannack Mill, Coverack Bridges, Helston. Tel: 0326 573316 (To, RH)

Cumbria
Bacchus Antiques, Longlands at Cartmel. Tel: 044 854 475 (Cor)

Ceramic Restorers, Domino Restorations, 129 Craig Walk, Windermere. Tel: 05394 45751 (Ce)

Derbyshire
Norman King, 24 Dinting Road, Glossop. Tel: 04574 2946 (Po)

Spurrier-Smith Antiques, 28b, 39-41 Church Street, Ashbourne. Tel: 0335 43669/42198 (M)

Devon
Bampton Telephone & General Museum of Communication and Domestic History, 4 Brook Street, Bampton. (Te)

Hill, Jonathan 2-4 Brook Street, Bampton. Tel: 0398 31310 (R)

Honiton Lace Shop, 44 High Street, Honiton. Tel: 0404 42416 (L&L)

Dorset
Chicago Sound Company, Northmoor House, Colesbrook, Gillingham. Tel: 0747 824338 (Ju)

Lionel Geneen Ltd., 781 Christchurch Road, Boscombe, Bournemouth. Tel: 0202 422961 (O)

Mitton, Mervyn A., 161 The Albany, Manor Road, Bournemouth. Tel: 0202 293767 (PMem)

Old Button Shop, Lytchett Minster. Tel: 0202 622169 (Bu)

Old Harbour Antiques, The Old Bakery, 3 Hope Square, Weymouth. Tel: 0305 777838 (Sh)

Yesterday's Tackle & Books, 42 Clingan Road, Southbourne. Tel: 0202 476586 (F)

Essex
Blackwells of Hawkwell, 733 London Road, Westcliff-on-Sea. Tel: 0702 72248 (DHF)

East Gates Antiques, 91a East Hill, Colchester. Tel: 0206 564474 (G)

G.K.R. Bonds Ltd., PO Box 1, Kelvedon. Tel: 03765 71711 (Scr)

It's About Time, 863 London Road, Westcliff-on-Sea. Tel: 0702 72574 (Ba)

R. F. Postcards, 17 Hilary Crescent, Rayleigh. Tel: 0268 743222 (Po)

Waine, A., Tweedale, Rye Mill Lane, Feering, Colchester. (ADC)

Old Telephone Co., The Granary Antiques Centre, Battlesbridge, Nr. Wickford. Tel: 0268 734005 (Te)

Gloucestershire
Acorn Antiques, Sheep Street, Stow-on-the-Wold. Tel: 0451 831519 (Ce)

Cotswold Motor Museum, The Old Mill, Bourton-on-the-Water. Tel: 0451 21255 (Au)

Greenwold, Lynn, Digbeth Street, Stow-on-the-Wold. Tel: 0451 30398 (J)

Lillian Middleton's Antique Dolls Shop, Days Stable, Sheep Street, Stow-on-the-Wold. Tel: 0451 31542 (Do)

Park House Antiques, Park Street, Stow-on-the-Wold. Tel: 0451 30159 (Do, DHF, TB)

Samarkand Galleries, 2 Brewery Yard, Stow-on-the-Wold. Tel: 0451 832322 (R&C)

Specialised Postcard Auctions, 25 Gloucester Street, Cirencester. Tel: 0285 659057 (Po)

The Trumpet, West End, Minchinhampton, Nr. Stroud. Tel: 0453 883027 (Col)

Hampshire
Art Deco China Centre, 62 Murray Road, Horndean. Tel: 0705 597440 (ADC)

Cobwebs, 78 Northam Road, Southampton. Tel: 0703 227458 (Ae, Au, Sh)

Evans & Partridge Auctioneers, Agriculture House, High Street, Stockbridge. Tel: 0264 810702 (F)

Gazelles, 31 Northam Road, Southampton. Tel: 0703 235291 (AD)

Goss & Crested China Ltd., 62 Murray Road, Horndean. Tel: 0705 597440 (G&CC)

Millers of Chelsea Ltd., Netherbrook House, Christchurch Road, Ringwood. Tel: 0425 472062 (P)

Romsey Medal Centre, 5 Bell Street, Romsey. Tel: 0794 512069 (A&M)

Toys Through Time, Fareham. Tel: 0329 288678 (Do)

Hereford & Worcester
Barometer Shop, New Street, Leominster. Tel: 0568 3652 (Ba)

BBM Jewellery & Coins, (W. V. Crook), 8-9 Lion Street, Kidderminster. Tel: 0562 744118 (I, J, Cns)

Button Museum, Kyrle Street, Ross-on-Wye. Tel: 0989 66089 (Bu)

Radiocraft, 56 Main Street, Sedgebarrow, Nr Evesham. Tel: 0386 881988 (R)

Hertfordshire
Ambeline Antiques, By George Antique Centre, St. Albans. Tel: 0727 53032/081-445 8025 (H/HP)

Coombs, P., 87 Gills Hill Lane, Radlett. Tel: 0923 856949 (Ca)

Forget Me Not, By George Antique Centre, 23 George Street, St. Albans. Tel: 0727 53032/0903 261172 (J)

Oriental Rug Gallery, 42 Verulam Road, St Albans. Tel: 0727 41046 (R&C)

Isle of Wight
Nostalgia Toy Museum, High Street, Godshill. Tel: 0983 730055 (To)

Vectis Model Auctions, Ward House, 12 York Avenue, East Cowes. Tel: 0983 292272 (To)

Kent
Amelia Dolls, Pantiles Spa Antiques, The Pantiles, Tunbridge Wells. Tel: 0892 541377/0342 713223 (Do)

Amherst Antiques, 23 London Road, Riverhead, Sevenoak. Tel: 0732 455047 (Tr)

Antiques & Interiors, 22 Ashford Road, Tenterden. Tel: 05806 5422 (PM, T)

Beaubush House Antiques,
95 High Street, Sandgate,
Folkestone.
Tel: 0303 49099
(SP)

Blackford, Rowena, at
Penny Lampard's,
Antique Centre, 31 High
Street, Headcorn.
Tel: 0622 890682/861360
(AD, K)

Burman, Valerie, 69 High
Street, Broadstairs.
Tel: 0843 862563
(ADC)

Candlestick & Bakelite,
30 Prescott Avenue, Petts
Wood, Orpington.
Tel: 081-467 3743
(Te)

Collectables, PO Box 130,
Rochester.
Tel: 0634 828767
(Col)

Dolls House Workshop,
54a London Road,
Teynham.
Tel: 0795 533445
(DHF)

Falstaff Antiques Motor
Museum,
63-67 High Street,
Rolvenden,
Nr. Cranbrook.
Tel: 0580 241234
(Au)

Hadlow Antiques, No. 1
The Pantiles, Tunbridge
Wells.
Tel: 0892 29858
(Do)

Heggie, Stuart, 58
Northgate, Canterbury.
Tel: 0227 470422
(Ca, St, R)

Kirkham, Harry, Garden
House Antiques, 118 High
Street, Tenterden.
Tel: 05806 3664
(F)

Kollectomania,
4 Catherine Street,
Rochester.
Tel: 0634 45099
(Ma)

Lace Basket, 1a East
Cross, Tenterden.
Tel: 05806 3923
(L&L, H/HP)

Lampard, Penny,
28 High Street, Headcorn
Tel: 0622 890682
(K)

Magpie's Nest, 14 Palace
Street, Canterbury.
Tel: 0227 764883
(Do, DHF)

Old Saddlers Antiques,
Church Road, Goudhurst,
Cranbrook.
Tel: 0580 211458
(J, M)

Page Angela Antiques,
Tunbridge Wells.
Tel: 0892 22217
(P)

Reeves, Keith & Veronica,
Burgate Antiques,
10c Burgate, Canterbury.
Tel: 0227 456500/0634
375098
(A&M)

Roses, 60 King Street,
Sandwich.
Tel: 0304 615303
(Col)

Serendipity, 168 High
Street, Deal.
Tel: 0304 369165/366536
(Ce)

Stevenson Brothers, The
Workshop, Ashford Road,
Bethersden, Ashford.
Tel: 0233 820363
(RH)

Strawsons Antiques,
33, 39 & 41 The Pantiles,
Tunbridge Wells.
Tel: 0892 30607
(TW)

Sturge, Mike, 39 Union
Street, Maidstone.
Tel: 0622 54702
(Po)

Up Country, Old Corn
Stores, 68 St. John's Road,
Tunbridge Wells.
Tel: 0892 23341
(K)

Variety Box, 16 Chapel
Place, Tunbridge Wells.
Tel: 0892 31868/21589
(BH, G&CC, Fa, G, H/HP,
Sew, S, TW)

Lancashire

A. S. Antiques, 26 Broad
Street, Pendleton, Salford.
Tel: 061-737 5938
(AD)

British Heritage
Telephones, 11 Rhodes
Drive, Unsworth, Bury.
Tel: 061-767 9259
(Te)

Bunn Roy W. Antiques,
34-36 Church Street,
Barnuldswick, Colne.
Tel: 0282 813703
(Ce, SP)

Lister Art Books, 22
Station Road, Banks,
Southport.
Tel: 0704 232033
(Bk)

Old Bakery The, 36
Inglewhite Road,
Longridge, Nr. Preston.
Tel: 0772 785411
(K)

Leicestershire

Charnwood Antiques,
Coalville, Leicester.
Tel: 0530 38530
(BP)

Jessups of Leicester Ltd.,
98 Scudamore Road,
Leicester.
Tel: 0533 320033
(Ca)

Williamson Janice, 9
Coverdale Road, Meadows
Wiston, Leicester.
Tel: 0533 812926
(Ce, D)

Lincolnshire

20th Century Frocks,
Lincolnshire Art Centre,
Bridge Street, Horncastle.
Tel: 06582 7794/06588
3638
(T)

Junktion, The Limes, Fen
Road, Stickford, Boston.
Tel: 0205 480087/480431
(To, T&MS)

Legends Rocking Horses,
Yew Tree Farmhouse,
Holme Road, Kirton
Holme, Boston.
Tel: 020 579 214
(To, RH)

Middlesex

Albert's Cigarette Card
Specialists, 113 London
Road, Twickenham.
Tel: 081-891 3067
(CC)

Ives, John, 5 Normanhurst
Drive, Twickenham.
Tel: 081-892 6265
(Bk)

Norfolk

Bluebird Arts, 1 Mount
Street, Cromer.
Tel: 0263 512384/78487
(Po)

Howkins, Peter, 39, 40 &
135 King Street, Great
Yarmouth.
Tel: 0493 844639
(J)

Kensington Pottery,
Winstanley Cats,
1 Grammar School Road,
North Walsham.
Tel: 0692 402962
(Ce, P)

Pundole, Neville, 1 White
House Lane, Attleborough.
Tel: 0953 454106
(ADC)

Trains & Olde Tyme Toys,
Aylsham Road, Norwich.
Tel: 0603 413585
(To)

Yesteryear Antiques,
24d Magdalen Street,
Norwich.
Tel: 0603 622908
(Ce, D)

North
Humberside

Marine Art Posters
Services, 42 Ravenspur
Road, Bilton, Hull.
Tel: 0482 874700/815115
(Sh)

Northamptonshire

Shelron, 9 Brackley Road,
Towcester.
Tel: 0327 50242
(Po)

Nottinghamshire

Breck Antiques, 726
Mansfield Road,
Nottingham.
Tel: 0602 605263
(Ce)

Keyhole The ,Dragonwyck,
Far Back Lane, Farnsfield,
Newark.
Tel: 0623 882590
(L&K)

Reflections of a Bygone
Age, 15 Debdale Lane,
Keyworth.
Tel: 06077 4079
(Po)

Vennett -Smith, T.,
11 Nottingham Road,
Gotham.
Tel: 0602 830541
(E,Po)

Vintage Wireless Shop,
The Hewarths, Sandiacre,
Nottingham.
Tel: 0602 393138
(R, TV

Oxfordshire

Clockwork & Steam,
The Old Marmalade
Factory, 27 Parkend
Street, Oxford.
Tel: 0865 200321
(To)

Comics & Showcase, 19-20
St. Clements Street,
Oxford.
Tel: 0865 723680
(Co)

Key Antiques, 11 Horse
Fair, Chipping Norton.
Tel: 0608 3777
(M)

Manfred Schotten, Crypt Antiques, 109 High Street, Burford.
Tel: 099 382 2302
(Go)

R.A.T.S., Unit 16, Telford Road, Bicester.
Tel: 0869 242161/40842
(T&MS)

Strange Peter, Restorer, The Willows, Sutton, Oxford.
Tel: 0865 882020
(Do)

Teddy Bears, 99 High Street, Witney.
Tel: 0993 702616
(TB)

Thames Gallery, Thameside, Henley-on Thames.
Tel: 0491 572449
(S)

Shropshire
Antiques on the Square, 2 Sandford Court, Church Stretton.
Tel: 0694 724111
(ADC)

Manser, F. C., & Son Ltd., 53 Wyle Cop, Shrewsbury.
Tel: 0743 51120
(CaC, Fa, S)

Nock Deighton, Saleroom Centre, Tasley, Bridgnorth.
Tel: 0746 762666
(F)

Rocking Horse Workshop, Ashfield House, The Foxholes, Wem.
Tel: 0939 32335
(RH)

Scot Hay House Antiques, 7 Nantwich Road, Woore.
Tel: 063 081 7118
(K)

Stretton Models, 12 Beaumont Road, Church Stretton.
Tel: 0694 723737
(To)

Summers Roger, 17 Daddlebrook, Hollinswood, Telford.
(BM)

Tiffany Antiques, Unit 3, Shrewsbury Antique Centre, 15 Princess Howe, The Square, Shrewsbury.
Tel: 0270 257425
and
Unit 15, Shrewsbury Antique Market, Frankwell Quay Warehouse, Shrewsbury.
Tel: 0270 257425
(Col, K)

Vintage Fishing Tackle Shop & Angling Art Gallery, 103 Longden Coleham, Shrewsbury.
Tel: 0743 69373
(F)

Staffordshire
Gordon The 'Ole Bottleman, 25 Stapenhill Road, Burton-on-Trent.
Tel: 0283 67213
(Bot)

Midwinter Antiques, 13 Brunswick Street, Newcastle-under-Lyme.
Tel: 0782 712483
(T)

Somerset
House, Bernard G., Mitre Antiques, Market Place, Wells.
Tel: 0749 72607
(Ba)

London Cigarette Card Co. Ltd., Sutton Road, Somerton.
Tel: 0458 73452
(CC)

Spencer & Co., Margaret, Dept AD, Chard Road, Crewkerne.
Tel: 0460 72362
(RH)

Yesterday's Paper, 40 South View, Holcombe Rogus, Wellington.
Tel: 0823 672774
(Co)

Suffolk
Crafers Antiques, The Hill, Wickham Market.
Tel: 0728 747347
(Ce, SP, Sew)

Hoad, W. L., 9 St. Peter's Road, Kirkley, Lowestoft.
Tel: 0502 587758
(CC)

Surrey
Burns, David, 116 Chestnut Grove, New Malden.
Tel: 081-949 7356
(S&MI)

Church Street Antiques, 15 Church Street, Godalming.
Tel: 0483 860894
(ADC, Com)

Dorking Dolls House Gallery, 23 West Street, Dorking.
Tel: 0306 885785
(Do)

Nostalgia Amusements, 22 Greenwood Close, Thames Ditton.
Tel: 081-398 2141
(Ju)

Sheppard Press, Unit 2, Monk's Walk, Farnham.
Tel: 0252 734347
(Bk)

Victoriana Dolls, Reigate.
Tel: 0737 249525
(Do)

West Street Antiques, 63 West Street, Dorking.
Tel: 0306 883487
(A&M)

Wych House Antiques, Wych Hill, Woking.
Tel: 04862 64636
(K)

Sussex
Barclay Antiques, 7 Village Mews, Little Common, Bexhill-on-Sea.
Tel: 0797 222734
(TW)

Bartholomew, John & Mary, The Mint Arcade, 71 The Mint, Rye.
Tel: 0797 225952
(Po)

Beech, Ron, Brambledean Road, Portslade, Brighton.
Tel: 0273 423355
(Ce, PL)

Bygones, Collectors Shop, 123 South Street, Lancing.
Tel: 0903 750051/763470
(Col, Po)

Chateaubriand Antique Centre, High Street, Burwash.
Tel: 0435 882535
(Cor, O, L&L)

Dolls Hospital, 17 George Street, Hastings.
Tel: 0424 444117/422758
(Do)

Ginns, Ray & Diane, PO Box 129, East Grinstead.
Tel: 0342 326041
(SP)

Keiron James Designs, St Dominic's Gallery, 4 South Street, Ditchling.
Tel: 0273 846411
(TB)

Lingard, Ann, Rope Walk Antiques, Rye.
Tel: 0797 223486
(K, Ti)

Old Mint House, Pevensey.
Tel: 0323 762337
(P)

Pearson, Sue, 13½ Prince Albert Street, Brighton.
Tel: 0273 29247
(Do, TB)

Recollect Studios, Dept. M, The Old School, London Road, Sayers Common.
Tel: 0273 833314
(Do)

Rin Tin Tin, 34 North Road, Brighton.
Tel: 0273 672424/733689
(eves)
(Col, T&MS)

Russell, Leonard, 21 King's Avenue, Mount Pleasant, Newhaven.
Tel: 0273 515153
(Ce, Com)

Sussex Commemorative Centre, 88 Western Road, Hove.
Tel: 0273 773911
(Ce)

Trains, 67 London Road, Bognor Regis.
Tel: 0243 864727
(To)

V.A.G. & Co., Possingworth Craft Centre, Brownings Farm, Blackboys, Uckfield.
Tel: 0323 507488
(A&M)

Verrall Brian R. & Co., The Old Garage, High Street, Handcross, Haywards Heath.
Tel: 0444 400678
(Au)

Wallis & Wallis, West Street Auction Galleries, Lewes.
Tel: 0273 480208
(A&M, To)

Tyne & Wear
Ian Sharp Antiques (Maling Ware), 23 Front Street, Tynemouth.
Tel: 091-296 0656
(Ce)

Warwickshire
Arbour Antiques Ltd., Poet's Arbour, Sheep Street, Stratford-upon-Avon.
Tel: 0789 293453
(A&M)

Art Deco Ceramics, Stratford Antique Centre, Ely Street, Stratford-upon-Avon.
Tel: 0789 297496/297244
(ADC)

Bowler, Simon, Smith Street Antique Centre, Warwick.
Tel: 0926 400554
(O)

Central Antique Arms & Militaria, Smith Street Antique Centre, 7 Smith Street, Warwick.
Tel: 0926 497864
(A&M)

Fab, 130 Queens Road, Nuneaton.
Tel: 0203 382399
(Col)

Jazz, Civic Hall, Rother Street, Stratford-upon-Avon.
Tel: 0789 298362
(ADC)

Lions Den, 31 Henley Street, Stratford-upon-Avon.
Tel: 0789 415802
(ADC, P)

Midlands Goss & Commemoratives, Warwick Antique Centre, 22 High Street, Warwick.
Tel: 0926 495704
(Ce, Com, G&CC)

Paull, Janice, 125 Warwick Road, Kenilworth.
Tel: 0926 55253
(P, LB)

Rich Designs, 11 Union Street, Stratford-upon-Avon.
Tel: 0789 772111
(ADC)

Time Machine, Paul M. Kennelly, 198 Holbrook Lane, Coventry.
Tel: 0203 663557
(To)

West Midlands

Doghouse The, 309 Bloxwich Road, Walsall.
Tel: 0922 30829
(K)

Moseley Railwayana Museum, Birmingham.
Tel: 021-449 9707
(Ra, To)

Mr Morgan, F11 Swincross Road, Old Swinford, Stourbridge.
Tel: 0384 397033
(TB)

Nostalgia & Comics, 14-16 Smallbrook, Queensway City Centre, Birmingham.
Tel: 021-643 0143
(Co)

Railwayana Collectors Journal, 7 Ascot Road, Moseley, Birmingham.
(Ra)

Sawyer, George, 11 Frayne Avenue, Kingswinford.
Tel: 0384 273847
(Po)

Walton & Hipkiss, 111 Worcester Road, Hagley, Stourbridge.
Tel: 0562 885555/886688
(Au)

Wiltshire

Coppins of Corsham Repairs, 1 Church Street, Corsham.
Tel: 0249 715404
(J)

Expressions, 17 Princess Street, Shrewsbury.
Tel: 0743 51731
(ADC)

Oxley, P. A., The Old Rectory, Cherhill, Nr. Calne.
Tel: 0249 816227
(Ba)

Relic Antiques, Lea, Malmesbury,
Tel: 0666 822332
(T&MS)

Wells, David, Salisbury Antique & Collectors Market, 37 Catherine Street, Salisbury.
Tel: 0425 476899
(Po, To)

Yorkshire

Barnett, Tim, Carlton Gallery, 60a Middle Street, Driffield.
Tel: 0482 443954
(ADC)

British Bottle Review, 2 Strafford Avenue, Elsecar, Nr. Barnsley.
Tel: 0226 745156/0709 879303
(Bot)

Camera House, Oakworth Hall, Colne Road, Oakworth.
Tel: 0535 642333
(Ca)

Clarke, Andrew, 42 Pollard Lane, Bradford.
Tel: 0274 636042
(To)

Crested China Company, Station House, Driffield.
Tel: 0377 47042
(G&CC)

Danby Antiques, 65 Heworth Road, York.
Tel: 0904 415280
(B)

Echoes, 650a Halifax Road, Eastwood, Todmorden.
Tel: 0706 817505
(T)

Haley, John & Simon, 89 Northgate, Halifax.
Tel: 0422 822148
(To, MB)

Hewitt, Muir, Halifax Antiques Centre, Queens Road, Gibbet Street, Halifax.
Tel: 0442 366657
(ADC)

In Retrospect, 2 Pavement, Pocklington, York.
Tel: 0759 304894
(P)

Memory Lane, 69 Wakefield Road, Sowerby Bridge.
Tel: 0422 833223
(TB)

National Railway Museum, Leeman Road, York.
Tel: 0904 621261
(Ra)

Rouse, Sue, The Dolls House, Gladstone Buildings, Hope Street, Hebden Bridge.
Tel: 0422 845606
(Do)

Sheffield Railwayana Auctions, 43 Little Norton Lane, Sheffield.
Tel: 0742 745085
(Ra)

Spencer Bottomley, Andrew, The Coach House, Thongsbridge, Holmfirth.
Tel: 0484 685234
(A&M)

Windmill Antiques, 4 Montpelier Mews, Harrogate.
Tel: 0423 530502
(B, M, RH)

Scotland

AKA Comics & Books,, 33 Virginia Street, Glasgow,
Tel: 041-552 8731
(Co)

Black Laurance, 45 Cumberland Street, Edinburgh.
Tel: 031-557 4543
(Ta)

Bow Well Antiques, 103 West Bow, Edinburgh.
Tel: 031-225 3335
(Gr, SC)

Edinburgh Coin Shop, 2 Polwarth Crescent, Edinburgh.
Tel: 031-229 3007/2915
(A&M)

Koto Buki, The Milestone, Balmedie, Aberdeen.
Tel: 0358 42414
(O)

Maxtone Graham, Jamie, Lyne Haugh, Lyne Station, Peebles.
Tel: 07214 304
(F)

Millars, 9-11 Castle Street, Kirkcudbright.
Tel: 0557 30236
(ADC)

Miller, Jess, PO Box 1, Birnam, Dunkeld, Perthshire.
Tel: 03502 522
(F)

Now & Then Classic Telephones, 7/9 Cross-causeway, Edinburgh.
Tel: 031-668 2927/0592 890235
(Te)

Stockbridge Antiques, 8 Deanhaugh Street, Edinburgh.
Tel: 031 332 1366
(Do, T)

Toys & Treasures, Wendy B. Austin-Bishop, 65 High Street, Grantown on Spey, Morayshire,
Tel: 0479 2449
(Do)

Whittingham Crafts Ltd., 8 Pentland Court, Saltire Centre, Glenrothes, Fife.
Tel: 0592 630433
(RH)

Wales

Ayers, Brindley John, 45 St. Anne's Road, Hakin, Milford Haven, Pembrokeshire.
Tel: 06462 78359
(F)

Biffins, Ty Newydd, Gwalchmai Uchaf, Anglesey.
Tel: 0407 720550
(Po)

Corgi Toys Ltd., Kingsway, Swansea Industrial Estate, Swansea.
Tel: 0792 586223
(To)

Forbidden Planet, 5 Duke Street, Cardiff.
Tel: 0222 228885
(Co)

Gibbs, Paul, 25 Castle Street, Conwy.
Tel: 0492 593429
(BH, ADC, Ti)

Howards Antiques, 10 Alexandra Road, Aberystwyth, Dyfed.
Tel: 0970 624973
(P)

MacPherson, Stuart & Pam, A.P.E.S., Ty Isaf, Pont y Gwyddel, Llanfair T.H., Abergele, Clwyd.
Tel: 074 579 365
(RH)

Victorian Fireplaces, (Simon Priestley), Ground Floor, Cardiff Antique Centre, 69/71 St Mary Street, Cardiff.
Tel: 0222 30970/226049
(Ti)

Watkins, Islwyn, 1 High Street/29 Market Street, Knighton, Powys.
Tel: 0547 520145/528940
(P)

Williams, Paul, Forge Antiques, Synod Inn, Llandysul, Dyfed.
(T)

CALENDAR OF FAIRS

MAY

Sat 1
Exeter Livestock Centre,
Matford Park Road, Marsh
Barton, Exeter, Devon
Devon County Antiques Fairs
Tel: 0363 82571

Sat 1-3
The East Berkshire Antiques
Fair, Hall Place, Burchett's
Green, Maidenhead
Tel: 0548 531356

Sat 1-3
Mammoth Fair, Donington
Park, Leics
Four In One Promotions
Tel: 0455 233495

Sun 2
Picketts-Lock Leisure Centre,
Picketts-Lock Lane, Edmonton,
London N9
Jax Fairs
Tel: 0444 400570

Sun 2-3
Ceramics Fair, The Great
Danes Hotel, Hollingbourne,
Nr Maidstone, Kent
Wakefield Fairs
Tel: 0634 723461

Sun 2-3
The Sutton Coldfield Antiques
Fair, Penn's Hall Hotel, Sutton
Coldfield,
W. Midlands
Tel: 0952 595622

Wed 5-11
The BADA Fair, Pavilion, The
Duke of Yorks' H.Q., Chelsea,
London SW3

Fri 7-9
The Tatton Park Paintings
Fair, Knutsford, Cheshire
Robert Bailey
Tel: 0277 362662

Fri 7-9
The 9th West & Wales Antique
Ceramics Fair, The New Inn,
Langstone, Nr. Newport, Gwent
Antiques in Britain Fairs
Tel: 0273 423355

Fri 7-9
The Tyneside Antiques Fair,
Redworth Hall, Newton
Aycliffe, Co. Durham
Country House Events
Tel: 0937 541065

Sat 8-9
Antiques Fair, Hagley Hall,
Stourbridge
Wakefield Fairs
Tel: 0634 723461

Sat 8-9
The Leicester County Antiques
Fair, Prestwold Hall, Nr.
Loughborough
Cooper Antiques Fairs
Tel: 0672 515558

Sat 8-15
The 29th Buxton Antiques Fair,
Pavilion Gardens, Buxton,
Derbyshire
Cultural Exhibitions
Tel: 0483 422562

Wed 12-13
Mammoth Fair, The
Racecourse, Chepstow, Gwent
Four In One Promotions
Tel: 0455 233495

Fri 14-16
Truro Antiques, Collectors' and
Book Fair, City Hall, Truro
West Country Antiques &
Collectors' Fairs
Tel: 0225 424677

Fri 14-16
The Edinburgh Ceramics Fair,
The Roxburghe Hotel,
Charlotte Sq., Edinburgh
Wakefield Fairs
Tel: 0634 723461

Sat 15-16
Euro Antiques Fair, The
Showground, Oswestry,
Shropshire
Tel: 0565 634614

Sat 15-16
The Scottish Antiques Super
Fair, Scottish Exhibition
Centre, Glasgow
Tel: 091 537 2893

Wed 19-23
The 3rd Spring Grasmere
Antiques Fair, Grasmere Hall,
Grasmere, Cumbria
Tel: 0748 824095

Sat 22-23
Mammoth Fair, Springwood
Park Showground, Kelso,
Scotland
Four In One Promotions
Tel: 0455 233495

Mon 24-25
Mammoth Fair, Royal
Highland Centre, Ingliston,
Edinburgh
Four In One Promotions
Tel: 0455 233495

Thurs 27-29
Lewes Antiques Fair, The Corn
Exchange, Lewes, East Sussex
Antiques in Britain Fairs
Tel: 0273 423355

Fri 28-31
The Antique Dealers' Fair of
Wales, The Orangery, Margan
Park, Port Talbot
Tel: 0202 604306

Fri 28-31
The Harlaxton Antiques Fair,
Harlaxton Manor, Grantham,
Lincs
Robert Bailey
Tel: 0277 362662

Sat 29-30
Newton Abbot Antiques,
Collectors' & Book Fair, The
Racecourse, Newton Abbot
West Country Antiques &
Collectors' Fairs
Tel: 0225 424677

Sat 29-31
Antiques Fair, Carlton Towers,
Goole, N. Yorks
Tel: 0742 351502

Sat 29-31
The 1st Langley Park Antiques
Fair, Nr Loddon, Norfolk
Tel: 0603 737631

Sun 30-31
Fine Art & Antiques Fair,
Bellhouse Hotel, Beaconsfield,
Bucks
Midas Fairs
Tel: 0753 886993

Mon 31
Harrow Leisure Centre,
Christchurch Avenue, Harrow,
Middx
Jax Fairs
Tel: 0444 400570

JUNE

Thurs 3-4
North Devon Antique Dealers'
Fair, Queen's Hall, Barnstaple,
Devon
West Country Antiques &
Collectors' Fairs
Tel: 0225 424677

Thurs 3-13
The 1993 Fine Art & Antiques
Fair, Olympia, London W14
Tel: 071 370 8211

Sat 5
Exeter Livestock Centre,
Matford Park Road, Marsh
Barton, Exeter, Devon
Devon County Antiques Fairs
Tel: 0363 82571

Sat 5-6
Antiques Fair, Lamport Hall,
Nr Northampton
C.J. Antiques Fairs
Tel: 0952 595403

Sat 5-6
Antiques Fair, Pavilion
Gardens, Buxton
Unicorn Fairs
Tel: 098 987 312

Sat 5-6
The West Berkshire Antiques
Fair, Englefield House, Nr
Theale, Berks
Tel: 0548 531356

Sun 6
The London International
Antique Dolls, Toys, Miniatures
& Teddy Bear Fair, Kensington
Town Hall, W8
Tel: 081 693 5432

Sun 6
Picketts-Lock Leisure Centre,
Picketts-Lock Lane, Edmonton,
London N9
Jax Fairs
Tel: 0444 400570

Tues 8
Newark & Nottinghamshire
Showground, Newark
International Antique &
Collectors Fair Co., Ltd.
Tel: 0636 702326

Tues 8-10
The 16th Annual Aberdeen
Antiques Fair, New Marcliffe
Hall, Queens Road, Aberdeen
Antiques in Britain Fairs
Tel: 0273 423355

Wed 9-19
The Grosvenor House Antiques
Fair, Grosvenor House, Park
Lane, London W1
sTel: 0799 526699

Thurs 10-12
Petersfield Antiques Fair,
Petersfield, Hants
Gamlin Exhibition Services
Tel: 0452 862557

Fri 11-13
The South-East Counties
Antique Dealers' Fair,
Goodwood House, West Sussex
Country House Events
Tel: 0937 541065

Fri 11-13
Elegant Homes Show, Royal
Baths & Assembly Rooms,
Harrogate, N. Yorks Tel: 081
445 5040

Fri 11-13
The London Ceramics Fair,
Cumberland Hotel, Marble
Arch, London W1
Wakefield Fairs
Tel: 0634 723461

Fri 11-14
The International Ceramics
Fair & Seminar, Park Lane
Hotel, Piccadilly, London W1
Tel: 071 734 5491

Sat 12-13
Mammoth Fair, Donington
Park, Leics
Four In One Promotions
Tel: 0455 233495

Fri 18-20
The Thoresby Antiques Fair,
Thoresby Park Exhibition
Centre,
Nr Ollerton, Notts
Whittington Exhibitions
Tel: 081 644 9327

Fri 18-20
Giant Antique Fair, Bingley
Hall, County Showground,
Stafford
Bowman Fairs
Tel: 0532 843333

Fri 18-21
P.B.F.A. Book Fair, Hotel
Russell, London WC1
Tel: 0763 248400

Sat 19-20
Trent Park Antiques &
Collectors' Fair, Oakwood
London N14
Tel: 0923 852817

Tues 22-24
London Antiquarian Book Fair,
Park Lane Hotel, London W1
Tel: 071 379 3041

Thurs 24-27
The Westminster Antiques
Fair, Horticultural Old Hall,
London SW1
Penman Antiques Fairs
Tel: 0444 482514

Sat 26-27
Antiques Fair, Westpoint
Exhibition Centre, Exeter,
Devon
Devon County Antiques Fairs
Tel: 0363 82571

Tues 29-30
Euro Antiques Fair, Essex Co.
Showground, Gt. Leighs, Nr
Chelmsford
Tel: 0565 634614

JULY

Sun 4
Newmarket Racecourse
International Antique &
Collectors Fair Co., Ltd.
Tel: 0636 702326

Mon 5-8
Elegant Homes Pavilion, Royal
Show, Stoneleigh,
Warwickshire
Tel: 081 445 5040

Tues 6-8
Shropshire Summer Antiques
Fair, Lion Hotel, Shrewsbury
Antiques in Britain Fairs
Tel: 0273 423355

Thurs 8-11
The Sussex Oak & Country
Fair, Barkham Manor Barn,
Piltdown, Nr Newick, West
Sussex
Penman Antiques Fairs
Tel: 0444 482514

Fri 9-10
International Tyne & Wear
Antiques & Collectors' Fair,
Gosforth Park, Newcastle
Great Northern Antiques Fairs
Tel: 0642 550268

Sat 10-11
Antiques Fair, Showground,
Shepton Mallet, Somerset
Tel: 0278 691616

Mon 12-13
Mammoth Fair, The
Racecourse, Chepstow, Gwent
Four In One Promotions
Tel: 0455 233495

Wed 14-19
The Cambridge Art &
Sculpture Fair, Cambridge
Tel: 0223 242946

Fri 16-18
The Chester Racecourse
Antiques Fair, Chester
Robert Bailey
Tel: 0277 362662

Sat 17-18
Antiques Fair, Rhodes Centre,
Bishops Stortford
Britannia Antiques Fairs
Tel: 0984 31668

Sat 17-18
The North Cotswolds Antiques
Fair, Stanway House, Nr
Winchcombe, Glos
Cooper Antiques Fairs
Tel: 0672 515558

Wed 21
South of England Showground,
Ardingly, Sussex
International Antique &
Collectors Fair Co., Ltd.
Tel: 0636 702326

Thurs 22-24
Antiques Fair, The Game Fair,
Edinburgh
Robert Bailey
Tel: 0277 362662

Thurs 22-24
Elegant Homes Pavilion, The
Game Fair, Edinburgh
Tel: 081 455 5040

Thurs 22-25
The 27th Annual Snape
Antiques Fair, The Maltings,
Snape, Suffolk
Anglian Arts & Antiques
Tel: 0986 872368

Sat 24-25
Mammoth Fair, Kent County
Showground, Detling, Nr
Maidstone
Four In One Promotions
Tel: 0455 233495

Tues 27-28
Great Northern International
Antiques & Collectors' Fair,
Yorkshire Showground,
Harrogate
Great Northern Antiques Fairs
Tel: 0642 550268

Tues 27-29
The 22nd Annual Edinburgh
Antiques Fair, Roxburghe Hotel
Antiques in Britain Fairs
Tel: 0273 423355

Fri 30-1 Aug
Elegant Homes Show,
Kensington Town Hall, London
W8   Tel: 081 445 5040

AUGUST

Tues 3-5
The 1st West Highland
Antiques Fair, Argyllshire
Gathering Halls, Oban
Antiques in Britain Fairs
Tel: 0273 423355

Thurs 5-8
The NEC August Fair, National
Exhibition Centre, Birmingham
Tel: 021 780 4141

Sat 7
Exeter Livestock Centre,
Matford Park Road, Marsh
Barton, Exeter, Devon
Devon County Antiques Fairs
Tel: 0363 82571

Sat 7-8
Mammoth Fair, Donington
Park, Leics
Four In One Promotions
Tel: 0455 233495

Tues 10
Newark & Nottinghamshire
Showground, Newark
International Antique &
Collectors Fair Co., Ltd.
Tel: 0636 702326

Fri 13-15
Giant Antique Fair, Bingley
Hall, County Showground,
Stafford
Bowman Fairs
Tel: 0532 843333

Fri 13-15
The South Cotswolds Antiques
Fair, Westonbirt School,
Tetbury
Cooper Antiques Fairs
Tel: 0672 515558

Sat 14-15
Mammoth Fair, Springwood
Park Showground, Kelso,
Scotland
Four In One Promotions
Tel: 0455 233495

Tues 17-18
Mammoth Fair, Royal
Highland Centre, Ingliston,
Edinburgh
Four In One Promotions
Tel: 0455 233495

Thurs 19-22
West London Antiques Fair,
Kensington Town Hall, London
W8
Penman Antiques Fairs
Tel: 0444 482514

Fri 20-21
Truro Antiques, Collectors' &
Book Fair, City Hall, Truro
West Country Antiques &
Collectors' Fairs
Tel: 0225 424677

Fri 20-22
The Petworth Antiques Fair,
Seaford College, West Sussex
Robert Bailey
Tel: 0277 362662

Sat 21-22
Euro Antiques Fair, The
Showground, Oswestry,
Shropshire
Tel: 0565 634614

Fri 27-28
Antiques & Staffordshire
Figures Fair, King Edward
Hall, Lindfield, Sussex
Antiques in Britain Fairs
Tel: 0273 423355

Fri 27-30
The Ilkley Antiques Fair, Kings
Hall, Ilkley,
W. Yorks
Robert Bailey
Tel: 0277 362662

Sat 28-29
Antiques Fair, Pavilion
Gardens, Buxton
Unicorn Fairs
Tel: 098 987 312

Sun 29-30
Antiques Fair, Dorking Halls,
Dorking
Tel: 081 874 3622

Sun 29-30
Antiques Fair, Lamport Hall,
Nr Northampton
C.J. Antiques Fairs
Tel: 0952 595403

Sun 29-30
Fine Art & Antiques Fair,
Bellhouse Hotel, Beaconsfield
Midas Fairs
Tel: 0753 886993

Sun 29-30
Antiques Fair, Elvaston Castle,
Derby
Tel: 0602 459321

Mon 30
Harrow Leisure Centre,
Christchurch Avenue, Harrow,
Middx
Jax Fairs
Tel: 0444 400570

SEPTEMBER

Thurs 2-4
The 27th Annual East Anglia
Antiques Fair, Athenaeum,
Bury St. Edmunds, Suffolk
Antiques in Britain Fairs
Tel: 0273 423355

Fri 3-5
The Hatfield House Antiques
Fair, Hatfield House, Herts
Robert Bailey
Tel: 0277 362662

Fri 3-5
Great Northern International
Antiques & Collectors' Fair,
Yorkshire Showground,
Harrogate
Great Northern Antiques Fairs
Tel: 0642 550268

Sat 4-5
Ceramics Fair, Royal Crown
Derby Museum, Derby
Wakefield Fairs
Tel: 0634 723461

Sat 4-5
Mammoth Fair, Donington
Park, Leics
Four In One Promotions
Tel: 0455 233495

Sat 4-5
City of Plymouth Antiques
Fair, The Pavilions, Plymouth
Tel: 0934 624854

Sat 4-5
The Loseley Antiques Fair,
Loseley House,
Nr Guildford
Tel: 0548 531356

Sun 5
Picketts-Lock Leisure Centre,
Picketts-Lock Lane, Edmonton,
London N9
Jax Fairs
Tel: 0444 400570

Tues 7-12
The London Antique Dealers'
Fair, Café Royal, Regent Street,
London W1
Jane Sumner
Tel: 0672 870727

Thurs 9-11
Petersfield Antiques Fair,
Petersfield, Hants
Gamlin Exhibition Services Tel:
0452 862557

Thurs 9-11
24th Annual Welsh Antiques
Fair, Castle of Brecon Hotel,
Brecon, Powys
Antiques in Britain Fairs
Tel: 0273 423355

Fri 10-12
The Carlton Towers Antiques &
Fine Art Fair, Nr Goole, N.
Yorks
Whittington Exhibitions
Tel: 081 644 9327

Sat 11
Exeter Livestock Centre,
Matford Park Road, Marsh
Barton, Exeter, Devon
Devon County Antiques Fairs
Tel: 0363 82571

Sat 11-12
Ceramics Fair, Felbridge Hotel,
East Grinstead, Sussex
Wakefield Fairs
Tel: 0634 723461

Sat 11-12
Mammoth Fair, Kent County
Showground, Detling, Nr
Maidstone
Four In One Promotions
Tel: 0455 233495

Sun 12
The London International
Antique Dolls, Toys, Minatures
& Teddy Bear Fair, Kensington
Town Hall, W8
Tel: 081 693 5432

Tues 14-19
The Decorative Antiques &
Textiles Fair, Chelsea Harbour,
London SW10
Tel: 071 624 5173

Tues 14-25
The Chelsea Antiques Fair, Old
Town Hall, King's Road,
London SW3
Penman Antiques Fairs
Tel: 0444 482514

Wed 15-19
The Tatton Park Antiques Fair,
Knutsford, Cheshire
Robert Bailey
Tel: 0277 362662

Sat 18
Salisbury Leisure Centre, The
Butts, Hulse Road, Salisbury,
Wilts
Devon County Antiques Fairs
Tel: 0363 82571

Sat 18-19
Antiques Fair, Ragley Hall,
Warwickshire
Wakefield Fairs
Tel: 0634 723461

Wed 22
South of England Showground,
Ardingly, Sussex
International Antique &
Collectors Fair Co., Ltd.,
Tel: 0636 702326

Wed 22-26
20th Century British Art Fair,
The Royal College of Art,
Kensington Gore, London SW7
Tel: 071 603 0165

Thurs 23-25
Ceramics Fair, Pittville Pump
Room, Cheltenham
Wakefield Fairs
Tel: 0634 723461

Fri 24-25
The 51st London Arms Fair,
Earls Court Park Inn
International, Lillie Road,
London SW6
Tel: 071 405 7933

Fri 24-25
Great Northern International
Fair, Gosforth Park, Newcastle
Great Northern Antiques Fair
Tel: 0642 550268

Fri 24-26
The Harrogate Antiques Fair,
Crown Hotel, Harrogate
Robert Bailey
Tel: 0277 362662

Fri 24-26
The Thoresby Antiques Fair,
Nr Ollerton, Notts
Whittington Exhibitions
Tel: 081 644 9327

Sat 25-26
38th Warwickshire County
Antiques Fair, Cricket Ground,
Edgbaston, Birmingham
Tel: 021 743 2259

Sat 25-26
The Cotswolds Oak and
Country Antiques Fair,
Painswick House, Glos
Cooper Antiques Fairs
Tel: 0672 515558

Sat 25-26
Trent Park Antiques &
Collectors' Fair, Oakwood,
London N14
Tel: 0923 852817

Sat 25-26
Mammoth Fair, Showground,
Peterborough
Four In One Promotions
Tel: 0455 233495

Sat 25-27
The Aberdeen Antiques & Fine
Art Fair, Exhibition Centre,
Bridge of Don, Aberdeen
Tel: 0202 604306

Tues 28-29
Euro Antiques Fair, Essex
County Showground,
Gt. Leighs
Tel: 0565 634614

Thurs 30-6 Oct
Northern Antiques Fair 1993,
Royal Baths Assembly Rooms,
Harrogate, N. Yorks
Tel: 0223 832852

OCTOBER

Fri 1-3
Ceramics Fair, Margam Park,
Port Talbot, W. Glamorgan
Wakefield Fairs
Tel: 0634 723461

Fri 1-3
Antiques & Decorative Arts at
Rudding House, Nr Harrogate,
N. Yorks
Country House Events
Tel: 0937 541065

Fri 1-3
Giant Fair, Bingley Hall, Co.
Showground, Stafford
Bowman Fairs
Tel: 0532 843333

Fri 1-3
Harlaxton Antiques Fair,
Harlaxton Manor, Grantham
Robert Bailey
Tel: 0277 362662

Fri 1-5
25th Surrey Antiques Fair,
Civic Hall, Guildford
Cultural Exhibitions
Tel: 0483 422562

Sat 2-3
Antiques Fair, Pavilion
Gardens, Buxton
Unicorn Fairs
Tel: 098 987 312

Sun 3
Picketts-Lock Leisure Centre,
Picketts-Lock Lane, Edmonton,
London N9
Jax Fairs
Tel: 0444 400570

Mon 4-5
Little Chelsea Antiques Fair,
Old Town Hall, King's Road,
London SW3
Ravenscott Fairs
Tel: 071 727 5045

Wed 6-7
Mammoth Fair, The
Racecourse, Chepstow, Gwent
Four In One Promotions
Tel: 0455 233495

Wed 6-10
The Park Lane Antiques Fair,
The Park Lane Hotel,
Piccadilly, London W1
Tel: 071 603 0165

Sat 9-10
Antiques Fair, Westpoint
Exhibition Centre, Exeter
Devon County Antiques Fairs
Tel: 0363 82571

Tues 12-14
23rd Annual Hereford Antiques
Fair, Hereford Moathouse,
Hereford
Antiques in Britain Fairs
Tel: 0273 423355

Tues 12-17
The LAPADA Show 1993,
Royal College of Art,
Kensington Gore, London SW7
Tel: 071 823 3511

Fri 15-17
The Antique Dealers' Fair of
Scotland, Hopetoun House,
South Queensferry
Country House Events
Tel: 0937 541065

Fri 15-17
Cheshire County Antiques Fair,
Arley Hall, Knutsford
Cooper Antiques Fairs
Tel: 0672 515558

Sat 16-17
Antiques Fair, Potterspury
Lodge School, Towcester,
Northants
Tel: 0925 595622

Sat 16-17
Antiques Fair, Rhodes Centre,
Bishops Stortford
Britannia Antiques Fairs
Tel: 0984 31668

Sat 16-17
Ceramics Fair, Dyson Perrins
Museum, Worcester
Wakefield Fairs
Tel: 0634 723461

Sat 16-17
Mammoth Fair, Donington
Park, Leics
Four In One Promotions
Tel: 0455 233495

Tues 19
Newark & Nottinghamshire
Showground, Newark
International Antique &
Collectors Fair Co., Ltd.
Tel: 0636 702326

Tues 19-23
Kenilworth Antiques Fair,
Chesford Grange, Kenilworth,
Warwicks
Jane Sumner
Tel: 0672 870727

Wed 20-24
The 24th Grasmere Annual
Autumn Antiques Fair,
Grasmere, Cumbria
Tel: 0798 824095

Thurs 21-23
The Cheltenham Antiques &
Fine Art Fair, Pittville Pump
Room
Whittington Exhibitions
Tel: 081 644 9327

Thurs 21-23
22nd Annual St Edmunds
Antiques Fair, Athenaeum,
Bury St. Edmunds
Anglian Arts & Antiques
Tel: 0986 872368

Fri 22-23
Truro Antiques, Collectors' &
Book Fair, City Hall, Truro
West Country Antiques &
Collectors' Fairs
Tel: 0225 424677

Fri 22-24
The Brighton Antiques Fair,
Brighton
Robert Bailey
Tel: 0277 362662

Fri 22-24
The Lancashire Antique
Dealers' Fair, Up Holland, Nr
Wigan
Country House Events
Tel: 0937 541065

Fri 22-24
Antiques Fair, Royal Concert
Hall, Glasgow
Great Northern Antiques Fairs
Tel: 0642 550268

Sat 23-24
Ceramics Fair, Worksop
College, Worksop, Notts
Wakefield Fairs
Tel: 0634 723461

Sat 23-24
Rutland County Antiques Fair,
Uppingham College
Cooper Antiques Fairs
Tel: 0672 515558

Sat 23-24
Antiques Fair, Sherborne
School, Dorset
Devon County Antiques Fairs
Tel: 0363 82571

Tues 26
Harrow Leisure Centre,
Christchurch Avenue, Harrow,
Middx
Jax Fairs
Tel: 0444 400570

Wed 27-30
Bath Antiques & Fine Art Fair,
The Assembly Rooms, Bath
Tel: 0823 323363

Thurs 28-30
The 36th Bi-Annual High
Wycombe Antiques Fair, Royal
Grammar School
Tel: 0494 673674

Thurs 28-30
2nd East Anglian Antique
Dealers' Fair, Langley School,
Loddon, Norfolk
Tel: 0603 737631

Thurs 28-31
The East Berkshire Antiques
Fair, Hall Place, Burchett's
Green, Maidenhead
Tel: 0548 531356

Fri 29-31
2nd Annual Nuneaton Antiques
Fair, The Chase Hotel, Higham
Lane, Nuneaton
Antiques in Britain Fairs
Tel: 0273 423355

Fri 29-31
Chelsea Brocante Fair, Old
Town Hall, King's Road,
London SW3
Tel: 0428 685452

Fri 29-31
Antiques Fair, Stonyhurst, Nr
Whalley, Lancs
Robert Bailey
Tel: 0277 362662

Sat 30-31
36th Luton Antiques Fair,
Putteridge Bury, Luton, Beds
Tel: 0462 434525

Sat 30-31
The Bedford County Antiques
Fair, Woburn Abbey
Cooper Antiques Fairs
Tel: 0672 515558

NOVEMBER

Tues 2-7
42nd Kensington Antiques
Fair, Town Hall, Kensington,
London W8
Cultural Exhibitions
Tel: 0483 422562

Wed 3
South of England Showground,
Ardingly
International Antique &
Collectors Fair Co., Ltd.,
Tel: 0636 702326

Fri 5-6
Wells Antiques Fair, The
Bishop's Palace, Wells,
Somerset
West Country Antiques &
Collectors' Fairs
Tel: 0225 424677

Fri 5-6
The Dorset County Antiques
Fair, Bryanston School,
Blandford Forum
Cooper Antiques Fairs
Tel: 0672 515558

Fri 5-7
Antiques Fair, Puckrup Hall
Hotel, Nr Tewkesbury, Glos
Wakefield Fairs
Tel: 0634 723461

Fri 5-7
Great Northern International
Antiques Fair, Yorkshire
Showground, Harrogate
Great Northern Antiques Fairs
Tel: 0642 550268

Fri 5-7
The Antique Dealers' Fair of
North Wales, Portmeirion,
Porthmadog, Gwynedd
Country House Events
Tel: 0937 541065

Fri 5-7
The Hatfield House Antiques
Fair, Hatfield, Herts
Robert Bailey
Tel: 0277 362662

Sat 6
Exeter Livestock Centre,
Matford Park Road, Marsh
Barton, Exeter, Devon
Devon County Antiques Fairs
Tel: 0363 82571

Sun 7
Picketts-Lock Leisure Centre,
Picketts-Lock Lane, Edmonton,
London N9
Jax Fairs
Tel: 0444 400570

Thurs 11-14
The Solihull Antiques Show,
Conference Centre, Solihull
Tel: 0562 700791

Fri 12-14
The West of Scotland Antiques
Fair, Cameron House, Balloch,
Loch Lomond
Country House Events
Tel: 0937 541065

Fri 12-14
Ceramics Fair, Crown Hotel,
Harrogate, N. Yorks
Wakefield Fairs
Tel: 0634 723461

Fri 12-14
Holker Hall Antiques Fair,
Holker Hall, Cartmel, Cumbria
Robert Bailey
Tel: 0277 362662

Fri 12-17
The International Art &
Antiques Fair, Harrods (3rd
Floor), Knightsbridge, London
SW1
Tel: 071 734 5491

Sat 13-14
Antiques Fair, Showground,
Shepton Mallet, Somerset
Tel: 0278 691616

Sat 13-14
Antiques Fair, Pavilion
Gardens, Buxton
Unicorn Fairs
Tel: 098 987 312

Sun 14
The London International
Antique Dolls, Toys, Miniatures
& Teddy Bear Fair, Kensington
Town Hall, W8
Tel: 081 693 5432

Wed 17-23
Fine Art & Antiques Fair,
Olympia, London W14
Tel: 071 370 8211

Fri 19-21
The Christmas South-East
Counties Antiques Fair,
Goodwood House, Sussex
Country House Events
Tel: 0937 541065

Fri 19-21
16th Annual Edinburgh Winter
Antiques Fair, Roxburghe
Hotel, Edinburgh
Antiques in Britain Fairs
Tel: 0273 423355

Sat 20-21
Newton Abbot Antiques,
Collectors' & Book Fair, The
Racecourse, Newton Abbot,
Devon
West Country Antiques &
Collectors' Fairs
Tel: 0225 424677

Tues 23-24
The 14th English-Speaking
Union Antiques Fair,
Dartmouth House, Charles St.,
London W1
Tel: 071 493 3328

Tues 23-25
Elegant Homes Show, Royal
Horticultural Halls, London
SW1
Tel: 081 445 5040

Wed 24-28
The Castle Howard Antiques
Fair, Castle Howard, Malton,
Yorks
Robert Bailey
Tel: 0277 362662

Wed 24-29
City Antiques & Fine Art Fair
1993, Barbican Centre, London
EC2
Tel: 081 660 8008

Fri 26-28
Ceramics Fair, Michael Herbert
Hall, Wilton, Wilts
Wakefield Fairs
Tel: 0634 723461

Fri 26-28
The Welsh Decorative &
Antiques Fair, Dyffryn House,
St. Nicholas, Cardiff Tel: 0202
604306

Sat 27
Exeter Livestock Centre,
Matford Park Road, Marsh
Barton, Exeter, Devon
Devon County Antiques Fairs
Tel: 0363 82571

Sat 27-28
The Leicester County Antiques
Fair, Prestwold Hall, Nr
Loughborough
Cooper Antiques Fairs
Tel: 0672 515558

Sat 27-28
The City of Plymouth Antiques
Fair, The Pavilions
Tel: 0934 624854

Mon 29-30
Little Chelsea Antiques Fair,
Old Town Hall, King's Road,
London SW3
Ravenscott Fairs
Tel: 071 727 5045

DECEMBER
Thurs 2-5
The Winter Westminster
Antiques Fair, Royal
Horticultural Halls, London
SW1
Penman Antiques Fairs
Tel: 0444 482514

Fri 3-5
The Hoghton Tower Antiques
Fair, Nr Preston, Lancs
Robert Bailey
Tel: 0277 362662

Sat 4-5
Mammoth Fair, Donington
Park, Leics
Four In One Promotions
Tel: 0455 233495

Sun 5
Picketts-Lock Leisure Centre,
Picketts-Lock Lane, Edmonton,
London N9
Jax Fairs
Tel: 0444 400570

Tues 7
Newark & Nottinghamshire
Showground, Newark
International Antique &
Collectors Fair Co., Ltd.
Tel: 0636 702326

Fri 10-12
Giant Antique Fair, Bingley
Hall, County Showground,
Stafford
Bowman Fairs
Tel: 0532 843333

Fri 10-12
The Ilkley Antiques Fair, Kings
Hall, Ilkley,
W. Yorks
Robert Bailey
Tel: 0277 362662

Fri 17-18
Truro Antiques, Collectors' &
Book Fair, City Hall, Truro
West Country Antiques &
Collectors' Fairs
Tel: 0225 424677

Mon 27-28
Antiques Fair, Pavilion
Gardens, Buxton
Unicorn Fairs
Tel: 098 987 312

Tues 28
Harrow Leisure Centre,
Christchurch Avenue, Harrow,
Middx
Jax Fairs
Tel: 0444 400570

Tues 28-29
Mammoth Fair, Sheffield
Arena, Sheffield
Four In One Promotions
Tel: 0455 233495

Tues 28-29
2nd Gwent Antiques Fair, The
New Inn, Langstone, Newport
Antiques in Britain Fairs
Tel: 0273 423355

Fri 31-2 Jan
The Petworth Antiques Fair,
Seaford College, West Sussex
Robert Bailey
Tel: 0277 362662

DIRECTORY OF MARKETS & CENTRES

London
Alfie's Antique Market,
13-25 Church Street, NW8.
Tel: 071-723 6066
Tues-Sat 10-6pm

Angel Arcade, 116-118
Islington High Street,
Camden Passage, N1.
Wed & Sat

Antiquarius Antique
Market, 131/141 King's
Road, Chelsea, SW3.
Tel: 071-351 5353
Mon-Sat 10-6pm

Antiques & Collectors
Corner, North Piazza,
Covent Garden, WC2.
Tel: 071-240 7405
9-5pm every day

Bermondsey Antiques
Market, Corner of Long
Lane & Bermondsey
Street, SE1.
Tel: 071-351 5353
Friday 5am-2pm

Bermondsey Antiques
Warehouse, 173
Bermondsey Street, SE1.
Tel: 071-407 2040/4250
9.30-5.30pm, Thurs 9.30-
8pm, Fri 7-5.30pm, closed
Sat & Sun.

Bond Street Antiques
Centre, 124 New Bond
Street, W1.
Tel: 071-351 5353
Mon-Fri 10-5.45pm, Sat
10-4pm

Camden Antiques Market,
Corner of Camden High
Street & Buck Street,
Camden Town, NW1.
Thurs 7-4pm

Camden Passage Antique
Centre, 12 Camden
Passage, Islington, N1.
Tel: 071-359 0190
Stalls Wed 8-3pm (Thurs
books 9-4pm), Sat 9-5pm

Chelsea Antiques Market,
245-253 King's Road, SW3.
Tel: 071-352
5689/9695/1424
10-6pm

Chenil Galleries, 181-183
King's Road, SW3.
Tel: 071-351 5353
Mon-Sat 10-6pm

Corner Portobello Antiques
Supermarket, 282, 284,
288, 290 Westbourne
Grove, W11.
Tel: 071-727 2027
Fri 12-4pm, Sat 7-6pm

Cutler Street Antiques
Market, Goulston Street,
Nr Aldgate End, E1.
Tel: 071-351 5353
Sun 7-2pm

Crystal Palace Collectors
Market, Jasper Road,
Westow Hill, Crystal
Palace, SE19.
Tel: 081-761 3735
Wed 9-4pm, Fri 9-5pm, Sat
9-4pm, Sun 11-4pm

Dixons Antique Centre,
471 Upper Richmond Road
West, East Sheen, SW14.
Tel: 081-878 6788
10-5.30pm, Sun 1.30-
5.30pm, Closed Wed.

Franklin's Camberwell
Antiques Market, 161
Camberwell Road, SE5.
Tel: 071-703 8089
10-6pm, Sun 1-6pm

Georgian Village Antiques
Market, 100 Wood Street,
Walthamstow, E17.
Tel: 081-520 6638
10-5pm, Closed Thurs.

Georgian Village, Islington
Green, N1.
Tel: 071-226 1571
Wed 10-4pm, Sat 7-5pm

Good Fairy Open Market,
100 Portobello Road, W11
Tel: 071-351 5950/221 8977
Sats only 5-5pm

Gray's Antique Market,
58 Davies Street, W1.
Tel: 071-629 7034
Mon-Fri 10-6pm

Gray's Mews,
1-7 Davies Street, W1.
Tel: 071-629 7034
Mon-Fri 10-6pm

Gray's Portobello, 138
Portobello Road, W11.
Tel: 071-221 3069
Sat 7-4pm

Greenwich Antiques
Market, Greenwich High
Road, SE10.
Sun 7.30-4.30 & Sat (June-
Sept)

Hampstead Antique
Emporium, 12 Heath
Street, Hampstead, NW3.
Tel: 071-794 3297
10-6pm, closed Mon & Sun.

Jubilee Market,
Covent Garden, WC2.
Tel: 071-836 2139
Open Mon

Kensington Church Street
Antiques Centre, 58-60
Kensington Church Street,
W8.
10-6

The London Silver Vaults,
Chancery House, 53-65
Chancery Lane, WC2.
Tel: 071-242 3844
9-5.30pm, Sat 9-12.30pm

The Mall Antiques Arcade,
359 Upper Street,
Islington, N1.
Tel: 071-354 2839
Tues, Thurs, Fri 10-5pm,
Wed 7.30-5pm, Sat 9-6pm

Northcote Road Antiques
Market, 155a Northcote
Road, Battersea, SW11.
Tel: 071-228 6850
10-6pm, Sun 12-5pm

Peckham Indoor Market,
Rye Lane Bargain Centre,
48 Rye Lane, Peckham,
SE15.
Tel: 071-246 3639
Tues-Sat

Pierrepoint Arcade,
Camden Passage, N1.
Tel: 071-359 0190
Wed & Sat

Portobello Road Market,
W11.
Sat 5.30-5pm

Rochefort Antique Gallery,
32/34 The Green,
Winchmore Hill, N21.
Tel: 081-886 4779/363 0910

Roger's Antiques Gallery,
65 Portobello Road, W11.
Tel: 071-351 5353
Sat 7-4pm

Steptoes Yard West
Market, 52a Goldhawk
Road, W12.
Tel: 071-602 2699
Fri, Sat & Sun

Streatham Traders &
Shippers Market, United
Reform Church Hall,
Streatham High Street,
SW16.
Tel: 071-764 3602
Tues 8-3pm

Wimbledon Market,
Car Park, Wimbledon
Greyhound Stadium,
Plough Lane, SW19.
Tel: 07268 17809
Sun.

Willesden Market, Car
Park, White Hart Public
House, Willesden, NW10.
Tel: 081-569 3889

World Famous Portobello
Market, 177 Portobello
Road & 1-3 Elgin Crescent,
W11.
Tel: 071-221 4964
Sat 5-6pm

York Arcade, 80 Islington
High Street, N1.
Tel: 071-833 2640
Wed & Sat 8-5pm

Avon
Bartlett Street Antique
Centre, 5-10 Bartlett
Street, Bath.
Tel: 0225 466689
Mon-Sat 9.30-5pm, Wed
Market 8-5pm

Bath Antiques Market,
Guinea Lane, off
Lansdown Road, Bath.
Wed 6.30-2.30pm

Bristol Antique Market, St
Nicholas Markets, The
Exchange, Corn Street,
Bristol.
Tel: 0272 224014
Fri 9-3pm

Clifton Antiques Market,
26/28 The Mall, Clifton,
Bristol.
Tel: 0272 741627
10-6pm, Closed Mon

Great Western Antique
Centre, Bartlett Street,
Bath.
Tel: 0225 424243
Mon-Sat 10-5pm, Wed
8.30-5pm

Bedfordshire
Dunstable Antique Centre,
38a West Street,
Dunstable.
Tel: 0582 696953

Woburn Abbey Antiques
Centre, Woburn.
Tel: 0525 290350
11-5pm Nov to Easter,
10-5.30pm Easter to Oct

Berkshire
Hungerford Arcade, High
Street, Hungerford.
Tel: 0488 683701
9.30-5.30pm, Sun 10-6pm

Reading Emporium, 1a
Merchant Place (off Friar
Street), Reading.
Tel: 0734 590290
10-5pm

Twyford Antiques Centre,
1 High Street, Twyford.
Tel: 0734 342161
Mon-Sat 9.30-5.30pm, Sun
10.30-5pm, Closed Wed

Buckinghamshire
Amersham Antique
Collectors Centre, 20-22
Whieldon Street, Old
Amersham.
Tel: 0494 431282
Mon-Sat 10-6pm

Antiques at Wendover, The
Old Post Office, 25 High
Street, Wendover.
Tel: 0296 625335
Mon-Sat 10-5.30pm, Sun
11-5.30pm

Bell Street Antiques
Centre, 20/22 Bell Street,
Princes Risborough.
Tel: 08444 3034
9.30-5.30pm, Sun 12-5pm

Market Square Antiques,
20 Market Place, Olney.
Tel: 0234 712172
Mon-Sat 10-5.30pm, Sun 2-
5.30pm

Olney Antiques Centre,
Rose Court, Olney.
Tel: 0234 712172
10-5.30pm, Sun 12-5.30pm

Tingewick Antiques
Centre, Main Street,
Tingewick.
Tel: 0280 847922
10.30-5pm every day

Winslow Antique Centre,
15 Market Square,
Winslow.
Tel: 0296 714540/714055
10-5

Cambridgeshire
Collectors Market, Dales
Brewery, Gwydir Street
(off Mill Road), Cambridge.
9.30-5pm

Fitzwilliam Antiques
Centre, Fitzwilliam Street,
Peterborough.
Tel: 0733 65415

Willingham Antiques &
Collectors Market, 25-29
Green Street, Willingham.
Tel: 0954 60283
10-5pm, Closed Thurs

Cheshire
Davenham Antique
Centre, 461 London Road,
Davenham, Nr. Northwick.
Tel: 0606 44350
Mon-Sat 10-5pm, Closed
Wed

Nantwich Antique Centre,
The Old Police Station,
Welsh Row, Nantwich.
Tel: 0270 624035
10-5.30pm, Closed Wed

Melody's Antique
Galleries, 30-32 City Road,
Chester.
Tel: 0244 328968
Mon-Sat 10-5.30pm

Stancie Cutler Antique &
Collectors Fairs, Nantwich
Civic Hall, Nantwich.
Tel: 0270 624288

Cornwall
New Generation Antique
Market, 61/62 Chapel
Street, Penzance.
Tel: 0736 63267
10-5pm

Waterfront Antique
Complex, 1st Floor, 4 Quay
Street, Falmouth.
Tel: 0326 311491
9-5pm

Cumbria
Carlisle Antique & Craft
Centre, Cecil Hall, Cecil
Street, Carlisle.
Tel: 0228 21970
Mon-Sat 9-5pm

Cockermouth Antiques
Market, Courthouse, Main
Street, Cockermouth.
Tel: 0900 824346
10-5pm

Derbyshire
Derby Antique Centre, 11
Friargate, Derby.
Tel: 0332 385002
Mon-Sat 10-5.30pm

Derby Antiques Market,
52-56 Curzon Street,
Derby.
Tel: 0332 41861
Mon-Sat 9-5pm, closed
Wed

Glossop Antique Centre,
Brookfield, Glossop.
Tel: 0457 863904
Thurs-Sun 10-5pm

Devon
The Antique Centre on the
Quay, Exeter.
Tel: 0392 214180
10-5pm

The Antique Centre,
Abingdon House, 136 High
Street, Honiton.
Tel: 0404 42108
Mon-Sat 10-5pm

Barbican Antiques Centre,
82-84 Vauxhall Street,
Barbican, Plymouth.
Tel: 0752 266927
9.30-5pm

Dartmoor Antiques Centre,
Off West Street,
Ashburton.
Tel: 0364 52182
Tues 9-4pm

Dorset
The Antique Centre, 837-
839 Christchurch Road,
East Boscombe,
Bournemouth.
Tel: 0202 421052
Mon-Sat 9.30-5.30pm

Barnes House Antiques Centre, West Row, Wimborne Minster.
Tel: 0202 886275
10-5pm

Bridport Antique Centre, 5 West Allington, Bridport.
Tel: 0308 25885
9-5pm

Gold Hill Antiques & Collectables,
3 Gold Hill Parade, Gold Hill, Shaftesbury.
Tel: 0747 54050

Sherborne Antique Centre, Mattar Arcade, 17 Newlands, Sherborne.
Tel: 0935 813464
9-5pm

R. A. Swift & Son, St Andrews Hall, 4c Wolverton Road (off Christchurch Road), Bournemouth.
Tel: 0202 394470
Mon-Fri 9-5.30pm

Wimborne Antique Centre, Newborough Road, Wimborne.
Tel: 0202 841251
Thurs 10-4pm, Fri 8.30-5pm, Sat 10-5pm, Sun 9.30-5pm

Essex
Abridge Antique Centre, Market Place, Abridge.
Tel: 0992 813113
10-5pm, Thurs 10-1pm

Battlesbridge Antiques Centre, The Green, Chelmsford Road, Battlesbridge, Nr Wickford.
Tel: 0268 764197

Essex Antiques Centre, Priory Street, Colchester.
Tel: 0206 871150
10-5.30pm

Grays Galleries Antiques & Collectors Centre, 23 Lodge Lane, Grays.
Tel: 0375 374883
10-5.30pm

Kelvedon Antiques Centre, 139 High Street, Kelvedon.
Tel: 0376 570896
Mon-Sat 10-5pm

Maldon Antiques & Collectors Market, United Reformed Church Hall, Market Hill, Maldon.
Tel: 07872 22826
1st Sat in month

Trinity Antiques Centre, 7 Trinity Street, Colchester.
Tel: 0206 577775
9.30-5pm

Townsford Mill Antiques Centre, The Causeway, Halstead.
Tel: 0787 474451
10-5pm, inc Sun

Gloucestershire
Antique Centre, London House, High Street, Moreton-in-Marsh.
Tel: 0608 51084
10-5pm

Charlton Kings Antique Centre, 199 London Road, Charlton Kings, Cheltenham.
Tel: 0242 510672
9.30-5.30pm

Cheltenham Antique Market, 54 Suffolk Road, Cheltenham.
Tel: 0242 529812
9.30-5.30pm

Cirencester Antique Market, Market Place, Cirencester.
Tel: 071-262 5003
Fri

Gloucester Antiques Centre, Severn Road, Gloucester.
Tel: 0452 529716
9.30-5pm, Sun 1-5pm

Cotswold Antiques Centre, The Square, Stow-on-the-Wold.
Tel: 0451 31585
10-5.30pm

Painswick Antique Centre, New Street, Painswick.
Tel: 0452 812431
10-5pm, Sat 9.30-5.30pm, Sun 11-5.30pm

Tewkesbury Antique Centre, Tolsey Hall, Tolsey Lane, Tewkesbury.
Tel: 0684 294091
9-5pm

Windsor House Antiques Centre, High Street, Moreton-in-Marsh.
Tel: 0608 50993
10-5.30pm, Sun 12-5.30pm

Hampshire
Creightons Antique Centre, 23-25 Bell Street, Romsey.
Tel: 0794 522758
9-6pm

Folly Antiques Centre, College Street, Petersfield.
Tel: 0730 64816
10-5pm, Thurs 10-1pm

Kingsley Barn Antique Centre, Church Lane, Eversley, Nr Wokingham.
Tel: 0734 328518
10.30-5pm, closed Mon

Lymington Antiques Centre, 76 High Street, Lymington.
Tel: 0590 670934
10-5pm, Sat 9-5pm

Squirrel Collectors Centre, 9 New Street, Basingstoke
Tel: 0256 464885
10-5.30pm

Hereford & Worcester
The Galleries Antiques Centre, Pickwicks, 503 Evesham Road, Crabbs Cross, Redditch.
Tel: 0527 550568
9.30-5pm, inc Sun

Hereford Antique Centre, 128 Widemarsh Street, Hereford.
Tel: 0432 266242
9-5pm, Sun 1-5pm

Leominster Antiques Market, 14 Broad Street, Leominster.
Tel: 0568 2189
10-5pm

Worcester Antiques Centre, Reindeer Court, Mealcheapen Street, Worcester.
Tel: 0905 610680/1
10-5pm

Hertfordshire
Antique & Collectors Market, Market Place, Hemel Hempstead.
Tel: 071-624 3214
Wed 9-2pm

Bushey Antiques Centre, 39 High Street, Bushey.
Tel: 081-95- 5040

By George! Antiques Centre, 23 George Street, St Albans
Tel: 0727 53032
10-5pm

The Herts & Essex Antique Centre, The Maltings, Station Road, Sawbridgeworth
Tel: 0279 722044
Tues-Fri 10-5pm, Sat & Sun 10-30-6pm, closed Mon

St Albans Antique Market, Town Hall, Chequer Street, St Albans
Tel: 0727 44957
Mon 9.30-4pm

Kent
The Antiques Centre, 120 London Road, Sevenoaks.
Tel: 0732 452104
9.30-5.30pm, Sat 10-5.30pm

Beckenham Antique Market, Old Council Hall, Bromley Road, Beckenham.
Tel: 081-777 6300
Wed 9.30-2pm

Bromley Antique Market, Widmore Road, Bromley.
Thurs 7.30-3pm

Burgate Antiques Centre, 10 Burgate, Canterbury.
Tel: 0227 456500
Mon-Sat 10-5pm

Castle Antiques Centre, 1 London Road, Westerham.
Tel: 0959 562492
Mon-Sat 10-5pm

Cranbrook Antiques Centre, 15 High Street, Cranbrook.
Tel: 0580 712173
10-5pm

Folkestone Market, Rotunda Amusement Park, Marine Parade, Folkestone.
Tel: 0850 311391
Sun

Hythe Antique Centre, 5 High Street, Hythe.
Tel: 0303 269043/269643
10-4pm, Sat 10-5pm
Closed Wed & Sun.

Malthouse Arcade, High Street, Hythe.
Tel: 0303 260103
Fri & Sat 10-6pm

Noah's Ark Antiques Centre, 5 King Street, Sandwich.
Tel: 0304 611144
10-5pm, closed Wed & Sun

Paraphernalia Antiques & Collectors Centre, 171 Widmore Road, Bromley.
Tel: 081-318 2997
10-5.30pm, Sun 10-2pm

Rochester Antiques & Flea Market, Corporation Street, Rochester.
Tel: 071 262 5003
Sat 8-1pm

Sandgate Antiques Centre, 61-63 High Street, Sandgate.
Tel: 0303 48987
10-6pm, Sun 11-6pm

Tenterden Antiques Centre, 66-66A High Street, Tenterden.
Tel: 05806 5885
10-5pm, inc Sun

Thanet Antiques Trade Centre, 45 Albert Street, Ramsgate.
Tel: 0843 597336
'9-5pm

Tudor Cottage Antiques Centre, 22-23 Shipbourne Road, Tonbridge.
Tel: 0732 351719
10-5.30pm

Tunbridge Wells Antique Centre, Union Square, The Pantiles, Tunbridge Wells.
Tel: 0892 533708
Mon-Sat 9.30-5pm

Lancashire
Blackpool Antiques Centre, 105-107 Hornby Road, Blackpool.
Tel: 0253 752514
9-5pm, closed Sat

Bolton Antiques Centre, Central Street, Bolton.
Tel: 0204 362694
9.30-5pm, inc Sun

Bygone Times, Times House, Grove Mill, The Green, Eccleston.
Tel: 0257 453780
8-6pm, inc Sun

Darwen Antique Centre, Provident Hall, The Green, Darwen.
Tel: 0254 760565
9.30-5pm, Sun 11-5pm, closed Tues

GB Antiques Centre, Lancaster Leisure Park, Wyresdale Road, Lancaster.
Tel: 0524 844734
10-5pm, inc Sun

Last Drop Antique & Collectors Fair, Last Drop Hotel, Bromley Cross, Bolton.
Sun 11-4pm

Levenshulme Antiques Hypermarket, Levenshulme Town Hall, 965 Stockport Road, Levenshulme, Manchester.
Tel: 061 224 2410
10-5pm

Memory Lane Antique Centre, Gilnow Lane, off Deane Road, Bolton.
Tel: 0204 380383
9-5pm, inc Sun

Preston Antique Centre, The Mill, New Hall Lane, Preston.
Tel: 0772 794498
Mon-Fri 8.30-5.30pm, Sat 10-4pm, Sun 9-4pm

Royal Exchange Shopping Centre, Antiques Gallery, St Anne's Square, Exchange Street, Manchester.
Tel: 061 834 3731/834 1427
Mon-Sat 9.30-5.30pm

Walter Aspinall Antiques, Pendle Antique Centre, Union Mill, Watt Street, Sabden, Nr Blackburn.
Tel: 0282 76311
9-5pm, weekends 11-4pm

Leicestershire
The Antiques Complex, St Nicholas Place, Leicester.
Tel: 0533 533343
9.30-5.30pm

Boulevard Antique & Shopping Centre, The Old Dairy, Western Boulevard, Leicester.
Tel: 0533 541201
10-6pm, Sun 2-5pm

Oxford Street Antiques Centre Ltd., 16-26 Oxford Street, Leicester.
Tel: 0533 553006
Mon-Fri 10-5.30pm, Sun 2-5pm

Lincolnshire
Boston Antiques Centre, 12 West Street, Boston.
Tel: 0205 361510
9-5pm, closed Thurs

Eastgate Antiques Centre, 6 Eastgate, Lincoln.
Tel: 0522 544404
9.30-5pm

Hemswell Antique Centre, Caenby Corner Estate, Hemswell Cliff, Nr Gainsborough.
Tel: 0427 668389
10-5pm, inc Sun

The Lincolnshire Antiques Centre, 26 Bridge Street, Horncastle
Tel: 0507 527794
9-5pm

Portobellow Row Antiques Centre, 93-95 High Street, Boston.
Tel: 0205 369456
10-4pm

Talisman Antiques, 51 North Street, Horncastle.
Tel: 0507 526893
10-5pm, closed Mon.

Stamford Antiques Centre, The Exchange Hall, Broad Street, Stamford.
Tel: 0780 62605
10-5pm

Talisman Antiques, Regent House, 12 South Market, Alford.
Tel: 0507 463441
10.30-4.30pm, closed Thurs.

Merseyside
Hoylake Antique Centre, 128-130 Market Street, Hoylake.
Tel: 051-632 4231
9.15-5.30pm

Middlesex
Hampton Village Antiques Centre, 76 Station Road, Hampton.
Tel: 081-979 5871
10-5.30pm

The Jay's Antique Centre, 25/29 High Street, Harefield.
Tel: 0895 824738
10-6pm, Wed 10-1pm

Norfolk
Angel Antique Centre, Pansthorn Farmhouse, Redgrave Road, South Lopham, Nr Diss.
Tel: 037 988 317
9.30-6pm, inc Sun

Antique & Collectors Centre, St Michael at Plea, Bank Plain, Norwich.
Tel: 0603 619129
9.30-5.00pm

Cloisters Antiques Fair, St Andrew's & Blackfriars Hall, St Andrew's Plain, Norwich.
Tel: 0603 628477
Wed 9.30-3.30pm

Coltishall Antiques Centre, High Street, Coltishall.
Tel: 0603 738306
10-5pm

Fakenham Antique Centre, Old Congregational Chapel, 14 Norwich Road, Fakenham.
Tel: 0328 862941
10-5pm, Thurs 9.5pm

Gostling's Antique Centre, 13 Market Hill, Diss.
Tel: 0379 650360
10-5pm, Thurs 10-7pm

Norwich Antiques & Collectors Centre, Quayside, Fye Bridge, Norwich.
Tel: 0603 612582
10-5pm

The Old Granary Antique & Collectors Centre, King Staithe Lane, off Queens Street, King's Lynn.
Tel: 0553 775509
10-5pm

Wells Antique Centre, The Old Mill, Maryland.
Tel: 0328 711433
10-5pm, inc Sun

Wymondham Antique Centre, No 1 Town Green, Wymondham.
Tel: 0953 604817
10-5pm

Northamptonshire

Antiques & Bric-a-Brac
Market, Market Square,
Town Centre,
Wellingborough.
Tel: 0905 611321
Tues 9-4pm

Finedon Antiques Centre,
Church Street, Finedon,
Nr Wellingborough.
Tel: 0933 681260
9.30-5.30pm, Sun 2-5

The Village Antique
Market, 62 High Street,
Weedon.
Tel: 0327 42015
9.30-5.30pm, Sun 10.30-
5.30pm

Northumberland

Colmans of Hexham, 15 St
Mary's Chare, Hexham.
Tel: 0434 603811/2
9-5pm

Nottinghamshire

Castle Gate Antiques
Centre, 55 Castle Gate,
Newark.
Tel: 0636 700076
9-5.30pm

Newark Antiques Centre,
Regent House, Lombard
Street, Newark.
Tel: 0636 605504
9.30-5pm, Sun 11-4

Newark Antique
Warehouse, Kelham Road,
Newark.
Tel: 0636 74869
8.30-5.30pm, Sat 10-4pm

Nottingham Antique
Centre, British Rail Goods
Yard, London Road,
Nottingham.
Tel: 0602 504504/505548
9-5pm, closed Sat

Top Hat Antiques Centre,
66-72 Derby Road,
Nottingham.
Tel: 0602 419143
9.30-5pm

Oxfordshire

Antique & Collectors
Market, Town Hall,
Thame.
Tel: 0844 28205
8.30-3.30pm, 2nd Tues of
month

Cotswold Gateway Antique
Centre, Cheltenham Road,
Burford Roundabout,
Burford.
Tel: 099 382 3678
10-5.30pm, Sun 2-5.30pm

Chipping Norton Antique
Centre, Ivy House, Middle
Row, Chipping Norton.
Tel: 0608 644212
10-5pm, inc Sun

Deddington Antique
Centre, Laurel House, Bull
Ring, Market Square,
Deddington.
Tel: 0869 38968
Mon-Sat 10-5pm

Friday Street Antique
Centre, 2 & 4 Friday
Street, Henley-on-Thames.
Tel: 0491 574104
9.30-5.30, Sun 11-5

Goring Antique Centre, 16
High Street, Goring-on-
Thames.
Tel: 0491 873300.
10-5pm, Sat 11-5pm, closed
Wed pm

Henley Antique Centre,
Rotherfield Arcade, 2-4
Reading Road, Henley-on-
Thames.
Tel: 0491 411468

The Lamb Arcade, High
Street, Wallingford.
Tel: 0491 35166/35048
10-5pm, Sat 10-5.30pm
Wed 10-4pm

Oxford Antiques Centre,
The Jam Factory, 27 Park
End Street, Oxford
Tel: 0865 251075
Mon-Sat 10-5pm and 1st
Sun every month

Oxford Antiques Market,
Gloucester Green, Oxford.
Tel: 0865 242216
Every Thurs

Span Antiques, 6 Market
Place, Woodstock.
Tel: 0993 811332
10-5pm, inc Sun, closed
Wed

Shropshire

Cleobury Mortimer
Antique Centre, Childe
Road, Cleobury Mortimer,
Nr Kidderminster.
Tel: 0299 270513
10-5pm, inc Sun, closed
Thurs

Ironbridge Antique Centre,
Dale End, Ironbridge.
Tel: 0952 433784
10-5pm, Sun 2-5pm

Pepper Lane Antique
Centre, Pepper Lane,
Ludlow.
Tel: 0584 876494
10-5pm

Shrewsbury Antique
Market, Frankwell Quay
Warehouse, Shrewsbury.
Tel: 0743 350916
9.30-5pm

Shrewsbury Antique
Centre, 15 Princess House,
The Square, Shrewsbury.
Tel: 0743 247704
9.30-5.30pm

St Leonards Antiques,
Corve Street, Ludlow.
Tel: 0584 875573
9-5pm

Stretton Antiques Market,
36 Sandford Avenue,
Church Stretton.
Tel: 0694 723718
9.30-5.30pm, Sun 10.30-
4.30pm

Telford Antique Centre,
High Street, Wellington,
Telford.
Tel: 0952 256450
10-5pm, Sun 2-5pm

Somerset

Bridgwater Antiques
Market, Marycourt
Shopping Mall,
Bridgwater.
Tel: 0823 451433
Friday 9-5pm, Sat 10-5pm

County Antiques Centre,
21/23 West Street,
Ilminster.
Tel: 0460 54151
10-5pm

Dulverton Antique Centre,
Lower Town Hall,
Dulverton.
Tel: 0398 23522
10-5pm

Guildhall Antique Market,
The Guildhall, Chard.
Thurs 9-3pm

Oscar's Antique Market,
13-15 Market Square,
Crewkerne.
Tel: 0460 72718
10-5.30pm

Taunton Silver Street
Antiques Centre, 27/29
Silver Street, Taunton.
Tel: 071-351 5353
Mon 9-4pm

Staffordshire

The Antique Centre,
128 High Street, Kinver.
Tel: 0384 877441
10-5.30pm

Antique Market,
The Stones,
Newcastle-under-Lyme.
Tel: 071-624 4848
Tues 9-4pm

Barclay House Antiques,
14-16 Howard Place,
Shelton, Stoke-on-Trent.
Tel: 0782 274747
9.30-6pm

Rugeley Antique Centre,
161/3 Main Road, Brereton,
Nr Rugeley.
Tel: 08895 77166
9-5pm

The Potteries Antique
Centre, Waterloo Road,
Cobridge, Stoke-on-Trent.
Tel: 0782 201455   9-6pm

Tudor of Lichfield Antique
Centre, Lichfield House,
Bore Street, Lichfield.
Tel: 0543 263951

Tutbury Mill Antiques,
6 Lower High Street,
Tutbury, Nr Burton-on-
Trent.
Tel: 0283 815999
9-5pm every day

Suffolk

The Barn, Risby, Bury St
Edmunds.
Tel: 0284 811126
10-5pm, inc Sun

Clare Antique Warehouse,
The Mill, Malting Lane,
Clare,
Nr. Sudbury.
Tel: 0787 278449
9.30-5.30pm

Debenham Antique
Centre, The Forresters
Hall, High Street,
Debenham.
Tel: 0728 860777
10-5.30pm, Sun 2-5pm

Long Melford Antiques
Centre, The Chapel
Maltings, Long Melford.
Tel: 0787 79287
9.30-5.30pm

Old Town Hall Antiques
Centre, High Street,
Needham Market.
Tel: 0449 720773
10-5pm

Snape Antiques and
Collectors' Centre, Snape
Maltings, Snape.
Tel: 0728 888038
10-6pm, inc Sun

Waveney Antiques Centre,
Peddars Lane, Beccles.
Tel: 0502 716147
10-5.30pm

Wrentham Antiques
Centre, 7 High Street,
Wrentham, Nr. Beccles.
Tel: 0502 75376
10-5.30pm, Sun 2-5.30pm

Surrey

Antiquarius Antique
Centre, 56 West Street,
Dorking.
Tel: 0306 743398
9.30-5.30pm

Antiques Arcade,
22 Richmond Hill,
Richmond.
Tel: 081-940 2035
10.30-5.30pm, closed Wed

Antiques & Interiors, 64
Station Road East, Oxted.
Tel: 0883 712806
9.30-5.30pm

The Antiques Arcade,
77 Bridge Road,
East Molesey.
Tel: 081-979 7954
10-5pm

The Antiques Centre, 22
Haydon Place, corner of
Martyr Road, Guildford.
Tel: 0483 67817
10-4pm, closed Mon & Wed

Cambridge Parade
Antiques, 229-231
Carshalton Road,
Carshalton.
Tel: 081-643 0014
10-5.30pm

Dorking Antiques Centre,
17/18 West Street,
Dorking.
Tel: 0306 740915
10-5.30pm

Duke's Yard Antique
Market, 1a Duke Street,
Richmond.
Tel: 081-332 1051
10-6pm, closed Mon

Farnham Antique Centre,
27 South Street, Farnham.
Tel: 0252 724475
9.30-5pm

Fern Cottage Antique
Centre, 28/30 High Street,
Thames Ditton.
Tel: 081-398 2281
10-5.30pm

Maltings Monthly Market,
Bridge Square, Farnham.
Tel: 0252 726234
First Sat in month

The Old Smithy Antique
Centre, 7 High Street,
Merstham.
Tel: 073764 2306
10-5pm

Reigate Antiques Arcade,
57 High Street, Reigate.
Tel: 0737 222654
10-5.30pm

Surrey Antiques Centre,
10 Windsor Street,
Chertsey.
Tel: 0932 563313
10-5pm

Sutton Market, West
Street, Sutton.
Tel: 081-661 1245
Tues & Sat

Victoria & Edward
Antiques Centre,
61 West Street, Dorking.
Tel: 0306 889645
9.30-5.30pm

Wood's Wharf Antiques
Bazaar, 56 High Street,
Haslemere.
Tel: 0428 642125
Mon-Sat 9.30-5pm

Sussex East

Antique Market, Leaf Hall,
Seaside, Eastbourne.
Tel: 0323 27530
Tues & Sat, 9-5pm

Bexhill Antiques Centre,
Quakers Mill, Old Town,
Bexhill.
Tel: 0424 210182/221940
10-5.30pm

Brighton Antiques Gallery,
41 Meeting House Lane,
Brighton.
Tel: 0273 26693/21059
10-5.30pm

Brighton Market, Jubilee
Shopping Hall, 44-47
Gardner Street, Brighton.
Tel: 0273 600574
9-5pm

Chateaubriand Antiques
Centre, High Street,
Burwash.
Tel: 0435 882535
10-5pm, Sun 2-5pm

Cliffe Antiques Centre, 47
Cliffe High Street, Lewes.
Tel: 0273 473266
9.30-5pm

Cliffe Gallery Antique
Centre, 39 Cliffe High
Street, Lewes.
Tel: 0273 471877
9.30-5pm

The Collectors Market,
The Enterprise Centre,
Station Parade,
Eastbourne.
Tel: 0323 32690

The Courtyard Antiques
Market, 13, 15 & 17 High
Street, Seaford.
Tel: 0323 892091
8.30-5.30pm

Foundry Lane Antiques
Centre, 15 Cliffe High
Street, Lewes.
Tel: 0273 475361
10-5pm, closed Mon

George Street Antiques
Centre, 47 George Street,
Old Town, Hastings.
Tel: 0424 429339
9-5pm Sun 11-4pm

The Hastings Antique
Centre, 59-61 Norman
Road, Hastings.
Tel: 0424 428561
10-5.30pm

Horsebridge Antiques
Centre, 1 North Street,
Horsebridge, Nr Hailsham.
Tel: 0323 844414
10-5pm

Kollect-O-Mania, 25
Trafalgar Street, Brighton.
Tel: 0273 694229
10-5pm

Lewes Antique Centre,
20 Cliffe High Street,
Lewes.
Tel: 0273 476148
9.30-5pm

Mint Arcade,
71 The Mint, Rye.
Tel: 0797 225952
10-5pm

Newhaven Flea Market,
28 South Way, Newhaven.
Tel: 0273 517207/516065
Open every day

The Old Town Hall,
Antique Centre, 52
Ocklynge Road,
Eastbourne.
Tel: 0323 416016
9.30-5pm, Sun 10.30-5pm

Pharoahs Antiques Centre,
28 South Street,
Eastbourne.
Tel: 0323 38655
10-5pm

Prinnys Antique Gallery,
3 Meeting House Lane,
Brighton.
Tel: 0273 204554
9.30-5pm

Seaford's Barn Collectors
Market & Studio Book
Shop, The Barn, Church
Lane, Seaford.
Tel: 0323 890010
Tues, Thurs & Sat
10-4.30pm

Sussex West

Almshouses Arcade,
19 The Hornet, Chichester.
9.30-4.30pm

Antiques & Collectors
Market, Old Orchard
Building,
Old House, Adversane,
Nr Billingshurst.
Tel: 0403 783594
Every day

Copthorne Group
Antiques, Copthorne Bank,
Crawley.
Tel: 0342 712802
Mon-Sat 10-5.30pm

Eagle House Antiques
Market, Market Square,
Midhurst.
Tel: 0730 812718

Mamies Antiques Centre, 5
River Road, Arundel.
Tel: 0903 882012
Thurs-Sun, 9-5pm

Midhurst Antiques
Market, Knockhundred
Row, Midhurst.
Tel: 0730 814231
9.30-5pm

Shirley, Mostyns Antique
Centre, 64 Brighton Road,
Lancing.
Tel: 0903 752961
Mon-Fri 10-5pm

Petworth Antique Market,
East Street, Petworth.
Tel: 0798 42073
10-5.30pm

Tarrant Street Antique
Centre, Nineveh House,
Tarrant Street, Arundel.
Tel: 0903 884307
9.30-5pm, Sun 11-5pm

Treasure House Antiques
& Collectors Market, 31b
High Street, Arundel.
Tel: 0903 883101
9-5pm

Upstairs Downstairs
Antique Centre, 29
Tarrant Street, Arundel.
Tel: 0903 883749
10.30-5pm, inc Sun

Tyne & Wear

Antique Centre Newcastle,
8 St Mary Place East,
Newcastle-upon-Tyne.
Tel: 091-232 9832
Tues-Sat 10-5pm

Blaydon Antique Centre,
Bridge House, Bridge
Street, Blaydon,
Nr Newcastle-upon-Tyne.
Tel: 091-414 3535
10-5pm

Vine Lane Antique
Market, 17 Vine Lane,
Newcastle-upon-Tyne.
Tel: 091-261 2963/232 9832
10-5.30pm

Warwickshire

The Antiques Centre, High
Street, Bidford-on-Avon.
Tel: 0789 773680
10-5pm, Sun 2-5.30pm,
closed Mon

Antiques Etc., 22 Railway
Terrace, Rugby.
10-5pm, closed Tues &
Wed

The Antique Arcade, 4
Sheep Street, Stratford-
upon-Avon.
Tel: 0789 297249
10-5.30pm

Dunchurch Antique
Centre, 16/16a Daventry
Road, Dunchurch, Nr
Rugby.
Tel: 0788 817147
10-5pm, inc Sun

Leamington Pine &
Antiques Centre, 20
Regent Street, Leamington
Spa.
Tel: 0926 429679
9-6pm

Smith Street Antiques
Centre, 7 Smith Street,
Warwick.
Tel: 0926 497864
10-5.30pm

Spa Antiques Market, 4
Windsor Street,
Leamington Spa.
Tel: 0926 22927
9.30-5.30pm

Stratford Antiques Centre,
60 Ely Street, Stratford-
upon-Avon.
Tel: 0789 204180
10-5.30pm

Vintage Antique Market,
36 Market Place, Warwick.
Tel: 0926 491527
10-5pm

Warwick Antique Centre,
20-22 High Street,
Warwick.
Tel: 0926 495704
6 days a week

West Midlands

Birmingham Antique
Centre, 141 Bromsgrove
Street, Birmingham.
Tel: 021-692 1414/622 2145
Thurs from 9am

The City of Birmingham
Antique Market, St
Martins Market,
Edgbaston Street,
Birmingham.
Tel: 021-267 4636
Mon 6.30-2pm

Stancie Cutler Antique &
Collectors Fair, Town Hall,
Sutton Coldfield.
Tel: 0270 624288
Wed monthly, 11-8pm

Walsall Antiques Centre,
7a The Digbeth Arcade,
Walsall.
Tel: 0922 725163/5
10-5pm

Wiltshire

Antique & Collectors
Market, 37 Catherine
Street, Salisbury.
Tel: 0722 326033
9-5pm

The Avon Bridge Antiques
& Collectors Market,
United Reform Church
Hall, Fisherton Street,
Salisbury.
Tues 9-4pm

London House Antique
Centre, High Street,
Marlborough.
Tel: 0672 52331
Mon-Sat 9.30-5.30pm

The Marlborough Parade
Antiques Centre, The
Parade, Marlborough.
Tel: 0672 515331
10-5pm, inc Sun

Micawber's, 53 Fisherton
Street, Salisbury.
Tel: 0722 337822
9.30-5pm, closed Wed

Yorkshire

The Ginnel, Harrogate
Antique Centre, off
Parliament Street,
Harrogate.
Tel: 0423 508857
9.30-5.30pm

Grove Collectors Centre,
Grove Road, Harrogate.
Tel: 0423 561680
10-4.30pm

Halifax Antiques Centre,
Queen's Road/Gibbet
Street, Halifax.
Tel: 0422 366657
Tues-Sat, 10-5pm

Malton Antique Market, 2
Old Maltongate, Malton.
Tel: 0653 692732
9.30-5, closed Thurs

Micklegate Antiques
Market, 73 Micklegate,
York.
Tel: 0904 644438
Wed & Sat, 10-5.30pm

Montpelier Mews Antique
Market, Montpelier Street,
Harrogate.
Tel: 0423 530484
9.30-5.30pm

Treasure House Antiques
Centre, 4-10 Swan Street,
Bawtry, Nr Doncaster.
Tel: 0302 710621
10-5pm, inc Sun

West Park Antiques
Pavilion, 20 West Park,
Harrogate.
Tel: 0423 61758
10-5pm, closed Mon

York Antique Centre, 2
Lendal, York.
Tel: 0904 641445
Mon-Sat 9.30-5.30pm

Scotland

Bath Street Antique
Galleries, 203 Bath Street,
Glasgow.
Tel: 041-248 4220
10-5pm, Sat 10-1pm

Corner House Antiques,
217 St Vincent Street,
Glasgow.
Tel: 041-248 2560
10-5pm

King's Court Antiques
Centre & Market, King
Street, Glasgow.
Tel: 041-423 7216
Tues-Sun

The Victorian Village, 53 &
57 West Regent Street,
Glasgow.
Tel: 041-332 0808
10-5pm, Sat 10-1pm

Wales

Cardiff Antique Centre,
69-71 St Mary Street,
Cardiff.
Tel: 0222 30970

Carew Market, Carew
Airfield on A477, Port
Talbot.
Tel: 0639 886822
Sun

Jacobs Antique Centre,
West Canal Wharf, Cardiff.
Tel: 0222 390939
Thurs & Sat 9.30-5pm

Offa's Dyke Antiques
Centre, 4 High Street,
Knighton, Powys.
Tel: 0547 528634/528940
Mon-Sat 10-5pm

Pembroke Antique Centre,
The Hall, Hamilton
Terrace, Pembroke.
Tel: 0646 687017
10-5pm

Port Talbot Market,
Jubilee Shopping Hall, 64-
66 Station Road, Port
Talbot, Glamorgan.
Tel: 0639 883184
Mon-Sat

Swansea Antique Centre,
21 Oxford Street, Swansea.
Tel: 0792 466854
10-5pm

Channel Islands

Union Street Antique
Market, 8 Union Street,
St Helier, Jersey.
Tel: 0534 73805/22475
10-5pm

A Noddy
kaleidoscope,
1960s, 9in
(23cm) long.
£5-6 *FAB*

INDEX

A Brimtoy clockwork train set, in original
£100-150 *STK*